CRISIS: A CONTEMPORARY READER

Crisis

A CONTEMPORARY READER

edited by PETER COLLIER

University of California, Berkeley

HARCOURT, BRACE & WORLD, INC.

New York · Chicago · San Francisco · Atlanta

Library of Congress Catalog Card Number: 69-17026

Printed in the United States of America

PREFACE

Crisis contains twenty-eight essays and four stories about America today. The portrait of our society that it presents is not traditional, and perhaps it is even a little asymmetrical and jagged at the edges. However, the book is not meant to be history or sociology. Rather, it is an impression of a culture in crisis.

No special theories about reading and writing lie behind this collection. It does assume, however, that students are interested in their environment and in the social gravity that pulls on them (often none too gently); that they are beginning to identify themselves as a minority within this society, threatened by what many of them have come to accept as an "establishment"; that they want the scholastic materials they work with to speak to reality as they perceive it. The threat of a racial holo-

caust, the emergence of a new social order, the choice between war and
peace—these are the issues students face, and *Crisis* attempts to present
them as forthrightly as possible within a short compass. The book, however, is not meant to be anything like a systematic survey of American
society. Nor is it meant to promote a sectarian political vision or bias,
unless, of course, printing an essay on police brutality without giving a
policeman equal time for a rebuttal is to be overly selective. But, then,
one of the assumptions of the book (and probably of the students who
will be reading it) is that such apologetics are served up in large daily
doses by the mass media, often without a real consideration of what is
involved, and that the student's cultural background will have given him
ample basis for understanding the opposition's case.

Even though the essays in this anthology are critical of the state
of the nation and often dissident in their mood, they are by no means
homogeneous in style, subject, or attitude. Some, like Norman Mailer's
irreverent dissection of the personality of Lyndon Johnson and Tom
Wolfe's clever polemic against America's appetite for violence, are imaginative; others—Dr. Alfred R. Lindesmith's discussion of marijuana and
Paul Goodman's critique of the Great Society, for example—are more
conventional instances of good expository writing. There are specimens of
reportage, such as Hunter S. Thompson's essay on the Hell's Angels and
Robert Stone's portrait of four deserters who chose exile rather than fight
in Vietnam; there are also works such as Norman Podhoretz's "My Negro
Problem—and Ours" and Bruno Bettelheim's "Joey: A 'Mechanical
Boy' " that are gaining recognition as contemporary prose classics. There
is, in short, diversity in tone and technique as well as in viewpoint and
subject matter.

Crisis is divided into four sections. The first, "Black and White—
Together?," is concerned with the racial dilemma; "Rites of Passage"
deals with the difficulty of what sociologist Edgar Z. Friedenberg calls
"coming of age in America"; "Culture and Anarchy" presents some of the
conflicts that lurk just below the surface of social order and asks whether
they erupt spontaneously or because of pressures created by social tension;
and, finally, "A State of the Nation" focuses on problems such as war
and peace, and poverty and plenty, which have always plagued societies
but which seem especially dramatic in America today.

All the selections are, I think, enjoyable and interesting. They are also
informative, and a number are first-hand accounts by men who were directly involved in the issues of which they write—LeRoi Jones, Stokely
Carmichael, Mario Savio, Lawrence Ferlinghetti, and William Styron, for
example. Each section of the book ends with a short story, which both summarizes and gives an imaginative dimension to the dialogue of that section.

The reader may have many questions after confronting these essays. If so, *Crisis* will have succeeded. No book can be "too controversial," and this one is no more so than contemporary America itself.

PETER COLLIER

CONTENTS

Preface   v

BLACK AND WHITE—TOGETHER?   1

ROBERT COLES • *The Last Ditch*   5

GENE MARINE • *White Power*   21

NORMAN PODHORETZ • *My Negro Problem—
and Ours*   33

KENNETH B. CLARK • *The Invisible Wall*   48

STOKELY CARMICHAEL · *Power and Racism*   58

LE ROI JONES · *What Does Nonviolence Mean?*   69

SOL STERN · *America's Black Guerrillas*   86

RALPH ELLISON · *Battle Royal*   95

RITES OF PASSAGE   111

BRUNO BETTELHEIM · *Joey: A "Mechanical Boy"*   115

EDGAR Z. FRIEDENBERG · *The Modern High School:
A Profile*   125

MARIO SAVIO · *An End to History*   141

JACK NEWFIELD · *The Beat Generation and the
Un-Generation*   146

AMERICAN FRIENDS SERVICE COMMITTEE ·
The Psychological Effects of the Draft   157

ROBERT STONE · *We Couldn't Swing with It:
The "Intrepid Four"*   173

LAWRENCE FERLINGHETTI · *Prison Diary*   189

PHILIP ROTH · *The Conversion of the Jews*   195

CULTURE AND ANARCHY   211

HENRY STEELE COMMAGER · *The University as
Employment Agency*   215

ED CRAY · *The Brutality*   224

TOM WOLFE · *Porno-violence*   238

HUNTER S. THOMPSON · *The Motorcycle Gangs:
Losers and Outsiders*   245

FRANKLIN RUSSELL · *A Madness of Nature*   256

ALFRED R. LINDESMITH · *The Marihuana Problem—
Myth or Reality?*   264

HARVEY COX • *Sex and Secularization* 283

HARVEY SWADOS • *Joe, the Vanishing American* 295

A STATE OF THE NATION 313

CAPTAIN JAMES MORRIS • *The Ambush* 317

THE EDITORS OF *RAMPARTS* • *The Redress of Their Grievances* 325

NORMAN MAILER • *Lyndon Johnson* 336

PAUL GOODMAN • *The Great Society* 343

PETER SCHRAG • *Appalachia: Again the Forgotten Land* 351

MARTIN GANSBERG • *38 Who Saw Murder Didn't Call the Police* 363

WILLIAM STYRON • *In the Jungle* 367

M. F. BEAL • *Survival* 376

black and white— together?

Writing in the early 1900s, Negro historian W. E. B. Du Bois predicted that the major problem of the twentieth century would be the color line. His words were prophetic enough: racial violence has become a condition of everyday life, and the alienation of the black man from white America has been acknowledged to be our preeminent domestic crisis.

Legal segregation and official Jim Crow are, by and large, gone. But gone too is the mood of optimism evoked by the nonviolent civil rights movement of the early sixties, which dedicated itself to gaining equal legal rights for black people, especially those in the South. Several subsequent long hot summers have forced on this country the realization that racial conflict is nationwide, not regional, and that inequitable laws are an expression of the racism engrained in the American character. The President's commission appointed to investigate recent ghetto uprisings noted that the United States, now more than ever, is in danger of splitting into two separate and unequal societies—one white, the other black. While many whites have begun to reevaluate the nature of their responsibility toward the dispossessed, and blacks—especially the young—are gaining a new sense of identity from brilliant spokesmen such as the late Malcolm X, the gulf separating black and white widens nonetheless. And such slogans as "We Shall Overcome" and "Black and White Together," once the marching songs of a civil rights movement that hoped to reconstruct America peacefully, are no longer spoken as confident assertions, but are inverted into questions, filled with a new doubt.

The essays in this section reflect the dark mood of disharmony and transition that characterizes the current dialogue on race in America. They do not offer easy solutions; rather, they suggest how deep the crisis is, and they pose some disturbing questions about it. Robert Coles, for instance, analyzes the character of a racial bigot in "The Last Ditch," in which he discusses a man who longs for mob violence against Negroes. A psychiatrist, Coles is forced to conclude that such bigotry would normally be regarded as individual sickness but that circumstances in America have made it an acceptable, even an expected response. Then, in "White Power," Gene Marine muses on how the concept of whiteness dominates our culture as a whole and suggests some of the types of racism this promotes. Norman Podhoretz's "My Negro Problem—and Ours" is a

blunt personal narrative about the way race affects even the most con-
cerned and well-intentioned of men.

"The Invisible Wall" is noted psychologist Kenneth B. Clark's dis-
cussion of the nature of a modern urban ghetto and its means of entrap-
ping its inhabitants. Stokely Carmichael, former chairman of the Student
Nonviolent Coordinating Committee (SNCC) and one of the men who
popularized the slogan "Black Power," indicates the political and social
aims of this new militancy in "Power and Racism." In "What Does Non-
violence Mean?" LeRoi Jones, celebrated poet and playwright, questions
the ability of nonviolent protest to break down the massive barriers be-
tween white and black. Then, in "America's Black Guerrillas," Sol Stern
reports on the young black militants who feel that the society which has
oppressed them is too corrupt for reform and must be overthrown.

The separation of black and white is given an imaginative perspec-
tive in the opening chapter of Ralph Ellison's classic novel, Invisible Man.
"Battle Royal" tells of a black teenager's bizarre experiences in a world
which fails to acknowledge his humanity.

ROBERT COLES

The Last Ditch

On August 5, 1964, a press service story quoted an FBI agent who
was working in the area of Neshoba County, Mississippi, where the
remains of three civil rights workers were found: "I wish I could have
a psychiatrist examine whoever did this right now and see what they'd
be thinking now that we've got the bodies."

I had heard a similar remark several weeks earlier from an agent in
McComb, Mississippi. A house occupied by several "integrationists"
had just been badly damaged by dynamite, and while I was looking

into some of the medical problems—two students were injured—
the officer was trying to find out who was responsible for the explosion. Standing near the debris with soda pop in our hands we talked
about the details of the incident. The officer assured me that it was a
serious attempt at murder rather than a mere effort to warn and
frighten, and then he turned his attention to explanations. Why
would people want to do this? He asked it, then I asked it, both of us
less curious than appalled. Yet, slowly the curiosity rose in him, and
well after we had finished our talk he came back to the question.
Why would anyone have nothing better to do in the middle of the
night than plant dynamite? He was clearly suggesting that only an
unhappy, a disturbed person would be awake so late, preparing that
kind of deed. Perhaps, he suggested, I had some thoughts on that
matter.

We each returned to our work, though I found myself ruminating
about how indeed I might have explained to him exactly what my
thoughts were. As I tried to lay that challenge to rest I kept on coming back to the chief capability we have in psychiatry, the case history.
Perhaps if we had had the time I would have been able to show him
what I felt to be the answer to his question by telling him about a
particular segregationist's life, including of course the life of his mind.

This man did not murder the three civil rights workers, or plant
dynamite in that home in the terror-stricken McComb area of Mississippi; but he has committed appallingly similar acts, in company with
many others. He has been in mobs and will not deny having seen
Negroes assaulted and killed as a result. I am sure he would satisfy
those agents and all of us as a prototype of the bigot who is a potential killer. I thought of him immediately that morning in McComb,
and again when I read the report of the government agent's dismayed
call for psychiatric help in Philadelphia.

I first met John, as I shall call him, while he was protesting the
archbishop's decision to admit some children who were Negro but
also Catholic to the parochial schools of New Orleans. It was a warm,
faintly humid early spring day, a Saturday too, and the next year's
school opening hardly seemed a timely worry. Up and down he
walked, picketing, tall, husky from the rear, an incipient paunch in
front. He wore a brown suit, slightly frayed at the cuffs, and on its
right shoulder rested his sign, wrought and lettered by himself:
"Fight Integration. Communists Want Negroes With Whites." His

shirt was starched and he wore a tie. He had brown eyes. He was bald but for the most meager line of black hair on his neck—baldness must have happened early and fast. His face was fleshy and largely unlined, and I thought, "Forty or forty-five."

Several of those in the picket line seemed unaware of the gazes they attracted. John, however, was the most engaging and communicative. Looking at people directly, he would talk with them if they showed the tiniest interest. He moved faster than the others, and seemed to be in charge, now signaling a new direction for walking, later approving or suggesting luncheon shifts.

We moved along the pavement side by side, he and I. Would I want a sign—he had several in reserve? I would rather talk with him; I was very much interested in his opinions. I felt it important that he, that they, not be misunderstood, and I would do my best to record fairly what he thought and wanted. I am a physician, I told him, a research physician specializing in problems of human adjustment under stress. A little amplification of this, and he laughed—it *was* a strain, the police and the scoffing people, and those reporters with the sly, obviously unfriendly questions. He would talk with reporters, any of them, so long as they were not niggers, not Communists, because he wanted to be heard. It was important to be heard or nothing could be accomplished. He wanted to do something, not merely have his say, and so he would surely talk with me if I were a teacher, if I wanted to report the truth to the educated. They needed the truth. I agreed. He was visibly impressed with certain credentials which, in my nervousness, I had offered: cards, pieces of paper which I now know were unnecessary for his cooperation. We began that day, later in the afternoon, signs put aside, over coffee. I arranged to meet him regularly, weekly, for several months at his home, or over coffee in a diner. He gradually told me about himself and his life, about what he believed and how he came to see things as he does.

He is a passionate segregationist ("you can put down the strongest, the strongest it's possible to be"). He has plans. He would like to exile most Negroes to Africa, perhaps sterilize a few quiet ones who would work at certain jobs fitting their animal nature, itself the work of God, he would emphasize. He would strip Jews of their fearful power, sending them off also, but to Russia, where they came from and yearn to return. There are other suspicious groups, Greeks, Lebanese—New Orleans is a port city, and he has worried about them leaving their boats. Do they try to *stay* on land? Unlike the niggers and Jews, whose clear danger to his city he had formulated for some time, he had not determined his exact position on such people, or his solution for them.

He was born in central Louisiana, say for example a town like Acme in Concordia Parish. The state is split into its southern, Catholic and French area and a northern section, basically Protestant and Anglo-Saxon. Typically, his father was the former and his mother Scotch-Irish, a wayward Baptist who embraced the Roman Church (the only term used for the Catholic Church in certain areas of the so-called Bible Belt) a few weeks before her marriage. Born their second child in the month America entered the First World War, he was sickly and fatherless his first year of life. While his father fought in Europe the boy was taken with what we now call "allergies," a timid stomach which mostly rejected milk, a cranky skin which periodically exploded red, raw, itchy, and was often infected by his responsive scratches. His sister was five years older, and she remembered all this. She and her mother, still alive, have told him about his fretful infancy, and he knew it well enough to be able to pass on their memories. His first memory was a whipping from his father's strap. With his father home from war, a second son and last child was born. John was three. He had pinched the infant, done enough wrong to the child's skin to cause a cry and attract his father's punishing attention. That was to happen many times, though he held a special place in his mind for this earliest occasion: "My brother and I started off on the wrong track, and we've never got along with one another."

His brother is tall and thin, ruddy-faced and blue-eyed like his mother, wears a white shirt to a bank teller's job near their hometown. John, dark and short like his father, has several "blue-shirt" skills which at various times he has used. "I can build a house myself" was his way of summarizing them: carpentry, electric work, plumbing, even bricklaying.

The childhood development of the boys forked: one neat, precise, his mother's favorite as well as her physical reflection; the other, by his own description, naughty, often idle or busy being scrappy. John in short was an overlooked and troubled middle child. He resembled his father, yet had hated him for as long as he can remember. Oddly, though, his manner, his temperament sound like the father's as he describes the man and shows pictures of him, now ten years dead, a large blustery fellow, open, opinionated, rumpled, a me-

chanic preoccupied with automobiles—under them daily, reading
magazines about them by night. He had storms within him, and
they fell upon his middle child, alone and arbitrarily, the boy felt.

Once John and I had talked long and hard—it seemed like a
whole day. I noticed it had actually been three hours. The length
of time measured a certain trust, a certain understanding that was
developing between us. I found myself knowing him, recognizing
some of the hardships he had endured, not just psychological ones,
but the hunger and jobless panic which must have entered so many
homes in a decade when I was scarcely born and he yet a child. I
felt guilty for a moment, torn between him and the simple but of
course complicated facts and experiences of his life, and him as he
now is, a shabby fanatic. He was feeling his own opening toward
me, and with considerable emotion in his voice, lifting his right hand
in a gesture which might well have been his father's, he interrupted
our talk of Huey Long's racial attitudes and how they compared
with those of his family: "Daddy [Southern fathers can be "daddy"
to their children forever without embarrassment] had a bad temper,
and I took it all myself. We had never had much money and bills
would set him going, but he wouldn't touch my mother, or my
brother or sister either. Yes" (I had asked), "my sister and brother
both favored Ma, and Daddy, he'd feel no good because he couldn't
get a week's pay, so he had to hit someone. Oh, he was for Huey
boy all the way, except Huey was soft on niggers, but I think Daddy
was, too. He used to say they were children, and we should protect
them. But if they're like kids, they're like bad ones, and just like animals, so they've got to be watched over. You wouldn't let a wild animal go free in your home or in school with your kids, would you? It's
right crazy how we forget that sometimes. Look at Harlem, and what
happens when they let them go. They rape and kill our women and
dirty the whole city up. I've been there and seen it. No" (prodded
again), "I don't blame Daddy, because, you see, in those days we
had them firm under our grip, so it was different and you didn't have
to worry about them. But look at now." We did talk about current
events for a few minutes, but each of us tired suddenly, and hardened.

Of course, from those old times to the present had been an
eventful period for him as well as for the Negro race. He almost died
twice. At seven he had a serious bout of pneumonia which—with
no help from antibiotics—almost killed him. He recalled gratefully
a Negro maid who cared for him through this, one of those (few

now) who knew and willingly lived in her "place." She died shortly after he recovered. Abruptly and looking still young ("I think she was around forty, but you can't tell with niggers"), she collapsed before his very eyes while preparing supper for him. It was by his description probably a stroke that took her, and she proved irreplaceable. They had paid her a pittance, but she had stayed with them for lack of better. About that time several Negro families started moving North, while others trekked south to New Orleans. Though his father had not really been able to pay Willi-Jean her established wages for many months, only death ended her loyalty and their comfort. "I got pneumonia again when I was twelve, and so did my brother. It nearly killed Ma taking care of us. She used to try to keep everything in its place, I think that's why it was so hard without Willi-Jean. With us sick on top of it, she almost didn't get through it all, she got so nervous."

In telling him of my interest in his medical history, I asked him several times to describe in further detail his fits of illness, and the care given him during those times. It seemed clear that he had, in fact, suffered badly at his mother's hands, neglected by her for his sister or brother, blamed by her for getting sick. The Negro woman's sudden death was actually a severe and deeply resented blow to him. His affections for her were hastily buried with her. He had to keep on his guard against his mother's personality, now no longer buffered by Willi-Jean. During one of our last talks he said, "You know, Doc, I think I *did* have a bad time with sickness when I was a kid. When I was twelve I almost died of pneumonia, and then I broke my leg a few weeks after that and lost that year of school." He had tried to run away from home before he contracted pneumonia, and after his recovery, too, until his lame leg made such attempts impossible for a while.

If his mother was nervous, oppressively ritualistic, and hardly his advocate, his father was a heavy drinker, temper-ridden, and fearfully unpredictable. When drunk he was moody. He also became brutal, and his middle son was his customary target. Declaring a truth whose painful implications he could not look at too closely, John once reflected, "I never figured why Daddy picked on me. We got along fine when he was sober, but when he got liquored up, I got it first and hardest. I looked like him and helped him most in fixing things around the house, but he never remembered things like that when

he was drunk." Not that his parents weren't "the nicest parents anyone could ever want." Any vision into their shortcomings, any criticism of them, had to be followed eventually by the atonement of
heavy sentiment. He had long ago learned how dangerous it was
to speak his mind. Perhaps his life, as we now see it, has been a
quest for that very possibility. "I used to be afraid to say anything
for fear it would get someone upset at home, so I just kept quiet and
ran my trains." Trains were his chief hobby for a little longer than is
usual, well into the early teens. He warmed while telling me about
his empire of them, and he became wistful afterward. I wanted to
hear of his childhood interests, and in speaking of them, he said am-
biguously, "I knew trains better than anyone in town."

By the last two years of high school he had found an easier time.
His mother reached menopause, surrendered in her war against dust
and for order, and became cheerless and distant. His father now
drank less, but had to struggle hard with another form of depression,
an economic one which he shared with his country. Amid all this
John strangely enough prospered. His sister married poorly, a marginal farmer soon dispossessed of his land. Slothful and malignant,
he beat her regularly, fathered two children by her, and left shortly
thereafter. She never remarried and has had to work hard to keep
her two children fed and clothed. John's brother had trouble with
learning. He left high school after one year, and for a time, nearly
penniless, he drew food and small coin from government relief programs. Recently he has managed a job in a bank, but his wife is a
heavy drinker, maybe worse, and they have five children. John says
they "live like pigs," and apparently this state of decay set in very
rapidly after their marriage. His brother's cleanest, most organized
moments are at his job.

John, however, graduated from high school, the first in his family
to do so, and went beyond that by securing a coveted job in the local hardware store. He had come to know its owner and his daughter,
too. Always interested in fixing things—bicycles, injured cars, falter-
ing plumbing, stray wires—he began in the hardware store as a willing and unpaid helper. The radio, new and mysterious, was his love,
and he tinkered endlessly with the various models. The store had
many other gadgets, and it also had his girl friend, the owner's daughter. He determined at about fifteen to marry her and did so at
twenty. At the time of his marriage he was a relatively prosperous

man, now wearing a white collar, regularly paid in dollars increasingly powerful out of their scarcity. ("My folks said I married real well, especially for those days.")

To hear him talk, the twelve months before and the twelve months after his wedding day were his best time. He remembers the pleasure and hope; but his nostalgia is brief, and is always tinctured with the bitterness which soon followed. His father-in-law's business collapsed, to be foreclosed by the handful of creditors who seemed to be gathering the entire countryside into their control. These provincial financiers, with their small banks all over the state, were controlled by Big Power and Big Money, both in New Orleans. Governor Huey had said so, and they killed him. John, with a wife and a boy of three months, had no choice but to try Huey's gambit—follow the Power, follow the Money. "We just up and moved. An uncle of my wife's thought he could get me work repairing radios. They were like TV today. No matter how poor you were, you needed some relaxation." John got a job and held it. He started by going into homes to repair wires or replace tubes. Soon he was selling radios themselves, all shapes and sizes on all kinds of payment plans. He was an exceptional salesman, seeing the radio as a box of easily summoned distraction for weary, uncertain people. He aimed at first not to sell but to explain, tracing with the future customer the webs and tangles of copper, informing his listener of their connections and rationale, pressing hard only at the end their whetted appetite, their need. ("Mostly they were people without cash.")

However, by the time a second world war was underway most Americans had radios, and his work slackened. In early 1942 he was the father of a four-year-old son, a two-year-old daughter. He owned a comfortable home in a distinctly middle-class area of white frame houses, each bulky, yet each a bit different. Most, though, had green shutters, high ceilings, thick walls, large, long windows, but no garage, all expressions of a warm, wet climate. More likely than not every residence had a single car so that the streets, palmy, well-paved, were lined on both sides just as from a plane's view the roofs asserted rows of radio antennae.

He still lives there, though many of his former neighbors have moved. For some the neighborhood was out of keeping with what they had recently become. They left for one-storied new houses in sprawling developments outside the city. The emigrants were replaced by others for whom the same neighborhood's value was defined by what they had just left. There are, however, a few who still prize those old houses, see their faintly shabby gentility and cherish their age and the memories they inspire. For John it is this way: "Those ranch houses are too expensive. Funny thing with a lot of the nigger lovers, they move out into the suburbs and then tell us how we should open our streets to them. I won't leave and I'd shoot to kill if they ever tried to buy a house nearby." (He cannot afford to leave. "They" are 2.4 miles away at their nearest.)

The war came as a relief. The economy was stagnant, floundering with too many unemployed. Poor people had bought their radios, and he was beginning to feel the pinch. ("Even the niggers had them. Some of them even had two.") Actually, he had sold many to Negroes in his years of salesmanship. He had collected money from them and taken showers after he came from their houses. Outweighing such services for Negroes was his participation in lynchings. He's been in two. His words: "We'd go home to see our folks, and you know in the country things are more direct, and there's no busybody reporters around. Once I heard one being organized, so I dropped by to see it." The other time was a rather spontaneous and informal affair. He noted that they "did it real quick like, the way you should. When you draw them out it makes it hard because you might get bad publicity. There are still lynchings around in farm country, I don't care what they tell you in the papers. We know how to take care of them when they get wise. We don't use rope, it's true, and get the crowds up we used to get. We may not always kill them, but we scare the Jesus out of them. You know the buckshot shootings you read about every now and then, it's the same thing as rope or fire. They know what'll happen if they get smart." Did he object at all to this? "Hell, no."

The Negroes were working for the Communists, any he would want to kill; I must know that. Had there been Communists in his town when he was a boy, during the twenties and thirties when lynchings were more public and common, some of them seen by him as a youth? Of course. The Communists took over in 1917, he knew the autumn month, but some of them had been working in this country even before that. He wasn't sure how far back, but he thought maybe twenty or thirty years, and they wanted to take this country, its free economy, for their prize. John was capable of broad, apocalyptic strokes: "This is a war between God and His Commandments and the Devil, and we may lose." I broached the subject of

loss. How could God lose? "To punish us." Why would he want to
do that? "We disobeyed him." Just an example or two—I was interested in them. "Nigger-loving."

In any case, he was glad to go to war in 1942, for he was accumu-
lating unpaid bills. He yearned for the East—he wanted to go fight
the Japs. He wasn't so sure about why we were fighting the Germans,
who were combating the Reds, and might be our allies if we would
have them. Hitler's enemies were his enemies: the Jews, moneyed,
slyly alien and the main support of the Negroes, inferior lackeys
who did their bidding for small reward. This was all communism,
personified in those hundreds of thousands of hook-nosed or black-
skinned natives who lived in New York, in Hollywood. They were
the capitalists, too; they controlled publishing houses, banks and the
stock exchanges. Their voices commanded a crippled, traitorous President's ear, bought the votes of errant, susceptible congressmen. "I
was never against the Germans. I was proven right. Look at us
now. They're our best protection against the Commies." Still, he
added, the Germans would be of small help if the UN and integration took over America.

He never fought, though he helped others fight. He did his service at an army camp in New Jersey, a very small distance from Manhattan's subversion, perversion—and fascination. He went to New
York all the time, to look, to see his enemy. He would always tell
his friends how well he knew his New York enemies, and his friends,
from what I could see, always seemed interested and stimulated by
the details he supplied.

From all those furloughs to Union Square, Harlem and Greenwich Village he managed to return home alive, heavier by fifteen
pounds, his balding completed. He worried about work after his discharge, with good reason. He came home to children grown older,
a wife with moderate rheumatoid arthritis ("her joints are stiff all
the time"). He was now irascible and sullen. His wife usually wanted
to stay away from him—out of pain, out of lack of response. She was
withdrawing into her narrowing world of routine care of the home
and the symptoms of a chronic, slowly crippling disease. To help her
she had a young Negro, a high school girl, not very experienced,
but not very expensive. (The price of Negroes was rising, along with
other postwar costs.) A mulatto, as thin and lissome—I gathered
from pictures I saw of her with his children—as her mistress was
fattening and severe, she stayed with them for three years, five part-

time days a week, until her marriage bore unexpectedly heavy demands of her own in twin sons.

During those years right after the war John found life confusing and hard; and he became bitter. He tried television-repair work, but couldn't "connect with it" as with radio. He drew unemployment relief for a while, short rations in the face of consuming inflation. Finally, nearly drowning in doctor's bills, in debt even for essentials like food and the most urgently needed clothing, his home heavily mortgaged, he found rescue in the state government, a clerk's job in a motor vehicle registration office. Now barely secure, in his mid-thirties, he was free to settle into concentrated, serious suspicion and hate. It was, after all, the decade of the fifties, when many of our countrymen would seek far and wide for subversives—and when the Supreme Court would declare segregated schools unconstitutional.

I met him, of course, well ripened in such zeal and involved in actions based upon it. From our first meeting it was clear that he relished talking, and talked well. He had found comfort for his views from his employer, a Louisiana state government whose legislature, in its very chambers, had carried on a mock funeral of a federal judge, a native son who had ordered four Negro girls into two elementary schools in New Orleans. The governor was a man whose chief merit seemed to be as a banjo player and singer whose theme song (composed by himself) was "You Are My Sunshine."

John dips constantly into the literature of segregation for support. It ranges all the way from the remarks of a scattering of biologists about a purported inferiority of the Negro on the basis of a supposedly lighter, smoother brain (fewer lines on the all-important frontal lobes) to the pathetic gibberish of the insane. He reads in such allied fields as the frantic anticommunism which holds the President and Supreme Court contaminated victims, even agents. There are always such diversions from the mainstream as the menacing ability fluorides have to erode America's freedom.

One of the first questions he had hurled at me, in our early tentative moments, was about his son. The young man was contemplating marriage and, a loyal Catholic, was about to attend a pre-marriage instruction course offered by their local church. The church was hell-bent on integration, however, and John feared the worst for and of his son. Did I believe "in integrated marriage courses"? I wanted to know more about this. Well, he would kill his son if a

Negro came into such a class and he, John Junior, remained. His customary composure cracked (one of the few times I was ever to see this, even when I knew him much better) and he shouted at me. I began to doubt whether he was "reasonable enough" for me ever to get to know "reasonably well." Yes, he'd kill his own son, he shouted. Would I? I thought not. Still, I told him I wanted to hear more about integrated marriage classes. Well, if I wanted to hear more, he would oblige.

The real truth was that he and his son hadn't been able to get along for many years, and for that matter he and his wife weren't now "together" as they used to be. Menopause along with arthritis had come to his wife, heightening with its flashing signals her sense of decline, pulling her from her husband into a separate bed. (He still remembered his mother's menopausal depression, and he mentioned it when talking about his wife's health.) Once scornful of even an aspirin, she now juggled and swallowed seven separate encapsulated remedies. Their daughter, *his* daughter, his great delight for years, had rewarded him with excellent school work and high achievement in pre-college tests. Yet her success in the form of a full scholarship had eventually transported her away from home. Now it was their son, an office worker by day and part-time college student by night, who was about to leave. His family was dissolving, his marriage disintegrating. He was lonely.

"My boy is a fool, and he always has been." He became angry at first, but later appeared to regret his own remark. His son, it seems, cared little about Negroes and their threatening postures. He and his son had fought about ways of dressing, table manners and hobbies; had fought all along as the boy tried his own ways and John resisted, tried to pinion the lad, fashion him in his father's image. Murderous thoughts by a father at the shameful possibility of his son's "church marriage class" becoming desegregated were but a final expression of long-standing turmoil.

It was against a background of such family problems that John ardently pursued a world as white and shadowless as possible. His work for most of the fifteen-odd years since the war had been uncertain or dull. He tired of temporary jobs selling in stores, then became bored with the security but confinement and meager pay of his state position. About a year before I met him he had run for a significant political office, claiming he would ferret out Communists in his district, export Negroes North or across the Atlantic, deprive

Jews of any local if hidden sovereignty, and keep a careful, alert eye upon Washington and New York. He lost, but polled a good vote. In the course of the campaign he met a man who shared his ideals. The man owned gas stations, more of them than he could operate by himself. ("He liked to watch the help, just like me. You can't trust a nigger out of the reach of your eye.") John, priding himself on his sharp vision, purchased one of the stations, mortgaging his house further. His wife was enraged; her arthritis worsened, a coincidence he noticed and wanted me to know about. Selling fuel was a tough but slimly profitable venture; a fortunate arrangement in some ways, however, because he was able to inform a fellow gasoline vendor, fast and angrily, about a Negro employee working for him whose child was one of the handful to initiate school desegregation. John helped organize the mobs around the city's desegregated schools. He was noisily attentive to those buildings, those nearly deserted and embattled buildings where a few Negro and white children stubbornly persisted in getting educated together. To enable the Negro attendant to lose his job was actually as heartening an experience as John had enjoyed in a long time, and he referred back to this accomplishment frequently. He liked disorder in the streets, but he was not one to pass up private spite or intrigue either.

In time, we began to understand the design of his life, how old threads appear in apparently new patterns. Remember John while very young: a dark and sulky boy whose black-haired, ill-humored father preferred his fair wife, daughter and younger son. John understood all too well arbitrary discrimination, the kind that appearances (height, build, complexion) stimulate. He was born in a state split among many lines—northern, Anglo-Saxon, light-skinned, Protestant country farmers on the one hand; southern, Catholic, Mediterranean types on the other, many of the thousands who lived in a wicked, international port city. His parents brought these different traditions together in an uneasy marriage, and the boy grew up a victim of this delicate arrangement. How accidental is it to find him years later moodily resenting dark people?

A psychiatric evaluation finds him oriented and alert, in no trouble about who or where he is—his name, the date and place of our talks. His mind works in understandable fashion. He does not hallucinate, and though we may consider his beliefs delusional, they are held in common with thousands of others, and do not seem insistently private or as incomprehensible as those in schizophrenic delusional systems. His thinking is not psychotic; it flows in orderly and logical steps, given certain assumptions that are shared by many others and thus have social rather than idiosyncratic sources.

He is intelligent, beyond question so. He grasps issues, relates them to others, takes stock of problems and tries to solve them. He has read widely and deeply, if with self-imposed restrictions. Much of what he reads gives him real encouragement. Full of references to God and country, encouraging virulent racism, recommending violence as possibly necessary in some future Armageddon of white versus black, Gentile versus Jew, biblical patriotism versus atheistic internationalism, this "literature" seeks an America which we hope will never exist, but it also collects its readers into a fellowship. One can call *all* these people crazy, but it is a shared insanity not an individual one. John works; he has a family and friends. He is fitful, alternately cheerless and buoyant. He is not shy or withdrawn; and he is in definite contact with many people, and responds to their feelings. Can we call him "sick"?

In one of those compact appraisals of an individual person we might say that John is not insane, not psychotic in any operational sense of the word; neither retarded nor delinquent. He has no police record, has committed no crimes as his society defines them, is even careful to obey laws on picketing or demonstrations where they exist or are enforced. (*His* kind of demonstration has often been encouraged by some officials of his state.) Absurdly xenophobic, an anti-Semitic, anti-Negro "paranoiac"? Yes, along with many, many thousands in his region. A frustrated, defeated man, a sometime political candidate, a feckless sidewalk crank, occasionally irritable and only rarely dangerous? Yes, but far from alone.

Born in a region long poor and defeated, into a family itself humble and moneyless, often at the mercy of capricious economic, social or political forces, the boy at home faced those first insecurities, those early rivalries, hates and struggles which often set the pattern for later ones. White man against black embodied all those childhood hatreds, all those desperate, anxious attempts children make to locate themselves and their identities amid the strivings of siblings, aid the conscious and unconscious smiles and grudges, animosities and predilections of their parents. He was an active child, a fighter who managed to survive perilous disease and hard times. When grown he had some initial modest success at home and at work, only to return from war into a sliding, middle-aged depression, a personal one, but one that plagued his family, and some of his friends, too. (The papers talked of a "dislocated, postwar economy.") Individual psychopathology, social conflict and economic instability, each has its separate causes. On the other hand the mind can connect them together, and for many people they are keenly felt as three aspects of one unhappy, unpredictable life.

I looked first to "psychopathology" for the answer to the riddle of John, and those like him; for an explanation of their frightful actions. Rather than seek after political, social or economic ills, I chose medical or psychiatric ones, the kind that seemed "real" to me. John's life shows that it can be understood best by looking at it in several ways, and one of them is certainly psychiatric. Yet I have to keep on reminding myself that I have seen mobs such as he joined collect in one city while in another they were nowhere to be found. While the incidence of individual psychopathology probably is relatively constant in all Southern cities, the quality of police forces and politicians has varied, and so have their ideas about what constituted law and order. I have seen avowed segregationists—some of them unstable individuals in addition—submit quietly to the most radical kinds of integrated society because they worked on a federal air base. American laws and jobs seemed curiously more influential than "deep-rooted" attitudes.

The FBI agent who spoke to me in McComb was standing in front of a dynamited house in the very heart of the most oppressive area in the South. James Silver's "closed society," the state of Mississippi, has a long history to fall back upon, one enforced by social, economic and political power; no corner of the state had been more loyal to its past. Certainly I and others with me were frightened, though perhaps the FBI agent was not, by the hateful, suspicious attitude we were meeting at the hands of many of the townspeople. The Negroes were scared, and many of the whites had a kind of murder in their eyes. In the face of all that, the agent posed a question only in terms of illness, of individual eccentricity.

In McComb, in Mississippi, at that time, a dynamited house and even three murdered youths were not unique. There were klans, councils and societies there whose daily words or deeds encouraged the burning of churches, the dynamiting of houses, the beating, ambushing and killing of men. A few weeks after the "incident" in McComb I examined a minister brutally beaten in a doctor's office in Leake County, Mississippi. The doctor—no redneck, not "ignorant"

—had literally pushed the minister and a young student with him into the hands of a gang *in his own office*. Every bit of evidence suggests a plot arranged by that doctor—he knew in advance the two men were coming because they had telephoned to ask for medical help. Shall we suggest psychiatric examinations for him and for all the others in the state—businessmen, newspaper editors, lawyers— who ignore, condone, encourage or fail to conceal their pleasure at such episodes?

I wonder about the eager emphasis given private, aberrant motives by some in our society. Many ignore crying, horrible, concrete social and political realities whose effects—as a matter of fact— might lead us to understand how John and others like him continue to plague us. It is easier, I suppose, to look for the madman's impulse and make explaining it the doctor's task.

The bestiality I have seen in the South cannot be attributed only to its psychotic and ignorant people. Once and for all, in the face of what we have seen this century, we must all know that the animal in us can be elaborately rationalized in a society until an act of murder is seen as self-defense and dynamited houses become evidence of moral courage. Nor is the confused, damaged South the only region of this country in need of that particular knowledge.

GENE MARINE

White Power

During the last week of August, WKBK-TV, Chicago, reviewed on its early evening news program the tense racial situation in the city, then branched out to film coverage of a riot in suburban Waukegan and a demonstration surrounded by hostile whites in nearby Wauwatosa, Michigan. As the announcer paused for breath, the screen switched to a Purex commercial, and a peremptory voice instructed me:

"Think about *white!*"

White Power. From *Ramparts*, November 1966. Originally titled "I've Got Nothing Against the Colored, Understand." Reprinted by permission of the publisher.

I had been thinking about white. In fact I was sick and tired of white. News reports of jeering, rock- and bottle-throwing whites, some of them waving Nazi flags or wearing Ku Klux Klan robes, had brought me to Chicago, sent me up and down white streets, into white restaurants and rectories and bars. White power. Turn into a cold and accurate and factual report the hundreds of conversations the sum of which, internally, is a sick and miserable despair.

I can't. But maybe I can tell you about some of white Chicago. I wish they were all Nazis: a sickness you can understand and try to cure. I wish they were all different, the product of some peculiar midwestern malady. I wish they didn't live next door to me no matter where I live.

You wouldn't believe Ashland Avenue, no matter what ghettoes you might know about in other cities. It runs north and south through Chicago; in the West Fifties it is the *de facto* eastern border of an all-white neighborhood called Gage Park; in the West Sixties and Seventies the eastern border of an all-white neighborhood called Chicago Lawn. I saw it first from a bus, and though it wasn't my destination I got off to stare. Because at that point you could build an 18-foot-high concrete wall down the middle of Ashland Avenue, and if you left room for the bus to get through you wouldn't need any other gap. Nobody ever crosses the line.

63rd from Justine to Ashland is any ghetto block in America. Sammy's Lounge, three doors from Ashland, screams the presence of a three-piece rhythm-and-blues group; across the street an unnamed, overheated restaurant sells links and ribs. There's a storefront church, a liquor store with more wine than whiskey in the window, a beauty salon with a heavy traffic in wigs. On a humid late afternoon in August, people—black people—stroll aimlessly or stand idly in little knots.

The next block, from Ashland to Marshfield, is equally typical. Three bars all bear the proud names of Irishmen. Teenage blonde girls pore avidly over an enormous selection of rock-and-roll and hair-do magazines in a drug store. A brightly lit, air-conditioned coffee shop offers ham and eggs at a bargain price until 11 A.M. In that block, too, people—white people—stand or stroll.

It may have been accidental, a striking chance symbolism, but on that evening I stood on the corner, watching a hundred Chicagoans strolling not just on 63rd Street but on Ashland Avenue itself. On the sidewalk on the west side of Ashland there was not one Negro; on the east side, not one white. No freeway, no park, no railroad tracks—just an invisible wall so familiar to the residents that no one even seemed to glance at it.

Eight blocks south and one month earlier—on Sunday, July 31— a column of civil rights demonstrators ignored the invisible wall at 71st and Ashland, and marched more than 20 blocks beyond it, to Marquette Park, where they stopped for lunch. The idea was to go on a few more blocks to Kedzie Avenue, then to turn north to the Fifties, where they would picket a real estate office accused of racial discrimination. They didn't make it.

In Marquette Park, a mob of jeering, shouting whites vied with a hastily augmented contingent of police, each trying to surround the demonstrators. Mobile television units roared to the scene in time to send across the country a picture of George Lincoln Rockwell and a group of his American Nazi cohorts, waving swastikas in the white crowd ("Grab that swastika and wave it up and down," a cameraman yelled to a white youth; the youth complied and was photographed by a dozen cameras). Ku Klux Klan robes appeared in the jeering circle. From behind the quickly formed police ranks, rocks began to fly. A brick hit Dr. Martin Luther King.

Finally, the marchers retreated, in a column of two's, eastward along the south side of 71st Street. The white crowd, shouting and hurling rocks and bottles, paralleled the march on the north side. Down the middle of the street, police walked and drove, choosing to maintain their line and keep the groups apart rather than to pursue individual rock-throwers.

Across the street, the whites tore up white property, ripping flagstones out of front yards to lob them over the line of police. The marchers ducked the largest stones and tried to ignore the rest. Youths raced back and forth trying whenever possible to catch the bottles: a rock simply hits, but a bottle can shatter against a wall and shower glass.

After 22 frightening, vicious blocks, the retreat reached and crossed Ashland Avenue. The police went with it, but not a single white heckler followed. The wall stood.

I talked with Father Mortimer Foley of St. Rita's Church in Chicago Lawn, nine blocks north of Marquette Park. I was a little impatient with Father Foley. I had already talked with Father John

Vysnauskas of St. Anthony's in Cicero, and Father Leonard Mattai of St. Attracta's. I'd been in all the lower-middle-class white parishes where demonstrators had met angry white violence in recent weeks.

There are other, better all-white neighborhoods in Chicago than Chicago Lawn; in fact, there are all-white neighborhoods into which the Lithuanians and Poles and Irish of Chicago Lawn can't move— "that class" isn't welcome. Maybe, in those neighborhoods, black marchers wouldn't be greeted with rocks and bottles—maybe. They weren't on one march into Chicago Heights, which is not quite so lower-middle-class. But I wanted to know who the rock-throwers were, and I went to Chicago Lawn.

You wind up in a neighborhood of tree-shaded streets and small, detached brick houses, each with its tiny lawn. The display window of Stiefel's Furniture Store tells you that the little houses are filled with cheap, unimaginative furniture whose design has little to do with taste either good or bad. In the California Bar—named for its proximity to California Avenue—you learn that a bad call against the White Sox was due to the fact that "that nigger umpire won't do anything for Chicago."

"It's such a tiny minority," Father Foley told me. "That's what you should write. A couple of bad apples that make the whole barrel look bad. It's you reporters that build it up."

He sat slightly hunched, as if he were hearing my confession—a big man, with thinning hair atop the bullet head that rose belligerently out of his cassock. "The people in this neighborhood don't want this," he insisted, "and the colored don't want it either. They don't want to live where they're not wanted. If nobody wanted you in a neighborhood, you wouldn't want to live there, would you?"

But the demonstrators didn't throw rocks and bottles, I said. Whites started the violence.

"They weren't from around here. They come from other parts of town. But you can't blame these people. I've got nothing against the colored, understand—but they don't know how to live in a neighborhood like this. They don't know how to take care of property. I'm not against integration—but we have to educate these people. Sure, we told our people to stay home when they had the marches—but you can't blame people for getting angry."

If the rock-throwers weren't from around here, why did you tell people to stay home?

"These are good people," Father Foley said stubbornly. "Policemen and schoolteachers and working men. Put yourself in their place. You've given 20 years to building up your property—you're in a nice neighborhood now, you have a little house worth fifteen or twenty thousand dollars maybe. Some colored moves into your block, and your property drops down two, three thousand dollars."

"That doesn't have to happen. Everybody doesn't have to sell and run."

"You know what those real estate people do."

"But you don't have to let them bust the block. You can decide to stay. The Church could even help to educate your parishioners."

"What am I supposed to say to a man when he's worked for 20 years and keeps up his house and his property, and one of the colored moves into the block? Now you know how they live—pretty soon their friends move in and there are six or seven families living in the house."

Father Foley spent much of his younger life in New York, and his favorite argument is that instead of demonstrating and agitating, the Negroes of Chicago should pull themselves out of segregation and misery by hard work and diligence—as the Jews pulled themselves out of the slums of New York's Lower East Side.

They fought their way up, I argued, with the help of the Garment Workers' Union and the Fur Workers and the Amalgamated Clothing Workers and District 65—with marches 10,000 strong and violence that was almost civil war in the garment center. They came out of the slums but they came out fighting—against the same discrimination that was all around us in St. Rita's Parish.

There are three and a half million people in Chicago, Illinois. One million of them are black. Mayor Richard Daley is proud of pointing out that Chicago has the largest number of middle-class Negroes of any city in the world. Take all the Negroes who own their own homes, or who have college educations, or who earn more than $6000 a year—the groups will overlap, of course—and they add up to 35 per cent of Chicago's Negro population.

These middle-class Negroes are the base for the Chicago Freedom Movement. The poor are not involved—but they watch. If Chicago's frightening reservoir of hatred spills over into more than sporadic local outbursts of violence, the 65 per cent who refuse to march will not refuse to fight, and everybody knows it.

In the 1959 elections, Daley won by a margin of 467,000 votes.

But in 1963, when Republican Benjamin Adamowski ran what one Chicago reporter called "a quiet racist campaign," Daley won by only 137,500 votes out of well over a million cast—and he got that margin only with solid support in Negro areas. Since then, the Movement has picketed Daley's home in a controversy over schools; in 1966, the June Democratic primaries saw Daley's machine candidates trail in middle-class Negro wards, their incumbencies saved only by big majorities in more tightly controlled areas.

Daley thus sits across a microcosm of the American Democratic party, his power shakily based on a coalition of welfare recipient ghetto Negroes (Illinois welfare law is generous and generously, if politically, administered), angry racist whites, a few active liberal intellectuals and the solid support of organized crime. The racists and the better educated Negroes are restive; the intellectuals yearn for freedom from the tight machine control; "the mob" simply doesn't want trouble. The businessmen of Chicago, having decided that they prefer middle-class Negro marches to lower-class Negro riots, are suddenly faced with the possibility of white riots. Everybody in Chicago thinks and breathes race, and walks in fear.

As they began to find their way in the confusing morass of Chicago politics, the politically oriented lieutenants of Dr. King, their early efforts having met with indifferent success, began to look for a pressure point that wouldn't involve a direct confrontation with Daley. They chose housing: Daley is already committed to Chicago's mild open-occupancy law, which is enforceable only against brokers (who of course always blame the owner). The demonstrations would be against the brokers, not against the city government. If there was white violence, Daley's police would have to protect the marchers— and thus anger the white voters. It was a carefully constructed box.

The Movement selected its targets carefully. They were all-white residential areas in which Daley's strength is already waning; in which broker-testing by white and Negro teams revealed actual discrimination; and in which housing is available at prices ghetto Negroes can afford.

In other neighborhoods, the demonstrators might have met a different response; but to go where Negroes can afford the housing means to go into the Polish and Irish and Czech and Lithuanian working-class neighborhoods, the parishes of the Father Foleys. The Movement announced its plans and began its marches. Except for the one "picnic march" into Chicago Heights, the demonstrators met the viciousness of white violence at every target.

Nazis? Klansmen? "No," says Neil Regan of the Chicago Commission on Human Relations. "Rockwell's got maybe 20 people. I'm not saying he couldn't organize some support maybe with the Poles and Lithuanians—but the Nazis are just too incompetent to organize anybody. We get into their meetings, and they don't know what they're doing. We investigated the Klan thing, too, but it was just a few guys from Ohio—they've got nothing going here.

"People ask me how come the Poles and the Czechs and the others aren't repelled by the Nazis—how come they don't remember the persecution at home. The old immigrants, of course, don't have anything to remember, and the kids, 20, 21, only know about it from television. But the new immigrants—people forget what our immigration policy has been. You don't get in unless you can prove you never had communist connections, you're absolutely an anti-communist. Who are the people who qualify? Hell, the immigrants in the last 15 years around here are fascists, and you'd better damn well know it."

The violence, Regan says, comes mostly from kids out looking for kicks. Waitess Sharon Cohn, who spends some of her spare time working with high school age students, says flatly, "It's JDs— the same kids who steal cars and raise hell all over." Negro newsman Lou House of WAAF, who has covered most recent racial demonstrations, says, "You see the same few white kids out in front at all the demonstrations."

But House adds, "Of course the kids can't make up that big a crowd. Things are ugly. These kids get out in front and start something, but then everybody joins in."

The planned climax of the Chicago Freedom Movement's "Open City" drive was a march into Cicero. Technically, all-white Cicero is outside Daley's jurisdiction; it's a separately incorporated city. But although the press usually calls it a "suburb," it is sociologically as much a part of Chicago as Flatbush is of Queens; white Cicero is, in fact, as much a part of Chicago as black Watts is of Los Angeles.

All but the very youngest of Cicero's 70,000 citizens have vivid memories of the bloody race riot that took place there in 1951; a Chicago Negro who has been on every 1966 march but one, and who has marched in the South as well, said seriously that he would rather

walk alone down a back road in Grenada, Mississippi, than down a
street in Cicero. During the summer just past, two young Negroes,
naively jobhunting in Cicero, were set upon by a group of whites
with baseball bats. One got away to the safety of the police station;
the other was beaten about the legs until both knees were broken
and he couldn't run, and then systematically pounded to death.

Cicero was once the home base of Al Capone. No one in
Chicago's Freedom Movement will say openly that this was a factor
in the strategy that selected it as a target, but there are still political
forces in Cicero who don't want the nation's attention drawn to
the wide-open suburb. Another factor is that Chicago police can provide no protection in Cicero; the Cicero force contains fewer than
100 men—meaning that in case of a march into Cicero, somebody
has to call out the National Guard, which for political reasons nobody wants either to do or not to do.

After the vicious violence in Marquette Park, in Belmont-Cragin,
on Ewing Avenue on the Southeast Side, the march into Cicero was
scheduled for Sunday, August 28. On the previous Friday, Daley and
a power-structure group concluded an agreement with King and the
Movement under the respectable auspices of the Chicago Conference on Religion and Race. Actually, the agreement said little; the
power structure, like the horse in *Animal Farm*, promised that "we
will work harder." Movement leaders, however, felt that the victory
was symbolically important; for the first time, Daley and the power
structure had been forced to concessions by direct action.

One militant group, the West Side Organization, called the agreement a "sellout" and said they'd march anyway, then postponed their
march a week until September 4. CORE and SNCC announced that
they would join WSO, but SNCC has little following in Chicago and
CORE has less. WSO ultimately withdrew from the march entirely—
and left CORE's Robert Lucas as the march leader, with about 200
followers drawn mostly from WSO.

Under the protection of 2000 National Guardsmen, Lucas and
his marchers made it through the rain of rocks and bottles back across
the tracks into Chicago, where waiting police charged the whites and
clubbed them away from the march. Only the bayonets and billy-
clubs kept the march from becoming a riot and probably a massacre.

The elevated train to Cicero, like any transporation in Chicago, takes you through part of the ghetto—but in this case it isn't

a slum you go through. It's an area of small, red-brick, two-story houses with tiny lawns, looking exactly like Cicero itself except that, right up to the city limits, the population is entirely black. The white resident of Cicero needs no imagination at all to look out his train window on the way home and see the future he fears.

I met Pete Vergiliano in a bar on West 24th Street. He was born and reared in Stickney, a part of Chicago proper. An Italian built more like a Slav, he won the Chicago Golden Gloves as a heavyweight a few years ago.

"Look, you have to know these people," Pete says. "The most important thing in the world to them is their home. It's maybe a crummy little house just like the house next door, but they busted their ass for 20 years to get that house, and they paint it and they take care of it and mow the lawn, and they live good in Cicero. Nobody bothers nobody. They like it the way it is, and they don't want any Negro—I mean nigger—to move in and louse it up."

"How about you?"

"Hell, I got nothing against Negroes—niggers. Only guy ever beat me bad was a nigger—whipped me three times. He was a good man. But I don't own a house. I wouldn't want them in if I did. They just live different, that's all. Let 'em keep to themselves."

"Would you throw rocks?"

The guitar player, Ron, looked up—suddenly a suspicious man regarding a stranger. "Let 'em come in here and you'll see who'll throw rocks," he said. "They can take over Chicago. They ain't gonna take over Cicero. This is a white town, buddy, and it's gonna stay that way."

By and large, though, Cicero is not an unfriendly place. There is not the warm hospitality that is found in the South—if you're white and not obviously interested in civil rights—but there is an unsuspicious openness. The hard-working, family-oriented people of Cicero would be good friends and good neighbors. What Pete Vergiliano said is true: the tiny houses are neat and carefully tended. When I took the last cigarette from a package at the residential corner of 50th Avenue and 23rd Place, I found myself automatically putting the crumpled package back into my pocket to keep from marring the careful neatness.

In front of one house, a green 1959 Chevrolet sat, rust evident on its underbody and the edges of its doors. At the next, a 1961 Rambler bore the scars of an old accident; wide strips of masking tape held one door in permanent place. A few minutes before, from the window of the "L," I had looked down on identical houses just outside Cicero, occupied by Negroes; I remembered one, its lawn not so neat as these, its window frames beginning to show the need of paint. In the driveway, two Negro men carefully polished a three-year-old Pontiac. The people of Cicero would have pointed to the Negro house, and said that its occupants didn't know how to take care of property.

Forced to a reason for his hostility, the white Chicagoan—or Ciceroan—returns again and again to his property, and, less often but often enough, to his safety. In Cicero at night, on the residential streets, you can still hear crickets; on a humid night in August, you can still meet two or three solitary strollers in as many blocks, some of them women, who don't cross the street or even seem agitated as you, a stranger, approach.

It is, in fact, not a part of a modern urban complex at all, but an American small town out of the 1930's, or perhaps out of the movies of the 1930's. Take away the consonant-heavy Czech names, and in Cicero there still seems to be a piece of Andy Hardy Americana. Jan Vrosak, whose father came from the old country and worked hard, can grow up on West 23rd Place, and marry the skinny kid in the next block who unexpectedly grew up to be pretty, and get a good job and have fat kids.

But across the tracks of the Chicago and Illinois Western, in a little house just like his, waits the black man. There is no telling Jan Vrosak that the black man lives very much like the resident of Cicero, that he may polish his car instead of painting his window sashes but that he too cares about good schools and the safety of the streets and church on Sunday. Jan Vrosak knows better: the black man is poised there waiting to take over, to turn his streets into jungles, to plunge the value of his property.

All over Chicago, white high school students are singing a doggerel song. It goes like this:

> I wish I were an Alabama trooper,
> That is what I really want to be,
> 'Cause if I were an Alabama trooper,
> I could kill a nigger le-gal-lee.

I don't know about you, but I can take just so much of this, and I'm not even black. I can take just so much property value and self-defense, just so much of Rons and Father Foleys. I get sick and angry. The surest way to get belted in the mouth right now is to walk up to me and say you've got nothing against the colored.

Yes, I know there are other whites in Chicago—but if they don't throw bottles, they did vote for Adamowski. I know, too, that there is at times a sad humor to be found in the whole scene. During a march in Belmont-Cragin, a group of Negroes were startled to be accosted from a passing car by a fat, angry woman who called, in a thick Lithuanian accent, "Vhy you don't go back vhere you come from?" In Harry's Lounge on Cicero Avenue, a Bohemian truck driver dropped a quarter into the juke box as he told me tightly, "I don't like nothin' about niggers—nothin' "; the first record he played was Ella Fitzgerald's vocal version of Ellington's "C Jam Blues." In the Sedgwick station of the Chicago "L," someone had scrawled a number of anti-Negro slogans across advertising posters; one read, "Down with civil writers."

But the moments of humor don't dispel the fog of despair; so I watched the Purex commercial and I did what it told me: I thought about white.

If the Gage Park Chicagoan's fears of the Negro are sexual, he doesn't know it. Maybe it's rooted in the half-true mythology about the Negro male's lust for white women, and the Great American Fear that somebody else (especially somebody black) might be better in bed—but if it is, it doesn't come out anywhere on the surface.

If the fears of the good neighbor of Cicero are rooted in the inescapable semantics of black and white—good, pure, clean white and evil, diseased, dirty black—then that doesn't come to the surface either. What does is ethnocentrism so rigid that he doesn't know it's there.

Somewhere at the bottom of the middle-class white liberal approach to all this, there is an unspoken dream: People are learning the truth about property values and block-busting. People are learning about the history of Negro family life and what we have done to it historically. People are learning what the problems are and what we have to do about them. People are learning . . .

But people aren't. There isn't any white backlash in Chicago. There was never any forward point to lash back from. You live in your own little world and you forget the miserable, sick despair of knowing that nothing you can say, no facts, no reasonable argument, will make any difference. In 100 years, maybe. In time to help the children of the ghetto Negro's children, maybe. But not today. If you want anything the white Chicagoan has, one way or another you just have to take it.

NORMAN PODHORETZ

My Negro Problem— and Ours

If we and . . . I mean the relatively conscious whites and the relatively conscious blacks, who must, like lovers, insist on, or create, the consciousness of the others—do not falter in our duty now, we may be able, handful that we are, to end the racial nightmare, and achieve our country, and change the history of the world.

JAMES BALDWIN

Two ideas puzzled me deeply as a child growing up in Brooklyn during the 1930's in what today would be called an integrated neighborhood. One of them was that all Jews were rich; the other was that all Negroes were persecuted. These ideas had appeared in print; therefore they must be true. My own experience and the evidence of my senses told they were not true, but that only confirmed what a daydreaming boy in the provinces—for the lower-class neighborhoods of New York belong as surely to the provinces as any rural town in North Dakota—discovers very early: *his* experience is unreal and the evidence of his senses is not to be trusted. Yet even a boy with a head full of fantasies incongruously synthesized out of Hollywood movies and English novels cannot altogether deny the reality of his own experience—especially when there is so much deprivation in that experience. Nor can he altogether gainsay the evidence of his own senses—especially such evidence of the senses as comes from being repeatedly beaten up, robbed, and in general hated, terrorized, and humiliated.

And so for a long time I was puzzled to think that Jews were supposed to be rich when the only Jews I knew were poor, and that Negroes were supposed to be persecuted when it was the Negroes who were doing the only persecuting I knew about—and doing it, moreover, to *me*. During the early years of the war, when my older sister joined a left-wing youth organization, I remember my astonishment at hearing her passionately denounce my father for thinking that Jews were worse off than Negroes. To me, at the age of twelve, it seemed very clear that Negroes were better off than Jews—indeed, than *all* whites. A city boy's world is contained within three or four square blocks, and in my world it was the whites, the Italians and Jews, who feared the Negroes, not the other way around. The Negroes were tougher than we were, more ruthless, and on the whole they were better athletes. What could it mean, then, to say that they were badly off and that we were more fortunate? Yet my sister's opinions, like print, were sacred, and when she told me about exploitation and economic forces I believed her. I believed her, but I was still afraid of Negroes. And I still hated them with all my heart.

It had not always been so—that much I can recall from early childhood. When did it start, this fear and this hatred? There was a kindergarten in the local public school, and given the character of the neighborhood, at least half of the children in my class must have been Negroes. Yet I have no memory of being aware of color differences at that age, and I know from observing my own children that they attribute no significance to such differences even when they

begin noticing them. I think there was a day—first grade? second
grade?—when my best friend Carl hit me on the way home from
school and announced that he wouldn't play with me any more
because I had killed Jesus. When I ran home to my mother crying for
an explanation, she told me not to pay any attention to such foolish-
ness, and then in Yiddish she cursed the *goyim* and the *schwartzes*,
the *schwartzes* and the *goyim*. Carl, it turned out, was a *schwartze*,
and so was added a third to the categories into which people were
mysteriously divided.

Sometimes I wonder whether this is a true memory at all. It is
blazingly vivid, but perhaps it never happened: can anyone really remember back to the age of six? There is no uncertainty in my mind,
however, about the years that followed. Carl and I hardly ever spoke,
though we met in school every day up through the eighth or ninth
grade. There would be embarrassed moments of catching his eye or
of his catching mine—for whatever it was that had attracted us to
one another as very small children remained alive in spite of the
fantastic barrier of hostility that had grown up between us, suddenly
and out of nowhere. Nevertheless, friendship would have been impossible, and even if it had been possible, it would have been un-
thinkable. About that, there was nothing anyone could do by the
time we were eight years old.

Item: The orphanage across the street is torn down, a city housing project begins to rise in its place, and on the marvelous vacant lot
next to the old orphanage they are building a playground. Much excitement and anticipation as Opening Day draws near. Mayor La-
Guardia himself comes to dedicate this great gesture of public be-
nevolence. He speaks of neighborliness and borrowing cups of sugar,
and of the playground he says that children of all races, colors, and
creeds will learn to live together in harmony. A week later, some of
us are swatting flies on the playground's inadequate little ball field.
A gang of Negro kids, pretty much our own age, enter from the other
side and order us out of the park. We refuse, proudly and indignantly,
with superb masculine fervor. There is a fight, they win, and we retreat, half whimpering, half with bravado. My first nauseating experience of cowardice. And my first appalled realization that there
are people in the world who do not seem to be afraid of anything,
who act as though they have nothing to lose. Thereafter the playground becomes a battleground, sometimes quiet, sometimes the

scene of athletic competition between Them and Us. But rocks are thrown as often as baseballs. Gradually we abandon the place and use the streets instead. The streets are safer, though we do not admit this to ourselves. We are not, after all, sissies—that most dreaded epithet of an American boyhood.

Item: I am standing alone in front of the building in which I live. It is late afternoon and getting dark. That day in school the teacher had asked a surly Negro boy named Quentin a question he was unable to answer. As usual I had waved my arm eagerly ("Be a good boy, get good marks, be smart, go to college, become a doctor") and, the right answer bursting from my lips, I was held up lovingly by the teacher as an example to the class. I had seen Quentin's face—a very dark, very cruel, very Oriental-looking face—harden, and there had been enough threat in his eyes to make me run all the way home for fear that he might catch me outside.

Now, standing idly in front of my own house, I see him approaching from the project accompanied by his little brother who is carrying a baseball bat and wearing a grin of malicious anticipation. As in a nightmare, I am trapped. The surroundings are secure and familiar, but terror is suddenly present and there is no one around to help. I am locked to the spot. I will not cry out or run away like a sissy, and I stand there, my heart wild, my throat clogged. He walks up, hurls the familiar epithet ("Hey, mo'f——r"), and to my surprise only pushes me. It is a violent push, but not a punch. Maybe I can still back out without entirely losing my dignity. Maybe I can still say, "Hey, c'mon Quentin, whaddya wanna do *that* for? I dint do nothin' to *you*," and walk away, not too rapidly. Instead, before I can stop myself, I push him back—a token gesture—and I say, "Cut that out, I don't wanna fight, I ain't got nothin' to fight about." As I turn to walk back into the building, the corner of my eye catches the motion of the bat his little brother has handed him. I try to duck, but the bat crashes colored lights into my head.

The next thing I know, my mother and sister are standing over me, both of them hysterical. My sister—she who was later to join the "progressive" youth organization—is shouting for the police and screaming imprecations at those dirty little black bastards. They take me upstairs, the doctor comes, the police come. I tell them that the boy who did it was a stranger, that he had been trying to get money from me. They do not believe me, but I am too scared to give them Quentin's name. When I return to school a few days later, Quentin avoids my eyes. He knows that I have not squealed, and he is ashamed. I try to feel proud, but in my heart I know that it was fear of what his friends might do to me that had kept me silent, and not the code of the street.

Item: There is an athletic meet in which the whole of our junior high school is participating. I am in one of the seventh-grade rapid-advance classes, and "segregation" has now set in with a vengeance. In the last three or four years of the elementary school from which we have just graduated, each grade had been divided into three classes, according to "intelligence." (In the earlier grades the divisions had either been arbitrary or else unrecognized by us as having anything to do with brains.) These divisions by IQ, or however it was arranged, had resulted in a preponderance of Jews in the "1" classes and a corresponding preponderance of Negroes in the "3's," with the Italians split unevenly along the spectrum. At least a few Negroes had always made the "1's," just as there had always been a few Jewish kids among the "3's" and more among the "2's" (where Italians dominated). But the junior high's rapid-advance class of which I am now a member is overwhelmingly Jewish and entirely white—except for a shy lonely Negro girl with light skin and reddish hair.

The athletic meet takes place in a city-owned stadium far from the school. It is an important event to which a whole day is given over. The winners are to get those precious little medallions stamped with the New York City emblem that can be screwed into a belt and that prove the wearer to be a distinguished personage. I am a fast runner, and so I am assigned the position of anchor man on my class's team in the relay race. There are three other seventh-grade teams in the race, two of them all Negro, as ours is all white. One of the all-Negro teams is very tall—their anchor man waiting silently next to me on the line looks years older than I am, and I do not recognize him. He is the first to get the baton and crosses the finishing line in a walk. Our team comes in second, but a few minutes later we are declared the winners, for it has been discovered that the anchor man on the first-place team is not a member of the class. We are awarded the medallions, and the following day our home-room teacher makes a speech about how proud she is of us for being su-

perior athletes as well as superior students. We want to believe that
we deserve the praise, but we know that we could not have won even
if the other class had not cheated.

That afternoon walking home, I am waylaid and surrounded by
five Negroes, among whom is the anchor man of the disqualified
team. "Gimme my medal, mo'f——r," he grunts. I do not have it
with me and I tell him so. "Anyway, it ain't yours," I say foolishly. He
calls me a liar on both counts and pushes me up against the wall on
which we sometimes play handball. "Gimme my mo'f——n' medal,"
he says again. I repeat that I have left it home. "Le's search the li'l
mo'f——r," one of them suggests, "he prolly got it *hid* in his mo'f——n'
pants." My panic is now unmanageable. (How many times had I
been surrounded like this and asked in soft tones, "Len' me a nickel,
boy." How many times had I been called a liar for pleading poverty
and pushed around, or searched, or beaten up, unless there happened
to be someone in the marauding gang like Carl who liked me across
that enormous divide of hatred and who would therefore say, "Aaah,
c'mon, le's git someone else, *this* boy ain't got no money on 'im.")
I scream at them through tears of rage and self-contempt, "Keep
your f——n' filthy lousy black hands offa me! I swear I'll get the cops."
This is all they need to hear, and the five of them set upon me. They
bang me around, mostly in the stomach and on the arms and shoulders, and when several adults loitering near the candy store down
the block notice what is going on and begin to shout, they run off
and away.

I do not tell my parents about the incident. My team-mates,
who have also been waylaid, each by a gang led by his opposite number from the disqualified team, have had their medallions taken from
them, and they never squeal either. For days, I walk home in terror,
expecting to be caught again, but nothing happens. The medallion
is put away into a drawer, never to be worn by anyone.

Obviously experiences like these have always been a common feature of childhood life in working-class and immigrant neighborhoods,
and Negroes do not necessarily figure in them. Wherever, and in
whatever combination, they have lived together in the cities, kids of
different groups have been at war, beating up and being beaten up:
micks against kikes against wops against spics against polacks.
And even relatively homogeneous areas have not been spared the
warring of the young: one block against another, one gang (called

in my day, in a pathetic effort at gentility, an "S.A.C.," or social-athletic club) against another. But the Negro-white conflict had—and no doubt still has—a special intensity and was conducted with a ferocity unmatched by intramural white battling.

In my own neighborhood, a good deal of animosity existed between the Italian kids (most of whose parents were immigrants from Sicily) and the Jewish kids (who came largely from East European immigrant families). Yet everyone had friends, sometimes close friends, in the other "camp," and we often visited one another's strange-smelling houses, if not for meals, then for glasses of milk, and occasionally for some special event like a wedding or a wake. If it happened that we divided into warring factions and did battle, it would invariably be half-hearted and soon patched up. Our parents, to be sure, had nothing to do with one another and were mutually suspicious and hostile. But we, the kids, who all spoke Yiddish or Italian at home, were Americans, or New Yorkers, or Brooklyn boys: we shared a culture, the culture of the street, and at least for a while this culture proved to be more powerful than the opposing cultures of the home.

Why, why should it have been so different as between the Negroes and us? How was it borne in upon us so early, white and black alike, that we were enemies beyond any possibility of reconciliation? Why did we hate one another so?

I suppose if I tried, I could answer those questions more or less adequately from the perspective of what I have since learned. I could draw upon James Baldwin—what better witness is there?—to describe the sense of entrapment that poisons the soul of the Negro with hatred for the white man whom he knows to be his jailer. On the the other side, if I wanted to understand how the white man comes to hate the Negro, I could call upon the psychologists who have spoken of the guilt that white Americans feel toward Negroes and that turns into hatred for lack of acknowledging itself as guilt. These are plausible answers and certainly there is truth in them. Yet when I think back upon my own experience of the Negro and his of me, I find myself troubled and puzzled, much as I was as a child when I heard that all Jews were rich and all Negroes persecuted. How could the Negroes in my neighborhood have regarded the whites across the street and around the corner as jailers? On the whole, the whites were not so poor as the Negroes, but they were quite poor enough, and the years were years of Depression. As for white hatred of the Negro,

how could guilt have had anything to do with it? What share had
these Italian and Jewish immigrants in the enslavement of the Negro?
What share had they—downtrodden people themselves breaking
their own necks to eke out a living—in the exploitation of the Negro?

No, I cannot believe that we hated each other back there in
Brooklyn because they thought of us as jailers and we felt guilty toward them. But does it matter, given the fact that we all went
through an unrepresentative confrontation? I think it matters profoundly, for if we managed the job of hating each other so well
without benefit of the aids to hatred that are supposedly at the root
of this madness everywhere else, it must mean that the madness is
not yet properly understood. I am far from pretending that I understand it, but I would insist that no view of the problem will begin to
approach the truth unless it can account for a case like the one I
have been trying to describe. Are the elements of any such view available to us?

At least two, I would say, are. One of them is a point we frequently come upon in the work of James Baldwin, and the other is
a related point always stressed by psychologists who have studied the
mechanisms of prejudice. Baldwin tells us that one of the reasons
Negroes hate the white man is that the white man refuses to *look*
at him: the Negro knows that in white eyes all Negroes are alike; they
are faceless and therefore not altogether human. The psychologists,
in their turn, tell us that the white man hates the Negro because he
tends to project those wild impulses that he fears in himself onto an
alien group which he then punishes with his contempt. What Baldwin does *not* tell us, however, is that the principle of facelessness is
a two-way street and can operate in both directions with no difficulty
at all. Thus, in my neighborhood in Brooklyn, *I* was as faceless to the
Negroes as they were to me, and if they hated me because I never
looked at them, I must also have hated them for never looking at
me. To the Negroes, my white skin was enough to define me as the
enemy, and in a war it is only the uniform that counts and not the
person.

So with the mechanism of projection that the psychologists talk
about: it too works in both directions at once. There is no question
that the psychologists are right about what the Negro represents
symbolically to the white man. For me as a child the life lived on the
other side of the playground and down the block on Ralph Avenue
seemed the very embodiment of the values of the street—free, in-

dependent, reckless, brave, masculine, erotic. I put the word "erotic" last, though it is usually stressed above all others, because in fact it came last, in consciousness as in importance. What mainly counted for me about Negro kids of my own age was that they were "bad boys." There were plenty of bad boys among the whites—this was, after all, a neighborhood with a long tradition of crime as a career open to aspiring talents—but the Negroes were *really* bad, bad in a way that beckoned to one, and made one feel inadequate. *We* all went home every day for a lunch of spinach-and-potatoes; *they* roamed around during lunch hour, munching on candy bars. In winter *we* had to wear itchy woolen hats and mittens and cumbersome galoshes; *they* were bareheaded and loose as they pleased. *We* rarely played hookey, or got into serious trouble in school, for all our street-corner bravado; *they* were defiant, forever staying out (to do what delicious things?), forever making disturbances in class and in the halls, forever being sent to the principal and returning uncowed. But most important of all, they were *tough*; beautifully, enviably tough, not giving a damn for anyone or anything. To hell with the teacher, the truant officer, the cop; to hell with the whole of the adult world that held *us* in its grip and that we never had the courage to rebel against except sporadically and in petty ways.

This is what I saw and envied and feared in the Negro: this is what finally made him faceless to me, though some of it, of course, was actually there. (The psychologists also tell us that the alien group which becomes the object of a projection will tend to respond by trying to live up to what is expected of them.) But what, on his side, did the Negro see in me that made me faceless to *him?* Did he envy me my lunches of spinach-and-potatoes and my itchy woolen caps and my prudent behavior in the face of authority, as I envied him his noon-time candy bars and his bare head in winter and his magnificent rebelliousness? Did those lunches and caps spell for him the prospect of power and riches in the future? Did they mean that there were possibilities open to me that were denied to him? Very likely they did. But if so, one also supposes that he feared the impulses within himself toward submission to authority no less powerfully than I feared the impulses in myself toward defiance. If I represented the jailer to him, it was not because I was oppressing him or keeping him down: it was because I symbolized for him the dangerous and probably pointless temptation toward greater repression, just as he symbolized for me the equally perilous tug toward greater freedom. I personally was to be rewarded for this repression with a new and better life in the future, but how many of my friends paid an even higher price and were given only gall in return.

We have it on the authority of James Baldwin that all Negroes hate whites. I am trying to suggest that on their side all whites—all American whites, that is—are sick in their feelings about Negroes. There are Negroes, no doubt, who would say that Baldwin is wrong, but I suspect them of being less honest than he is, just as I suspect whites of self-deception who tell me they have no special feeling toward Negroes. Special feelings about color are a contagion to which white Americans seem susceptible even when there is nothing in their background to account for the susceptibility. Thus everywhere we look today in the North we find the curious phenomenon of white middle-class liberals with no previous personal experience of Negroes—people to whom Negroes have always been faceless in virtue rather than faceless in vice—discovering that their abstract commitment to the cause of Negro rights will not stand the test of a direct confrontation. We find such people fleeing in droves to the suburbs as the Negro population in the inner city grows; and when they stay in the city we find them sending their children to private school rather than to the "integrated" public school in the neighborhood. We find them resisting the demand that gerrymandered school districts be re-zoned for the purpose of overcoming de facto segregation; we find them judiciously considering whether the Negroes (for their own good, of course) are not perhaps pushing too hard; we find them clucking their tongues over Negro militancy; we find them speculating on the question of whether there may not, after all, be something in the theory that the races are biologically different; we find them saying that it will take a very long time for Negroes to achieve full equality, no matter what anyone does; we find them deploring the rise of black nationalism and expressing the solemn hope that the leaders of the Negro community will discover ways of containing the impatience and incipient violence within the Negro ghettos.[1]

But that is by no means the whole story; there is also the phenomenon of what Kenneth Rexroth once called "crow-jimism." There

---

[1] For an account of developments like these, see "The White Liberal's Retreat" by Murray Friedman in the January 1963 *Atlantic Monthly*.

are the broken-down white boys like Vivaldo Moore in Baldwin's *Another Country* who go to Harlem in search of sex or simply to brush up against something that looks like primitive vitality, and who are so often punished by the Negroes they meet for crimes that they would have been the last ever to commit and of which they themselves have been as sorry victims as any of the Negroes who take it out on them. There are the writers and intellectuals and artists who romanticize Negroes and pander to them, assuming a guilt that is not properly theirs. And there are all the white liberals who permit Negroes to blackmail them into adopting a double standard of moral judgment, and who lend themselves—again assuming the responsibility for crimes they never committed—to cunning and contemptuous exploitation by Negroes they employ or try to befriend.

And what about me? What kind of feelings do I have about Negroes today? What happened to me, from Brooklyn, who grew up fearing and envying and hating Negroes? Now that Brookyn is behind me, do I fear them and envy them and hate them still? The answer is yes, but not in the same proportions and certainly not in the same way. I now live on the upper west side of Manhattan, where there are many Negroes and many Puerto Ricans, and there are nights when I experience the old apprehensiveness again, and there are streets that I avoid when I am walking in the dark, as there were streets that I avoided when I was a child. I find that I am not afraid of Puerto Ricans, but I cannot restrain my nervousness whenever I pass a group of Negroes standing in front of a bar or sauntering down the street. I know now, as I did not know when I was a child, that power is on my side, that the police are working for me and not for them. And knowing this I feel ashamed and guilty, like the good liberal I have grown up to be. Yet the twinges of fear and the resentment they bring and the self-contempt they arouse are not to be gainsaid.

But envy? Why envy? And hatred? Why hatred? Here again the intensities have lessened and everything has been complicated and qualified by the guilts and the resulting over-compensations that are the heritage of the enlightened middle-class world of which I am now a member. Yet just as in childhood I envied Negroes for what seemed to me their superior masculinity, so I envy them today for what seems to me their superior physical grace and beauty. I have come to value physical grace very highly, and I am now capable of aching with all my being when I watch a Negro couple on the dance floor, or a Negro playing baseball or basketball. They are on the kind of terms with their own bodies that I should like to be on with mine, and for that precious quality they seemed blessed to me.

The hatred I still feel for Negroes is the hardest of all the old feelings to face or admit, and it is the most hidden and the most overlarded by the conscious attitudes into which I have succeeded in willing myself. It no longer has, as for me it once did, any cause or justification (except, perhaps, that I am constantly being denied my right to an honest expression of the things I earned the right as a child to feel). How, then, do I know that this hatred has never entirely disappeared? I know it from the insane rage that can stir in me at the thought of Negro anti-Semitism; I know it from the disgusting prurience that can stir in me at the sight of a mixed couple; and I know it from the violence that can stir in me whenever I encounter that special brand of paranoid touchiness to which many Negroes are prone.

This, then, is where I am; it is not exactly where I think all other white liberals are, but it cannot be so very far away either. And it is because I am convinced that we white Americans are—for whatever reason, it no longer matters—so twisted and sick in our feelings about Negroes that I despair of the present push toward integration. If the pace of progress were not a factor here, there would perhaps be no cause for despair: time and the law and even the international political situation are on the side of the Negroes, and ultimately, therefore, victory—of a sort, anyway—must come. But from everything we have learned from observers who ought to know, pace has become as important to the Negroes as substance. They want equality and they want it *now*, and the white world is yielding to their demand only as much and as fast as it is absolutely being compelled to do. The Negroes know this in the most concrete terms imaginable, and it is thus becoming increasingly difficult to buy them off with rhetoric and promises and pious assurances of support. And so within the Negro community we find more and more people declaring—as Harold R. Isaacs recently put it in an article in *Commentary*—that they want *out*: people who say that integration will never come, or that it will take a hundred or a thousand years to come, or that it will come at too high a price in suffering and struggle for the pallid and sodden life of the American middle class that at the very best it may bring.

The most numerous, influential, and dangerous movement that has grown out of Negro despair with the goal of integration is, of course, the Black Muslims. This movement, whatever else we may say about it, must be credited with one enduring achievement: it inspired James Baldwin to write an essay which deserves to be placed among the classics of our language. Everything Baldwin has ever been trying to tell us is distilled in *The Fire Next Time* into a statement of overwhelming persuasiveness and prophetic magnificence. Baldwin's message is and always has been simple. It is this: "Color is not a human or personal reality; it is a political reality." And Baldwin's demand is correspondingly simple: color must be forgotten, lest we all be smited with a vengeance "that does not really depend on, and cannot really be executed by, any person or organization, and that cannot be prevented by any police force or army: historical vengeance, a cosmic vengeance based on the law that we recognize when we say, 'Whatever goes up must come down.' " The Black Muslims Baldwin portrays as a sign and a warning to the intransigent white world. They come to proclaim how deep is the Negro's disaffection with the white world and all its works, and Baldwin implies that no American Negro can fail to respond somewhere in his being to their message: that the white man is the devil, that Allah has doomed him to destruction, and that the black man is about to inherit the earth. Baldwin of course knows that this nightmare inversion of the racism from which the black man has suffered can neither win nor even point to the neighborhood in which victory might be located. For in his view the neighborhood of victory lies in exactly the opposite direction: the transcendence of color through love.

Yet the tragic fact is that love is not the answer to hate—not in the world of politics, at any rate. Color is indeed a political rather than a human or a personal reality and if politics (which is to say power) has made it into a human and personal reality, then only politics (which is to say power) can unmake it once again. But the way of politics is slow and bitter, and as impatience on the one side is matched by a setting of the jaw on the other, we move closer and closer to an explosion and blood may yet run in the streets.

Will this madness in which we are all caught never find a resting-place? Is there never to be an end to it? In thinking about the Jews I have often wondered whether their survival as a distinct group was worth one hair on the head of a single infant. Did the Jews have to survive so that six million innocent people should one day be burned

in the ovens of Auschwitz? It is a terrible question and no one, not
God himself, could ever answer it to my satisfaction. And when I
think about the Negroes in America and about the image of integration as a state in which the Negroes would take their rightful place
as another of the protected minorities in a pluralistic society, I wonder whether they really believe in their hearts that such a state can
actually be attained, and if so *why* they should wish to survive as a
distinct group. I think I know why the Jews once wished to survive
(though I am less certain as to why we still do): they not only believed that God had given them no choice, but they were tied to a
memory of past glory and a dream of imminent redemption. What
does the American Negro have that might correspond to this? His
past is a stigma, his color is a stigma, and his vision of the future is
the hope of erasing the stigma by making color irrelevant, by making
it disappear as a fact of consciousness.

I share this hope, but I cannot see how it will ever be realized
unless color does *in fact* disappear: and that means not integration,
it means assimilation, it means—let the brutal word come out—miscegenation. The Black Muslims, like their racist counterparts in the
white world, accuse the "so-called Negro leaders" of secretly pursuing miscegenation as a goal. The racists are wrong, but I wish they
were right, for I believe that the wholesale merger of the two races
is the most desirable alternative for everyone concerned. I am not
claiming that this alternative can be pursued programmatically or
that it is immediately feasible as a solution; obviously there are
even greater barriers to its achievement than to the achievement of
integration. What I am saying, however, is that in my opinion
the Negro problem can be solved in this country in no other way.

I have told the story of my own twisted feelings about Negroes
here, and of how they conflict with the moral convictions I have since
developed, in order to assert that such feelings must be acknowledged as honestly as possible so that they can be controlled and ultimately disregarded in favor of the convictions. It is *wrong* for a man
to suffer because of the color of his skin. Beside that clichéd proposition of liberal thought, what argument can stand and be respected? If the arguments are the arguments of feeling, they must
be made to yield; and one's own soul is not the worst place to begin
working a huge social transformation. Not so long ago, it used to be
asked of white liberals, "Would you like your sister to marry one?"

When I was a boy and my sister was still unmarried I would certainly have said no to that question. But now I am a man, my sister is already married, and I have daughters. If I were to be asked today whether I would like a daughter of mine "to marry one," I would have to answer: "No, I wouldn't *like* it at all. I would rail and rave and rant and tear my hair. And then I hope I would have the courage to curse myself for raving and ranting, and to give her my blessing. How dare I withhold it at the behest of the child I once was and against the man I now have a duty to be?"

KENNETH B. CLARK

The Invisible Wall

"Ghetto" was the name for the Jewish quarter in sixteenth-century Venice. Later, it came to mean any section of a city to which Jews were confined. America has contributed to the concept of the ghetto the restriction of persons to a special area and the limiting of their freedom of choice on the basis of skin color. The dark ghetto's invisible walls have been erected by the white society, by those who have power, both to confine those who have *no* power and to perpetuate their powerlessness. The dark ghettos are social, political, educational, and—above all—economic colonies. Their inhabitants are subject peoples, victims of the greed, cruelty, insensitivity, guilt, and fear of their masters.

The objective dimensions of the American urban ghettos are overcrowded and deteriorated housing, high infant mortality, crime, and disease. The subjective dimensions are resentment, hostility, despair, apathy, self-depreciation, and its ironic companion, compensatory grandiose behavior.

The ghetto is ferment, paradox, conflict, and dilemma. Yet within its pervasive pathology exists a surprising human resilience. The ghetto is hope, it is despair, it is churches and bars. It is aspiration for change, and it is apathy. It is vibrancy, it is stagnation. It is courage, and it is defeatism. It is cooperation and concern, and it is suspicion, competitiveness, and rejection. It is the surge toward assimilation, and it is alienation and withdrawal within the protective walls of the ghetto.

The pathologies of the ghetto community perpetuate themselves through cumulative ugliness, deterioration, and isolation and strengthen the Negro's sense of worthlessness, giving testimony to his impotence. Yet the ghetto is not totally isolated. The mass media —radio, television, moving pictures, magazines, and the press—penetrate, indeed, invade the ghetto in continuous and inevitable communication, largely one-way, and project the values and aspirations, the manners and the style of the larger white-dominated society. Those who are required to live in congested and rat-infested homes are aware that others are not so dehumanized. Young people in the ghetto are aware that other young people have been taught to read, that they have been prepared for college, and can compete successfully for white-collar, managerial, and executive jobs. Whatever accommodations they themselves must make to the negative realities which dominate their own lives, they know consciously or unconsciously that their fate is not the common fate of mankind. They tend to regard their predicament as a consequence of personal disability or as an inherent and imposed powerlessness which all Negroes share.

The privileged white community is at great pains to blind itself to conditions of the ghetto, but the residents of the ghetto are not themselves blind to life as it is outside of the ghetto. They observe that others enjoy a better life, and this knowledge brings a conglomerate of hostility, despair, and hope. If the ghetto could be contained totally, the chances of social revolt would be decreased, if not eliminated, but it cannot be contained and the outside world intrudes. The Negro lives in part in the world of television and motion pictures, bombarded by the myths of the American middle class, often believing as literal truth their pictures of luxury and happiness, and yet at the same time confronted by a harsh world of reality where the dreams do not come true or change into nightmares. The discrepancy between the reality and the dream burns into their consciousness. The oppressed can never be sure whether their failures reflect personal inferiority or the fact of color. This persistent and agonizing conflict dominates their lives.

The young people in Harlem, in the Negro ghettos of Chicago, Washington, Cleveland, Detroit, Los Angeles, and other cities, who persist, in spite of obstacles, in seeking an education, who insist upon going to night school and then the day session of a municipal college, whose parents, friends, or teachers encourage and support them demonstrate that a positive resolution of the ghetto's nuclear conflict is possible. But many resolve the conflict negatively—in either a passive or defiant way. Those within the ghetto who are defeated—those who accept the "evidence" of their personal inferiority and impotence, those who express a pervasive sense of personal failure through stagnation and despair, who drop out of school, who depend on marijuana and narcotics—demonstrate a passively negative and self-destructive solution.

The overt delinquent, the acting-out rebel, on the other hand, seeks his salvation in defiant, aggressive, and in the end self-destructive forms. Because the larger society has clearly rejected him, he rejects—or appears to reject—the values, the aspirations, and techniques of that society. His conscious or unconscious argument is that he cannot hope to win meaningful self-esteem through the avenues ordinarily available to more privileged individuals. These avenues have been blocked for him through inadequate education, through job discrimination, and through a system of social and political power which is not responsive to his needs. When a warlord of one of the last of Harlem's active fighting gangs was asked why he did not "go downtown and get a job," he laughed and replied:

> Oh come on. Get off that crap. I make $40 or $50 a day selling marijuana. You want me to go down to the garment district and push one of those trucks through the street and at the end of the week take home $40 or $50 if I'm lucky? They don't have animals doing what

you want me to do. There would be some society to protect animals if anybody had them pushing them damn trucks around. I'm better than an animal, but nobody protects me. Go away, mister. I got to look out for myself.

Such rebels are scornful of what they consider the hypocrisy and the dishonesty of the larger society. They point to corruption and criminal behavior among respected middle-class whites. Almost every delinquent or marginal adolescent in a Negro urban ghetto claims to know where and how the corrupt policeman accepts graft from the numbers runners and the pimps and the prostitutes. The close association, collaboration, and at times identity, of criminals and the police is the pattern of day to-day life in the ghetto as these young people come to know and accept it. Not only do they not respect the police, but they see the police as part of their own total predicament.

Large numbers of other ghetto youth, however, are caught in the paradox of the ghetto unable to resolve their personal conflicts either in positive and socially acceptable forms of adjustment or in direct and assertive antisocial behavior. They are aware of the values and standards of the larger society, but they know that they are not personally equipped to meet its demands. They have neither succumbed totally to pathology nor have they been able to emerge from it. As adults they live out lives they feel helpless to change, in a kind of unstable equilibrium, aware of their plight and yet accepting it. They are the ones who listen to Malcolm X but do not join; who vote Democratic if they bother to register but recognize at the same time that City Hall will do little for them. They are momentarily stimulated by the verbal militance of certain Negro newspaper editors and soapbox orators; they gain vicarious satisfaction through temporary identification with the flamboyance and antiwhite verbal extremisms of charismatic Negro politicians. They send their children to bad public schools reluctantly because they do not have the money for private schools. They are the great potential who could engage in constructive social action or who could become the pawns of the demagogues. They have no inner-determined direction. Whoever develops any movement toward power in the ghetto finally does so through winning the allegiance of this group—the largest in the ghetto—not of the semicriminal and certainly not of the elite and comfortable.

The ferment within Negro communities throughout the nation —hitherto more obvious in certain Southern communities, but be-

ginning to express itself with increasing intensity and even spasmodic
ferocity in such Northern urban communities as Chicago, Boston,
Philadelphia, Rochester, and New York—suggests that the past cycle,
in which personal and community powerlessness reinforces each
other, is being supplanted by a more forceful pattern of personal and
community action. This is proof that the reservoir of energy was
there, ready to be stirred by hope, for effective or even sporadic protest could never have emerged out of total stagnation.

Although the civil rights movement gives Negroes more leverage,
enabling many to channel their energies into constructive protest,
there is a possibility that these energies could also be diluted into
meaningless catharsis. Demonstrations that do not lead to results
may become only one more safety valve—as the church has long
been for Negroes—releasing Negro energies without the transformation of society, without any actual change in their relative status.

If mobilized community power and protest do succeed in winning concrete positive changes, Negro self-confidence and pride will
grow, and a new cycle of greater personal and community effectiveness should emerge. But it would not be realistic for the white community to expect protest to subside in the face of gains, for the closer
the Negro community gets to the attainment of its goals—the removal of the causes and effects of racial exploitation and powerlessness—the more impatient will Negroes become for total equality.
In the complex turbulence of the Negro ghetto, and consistent with
the affirmative dynamics of the civil rights thrust, success feeds hope
and provides the strength and the motivation for further activity.
This, in turn, makes existing barriers even more intolerable. Accelerated impatience and the lowering of the threshold of frustration toward remaining inequities, paradoxically increase the chances of racial tensions and ferment and conflict. Failure would reinforce the
sense of stagnation and despair and establish as fact the sense of personal and group powerlessness. A truly hopeless group makes no demands and certainly does not insist upon stark social confrontations.

The summer of 1964 brought violent protests to the ghettos of
America's cities, not in mobilization of effective power, but as an
outpouring of unplanned revolt. The revolts in Harlem were not led
by a mob, for a mob is an uncontrolled social force bent on irrational
destruction. The revolts in Harlem were, rather, a weird social defiance. Those involved in them were, in general, not the lowest
class of Harlem residents—not primarily looters and semicriminals

—but marginal Negroes who were upwardly mobile, demanding a higher status than their families had. This was not a race riot in the sense that mobs of whites were assaulting mobs of Negroes or vice versa, yet the fact of race was pervasive. The 1964 Harlem riot was indeed in many respects more frightening than a race riot and the participants' deliberate mockery more threatening than a mob. Small groups of young people seemed to take delight in taunting the police, whose white faces were accentuated by their white helmets: "Here's a nigger, kill me." Even those Negroes who threw bottles and bricks from the roofs were not in the grip of a wild abandon, but seemed deliberately to be prodding the police to behave openly as the barbarians that the Negroes felt they actually were. You cannot hear conversations of a mob, but during the disturbance in Harlem, groups of young people discussed their plans: "I'll go home and come back tomorrow. Whitey will still be here." "I don't want to be killed tonight; tomorrow will be all right." There was an eerie, surrealistic quality, a silence within the din, punctuated by gunfire and sporadic shattering of glass, a calm within the chaos, a deliberateness within the hysteria. The Negro seemed to feel nothing could happen to him that had not happened already; he behaved as if he had nothing to lose. His was an oddly controlled rage that seemed to say, during those days of social despair, "We have had enough. The only weapon you have is bullets. The only thing you can do is to kill us." Paradoxically, his apparent lawlessness was a protest against lawlessness directed against *him*. His acts were a desperate assertion of his desire to be treated as a man. He was affirmative up to the point of inviting death; he insisted upon being visible and understood. If this was the only way to relate to society at large, he would die rather than be ignored.

At times of overt social unrest, many white persons who claim to be in favor of civil rights and assert that they are "friends" of the Negro will admonish the Negro not to engage in disruptive and lawless demonstrations lest he incite racism and reverse the progress made in his behalf. These often well-meaning requests may reflect the unconscious condescension of benign prejudices. They demonstrate mistaken assumptions concerning the nature and dynamics of Negro protest. It is argued, for example, that Negroes should "choose" only those techniques, tactics, and demonstrations which do not inconvenience the dominant white society; the oppressed are urged to be concerned about the comfort and sensitivities of those they regard as their oppressors. The implication is that if they do not, middle-class whites will use their own power to retaliate against all Negroes. Negroes are increasingly reminded of the sting of the "white backlash." Many middle-class Negroes as well as whites accept these arguments and behave accordingly. Yet the threat is not new. The struggle of those with power to deny power to those who have none is age-old, and accommodation and appeasement have not resolved it. The "white backlash" is a new name for an old phenomenon, white resistance to the acceptance of the Negro as a human being. As the Negro demands such status—as he develops more and more effective techniques to obtain it, and as these techniques come closer to success—the resistance to his demands rises in intensity and alarm. The forms it takes vary from the overt and barbaric murders and bombings to the more subtle innuendo of irritation and disparagement.

Many whites also assume that a governing group of Negro leaders chooses tactics for the Negro masses. Yet leaders of the stature and responsibility of Roy Wilkins and Whitney M. Young, Jr., James Farmer or Martin Luther King cannot impose tactics upon the masses of marginal Negroes, who are not disciplined members of any group. And the masses of Negroes do not "choose" tactics at all. They respond to the pressures of their lives and react spontaneously to incidents which trigger explosions or demonstrations. When a bewildered white liberal asks why, in the face of the passage of the Civil Rights Bill of 1964, "they" still revolt—and not in the dignified, respectable nonviolent way of the earlier student sitins—he betrays his own alienation from the Negroes whose cause he espouses. The Civil Rights Act was so long coming it served merely to remind many Negroes of their continued rejected and second-class status. Even well-meaning whites continue to see and talk of Negroes as "they," clearly differentiated from "we," the "outgroup" from the "ingroup." As long as this alienation remains, the masses of whites will be irritated and inconvenienced by any meaningful activity by Negroes to change their status. No real revolt can be convenient for the privileged; no real revolt can be contained within comfortable bounds or be made respectable.

In the face of the growing unrest, careful, thoughtful, and realistic planning becomes starkly imperative. Some whites would react to renewed protest by warning Negroes not to go too far too fast, not to alienate the white liberals who have, even if often timidly, supported them. To others, less well-intentioned, Negro unrest is but confirmation of their own prejudice: Negroes are, after all, behaving as the uncivilized do. But unrest *is* a characteristic of civilization, and to fight against oppression—even unwisely—is a sign that men have begun to hope. As studies on social disasters have demonstrated, people who feel there is no escape submit to their fate; it is those who see an exit sign and an open door who struggle to reach it.

Furthermore, energies devoted to a struggle for constructive social change are clearly not simultaneously available for antisocial and self-destructive patterns of behavior. In those communities such as Montgomery, Alabama, where Negroes mobilized themselves for sustained protest against prevailing racial injustice, *the incidence of antisocial behavior and delinquency decreased almost to a vanishing point during the period of protest.*

The Negro cannot any longer feel, if he ever did, that he should have to prove himself "worthy" in order to gain his full freedom— the rights guaranteed to all other American citizens, including those most recently naturalized. The Negro cannot be asked to prove that he "deserves" the rights and responsibilities of democracy, nor can he be told that others must first be persuaded "in heart and mind" to accept him. Such tests and trials by fire are not applied to others. To impose them on the Negro is racist condescension. It is to assume that the Negro is a special type of human being who must pass a special test before admission to a tenuous status worthy of governmental protection. It is to place upon the Negro a peculiar burden reflecting and exploiting his powerlessness, and it is, paradoxically, to deny him the essential human rights of frailty and imperfection. The experience of inferior racial status has not transformed the Negro into a super human being. To demand that he demonstrate virtues not ordinarily found in more privileged people, before he may enjoy the benefits of democracy, is not only irrational and inconsistent but gratuitously cruel. And above all it is evidence that the invisible wall is opaque from outside in.

No one ought to expect the transition from a system of injustice to a system of social justice to occur without personal and social trauma for the Negro as well as the white. The intensification of conflict and resistance inherent in the immediacy of the Negro's demands, and the dramatic methods which he is now using to attain his goals, understandably obscure some of the more profound human problems involved in progressing from a racially segregated to a non-

segregated society. But, when the cries of anguish of the segregationists have subsided, as they will eventually, the Negro will be confronted with his own inner anxieties, conflicts, and challenges as he
dares to move into a society of open competition. It will then be
clear that though the problems of adjusting to change are difficult
for whites, in even more insidious ways they are quite painful for
Negroes. The invisible walls of a segregated society are not only damaging but protective in a debilitating way. There is considerable psychological safety in the ghetto; there one lives among one's own and
does not risk rejection among strangers. One first becomes aware of
the psychological damage of such "safety" when the walls of the
ghetto are breached and the Negro ventures out into the repressive,
frightening white world. Some Negroes prefer to stay in the ghetto,
particularly those who have developed seemingly effective defenses to
protect themselves against hurt, those who fear for their children,
and those who have profited from the less competitive segregated society. Other Negroes, particularly the young, are militant in their efforts to crash the remaining barriers of race. But even among this
group it is not always easy to tell who is totally committed and willing to assume the risks and who is only talking militance. Most
Negroes take the first steps into an integrated society tentatively and
torn with conflict. To be the first Negro who is offered a job in a
company brings a sense of triumph but also the dread of failure. To
be the "show" Negro, the symbol of a new-found policy of racial
democracy in an educational institution, private industry, or governmental agency, imposes demands for personal restraint, balance, and
stability of character rare among any group of mere human beings.
For a Negro to be offered friendship and to find himself unable to
accept it fully, to find that he is himself in the grip of hitherto un-
realized racial prejudice—or, more precisely racial anger—is to look
into the hidden recesses of his own mind. A person—or a race—who
has been forced to be ashamed of his identity cannot easily accept
himself simply as a human being and surrender either the supportive
group identification or hostility toward those who have rejected him.

The newly emerging Negro—the assertive, militant, defiant, self-
affirming Negro seeking his identity—will probably at first seem a
caricature, a person who wears the mask of race with its fixed artificial expression. No more than the white bigot who succumbs to his
passion of hatred and fear, or the white "liberal" who struggles to rec-
oncile his affirmation of racial justice with his visceral racism, has

the Negro escaped domination of his own individuality by the role of race. Only when the need to play such a role is no longer urgent will the individual Negro and white feel free to be merely themselves, without defenses.

STOKELY CARMICHAEL

Power and Racism

One of the tragedies of the struggle against racism is that up to now there has been no national organization which could speak to the growing militancy of young black people in the urban ghetto. There has been only a civil rights movement, whose tone of voice was adapted to an audience of liberal whites. It served as a sort of buffer zone between them and angry young blacks. None of its so-called leaders could go into a rioting community and be listened to. In a sense, I blame ourselves—together with the mass media—for what

Power and Racism. From *The New York Review of Books*, September 22, 1966. Originally titled "What We Want." Reprinted by permission of the Student Nonviolent Coordinating Committee.

has happened in Watts, Harlem, Chicago, Cleveland, Omaha. Each time the people in those cities saw Martin Luther King get slapped, they became angry; when they saw four little black girls bombed to death, they were angrier; and when nothing happened, they were steaming. We had nothing to offer that they could see, except to go out and be beaten again. We helped to build their frustration.

For too many years, black Americans marched and had their heads broken and got shot. They were saying to the country, "Look, you guys are supposed to be nice guys and we are only going to do what we are supposed to do—why do you beat us up, why don't you give us what we ask, why don't you straighten yourselves out?" After years of this, we are at almost the same point—because we demonstrated from a position of weakness. We cannot be expected any longer to march and have our heads broken in order to say to whites: come on, you're nice guys. For you are not nice guys. We have found you out.

An organization which claims to speak for the needs of a community—as does the Student Nonviolent Coordinating Committee —must speak in the tone of that community, not as somebody else's buffer zone. This is the significance of black power as a slogan. For once, black people are going to use the words they want to use—not just the words whites want to hear. And they will do this no matter how often the press tries to stop the use of the slogan by equating it with racism or separatism.

An organization which claims to be working for the needs of a community—as SNCC does—must work to provide that community with a position of strength from which to make its voice heard. This is the significance of black power beyond the slogan.

Black power can be clearly defined for those who do not attach the fears of white America to their questions about it. We should begin with the basic fact that black Americans have two problems: they are poor and they are black. All other problems arise from this two-sided reality: lack of education, the so-called apathy of black men. Any program to end racism must address itself to that double reality.

Almost from its beginning, SNCC sought to address itself to both conditions with a program aimed at winning political power for impoverished Southern blacks. We had to begin with politics because black Americans are a propertyless people in a country where property is valued above all. We had to work for power, because this country does not function by morality, love, and nonviolence, but by power. Thus we determined to win political power, with the idea of moving on from there into activity that would have economic effects. With power, the masses could *make or participate in making* the decisions which govern their destinies, and thus create basic change in their day-to-day lives.

But if political power seemed to be the key to self-determination, it was also obvious that the key had been thrown down a deep well many years earlier. Disenfranchisement, maintained by racist terror, made it impossible to talk about organizing for political power in 1960. The right to vote had to be won, and SNCC workers devoted their energies to this from 1961 to 1965. They set up voter registration drives in the Deep South. They created pressure for the vote by holding mock elections in Mississippi in 1963 and by helping to establish the Mississippi Freedom Democratic Party (MFDP) in 1964. That struggle was eased, though not won, with the passage of the 1965 Voting Rights Act. SNCC workers could then address themselves to the question: "Who can we vote for, to have our needs met —how do we make our vote meaningful?"

SNCC had already gone to Atlantic City for recognition of the Mississippi Freedom Democratic Party by the Democratic convention and been rejected; it had gone with the MFDP to Washington for recognition by Congress and been rejected. In Arkansas, SNCC helped thirty Negroes to run for School Board elections; all but one were defeated, and there was evidence of fraud and intimidation sufficient to cause their defeat. In Atlanta, Julian Bond ran for the state legislature and was elected—twice—and unseated—twice. In several states, black farmers ran in elections for agricultural committees which make crucial decisions concerning land use, loans, etc. Although they won places on a number of committees, they never gained the majorities needed to control them.

All of the efforts were attempts to win black power. Then, in Alabama, the opportunity came to see how blacks could be organized on an independent party basis. An unusual Alabama law provides that any group of citizens can nominate candidates for county office and, if they win 20 per cent of the vote, may be recognized as a county political party. The same then applies on a state level. SNCC went to organize in several counties such as Lowndes, where black

people—who form 80 per cent of the population and have an average annual income of $943—felt they could accomplish nothing
within the framework of the Alabama Democratic Party because of
its racism and because the qualifying fee for this year's elections was
raised from $40 to $500 in order to prevent most Negroes from becoming candidates. On May 3, five new county "freedom organizations" convened and nominated candidates for the offices of sheriff,
tax assessor, members of the school boards. These men and women
are up for election in November—if they live until then. Their
ballot symbol is the black panther: a bold, beautiful animal, repre-
senting the strength and dignity of black demands today. A man
needs a black panther on his side when he and his family must endure—as hundreds of Alabamians have endured—loss of job, evic-
tion, starvation, and sometimes death, for political activity. He may
also need a gun and SNCC reaffirms the right of black men everywhere to defend themselves when threatened or attacked. As for ini-
tiating the use of violence, we hope that such programs as ours will
make that unnecessary; but it is not for us to tell black communities
whether they can or cannot use any particular form of action to resolve their problems. Responsibility for the use of violence by black
men, whether in self defense or initiated by them, lies with the white
community.

This is the specific historical experience from which SNCC's call
for "black power" emerged on the Mississippi march last July. But
the concept of "black power" is not a recent or isolated phenomenon:
It has grown out of the ferment of agitation and activity by different
people and organizations in many black communities over the years.
Our last year of work in Alabama added a new concrete possibility.
In Lowndes County, for example, black power will mean that if a
Negro is elected sheriff, he can end police brutality. If a black man
is elected tax assessor, he can collect and channel funds for the building of better roads and schools serving black people—thus advancing the move from political power into the economic arena. In such
areas as Lowndes, where black men have a majority, they will attempt to use it to exercise control. This is what they seek: control.
Where Negroes lack a majority, black power means proper represen-
tation and sharing of control. It means the creation of power bases
from which black people can work to change statewide or nationwide
patterns of oppression through pressure from strength—instead of
weakness. Politically, black power means what it has always meant

to SNCC: the coming-together of black people to elect representatives and *to force those representatives to speak to their needs*. It does not mean merely putting black faces into office. A man or woman who is black and from the slums cannot be automatically expected to speak to the needs of black people. Most of the black politicians we see around the country today are not what SNCC means by black power. The power must be that of a community, and emanate from there.

SNCC today is working in both North and South on programs of voter registration and independent political organizing. In some places, such as Alabama, Los Angeles, New York, Philadelphia, and New Jersey, independent organizing under the black panther symbol is in progress. The creation of a national "black panther party" must come about; it will take time to build, and it is much too early to predict its success. We have no infallible master plan and we make no claim to exclusive knowledge of how to end racism; different groups will work in their own different ways. SNCC cannot spell out the full logistics of self-determination but it can address itself to the problem by helping black communities define their needs, realize their strength, and go into action along a variety of lines which they must choose for themselves. Without knowing all the answers, it can address itself to the basic problem of poverty; to the fact that in Lowndes County, 86 white families own 90 per cent of the land. What are black people in that county going to do for jobs, where are they going to get money? There must be reallocation of land, of money.

Ultimately, the economic foundations of this country must be shaken if black people are to control their lives. The colonies of the United States—and this includes the black ghettoes within its borders, north and south—must be liberated. For a century, this nation has been like an octopus of exploitation, its tentacles stretching from Mississippi and Harlem to South America, the Middle East, southern Africa, and Vietnam; the form of exploitation varies from area to area but the essential result has been the same—a powerful few have been maintained and enriched at the expense of the poor and voiceless colored masses. This pattern must be broken. As its grip loosens here and there around the world, the hopes of black Americans become more realistic. For racism to die, a totally different America must be born.

This is what the white society does not wish to face; this is why that society prefers to talk about integration. But integration speaks not at all to the problem of poverty, only to the problem of blackness. Integration today means the man who "makes it," leaving his black brothers behind in the ghetto as fast as his new sports car will take him. It has no relevance to the Harlem wino or to the cottonpicker making three dollars a day. As a lady I know in Alabama once said, "the food that Ralph Bunche eats doesn't fill my stomach."

Integration, moreover, speaks to the problem of blackness in a despicable way. As a goal, it has been based on complete acceptance of the fact that *in order to have* a decent house or education, blacks must move into a white neighborhood or send their children to a white school. This reinforces, among both black and white, the idea that "white" is automatically better and "black" is by definition inferior. This is why integration is a subterfuge for the maintenance of white supremacy. It allows the nation to focus on a handful of Southern children who get into white schools, at great price, and to ignore the 94 per cent who are left behind in unimproved all-black schools. Such situations will not change until black people have power —to control their own school boards, in this case. Then Negroes become equal in a way that means something, and integration ceases to be a one-way street. Then integration doesn't mean draining skills and energies from the ghetto into white neighborhoods; then it can mean white people moving from Beverly Hills into Watts, white people joining the Lowndes County Freedom Organization. Then integration becomes relevant.

Last April, before the furor over black power, Christopher Jencks wrote in a *New Republic* article on white Mississippi's manipulation of the anti-poverty program:

> The war on poverty has been predicated on the notion that there is such a thing as *a community* which can be defined geographically and mobilized for a collective effort to help the poor. This theory has no relationship to reality in the Deep South. In every Mississippi county there are *two* communities. Despite all the pious platitudes of the moderates on both sides, these two communities habitually see their interests in terms of conflict rather than cooperation. Only when the Negro community can muster enough political, economic and professional strength to compete on somewhat equal terms, will Negroes believe in the possibility of true cooperation and whites accept its necessity. En route to integration, the Negro community needs to develop greater independence—a chance to run its own affairs and not

cave in whenever "the man" barks . . . Or so it seems to me, and to most of the knowledgeable people with whom I talked in Mississippi. To OEO, this judgment may sound like black nationalism . . .

Mr. Jencks, a white reporter, perceived the reason why America's anti-poverty program has been a sick farce in both North and South. In the South, it is clearly racism which prevents the poor from running their own programs; in the North, it more often seems to be politicking and bureaucracy. But the results are not so different: In the North, non-whites make up 42 per cent of all families in metropolitan "poverty areas" and only 6 per cent of families in areas classified as not poor. SNCC has been working with local residents in Arkansas, Alabama, and Mississippi to achieve control by the poor of the program and its funds; it has also been working with groups in the North, and the struggle is no less difficult. Behind it all is a federal government which cares far more about winning the war on the Vietnamese than the war on poverty; which has put the poverty program in the hands of self-serving politicians and bureaucrats rather than the poor themselves; which is unwilling to curb the misuse of white power but quick to condemn black power.

To most whites, black power seems to mean that the Mau Mau are coming to the suburbs at night. The Mau Mau are coming, and whites must stop them. Articles appear about plots to "get Whitey," creating an atmosphere in which "law and order must be maintained." Once again, responsibility is shifted from the oppressor to the oppressed. Other whites chide, "Don't forget—you're only 10 per cent of the population; if you get too smart, we'll wipe you out." If they are liberals, they complain, "what about me?—don't you want my help any more?" These are people supposedly concerned about black Americans, but today they think first of themselves, of their feelings of rejection. Or they admonish, "you can't get anywhere without coalitions," without considering the problems of coalition with whom?; on what terms? (coalescing from weakness can mean absorption, betrayal); when? Or they accuse us of "polarizing the races" by our calls for black unity, when the true responsibility for polarization lies with whites who will not accept their responsibility as the majority power for making the democratic process work.

White America will not face the problem of color, the reality of it. The well-intended say: "We're all human, everybody is really decent, we must forget color." But color cannot be "forgotten" until its weight is recognized and dealt with. White America will not ac-

knowledge that the ways in which this country sees itself are con-
tradicted by being black—and always have been. Whereas most of
the people who settled this country came here for freedom or for
economic opportunity, blacks were brought here to be slaves. When
the Lowndes County Freedom Organization chose the black panther
as its symbol, it was christened by the press "the Black Panther
Party"—but the Alabama Democratic Party, whose symbol is a
rooster, has never been called the White Cock Party. No one ever
talked about "white power" because power in this country *is* white.
All this adds up to more than merely identifying a group phenomenon
by some catchy name or adjective. The furor over that black panther
reveals the problems that white America has with color and sex; the
furor over "black power" reveals how deep racism runs and the great
fear which is attached to it.

Whites will not see that I, for example, as a person oppressed because of my blackness, have common cause with other blacks who
are oppressed because of blackness. This is not to say that there are
no white people who see things as I do, but that it is black people I
must speak to first. It must be the oppressed to whom SNCC ad-
dresses itself primarily, not to friends from the oppressing group.

From birth, black people are told a set of lies about themselves.
We are told that we are lazy—yet I drive through the Delta area
of Mississippi and watch black people picking cotton in the hot sun
for fourteen hours. We are told, "If you work hard, you'll succeed"—
but if that were true, black people would own this country. We are
oppressed because we are black—not because we are ignorant, not
because we are lazy, not because we're stupid (and got good rhythm),
but because we're black.

I remember that when I was a boy, I used to go to see Tarzan movies on Saturday. White Tarzan used to beat up the black natives. I
would sit there yelling, "Kill the beasts, kill the savages, kill 'em!" I
was saying: Kill *me*. It was as if a Jewish boy watched Nazis taking
Jews off to concentration camps and cheered them on. Today, I
want the chief to beat hell out of Tarzan and send him back to Europe. But it takes time to become free of the lies and their shaming
effect on black minds. It takes time to reject the most important lie:
that black people inherently can't do the same things white people
can do, unless white people help them.

The need for psychological equality is the reason why SNCC

today believes that blacks must organize in the black community. Only black people can convey the revolutionary idea that black people are able to do things themselves. Only they can help create in the community an aroused and continuing black consciousness that will provide the basis for political strength. In the past, white allies have furthered white supremacy without the whites involved realizing it—or wanting it, I think. Black people must do things for themselves; they must get poverty money they will control and spend themselves, they must conduct tutorial programs themselves so that black children can identify with black people. This is one reason Africa has such importance: The reality of black men ruling their own nations gives blacks elsewhere a sense of possibility, of power, which they do not now have.

This does not mean we don't welcome help, or friends. But we want the right to decide whether anyone is, in fact, our friend. In the past, black Americans have been almost the only people whom everybody and his momma could jump up and call their friends. We have been tokens, symbols, objects—as I was in high school to many young whites, who liked having "a Negro friend." We want to decide who is our friend, and we will not accept someone who comes to us and says: "If you do X, Y, and Z, then I'll help you." We will not be told whom we should choose as allies. We will not be isolated from any group or nation except by our own choice. We cannot have the oppressors telling the oppressed how to rid themselves of the oppressor.

I have said that most liberal whites react to "black power" with the question, What about me?, rather than saying: Tell me what you want me to do and I'll see if I can do it. There are answers to the right question. One of the most disturbing things about almost all white supporters of the movement has been that they are afraid to go into their own communities—which is where the racism exists— and work to get rid of it. They want to run from Berkeley to tell us what to do in Mississippi; let them look instead at Berkeley. They admonish blacks to be nonviolent; let them preach nonviolence in the white community. They come to teach me Negro history; let them go to the suburbs and open up freedom schools for whites. Let them work to stop America's racist foreign policy; let them press this government to cease supporting the economy of South Africa.

There is a vital job to be done among poor whites. We hope to see, eventually, a coalition between poor blacks and poor whites. That is the only coalition which seems acceptable to us, and we see such a coalition as the major internal instrument of change in American society. SNCC has tried several times to organize poor whites; we are trying again now, with an initial training program in Tennessee. It is purely academic today to talk about bringing poor blacks and whites together, but the job of creating a poor-white power bloc must be attempted. The main responsibility for it falls upon whites. Black and white can work together in the white community where possible; it is not possible, however, to go into a poor Southern town and talk about integration. Poor whites everywhere are becoming more hostile—not less—partly because they see the nation's attention focused on black poverty and nobody coming to them. Too many young middle-class Americans, like some sort of Pepsi generation, have wanted to come alive through the black community; they've wanted to be where the action is—and the action has been in the black community.

Black people do not want to "take over" this country. They don't want to "get Whitey"; they just want to get him off their backs, as the saying goes. It was for example the exploitation by Jewish landlords and merchants which first created black resentment toward Jews—not Judaism. The white man is irrelevant to blacks, except as an oppressive force. Blacks want to be in his place, yes, but not in order to terrorize and lynch and starve him. They want to be in his place because that is where a decent life can be had.

But our vision is not merely of a society in which all black men have enough to buy the good things of life. When we urge that black money go into black pockets, we mean the communal pocket. We want to see money go back into the community and used to benefit it. We want to see the cooperative concept applied in business and banking. We want to see black ghetto residents demand that an exploiting landlord or storekeeper sell them, at minimal cost, a building or a shop that they will own and improve cooperatively; they can back their demand with a rent strike, or a boycott, and a community so unified behind them that no one else will move into the building or buy at the store. The society we seek to build among black people, then, is not a capitalist one. It is a society in which the spirit of community and humanistic love prevail. The word love is suspect; black expectations of what it might produce have been betrayed too often. But those were expectations of a response from the white community, which failed us. The love we seek to encourage is within the black community, the only American community where men call each other "brother" when they meet. We can build a community of love only where we have the ability and power to do so: among blacks.

As for white America, perhaps it can stop crying out against "black supremacy," "black nationalism," "racism in reverse," and begin facing reality. The reality is that this nation, from top to bottom, is racist; that racism is not primarily a problem of "human relations" but of an exploitation maintained—either actively or through silence—by the society as a whole. Camus and Sartre have asked, can a man condemn himself? Can whites, particularly liberal whites, condemn themselves? Can they stop blaming us, and blame their own system? Are they capable of the shame which might become a revolutionary emotion?

We have found that they usually cannot condemn themselves, and so we have done it. But the rebuilding of this society, if at all possible, is basically the responsibility of whites—not blacks. We won't fight to save the present society, in Vietnam or anywhere else. We are just going to work, in the way *we* see fit, and on goals *we* define, not for civil rights but for all our human rights.

LE ROI JONES

What Does
Nonviolence Mean?

There is a war going on now in the United States. Anyone who
does not understand how this could be possible is more naïve, fortunately or unfortunately, than one would think this century would
permit.

Recently in that war, four Negro children were blown to bits
while they were learning to pray. The leader of the Jackson, Mississippi, NAACP (himself a reluctant convert to "the doctrines of
nonviolence") was assassinated in front of his home. Police dogs,

What Does Nonviolence Mean? From Home: Social Essays by LeRoi Jones. Reprinted by permission of William Morrow and Company, Inc. Copyright ©
1961, 1962, 1963, 1964, 1965, 1966 by LeRoi Jones.

fire hoses, blackjacks, have been used on Negroes, trying to reinforce a simple and brutal social repression. And all these terroristic tactics are used, finally, toward the same end: to make young bucks and tottering school marms confess to the same lie the racks and iron maidens of the Inquisition demanded—that there is something other than reality. While a Negro is under a hose or thrown against a building by some dumb brute, he is supporting that lie as well as the lie of his own inferiority. The inferiority of the suppliant. The readiness of the weak to repeat themselves. To be no more than weak, or no smarter than their torturers. Yet in spite of this, and in the face of such brutality, certain elements in America ask the Negro to be Nonviolent. But who are these elements, and what are they really asking?

On all levels the white man insists that there is no Negro in America like the one that claims now to be here. Or at least there has been a constant and unfailing effort on the part of almost every white man in America (and the West) to have his own qualified version of a black man exist, and not just any black man who might like to appear under his own volition. To the Southern white (and many Northerners) the sit-ins are liars, the pickets and boycotters, all are fiendish liars. There is no such Negro who would want anything but what we've always given them, the white Southerner says. The Negro who wants the foot off his neck must be inspired by Communists. It is a simple lie to say otherwise, they say. We know what Negroes are, what they want. Governor Wallace, on television, admonishes his black housekeeper warmly, "Y'all take care of everything, heah?" The old woman smiles, and goes off to take care of his baby. That is the Negro that really exists for him. No other. The smiling convicts raking up leaves in his yard. He waves as he crosses to his car. More real Negroes. He is on his way to the University to make the fake Negroes disappear.

The liberal white man insists also that there is no such thing as a Negro, except the thing he has invented. They are simply underprivileged, the have-nots, the emerging. They are the same as we, given an education, a livelihood, etc. And this is the rhetoric. But where did all these underprivileged people, these have-nots, come from? What, for instance, are all these black people doing in this country in the first place? It is questions like these that the rhetoric is supposed to erase from the liberal white man's mind. The fact that the Negro was brought here as an African slave, and that he labored some two hundred years in slavery, is by now supposedly forgotten. (During slavery a liberal, or a moderate, was a man who didn't want the slaves beaten. But he was not asking that they be freed.) Certainly the Negro middle class has forgotten, or at least it is their job to pretend they have forgotten, and for this reason even the low moan of blues from some un-American tenement is almost as much of a social affront as a sign on a water fountain. This is the missionaries' legacy, the last pure remnant of the slave mentality—cultural shame.

What the liberal white man does is to open a door into the glittering mainstream of white American life as a possibility for the middle-class black man. All the Negro need do is renounce his history as pure social error and strive with the rest of the strivers, so that he too can help in erecting a monolithic syndrome of predictable social values, based on the economic power and hegemony of the American (Western) white man.

In order for the Negro to achieve what I will call an "equality of means," that is, at birth to be able to benefit by everything of value in the society, of course, the society would have to change almost completely. What the liberal white man wants is to change the Negro so he can be included in the existing system. Richard Nixon is an example of what the liberal wants the Negro to become. A drab lower middle-class buffoon who has no more political power or cultural significance than his social interment petty ambition allows. Very few American white men want the system itself changed, and that change complete, or occurring with the rudeness of sudden reality. Abracadabra, a family of twelve Negroes is living in the next lot. What shall we do? the cry goes up from the kindest hearts.

It is the same kind of spurious and pragmatic realism that motivates most American "reformers," e.g., most of the socio-economic policies of Roosevelt's New Deal were not meant to change the society, but to strengthen the one that existed. Roosevelt, in this sense, like a man who when fire breaks out in his apartment immediately builds a stove around it, gave a flexibility to the American ruling class that it could not have survived without.

So far the most serious battles in the war I spoke of are being waged between two classes of white men, although the middle-class Negroes are the semi-conscious pawns in these struggles. (The rest of the black population are pawns by default.) The battles are being waged now, have been waged for the last three hundred years, be-

tween those white men who think the Negro is good for one thing
and those who think he is good for another. This same fight went on
during the early days of slavery between the missionaries, those who
would give the slave Christianity, thereby excusing the instance
of slavery as a moral crusade (with concomitant economic advantages) and those who felt that as animals the black men had no
need for God, since as animals they had no souls. The fight continues today, with the same emphasis. Except in earlier times the liberal forces, the God-carriers, had only the house slave, or occasional
freedman, to show off as end products of a benevolent Christian
ethic, but now the Kennedys and the Rockefellers have a full-fledged
black bourgeosie to gesture toward as an indication of what the social utopia of the West should look like.

So the war goes on, from battle to battle, but with essentially the
same things at stake, and for the same reasons. The forces of naked
repression, on the one hand, have always been out in the open.
What they want, have wanted, is common knowledge to Negroes
once Negroes have gotten old enough to find out that the world
as they will come to know it is basically unfriendly if you are black.
Each "class" (of white people) has its own method of making that
world unfriendly, which makes the quarrel. But nothing is really to
be changed. Complete socio-economic subjugation is the goal of
both white forces. What the liberal sees as evil about this program
is the way it is being carried out. Liberals want to be leaders rather
than rulers.

The black middle class, and its spiritual forebears, the freedmen
and house slaves, have always "fought" to maintain some hegemony
and privilege, and as a privileged class within the American system
as defined by the Liberal/Missionary class of American white men.
And because of this they have always had to be pawns and tokens in
the white class war that constantly goes on over the question of what
to do with Negroes. The NAACP, SCLC, CORE, and any other
group who advocate moral suasion as their weapon of change (reform) have been members of the Negro middle class, or at least
bound by that class's social sentiments. These organizations, and
others like them, are controlled by the Negro middle class and sponsored by white liberal monies. All these people treat history as if it
were autonomous and had nothing to do with people or ideas. Old
slavery, for instance, and its legacy, contemporary social and economic slavery, are looked at as hideous accidents for which no one

should be blamed. (The liberal mind is such that it is already trying to persuade us that no one was to blame for Hitler, or for that matter, Joe McCarthy, but "the times.") But the fact is that Negroes in America are still either field slaves or house slaves, the mode of oppression depending on the accident of social breeding, one group having easy chairs in its cells.

The puppet uses to which the historic Liberal/Missionary syndrome has put the black middle class have grown more bizarre through the years simply because of the increasing dead weight of the black poor which this artificial middle class is supposed to exorcise. But this weight, if anything, has gotten heavier, and is felt by all the elements of this society. The Welfare State was the reformer's answer. It was, and is, like a rotten blimp attached to the sleek new airliner. Thirty-five dollars a month and carfare to the Welfare office is available to each poor Negro who rides in this quasi-lighter-than-air ship called Ghetto. Each scream of agony that comes from the airship causes the black middle class, who ride in a special airtight compartment of the airliner, to ask for more Zwiebacks in their gleaming bowls. So that now there must be a Negro Asst. Press Secretary, a proposed Negro chief of Urban Affairs, a Negro for housing, etc., all of which creates a tiny transistor-like industry, for the placing of Negro tokens.

Booker Washington prepared the way for such utilization of Negroes. Martin Luther King, as a faceless social factor, is the same man. Both men are simply public servants. Washington solidified the separate but equal lie, when that lie was of value to the majority of intelligent white men. King's lie is that there is a moral requirement to be met before entrance into the secular kingdom of plenty. This is the reason Washington said Negroes had to labor in the wings in the first place: to *get ready* for this entrance. Rev. King, who is formed very clearly and expertly from the same missionary fabric, comes bearing the same message of goodwill—that once this moral requirement is met by all Negroes (*i.e.*, the poor and brutalized will immediately rise once they understand this) then they might pass easily and joyously into that burning building which he insists on calling Heaven, even though gasoline is being spread on the blaze on all sides by every suffering man in the world. The reward for piety and high moral concern then is to be a membership in Gomorrah.

In this sense King's main function (as was Washington's) is to be an agent of the middle-class power structure, black and white.

He has functioned in Montgomery, Albany, Birmingham, etc. (as has the Negro middle class in general) as a buffer, an informer, a cajoler against action not sanctioned by white Intelligence, however innocently these functions might collect as moral imperatives in his own mind. "Let it be our blood," he has said repeatedly to Negroes, and his sincerity on this point is not to be questioned. He is screaming out to the blimp with the loudspeaker of recent agonies. He is a hand-picked leader of the oppressed, but only the pickers are convinced.

For every token offered in the general interest of keeping goodwill between the black middle class and the Liberal/Missionary power structure, the gap between this invented bourgeoisie and the majority of black men in this country is widened. The tokens are more and more bizarre, have more and more supposed power and influence, but at each instance the poor black man gets even statistically poorer and less accessible to utopian propaganda. But the public servant function of the black middle class, especially as indicated by the performance of its chiefs like King, Roy Wilkins, Whitney Young, etc., is one of communication and control. That is, they present the "demands" of the black middle class to the white ruling class, and in exchange, as payment for the meeting of some of these demands—usually such social treachery as token integration which involves the creation of a lucrative civil rights *industry*—they relay that ruling class's wishes to the great mass of Negroes, while making sure that none of this mass becomes autonomous enough to make demands of its own.

The various vigilante middle-class groups like the first student sit-ins and the more militant chapters of CORE and SNCC began autonomously enough, but very soon they came into the fold of the mainstream moral suasion groups of which King is the titular if not actual head. The reduction of the Student Non-Violent Coordinating Committee to mere membership on the rolls of this main black middle-class reform element was signified quite blatantly by the censorship of its chairman's, John Lewis', speech at the March On Washington ceremonies. The Montgomery bus boycotts and later disorders, as well as the Birmingham near-violence before and after the bombings, were all quickly mounted by King, and brought to sanctimonious halts. Hours after the Birmingham bombings, King was already there, moving through crowds of Negroes, bringing them the word. Before that, when the Negroes were marching in that same city, King and the others, the leaders, swore that the white men were willing to bargain, if only the moral commitment could be made by black men. Absence of violence was the commitment these leaders asked, have always asked, and again it was given, by poor and lower middle-class Negroes and those strivers who had to be on the scene. And if word got back to the leaders that the silent weight, the poor blacks, were uneasy at being left to rot in the same ghettoes (without the slightest hope or chance of their misery being eased, except by making that symbolic leap into Bourgeois commitment, which is the local utopia) and dwelt by such uneasiness upon the impossibility of such advice, then King would walk among them praying, seeking to involve the most oppressed people in this country in a sham ethic that only has value for the middle-class power structure, and that even in those uses remains artificial, except as it maintains local and national social evils with an admirable stability. When this uneasiness would manifest itself as actuality or actual possibility, then these bearers of the missionary legacy would quickly seek to turn whatever energy that existed into confusion, and always shame. "Let it be our blood," King says to the poor, making an opportunistic identification he trusts even "backward" white people will understand as *leadership*. And when that cry of "passive resistance" is translated into common social activity, it means very simply, "Do as you have been doing, and some white miracle will prove your suffering was accidental, and finally worthwhile."

Violence or nonviolence as actualities have never been real categories. Rather, their use is symbolic in discussing possible goals of any Negro "progress" in this country (and the white West). Negroes, except for isolated, *i.e.*, limitedly organized and unconnected, incidents, have never been anything else but nonviolent. There have been race riots, when the "liberalizing" elements of the white power structure have been briefly stalemated, and the brainwashed lower-class and lower middle-class whites have clashed with those economically similar groups of Negroes. (In purely idealistic terms the real tragedy is that these two groups could not find goals that were mutually attainable in some kind of egalitarian "revolution" that would simply kill off their mutual oppressors and resurrect a "system" that would be workable for men who could utilize all their energies within it. Such a revolution was possible at the end of the Civil War. Marx did not study the racial situation in America closely enough, nor its macrocosm which has been worldwide since the white man realized, as E. Franklin Frazier says in his book *Race and Culture Contacts in the Modern World*, ". . . the extension of control over the colored peoples of the world." But the suspicions bred out of race ties, and in some cases inculcated in lower-class whites by upper-class whites purely for their own economic advantage, *e.g.*, at the end of the Civil War, are much stronger than any purely political method of organization.)

But for the most part there has been no violence from the black man. American Indians tried violently to defend their lands from white expansionism, but the material superiority of Western culture, and of the peculiar aggressiveness of humanist industrialism, was, of course, much too powerful. It is a humanist industrialism that has always longed for the twentieth century, *i.e.*, a century when man really is the measure, and literally has his fate clutched quite tightly in his spastic hands. A century where the only gods are immediately useful, and grow angry only as their worshipers do. The moral priggishness of the Western white man, which grows to insane proportions in America, is displayed religiously in every part of the world he has exploited. The ritual murders in the name of reason and progress go on every hour, in every part of the globe. How many nonwhite peoples have been killed in Asia, in Africa, in Latin America, just since 1945, in the name of some almost mystical need for a consistently accommodating order? The "Free World" is merely that part of the world in which the white man is free to do as he wants with the rest of the people there. And he has ruled this way since the Elizabethans.

When the white man says *violence*, he means first of all violence to his system, the possibility of outright war to change the political and economic categories of rule. But this has to do with thought, primarily, rather than the actual utilization of arms by Negroes to attain some arbitrary political and economic goals. The middle-class Negro's first word on the subject of violence, as it is sheepishly (and unintentionally) given reference as a possibility in the real world, is that, "We couldn't win anyway." But the real idea expressed here is that the bourgeois black man does not believe he could benefit by a total withdrawal from white society, which could be manifest by simple political rebellion. And in this sense any attempt at such rebellion represents "violence." (In the same sense, the political overtones of the Muslim movement represent this kind of violence against the liberal middle-class missionary power structure, as withdrawal and actual political rebellion. This is why the intelligent white man and the middle-class Negro are so frightened of this group. Because, certainly, the only real terror in Elijah Muhammad's program is the fact that even though it utilizes a fancied ethnic hegemony as its catalyst, its "goals" and its version of U.S. social history are quite practical, as even a thinker like Thomas Jefferson has attested. "The slave . . . when freed . . . is to be removed beyond the reach of mixture. . . .")

But a political rebellion within the existing social structure is impossible. Any energy seen to exist within the superstructure of American society is almost immediately harnessed within acceptable motifs, and shaped for use by the mainstream, whether the results of this process are called Swing music or CORE. The intent is the same: *white music*. There is no way the black man can be heard, or seen clearly, in the existing system. Muslims would be rounded up and dropped in the Grand Canyon before any kind of territorial gift would be made. Absolutely no "violence," no real social or political rebellion, will be tolerated by the static center, and for this reason this center assumes a flexibility which allows it to sweep from right to left without actually moving at all. It merely gets stronger and essentially more intransigent. "We will risk our cities to defend Berlin," is one answer.

Since Negroes have never tried to mount any organized physical violence, and any political violence to the system is, by the nature of the black man's oppression, almost impossible (even though there are attempts from time to time, such as the new all black Freedom Now party, which by the very exclusivity of its form proposes a very practical dissent, hence violence, to the existing party system), one might wonder just why it is so necessary for white liberals and the Negro middle class to exhort Negroes constantly to follow a path that, willingly or not, they have always followed? It would seem, if one examines the history of black men in the West, and especially in the United States, that they have most often been objects of violence rather than perpetrators. It would seem too that if there were any need to caution some group against violence, and influence them toward a path of righteous passivity and moral indignation, it would be the white man, at this point, who needed such persuasion. As exiled ex-NAACP leader Robert Williams has said, "How much money has been expended to convert the racist brutes of the social jungle of the South to the ism of nonviolence and love? How many nonviolent workshops are being conducted in Ku Klux Klan dominated communities and racist strongholds of hate and violence against Afro-Americans?"

Nonviolence, as a theory of social and political demeanor concerning American Negroes, means simply a continuation of the *status quo*. As this "theory" is applied to define specific terms of personal conduct Negroes are supposed to utilize, it assumes, again, the nature of that mysterious moral commitment Negro leaders say the black man must make to participate as a privileged class among the oppressed. Nonviolence on this personal (moral) level is the most sinister application of the Western method of confusing and subjugating peoples by convincing these peoples that the white West knows what is best for them. Since the Negro exists at a particular place in American society, which has been constantly redefined by the warring elements in white society, Nonviolence and Passive Resistance are only the echoes of a contemporary redefinition of the Negro's place, as seen by the most powerful of those elements, the industrial-liberal née missionary element, which since the Civil War has held the upper hand in the overall power structure of the society. But even couched in purely secular terms, the emphasis on passive resistance and moral suasion is an undiluted leftover from the missionary era, and its intentions are exactly the same. Only God has been replaced, as he has all over the West, with respectability and air conditioning. The Negro must have both before he is "ready" for equality is the way another answer goes. To enter into the mainstream of American society the Negro *must* lose all identity as a Negro, as a carrier of possible dissent. He must even assume a common cultural liability, and when the time comes for this white society to die, he will be asked to die with it, and for the same reasons it will die. But there is no indication that the poor have any such communal suicide in mind, not that they have any theories or bodies of social reasoning to the contrary; it is merely that in most parts of America the social system still hews to the intransigence of its beginnings and no real advance into that mainstream is really being offered. The white liberal's plan is still too academic to really work. But then what *will* happen? What will Negroes do? Are there any alternatives?

*

All black political thrusts, that is, any that could issue from the
actual needs of the masses of Negroes are blocked, either by the
sham "leadership" of the middle-class Negro, whose whole tradition
is based on selling out his poorer brothers, or by the intransigence of
those whites who are "behind the times," as any liberal spokesman
will tell them. An America made up strictly of such backward types
of white men would survive only a few more years before internal
disorder and/or external pressures resulted in out-and-out racial wars.
(Asia, Africa, Latin America, and Black America versus the white
West.) But the feigned flexibility of the center permits a certain
toughness, for the American way that will take some pushing to topple completely. Nonviolence is such a feigned flexibility. It allows
some gesture of social and political "protest," but offers no real alternative to the existing order. But, again, what is the black man's alternative? Very simply, either he must find some way to do political
and social violence to the existing system, even though he is hampered at every step by the black middle-class and the white power
structure, or an actual physical violence will result.

When those four children were killed in the Birmingham bombing, the US Steel plant in that city should have been shut down by
Negroes. Black workers should have walked out of every job they
hold in the city. A general strike should have been called. An attempt
should have been made to shut down completely the city's industrial
resources. That city should have died, should have been killed by
Negroes. At this writing the bombers have still not been found, and
no attempts have been made toward finding an "equitable" position
for Negroes in that city, if that's what was supposed to have happened. All of this happened two or three weeks after the great March
On Washington. And nothing else could have shown the moral sham
involved in that lugubrious display as horribly as that bombing.
Martin Luther King arrived in Brimingham hours after the bombing
to quiet the crowds and give a quiet light of hope to the middle
class. But no real hope or stance is offered by black leaders in the face
of such treachery. Talks in poolrooms with "the 4th St. toughs,"
about the dignity of man, to men whose dignity consists in their
constant resistance to the yoke of cultural compromise white men
call their place. One young slick-haired cat chalking his cue and looking straight into the television camera, after that same bombing,
said, "There's a whole lotta' people ain't gonna stand for much

more 'a this." Meaning: "I am not the president's Assistant Press Secretary nor the first Negro to appear in a Chemical Corn Bank television commercial, but nobody's gonna run over me because of it."

The point is, I think, that the poor black realizes, at least instinctively, that no matter what deal goes down, *i.e.*, no matter which side "wins out," the "Crackers" or the Government, no help at all is being offered to him. The desegregation of schools has been largely a lie, the increase of employment among chronically unemployed Negroes has also not happened. The battle of housing is to determine whether a Negro who is able to buy a $12,000 house can live in it. There is no doubt that soon he might be able to, but that means little to most Negroes. At this moment even the administration's long touted civil rights bill is being systematically compromised by its supposed sponsors, not that it was very strong to begin with. A television commentator says it is a "reasonable" bill. Wish to God this man were black so he could get a good idea just how reasonable the bill is. Such a bill at its strongest is only a token, and has no practical application at all.

In the United Nations a few days ago only the United States, Great Britain, France, and the white "Free World" abstained from voting on a resolution to make illegal any organization that promotes race prejudice. In Latin America governments change hands monthly, and no matter how repressive, illegal, and non-representative a government might be, as long as it plays ball with the United States, is "anti-Communist," we say nothing. It is only in Cuba that something is going on of which we disapprove. But why? In South Vietnam and South Korea the United States supports the most brutal governments in the world. Part of the sugar quota is transferred to South Africa. We sign a new contract with Franco. And this is the society Rev. King wants to get the poor Negro ready to enter. Better Hell itself. But "partnership" in Gomorrah is the best thing offered by the white man to the Negro in America today. This is in essence what the promoters of Nonviolence represent to the Negro masses. The March On Washington, for instance, began as an idea of protest against the system, but was quickly turned into a night-club act, and a "moral victory" for the middle classes, with marines and plainclothesmen on the scene just to make sure the audience liked the show they were going to put on.

Nonviolence then is not a protest at all, in the context it has been promoted into in America. It has to do with India too, just as Rev. King thinks it does. And just *what* did nonviolence accomplish there? The Germans were our enemies and they are better off than the great majority of Indians. Plague and hunger still ravage India: and for all the lies and rhetoric that issue from the West about that country's independence and the political individuality of Mr. Nehru, India for all practical purposes is still a crown colony. It is still very much exploited by Great Britain and the rest of the Western world.

Not only does Nonviolence usually mean no action at all, but it is not nor is it likely to be a useful moral concept in the impossible social environment of America, especially not the American South. One cannot draw analogies between American liberal proposals for Negro Nonviolence and the recent Algerian quietism under the terror of the OAS, simply because the Algerians were waiting for the French to clear out. It was a simple case of resisting a greater malice, knowing that the French troops would return if too many Colons were killed in retribution for the many Algerians who were killed during that period. It was a qualified military tactical device, which kept the French from marching back at the flank. But the Negro's "goal" has never, except in the late stages of slavery, been as clearly delineated as was the Algerians' in that situation. Nonviolence in the American context means, at its most honest evocation, a proposed immersion into the mainstream of a bankrupt American culture, and that's all. And as I have said, even the proposition is, finally, a fake. No such immersion is even possible. It is much too late.

A closer analogy is the fate of the European Jews, and more specifically the fate of German Jews at the hands of Adolph Hitler. The German Jews, at the time of Hitler's rise to power, were the most assimilated Jews in Europe. They believed, and with a great deal of emotional investment, that they were Germans. The middle-class German Jew, like the middle-class American Negro, had actually moved, in many instances, into the mainstream of the society, and wanted to believe as that mainstream did. Even when the anti-Jewish climate began to thicken and take on the heaviness of permanence, many middle-class Jews believed that it was only the poor Jews, who, perhaps rightly so, would suffer in such a climate.

Like these unfortunate Jews the middle-class Negro has no real program of rebellion against the *status quo* in America, quite frankly, because he believes he is pretty well off. The blatant cultural assassination, and the social and economic exploitation of most Negroes in this society, does not really impress him. The middle-class Negro's goal, like the rest of the American middle class, is to be ignorant comfortably.

What other goals can the Negro realize in America? The "out of date" white man, who is perhaps in one manner of speaking more honest, is offering the Negro nothing at all, except what has always been offered the black man in white society. He is saying if the Negro wants *anything* further than what the white man has always given he is going to have to take it. And this kind of white man will take steps immediately to see that such taking remains, as it has always remained, in the context of an "orderly" American society, unheard of. The liberal white man does not even offer the possibility of such "taking." His only goal for the Negro is that the Negro remain nonviolent. In exchange for this nonviolence this liberal power structure will send an army into Mississippi to see that its symbols are accepted by white and black alike, but in essence this is all this power structure offers and what it hopes Negroes will continue to accept. It offers Negroes nothing further in their or its lifetime. Nonviolence, then, is not being offered as a means to an end, but as the end in itself.

The Negro's real problem remains in finding some actual goal to work toward. A complete equality of means is impossible in the present state of American society. And even if it were possible, the society is horrible enough without Negroes swelling its ranks. The only genuine way, it seems to me, for the Negro to achieve a personal autonomy, this equality of means, would be as a truly active moralizing force within or *against* American society as it now stands. In this sense I advocate a violence, a literal murdering of the American socio-political stance, not only as it directly concerns American Negroes, but in terms of its stranglehold on most of the modern world.

The Negro must take an extreme stance, must attack the white man's system, using his own chains to help beat that system into submission and actual change. The black man is the only revolutionary force in American society today, if only by default. The supposed Christian ideal of Nonviolence is aimed at quieting even this most natural of insurrectionary elements. As an actual moral category all rational men are essentially nonviolent, except in defense of their lives. To ask that the black man not even defend himself (as Robert Williams tried to defend himself and the rest of the black community of Monroe, North Carolina, a few years ago, before he was framed in a bogus kidnapping charge by local whites with the aid of the Federal Government) is to ask that that black man stay quiet in his chains while the most "liberal" elements in this country saw away at those chains with make-believe saws. The Negro, again, in this instance, is asked to be what the white man makes of him. Not only does the white man oppress the Negro, but he is even going to tell him how to react under the oppression. Surely, however, the most patiently Christian man must realize that self-defense in any situation is honest and natural. It is also obligatory, otherwise there is no use in asking for any right since the asker will probably not be around to benefit by its granting.

But if the most violent political and social protests are muffled (and the exile of Robert Williams seems to me one notable example of such muffling; the attempted jailing of newsman William Worthy for trying to find out about China and Cuba another) and the moral bankruptcy of the black middle class continues to be used by the white ruling class as its cynical symbol of Negro "progress," then it seems to me that quite soon an actual physical violence *will* break out. For every lie that the liberal power structure tells itself, the black bourgeoisie, and the rest of the world about the majority of Negroes in this country alienates that majority even more critically. By not allowing a real "grassroots" protest to issue from the core of the oppressed black masses, the American white man is forcing another kind of protest to take shape. One that will shake this whole society at its foundations, and succeed in changing it, if only into something worse.

Soon, for every sham gesture like the March On Washington or the still impending "deal" King and the other black "leaders" made with white Birmingham, there may be twice that many acts of unorganized responsive violence. How much longer does anyone in this country, black or white, think that the "4th St. toughs," *i.e.*, the oppressed black man, who has made no deals with the white power structure, nor received any favors, is going to run from policeman and dogs, or stand by and watch while "unknown assailants" blow up their pitiful homes? Is it possible that the American white man knows so little about Negroes, from whatever level he does his observing, that he thinks these Negroes believe or have ever believed in the justice and morality of the white man? Left to their own devices, the masses of Negroes will finally strike back, perhaps even

kill, in a vertiginous gesture of fear and despair. Their anger will
not even matter, since it has been a hopelessly familiar element in
their emotional lives.

Nonviolence can be your "goal" if you are already sitting in a
comfortable house being brought the news of your oppression over
television. It *can* be the normal conduct of rational men if they can
believe in the literalness and effectiveness of what they are trying to accomplish by such conduct. But walk, on any night, from one
end of 125th Street (in New York's Harlem) to the other, and count
the hundred policemen and figure out the climate of rational conduct that is being cultivated by such an environment.

A legitimate Negro protest movement unstalemated by the
sham of tokenism and filthy bourgeois intention might succeed in
remaking this society, and establishing an honest connection between it and the rest of the nonwhite world. But most of the leaders
of what passes as such protest, the middle-class Negroes and white
liberals, who have access to courtrooms and picket lines, have already
sold their souls. Finally, it would seem that for the mass of Negroes
such leadership as they need will be spawned within their own ranks,
bolstered by those young Negroes from the middle class who recognize themselves the hopelessness of their social connections. But
this leadership is most likely to take solid form only in the most repressive and irrational of circumstances. The most horrible vision I
have is that the white man, in growing terror of those suddenly
ubiquitous acts of unorganized violence to which the most oppressed
black men might resort, will become even more repressive, and even
the veneer of the liberal establishment will be stripped away (in much
the same way that such veneer has been worn away in international
affairs or in dealing with the possibility of actual domestic political
dissent. The Communist party is already outlawed. Mail is being
opened. Phones are being tapped. The penalty for traveling to Cuba
is five years in prison and five thousand dollars fine, they say. Where
will such insanity lead?). And in such instances these unconnected
acts of responsive violence would increase, and perhaps even gradually find their connection. The result of such chaos is anybody's
guess. Guerrilla warfare, concentration camps? But one of our congressmen has said recently that our only real ally in Africa is South
Africa. And the only "foolproof" way to completely stop legitimate
Negro protest, especially as it grows more agitated by the lies and
malice of most of America, and agitated, I am saying, into actual

bloodletting, would be to follow the South African example (or Hitler's). I hope this is ugly fantasy too. But there are very few white men in this country who are doing anything to prevent this. The present emphasis on Nonviolence rather than honest attempts at socio-economic reconstruction will only speed the coming of such horror.

SOL STERN

America's Black Guerrillas

"We are already at war . . . The racist dog police must withdraw from the black community. . . ."

The speaker was Huey P. Newton, the 25-year-old leader of the Black Panthers of California. It was two months ago, before Newark and Detroit, before the Black Revolution in this country had taken its latest and most fateful turn into urban guerrilla warfare.

I thought about those words two months later as I watched the Battle of Detroit on television. All the talk about guerrilla warfare which had seemed so unreal became vivid as I watched tanks

America's Black Guerrillas. From *Ramparts*, July 1967. Reprinted by permission of the publisher.

and armored cars move through the streets of Detroit, rattling their machine-guns against tenement buildings. It was like some phantasmagorical historical dream in which an American city was reenacting the Warsaw Ghetto 1943, Budapest 1956, Santo Domingo 1965. If such an analogy is objectively inappropriate, if the National Guard and paratroopers were not the Wehrmacht or the Red Army, the important fact, the fact that most whites fail to perceive, is that the cops were considered a foreign occupying army by the black men who were willing to pit their rifles against tanks. The snipers thus turned themselves in the eyes of many of their black comrades into "freedom fighters."

If Newark and Detroit did nothing else, they at least forced a more accurate vocabulary upon the press and public officials. What had merely been "riots" in Harlem and Watts, what had been traditionally analyzed as primitive reactions to heat and frustration, was now in Detroit clearly recognizable as an uprising with revolutionary overtones. (Governor Hughes of New Jersey set the precedent by referring to Newark as an "insurrection." A newspaperman in Newark told me that the real explanation for the governor's enlightenment lies in the fact that the Prudential Insurance Company is Newark's biggest industry, and the insurance companies are off the hook for liabilities if the damage is caused by an insurrection.)

Still, much nonsense was written by way of explanation of the insurrections; a new, crude version of economic determinism takes the place of the vaguer explanations of "heat" and "frustration." Negroes riot, the press and the urban sociologists now almost unanimously agree, because they lack housing or education or jobs. Thus a new riot prevention mystique grows, abetted even by "moderate" civil rights leaders, which suggests that a little more poverty money spent, a police review board, better schools, an extra swimming pool, will have a direct effect on the propensity to loot and snipe in the ghetto. It is a dangerous liberal myth, not because it is not well-intentioned, but because it is already outdated and ignores the real, new factor in the Black Revolution—the black urban guerrilla.

The black guerrilla will not come down off his sniper's perch or stop making molotov cocktails because of a little more welfare money in the ghetto, since he has probably already rejected a job with the poverty program—or perhaps he *has* a job with the poverty program by day and still wants to burn down City Hall by night. His hatred of the system will not be affected by a better school in the ghetto, since he has probably been through the best schools and rejected their values. He takes part in insurrections in Detroit and Newark not because of a sudden incident that sets off a smoldering frustration, but because he has long-range plans to disrupt and wreak havoc on the system that he feels produced the ghetto in this country and oppression all over the world—even if those plans mean the loss of his life. He is like Samson among the Philistines, bound and alone among many, but hopefully strong enough to pull the whole house down.

The secret and anonymous interview with some of the Newark snipers published in *Life* magazine shows that they are middle class young men who organized themselves after doing civil rights work in Mississippi in 1965. One of them was reported to be a law student in an eastern university. Perhaps there was a bit of *Life* hyperbole hidden in the interview, but it had the ring of authenticity. For it is not the poorest, least-educated blacks, but a better-educated, indeed almost middle class, radical black intelligentsia that forms the vanguard of America's black guerrillas.

The *Life* interview was couched in familiar language. I had first heard this vernacular from the Black Panthers in the relaxed atmosphere of a San Francisco living room. The Panthers, a group of armed Negroes who make their home in the San Francisco Bay Area, consider themselves a political party, and their official name is the Black Panther Party for Self Defence. They first made local headlines when they appeared in public, in groups of about 20, armed with loaded shotguns and pistols, escorting the widow of Malcolm X around the city. Local cops were dumbfounded to discover that there was no law which prohibited the Panthers from carrying loaded weapons so long as they were unconcealed, a legal fact which the Panthers had carefully researched and briefed themselves on. That situation produced some dramatic confrontations between the cops and the Panthers, like one scene I witnessed: A cop approached a Panther and asked him to hand over his gun. The Panther asked, "Am I under arrest?" The cop answered, "No." The Panther replied, "Then get your . . . hands off my gun."

It was a dangerous act of bravado, but it typified the embattled mentality of the new black guerrillas. Behind it was a deadly serious purpose. The Panthers' public display of guns had both a real and a symbolic meaning—real because they believe that they will have to use the guns eventually against the power structure, yet symbolic because of the political effect on the black community of a few blacks openly carrying guns.

"Ninety per cent of the reason we carried guns in the first place," says Panther leader Huey P. Newton, "was educational. We set the example. We made black people aware that they have the right to carry guns."

Newton and his co-leader, 30-year-old Bobby Seale, quietly tried to explain to me why the black people have to have guns and what they must do with them. They see the United States as the center of an imperialist system which suppresses the world-wide revolution of colored people, of which American Negroes are only one part. But, says Huey Newton, "We can stop the machinery. We can stop the imperialists from using it against black people all over the world. We are in a strategic position in this country, and we won't be the only group rebelling against the oppressor here."

The Panthers are only a small cadre in the Negro community. Their membership figures are hard to come by. When you ask them, they answer by quoting Malcolm X: "Those who know don't say and those who say don't know." Nevertheless, it has not affected their revolutionary fervor or their confidence. Theirs is a vision of an American apocalypse in which all of the blacks are forced to unite for survival against the white oppressors. Huey Newton puts it this way: "At the height of the resistance they are going to be slaughtering black people indiscriminately. We are sure that at that time Martin Luther King will be a member of the Black Panthers through necessity. He and others like him will have to band together with us just to save themselves."

There has always been something of the rhetoric of Armageddon among Negro militants, but it has never had such a serious ring. Once it was more a matter of literary allusion and wish-fulfillment of revenge, as in the plays of LeRoi Jones or the essays of James Baldwin. But Detroit has made it suddenly a very real business.

In Detroit on the Tuesday night of the outbreak, the most modern symbol of counter-insurgency, the helicopter, went into action. The Pentagon sent in 25 Army choppers to assist the soldiers in ferreting out the guerrillas from the tangled jungle of tenement buildings. One resident of the ghetto said, "They came flying in low just over the rooftops, shining their big searchlights up and down the building. Once I saw one of them open fire. A soldier riding in front used an automatic weapon—he was firing at one of the rooftops."

But the guerrillas, according to reporters on the scene, struck back like Viet Cong by "laying siege to four separate police and fire stations." The only thing missing in the script were the satchel charges.

Detroit was a revolutionary battlefront. It was treated by the authorities not like a mere outbreak of criminal lawlessness, answerable by measured justice, but like a revolution that had to be suppressed by anti-population measures. Days after the fighting had ceased, 5000 men, women and children languished in Michigan's overcrowded jails. The injured never had their wounds treated. No one had been released on his own recognizance. Bail was set at an average of $5000. Even when it was possible for families and friends to raise the money to release a prisoner, they usually could not find him, for there was no central record of where each prisoner was being kept.

There is something of Detroit in the street corner rallies held by the Black Panthers in the black communities of the Bay Area. At these rallies small groups of young bloods gather to hear Bobby Seale and Newton tell them how, when the time comes, they can "take care of business" in groups of threes and fours. The "business" they are talking about is "executing white racist cops" or dropping molotov cocktails into stragetic industrial installations. It is all suddenly very real and serious when you ask Huey Newton, who looks younger than his 25 years, why they talk of killing a couple of cops, and he tells you confidently that when the time comes, it won't be just the killing of a couple of cops but part of a whole nationally coordinated effort aimed at the entire "white occupying army." And it is, finally, very serious when you ask him what he thinks will happen to him and he answers, "I am going to be killed."

Where do they come from, these articulate and well-educated young men who have become black Kamikazes? And why have they become revolutionaries in the most unlikely place for revolution in the world? Huey Newton graduated from the excellent and integrated Berkeley High School, went to a two-year college, eventually spent a year in law school. Stokely Carmichael went to Bronx Science High School, probably the best prep-school for success in the U.S. Somewhere in the recent history of the country they, along with countless other young black men, decided that it was no use trying to liberate their people by appealing to the good sense and conscience of their white neighbors; instead, they became convinced that their freedom could only be wrested through force and turmoil.

It is all somehow summed up by the answer Stokely Carmichael gave at a conference in London to the young hippies who asked him how they could help the Black Revolution. His sardonic answer was, "Well, I'll tell you what, when the police come into the ghettos to shoot us down in the streets, you can help us fight the police by throwing flowers at them."

Perhaps back in the early days of the movement Carmichael did believe in the power of flowers. If he now stands in Havana, surrounded by the veterans of the international revolution, publicly welcoming the emergence of guerrilla warfare in the United States, it is neither because he has been subverted by Peking propaganda or because he has flipped his lid. He has simply come to believe that America can only be regenerated as part of a world revolutionary process.

It is easy to bemoan the change in Carmichael and SNCC, as many liberals have been doing lately, and nostalgically recall the days when SNCC and the civil rights movement seemed to be a community of love. But one must remember that SNCC moved in its current direction as a result of careful, often anguished, deliberation by intelligent and dedicated young men and women who had tested their ideas in the crucibles of Southern and Northern jails.

In an exclusive interview with a *Ramparts* reporter recently, Rap Brown mused about the changing mood in SNCC. "That whole nonviolence thing was nothing but a preparation for genocide," he said. "At one point, not so long ago, the man could have sent a message to black people, saying meet me at such and such a concentration camp, and black people would have been there—on time!"

Asked about SNCC's attitude toward the rebellions, Brown answered that he was satisfied that they "were becoming more sophisticated on their own." He mentioned with pleasure the fact that in Tampa, for example, the police could not contain the actions in the ghetto area and that sniper fire against police was on the increase. He said this trend would continue, putting it, simply, that "people in the black community are coming to accept that tactic [guerrilla warfare], and as counter-revolutionary violence escalates against black people, revolutionary violence will rise to meet it."

On second thought, Brown said, "The trouble with black folks is that they wanna loot—they don't want to shoot! [But that was before Detroit.] But black folks are not looting—they have a right to everything they take . . . this country has looted everything it has, beginning with black people."

Asked what exactly SNCC did when a rebellion broke out, Brown replied, "We do then what we always do—help the people get organized, tell them how to get the most out of it. We tell them they got the man by the balls, now the thing is to get the most out of it. You see how they got the hunkies promising them jobs now."

The turning point for Brown, as with so many others of his generation in SNCC, the point at which they began to understand that the system wasn't worth integrating into, came at the 1964 Democratic National Convention—when the Convention refused to seat the delegation from the Mississippi Freedom Democratic Party. Brown recalled this bitterly and was particularly vituperous about the hatchet job performed on the MFDP by Hubert Humphrey.

And so SNCC and Rap Brown have left the comfortable traditions of loyal opposition and gone their own way. They have moved toward an exclusive concern with black people. They are not racists, only pro-black, and very pessimistic about what they see coming out of the white community. "The only encouraging thing that has happened with white people," said Brown, "is when those white people in Los Angeles got beat up by the cops and started hollering about police brutality—hell, we told them that years ago, but they had to get their heads whipped before they could see it." The only other encouraging thing in the white community, he said chuckling, is that Lurleen Wallace has cancer.

It is not their own aberration but society's that this generation of young Negroes, who came to maturity in an organization founded on the principles of Gandhi, have come out sounding like Robert Williams. Williams is the American Negro who has lived as a political exile for the last half dozen years—first in Cuba, then in China— where he directed messages via a newsletter to American Negroes urging them to take up armed guerrilla warfare in the cities. In the late 1950's, Williams had been president of the Monroe, North Carolina, branch of the NAACP. He set off a furor in the national civil rights movement and turned himself into a pariah by suggesting that Negroes shoot back when armed bands of white rednecks start shooting up the Negro section of town. That was just a short time ago;

black America has lived through much since the simple proposal of armed self-defense could provoke so much tumult.

Today bands of young Negroes around the country are preparing themselves for guerrilla warfare in the cities. The theory is chillingly simple. The ghetto is a vast sea in which the guerrilla can swim. He can venture forth to sabotage the installations of the government, or, hidden in the ghetto, he can hold down a whole company of infantry and then disappear into the crowded city. The guerrilla knows that he can never hope to overturn the government by such tactics, but his perspective is a world-wide one. America, the suppressor of world revolution, becomes over-extended. Every soldier that must be garrisoned at home to keep the lid on the ghetto is one less that can be sent overseas to suppress another colored revolution. As the pressure on America mounts, it must either come to terms with the revolution both overseas and at home or turn itself into a fascist garrison state and thus at least show the world its true color.

Whether or not the guerrilla warfare in Detroit was actively planned beforehand, the results of that warfare must have confirmed many a black revolutionary's belief in the potential of such tactics. He could not fail to have noticed the symbolic fact that two brigades of the 101st Airborne had to be dispatched to Detroit. The 101st third brigade was off in Vietnam fighting the Viet Cong. All together over 10,000 troops, plus 2000 police officers, were tied up by the four-day incident. At one point, over 140 square blocks of the city were under the complete control of the rioters and snipers. The police and the National Guardsmen had been completely routed, and only when they came back with tanks and .50 caliber machine-guns blazing were they able to reestablish control. And yet there were probably never more than a handful of snipers.

The spirit of Detroit is the spirit of the Black Panthers, of Rap Brown, of Stokely Carmichael—not because they participated in the Detroit revolution or planned it, or even knew about it, but because there is a new revolutionary consensus among militant blacks that is producing guerrilla fighters. It is wild and suicidal and romantic and very irrational. It is the spirit of revolution, and since America has shown very little capacity for understanding or coping with the forces of revolution abroad, it is unlikely that it will show much understanding of the new revolutionary spirit at home. When Ronald Reagan called the guerrillas of Detroit "mad dogs" he was at least reacting honestly—expressing a sentiment that was shared by the average white American. One deals with "mad dogs" by shooting them down quickly and peremptorily and America will be tempted to do just that with the blacks, thus sparing itself the necessity of trying to find out *why* young men become guerrillas in the most "successful" country in the world. When a few more jobs are created, and a few swimming pools built in the ghettos and the rebellion does not cease, Americans will be even more furious at the "mad dogs."

America will also be tempted to find scapegoats. Last year it was Stokely Carmichael. This year it is Rap Brown. Next year it may well be Mao Tse-tung. Some enterprising newspaperman or congressman with help from J. Edgar Hoover will probably discover that some of the captured guerrillas have been reading Mao or once belonged to a political group that defended the Chinese Revolution.

But then America will be deceiving itself further. If Rap Brown is jailed, SNCC will find another leader who will sound the same tones, not because he will have taken his cue from some foreign ideology, but because he has gone through an American experience and come out of it a revolutionary. The black guerrillas have become convinced that it is impossible to achieve decent human values within this system and that it must therefore be overthrown. If America in its arrogance refuses to confront this elemental fact, then the revolutionaries will have had the last laugh. For if it merely tries to purge itself of what it considers a foreign element in its midst, America will have lost its last chance to understand the horrors of ghetto life that produce black revolutionaries. And it is that failure of understanding which produces the Detroits in the first place.

RALPH ELLISON

Battle Royal

It goes a long way back, some twenty years. All my life I had been looking for something, and everywhere I turned someone tried to tell me what it was. I accepted their answers too, though they were often in contradiction and even self-contradictory. I was naïve. I was looking for myself and asking everyone except myself questions which I, and only I, could answer. It took me a long time and much painful boomeranging of my expectations to achieve a realization everyone else appears to have been born with: That I am nobody but myself. But first I had to discover that I am an invisible man!

And yet I am no freak of nature, nor of history. I was in the cards, other things having been equal (or unequal) eighty-five years ago. I am not ashamed of my grandparents for having been slaves. I am only ashamed of myself for having at one time been ashamed. About eighty-five years ago they were told that they were free, united with others of our country in everything pertaining to the common good, and, in everything social, separate like the fingers of the hand. And they believed it. They exulted in it. They stayed in their place, worked hard, and brought up my father to do the same. But my grandfather is the one. He was an odd old guy, my grandfather, and I am told I take after him. It was he who caused the trouble. On his deathbed he called my father to him and said, "Son, after I'm gone I want you to keep up the good fight. I never told you, but our life is a war and I have been a traitor all my born days, a spy in the enemy's country ever since I give up my gun back in the Reconstruction. Live with your head in the lion's mouth. I want you to overcome 'em with yeses, undermine 'em with grins, agree 'em to death and destruction, let 'em swoller you till they vomit or bust wide open." They thought the old man had gone out of his mind. He had been the meekest of men. The younger children were rushed from the room, the shades drawn and the flame of the lamp turned so low that it sputtered on the wick like the old man's breathing. "Learn it to the younguns," he whispered fiercely; then he died.

But my folks were more alarmed over his last words than over his dying. It was as though he had not died at all, his words caused so much anxiety. I was warned emphatically to forget what he had said and, indeed, this is the first time it has been mentioned outside the family circle. It had a tremendous effect upon me, however. I could never be sure of what he meant. Grandfather had been a quiet old man who never made any trouble, yet on his deathbed he had called himself a traitor and a spy, and he had spoken of his meekness as a dangerous activity. It became a constant puzzle which lay unanswered in the back of my mind. And whenever things went well for me I remembered my grandfather and felt guilty and uncomfortable. It was as though I was carrying out his advice in spite of myself. And to make it worse, everyone loved me for it. I was praised by the most lily-white men of the town. I was considered an example of desirable conduct—just as my grandfather had been. And what puzzled me was that the old man had defined it as *treachery*. When I was praised for my conduct I felt a guilt that in some way I was doing something that was really against the wishes of the white folks, that if they had understood they would have desired me to act just the opposite, that I should have been sulky and mean, and that that really would have been what they wanted, even though they were fooled and thought they wanted me to act as I did. It made me afraid that some day they would look upon me as a traitor and I would be lost. Still I was more afraid to act any other way because they didn't like that at all. The old man's words were like a curse. On my graduation day I delivered an oration in which I showed that humility was the secret, indeed, the very essence of progress. (Not that I believed this—how could I, remembering my grandfather?—I only believed that it worked.) It was a great success. Everyone praised me and I was invited to give the speech at a gathering of the town's leading white citizens. It was a triumph for our whole community.

It was in the main ballroom of the leading hotel. When I got there I discovered that it was on the occasion of a smoker, and I was told that since I was to be there anyway I might as well take part in the battle royal to be fought by some of my schoolmates as part of the entertainment. The battle royal came first.

All of the town's big shots were there in their tuxedoes, wolfing down the buffet foods, drinking beer and whiskey and smoking black cigars. It was a large room with a high ceiling. Chairs were arranged in neat rows around three sides of a portable boxing ring. The fourth side was clear, revealing a gleaming space of polished floor. I had some misgivings over the battle royal, by the way. Not from a distaste for fighting, but because I didn't care too much for the other fellows who were to take part. They were tough guys who seemed to have no grandfather's curse worrying their minds. No one could mistake their toughness. And besides, I suspected that fighting a battle royal might detract from the dignity of my speech. In those pre-invisible days I visualized myself as a potential Booker T. Washington. But the other fellows didn't care too much for me either, and there were nine of them. I felt superior to them in my way, and I didn't like the manner in which we were all crowded together into the servants' elevator. Nor did they like my being there. In fact, as the warmly lighted floors flashed past the elevator we had words over the fact that I, by taking part in the fight, had knocked one of their friends out of a night's work.

We were led out of the elevator through a rococo hall into an anteroom and told to get into our fighting togs. Each of us was issued a pair of boxing gloves and ushered out into the big mirrored hall, which we entered looking cautiously about us and whispering, lest we might accidentally be heard above the noise of the room. It was foggy with cigar smoke. And already the whiskey was taking effect. I was shocked to see some of the most important men of the town quite tipsy. They were all there—bankers, lawyers, judges, doctors, fire chiefs, teachers, merchants. Even one of the more fashionable pastors. Something we could not see was going on up front. A clarinet was vibrating sensuously and the men were standing up and moving eagerly forward. We were a small tight group, clustered together, our bare upper bodies touching and shining with anticipatory sweat; while up front the big shots were becoming increasingly excited over something we still could not see. Suddenly I heard the school superintendent, who had told me to come, yell, "Bring up the shines, gentlemen! Bring up the little shines!"

We were rushed up to the front of the ballroom, where it smelled even more strongly of tobacco and whiskey. Then we were pushed into place. I almost wet my pants. A sea of faces, some hostile, some amused, ringed around us, and in the center, facing us, stood a magnificent blonde—stark naked. There was a dead silence. I felt a blast of cold air chill me. I tried to back away, but they were behind me and around me. Some of the boys stood with lowered heads, trembling. I felt a wave of irrational guilt and fear. My teeth chattered, my skin turned to goose flesh, my knees knocked. Yet I was strongly attracted and looked in spite of myself. Had the price of looking been blindness, I would have looked. The hair was yellow like that of a circus kewpie doll, the face heavily powdered and rouged, as though to form an abstract mask, the eyes hollow and smeared a cool blue, the color of a baboon's butt. I felt a desire to spit upon her as my eyes brushed slowly over her body. Her breasts were firm and round as the domes of East Indian temples, and I stood so close as to see the fine skin texture and beads of pearly perspiration glistening like dew around the pink and erected buds of her nipples. I wanted at one and the same time to run from the room, to sink through the floor, or go to her and cover her from my eyes and the eyes of the others with my body; to feel the soft thighs, to caress her and destroy her, to love her and murder her, to hide from her, and yet to stroke where below the small American flag tattooed upon her belly her thighs formed a capital V. I had a notion that of all in the room she saw only me with her impersonal eyes.

And then she began to dance, a slow sensuous movement; the smoke of a hundred cigars clinging to her like the thinnest of veils. She seemed like a fair bird-girl girdled in veils calling to me from the angry surface of some gray and threatening sea. I was transported. Then I became aware of the clarinet playing and the big shots yelling at us. Some threatened us if we looked and others if we did not. On my right I saw one boy faint. And now a man grabbed a silver pitcher from a table and stepped close as he dashed ice water upon him and stood him up and forced two of us to support him as his head hung and moans issued from his thick bluish lips. Another boy began to plead to go home. He was the largest of the group, wearing dark red fighting trunks much too small to conceal the erection which projected from him as though in answer to the insinuating low-registered moaning of the clarinet. He tried to hide himself with his boxing gloves.

And all the while the blonde continued dancing, smiling faintly at the big shots who watched her with fascination, and faintly smiling at our fear. I noticed a certain merchant who followed her hungrily, his lips loose and drooling. He was a large man who wore diamond studs in a shirtfront which swelled with the ample paunch underneath, and each time the blonde swayed her undulating hips he ran his hand through the thin hair of his bald head and, with his arms upheld, his posture clumsy like that of an intoxicated panda, wound his belly in a slow and obscene grind. This creature was completely hypnotized. The music had quickened. As the dancer flung herself about with a detached expression on her face, the men began reaching out to touch her. I could see their beefy fingers sink into the soft flesh. Some of the others tried to stop them and she began to move around the floor in graceful circles, as they gave chase, slipping and sliding over the polished floor. It was mad. Chairs went crashing, drinks were spilt, as they ran laughing and howling after her. They caught her just as she reached a door, raised her from the floor, and tossed her as college boys are tossed at a hazing, and above her red, fixed-smiling lips I saw the terror and disgust in her eyes, almost like my own terror and that which I saw in some of the other boys. As I watched, they tossed her twice and her soft breasts seemed to flatten against the air and her legs flung wildly as she spun. Some of the more sober ones helped her to escape. And I started off the floor, heading for the anteroom with the rest of the boys.

Some were still crying and in hysteria. But as we tried to leave we were stopped and ordered to get into the ring. There was nothing to do but what we were told. All ten of us climbed under the ropes and allowed ourselves to be blindfolded with broad bands of white cloth. One of the men seemed to feel a bit sympathetic and tried to cheer us up as we stood with our backs against the ropes. Some of us tried to grin. "See that boy over there?" one of the men said. "I want you to run across at the bell and give it to him right in the belly. If you don't get him, I'm going to get you. I don't like his looks." Each of us was told the same. The blindfolds were put on. Yet even then I had been going over my speech. In my mind each word was as bright as flame. I felt the cloth pressed into place, and frowned so that it would be loosened when I relaxed.

But now I felt a sudden fit of blind terror. I was unused to darkness. It was as though I had suddenly found myself in a dark room filled with poisonous cottonmouths. I could hear the bleary voices yelling insistently for the battle royal to begin.

"Get going in there!"

"Let me at the big nigger!"

I strained to pick up the school superintendent's voice, as though to squeeze some security out of that slightly more familiar sound.

"Let me at those black sonsabitches!" someone yelled.

"No, Jackson, no!" another voice yelled. "Here, somebody, help me hold Jack."

"I want to get at that ginger-colored nigger. Tear him limb from limb," the first voice yelled.

I stood against the ropes trembling. For in those days I was what they called ginger-colored, and he sounded as though he might crunch me between his teeth like a crisp ginger cookie.

Quite a struggle was going on. Chairs were being kicked about and I could hear voices grunting as with a terrific effort. I wanted to see, to see more desperately than ever before. But the blindfold was as tight as a thick skin-puckering scab and when I raised my gloved hands to push the layers of white aside a voice yelled, "Oh, no you don't, black bastard! Leave that alone!"

"Ring the bell before Jackson kills him a coon!" someone boomed in the sudden silence. And I heard the bell clang and the sound of feet scuffling forward.

A glove smacked against my head. I pivoted, striking out stiffly as someone went past, and felt the jar ripple along the length of my arm to my shoulder. Then it seemed as though all nine of the boys had turned upon me at once. Blows pounded me from all sides while I struck out as best I could. So many blows landed upon me that I wondered if I were not the only blindfolded fighter in the ring, or if the man called Jackson hadn't succeeded in getting me after all.

Blindfolded, I could no longer control my emotions. I had no dignity. I stumbled about like a baby or a drunken man. The smoke had become thicker and with each new blow it seemed to sear and further restrict my lungs. My saliva became like hot bitter glue. A glove connected with my head, filling my mouth with warm blood. It was everywhere. I could not tell if the moisture I felt upon my body was sweat or blood. A blow landed hard against the nape of my neck. I felt myself going over, my head hitting the floor. Streaks of blue light filled the black world behind the blindfold. I lay prone, pretending that I was knocked out, but felt myself seized by hands and yanked to my feet. "Get going, black boy! Mix it up!" My arms were like lead, my head smarting from blows. I managed to feel my way to the ropes and held on, trying to catch my breath. A glove landed in my midsection and I went over again, feeling as though the smoke had become a knife jabbed into my guts. Pushed this way and that by the legs milling around me, I finally pulled erect and discovered that I could see the black, sweat-washed forms weaving in the smoky-blue atmosphere like drunken dancers weaving to the rapid drum-like thuds of blows.

Everyone fought hysterically. It was complete anarchy. Everybody fought everybody else. No group fought together for long. Two, three, four, fought one, then turned to fight each other, were themselves attacked. Blows landed below the belt and in the kidney, with the gloves open as well as closed, and with my eye partly opened now there was not so much terror. I moved carefully, avoiding blows, although not too many to attract attention, fighting from group to group. The boys groped about like blind, cautious crabs crouching to protect their mid-sections, their heads pulled in short against their shoulders, their arms stretched nervously before them, with their fists testing the smoke-filled air like the knobbed feelers of hypersensitive snails. In one corner I glimpsed a boy violently punching the air and heard him scream in pain as he smashed his hand against a ring post. For a second I saw him bent over holding his hand, then going down as a blow caught his unprotected head. I played one group against the other, slipping in and throwing a punch then stepping out of range while pushing the others into the melee to take the blows blindly aimed at me. The smoke was agonizing and there were no rounds, no bells at three minute intervals to relieve our exhaustion. The room spun round me, a swirl of lights, smoke, sweating bodies surrounded by tense white faces. I bled from both nose and mouth, the blood spattering upon my chest.

The men kept yelling, "Slug him, black boy! Knock his guts out!" "Uppercut him! Kill him! Kill that big boy!"

Taking a fake fall, I saw a boy going down heavily beside me as though we were felled by a single blow, saw a sneaker-clad foot shoot into his groin as the two who had knocked him down stumbled upon him. I rolled out of range, feeling a twinge of nausea.

The harder we fought the more threatening the men became. And yet, I had begun to worry about my speech again. How would it go? Would they recognize my ability? What would they give me?

I was fighting automatically when suddenly I noticed that one after another of the boys was leaving the ring. I was surprised, filled with panic, as though I had been left alone with an unknown danger. Then I understood. The boys had arranged it among themselves. It was the custom for the two men left in the ring to slug it out for the winner's prize. I discovered this too late. When the bell sounded two men in tuxedoes leaped into the ring and removed the blindfold. I found myself facing Tatlock, the biggest of the gang. I felt sick at my stomach. Hardly had the bell stopped ringing in my ears than it clanged again and I saw him moving swiftly toward me. Thinking of nothing else to do I hit him smash on the nose. He kept coming, bringing the rank sharp violence of stale sweat. His face was a black blank of a face, only his eyes alive—with hate of me and aglow with a feverish terror from what had happened to us all. I became anxious. I wanted to deliver my speech and he came at me as though he meant to beat it out of me. I smashed him again and again, taking his blows as they came. Then on a sudden impulse I struck him lightly and as we clinched, I whispered, "Fake like I knocked you out, you can have the prize."

"I'll break your behind," he whispered hoarsely.

"For *them?*"

"For *me,* sonofabitch."

They were yelling for us to break it up and Tatlock spun me half around with a blow, and as a joggled camera sweeps in a reeling scene, I saw the howling red faces crouching tense beneath the cloud of blue-gray smoke. For a moment the world wavered, unraveled, flowed, then my head cleared and Tatlock bounced before me. That fluttering shadow before my eyes was his jabbing left hand. Then falling forward, my head against his damp shoulder, I whispered,

"I'll make it five dollars more."

"Go to hell!"

But his muscles relaxed a trifle beneath my pressure and I breathed, "Seven?"

"Give it to your ma," he said, ripping me beneath the heart.

And while I still held him I butted him and moved away. I felt myself bombarded with punches. I fought back with hopeless desperation. I wanted to deliver my speech more than anything else in the world, because I felt only these men could judge truly my ability, and now this stupid clown was ruining my chances. I began fighting carefully now, moving in to punch him and out again with my greater speed. A lucky blow to his chin and I had him going too—until I heard a loud voice yell, "I got my money on the big boy."

Hearing this, I almost dropped my guard. I was confused: Should I try to win against the voice out there? Would not this go against my speech, and was not this a moment for humility, for nonresistance? A blow to my head as I danced about sent my right eye popping like a jack-in-the-box and settled my dilemma. The room went red as I fell. It was a dream fall, my body languid and fastidious as to where to land, until the floor became impatient and smashed up to meet me. A moment later I came to. An hypnotic voice said FIVE emphatically. And I lay there, hazily watching a dark red spot of my own blood shaping itself into a butterfly, glistening and soaking into the soiled gray world of the canvas.

When the voice drawled TEN I was lifted up and dragged to a chair. I sat dazed. My eye pained and swelled with each throb of my pounding heart and I wondered if now I would be allowed to speak. I was wringing wet, my mouth still bleeding. We were grouped along the wall now. The other boys ignored me as they congratulated Tatlock and speculated as to how much they would be paid. One boy whimpered over his smashed hand. Looking up front, I saw attendants in white jackets rolling the portable ring away and placing a small square rug in the vacant space surrounded by chairs. Perhaps, I thought, I will stand on the rug to deliver my speech.

Then the M.C. called to us, "Come on up here boys and get your money."

We ran forward to where the men laughed and talked in their chairs, waiting. Everyone seemed friendly now.

"There it is on the rug," the man said. I saw the rug covered with coins of all dimensions and a few crumpled bills. But what excited me, scattered here and there, were the gold pieces.

"Boys, it's all yours," the man said. "You get all you grab."

"That's right, Sambo," a blond man said, winking at me confidentially.

I trembled with excitement, forgetting my pain. I would get the gold and the bills, I thought. I would use both hands. I would throw my body against the boys nearest me to block them from the gold.

"Get down and around the rug now," the man commanded, "and don't anyone touch it until I give the signal."

"This ought to be good," I heard.

As told, we got around the square rug on our knees. Slowly the man raised his freckled hand as we followed it upward with our eyes.

I heard, "These niggers look like they're about to pray!"

Then, "Ready," the man said. "Go!"

I lunged for a yellow coin lying on the blue design of the carpet, touching it and sending a surprised shriek to join those rising around me. I tried frantically to remove my hand but could not let go. A hot, violent force tore through my body, shaking me like a wet rat. The rug was electrified. The hair bristled up on my head as I shook myself free. My muscles jumped, my nerves jangled, writhed. But I saw that this was not stopping the other boys. Laughing in fear and embarrassment, some were holding back and scooping up the coins knocked off by the painful contortions of the others. The men roared above us as we struggled.

"Pick it up, goddamnit, pick it up!" someone called like a bass-voiced parrot. "Go on, get it!"

I crawled rapidly around the floor, picking up the coins, trying to avoid the coppers and to get greenbacks and the gold. Ignoring the shock by laughing, as I brushed the coins off quickly, I discovered that I could contain the electricity—a contradiction, but it works. Then the men began to push us onto the rug. Laughing embarrassedly, we struggled out of their hands and kept after the coins. We were all wet and slippery and hard to hold. Suddenly I saw a boy lifted into the air, glistening with sweat like a circus seal, and dropped, his wet back landing flush upon the charged rug, heard him yell and saw him literally dance upon his back, his elbows beating a frenzied tattoo upon the floor, his muscles twitching like the flesh of a horse stung by many flies. When he finally rolled off, his face was gray and no one stopped him when he ran from the floor amid booming laughter.

"Get the money," the M.C. called. "That's good hard American cash!"

And we snatched and grabbed, snatched and grabbed. I was careful not to come too close to the rug now, and when I felt the hot whiskey breath descend upon me like a cloud of foul air I reached out and grabbed the leg of a chair. It was occupied and I held on desperately.

"Leggo nigger! Leggo!"

The huge face wavered down to mine as he tried to push me free. But my body was slippery and he was too drunk. It was Mr. Colcord, who owned a chain of movie houses and "entertainment palaces." Each time he grabbed me I slipped out of his hands. It became a real struggle. I feared the rug more than I did the drunk, so I held on, surprising myself for a moment by trying to topple *him* upon the rug. It was such an enormous idea that I found myself actually carrying it out. I tried not to be obvious, yet when I grabbed his leg, trying to tumble him out of the chair, he raised up roaring with laughter, and, looking at me with soberness dead in the eye, kicked me viciously in the chest. The chair leg flew out of my hand and I felt myself going and rolled. It was as though I had rolled through a bed of hot coals. It seemed a whole century would pass before I would roll free, a century in which I was seared through the deepest levels of my body to the fearful breath within me and the breath seared and heated to the point of explosion. It'll all be over in a flash, I thought as I rolled clear. It'll all be over in a flash.

But not yet, the men on the other side were waiting, red faces swollen as though from apoplexy as they bent forward in their chairs. Seeing their fingers coming toward me I rolled away as a fumbled football rolls off the receiver's fingertips, back into the coals. That time I luckily sent the rug sliding out of place and heard the coins ringing against the floor and the boys scuffling to pick them up and the M.C. calling, "All right, boys, that's all. Go get dressed and get your money."

I was limp as a dish rag. My back felt as though it had been beaten with wires.

When we had dressed the M.C. came in and gave us each five dollars, except Tatlock, who got ten for being last in the ring. Then he told us to leave. I was not to get a chance to deliver my speech, I thought. I was going out into the dim alley in despair when I was stopped and told to go back. I returned to the ballroom, where the men were pushing back their chairs and gathering in groups to talk.

The M.C. knocked on a table for quiet. "Gentlemen," he said, "we almost forgot an important part of the program. A most serious part, gentlemen. This boy was brought here to deliver a speech which he made at his graduation yesterday . . ."

"Bravo!"

"I'm told that he is the smartest boy we've got out there in Greenwood. I'm told that he knows more big words than a pocket-sized dictionary."

Much applause and laughter.

"So now, gentlemen, I want you to give him your attention."

There was still laughter as I faced them, my mouth dry, my eye throbbing. I began slowly, but evidently my throat was tense, because they began shouting, "Louder! Louder!"

"We of the younger generation extol the wisdom of that great leader and educator," I shouted, "who first spoke these flaming words of wisdom: 'A ship lost at sea for many days suddenly sighted a friendly vessel. From the mast of the unfortunate vessel was seen a signal: "Water, water; we die of thirst!" The answer from the friendly vessel came back: "Cast down your bucket where you are." The captain of the distressed vessel, at last heeding the injunction, cast down his bucket, and it came up full of fresh sparkling water from the mouth of the Amazon River.' And like him I say, and in his words, 'To those of my race who depend upon bettering their condition in a foreign land, or who underestimate the importance of cultivating friendly relations with the Southern white man, who is his next-door neighbor, I would say: "Cast down your bucket where you are"—cast it down in making friends in every manly way of the people of all races by whom we are surrounded. . . .' "

I spoke automatically and with such fervor that I did not realize that the men were still talking and laughing until my dry mouth, filling up with blood from the cut, almost strangled me. I coughed, wanting to stop and go to one of the tall brass, sand-filled spittoons to relieve myself, but a few of the men, especially the superintendent, were listening and I was afraid. So I gulped it down, blood, saliva and all, and continued. (What powers of endurance I had during those days! What enthusiasm! What a belief in the rightness of things!) I spoke even louder in spite of the pain. But still they talked and still they laughed, as though deaf with cotton in dirty ears. So I spoke with greater emotional emphasis. I closed my ears and swallowed blood until I was nauseated. The speech seemed a hundred times as long as before, but I could not leave out a single word. All had to be said, each memorized nuance considered, rendered. Nor was that all. Whenever I uttered a word of three or more syllables a group of voices would yell for me to repeat it. I used the phrase "social responsibility" and they yelled:

"What's that word you say, boy?"

"Social responsibility," I said.

"What?"

"Social . . ."

"Louder."

". . . responsibility."

"More!"

"Respon—"

"Repeat!"

"—sibility."

The room filled with the uproar of laughter until, no doubt, dis tracted by having to gulp down my blood, I made a mistake and yelled a phrase I had often seen denounced in newspaper editorials, heard debated in private.

"Social . . ."

"What?" they yelled.

". . . equality—"

The laughter hung smokelike in the sudden stillness. I opened my eyes, puzzled. Sounds of displeasure filled the room. The M.C. rushed forward. They shouted hostile phrases at me. But I did not understand.

A small dry mustached man in the front row blared out, "Say that slowly, son!"

"What, sir?"

"What you just said!"

"Social responsibility, sir," I said.

"You weren't being smart, were you, boy?" he said, not unkindly.

"No, sir!"

"You sure that about 'equality' was a mistake?"

"Oh, yes, sir," I said. "I was swallowing blood."

"Well, you had better speak more slowly so we can understand. We mean to do right by you, but you've got to know your place at all times. All right, now, go on with your speech."

I was afraid. I wanted to leave but I wanted also to speak and I was afraid they'd snatch me down.

"Thank you, sir," I said, beginning where I had left off, and having them ignore me as before.

Yet when I finished there was a thunderous applause. I was surprised to see the superintendent come forth with a package wrapped in white tissue paper, and, gesturing for quiet, address the men.

"Gentlemen, you see that I did not overpraise the boy. He makes a good speech and some day he'll lead his people in the proper paths. And I don't have to tell you that that is important in these days and times. This is a good, smart boy, and so to encourage him in the right direction, in the name of the Board of Education I wish to present him a prize in the form of this . . ."

He paused, removing the tissue paper and revealing a gleaming calfskin brief case.

". . . in the form of this first-class article from Shad Whitmore's shop."

"Boy," he said, addressing me, "take this prize and keep it well. Consider it a badge of office. Prize it. Keep developing as you are and some day it will be filled with important papers that will help shape the destiny of your people."

I was so moved that I could hardly express my thanks. A rope of bloody saliva forming a shape like an undiscovered continent drooled upon the leather and I wiped it quickly away. I felt an importance that I had never dreamed.

"Open it and see what's inside," I was told.

My fingers a-tremble, I complied, smelling the fresh leather and finding an official-looking document inside. It was a scholarship to the state college for Negroes. My eyes filled with tears and I ran awkwardly off the floor.

I was overjoyed; I did not even mind when I discovered that the gold pieces I had scrambled for were brass pocket tokens advertising a certain make of automobile.

When I reached home everyone was excited. Next day the neighbors came to congratulate me. I even felt safe from grandfather, whose deathbed curse usually spoiled my triumphs. I stood beneath his photograph with my brief case in hand and smiled triumphantly into his stolid black peasant's face. It was a face that fascinated me. The eyes seemed to follow everywhere I went.

That night I dreamed I was at a circus with him and that he refused to laugh at the clowns no matter what they did. Then later he told me to open my brief case and read what was inside and I did, finding an official envelope stamped with the state seal; and inside the envelope I found another and another, endlessly, and I thought I would fall of weariness. "Them's years," he said. "Now open that one." And I did and in it I found an engraved document containing a short message in letters of gold. "Read it," my grandfather said. "Out loud."

"To Whom It May Concern," I intoned. "Keep This Nigger-Boy Running."

I awoke with the old man's laughter ringing in my ears.

. . .

rites

of

passage

Every era probably has what sociologists call "the generation gap." But never before have so many people in our society found it so difficult to accommodate to the symbols and attitudes of the culture at large. Many are forced into positions of alienation and even rebellion, identifying society and prevailing social attitudes as their enemy and willingly seeing themselves as outlaws. Such rebellion has always been considered a temporary stage in the passage from adolescence to "maturity" and "responsibility"; but in the sixties it has become a permanent condition for whole groups of people, and the traditional vocabulary for defining man's relationship to society is, to many, obsolete. Young people are especially aware of this and are refusing to grow up in the ways that Paul Goodman, one of their spokesmen, has called "absurd."

This section presents essays describing this mood of change and rebellion and some of the reasons for it. In "Joey: A 'Mechanical Boy,'" Bruno Bettelheim discusses a severely disturbed child who was so confused and starved for tenderness and affection that he imagined himself to be a machine. This study is rich in specific detail about Joey and children like him, but it also implies that his choice of symbols by which to express his alienation was no accident in this mechanical age.

In "The Modern High School: A Profile," Edgar Z. Friedenberg discusses high school life today. Through a painstaking analysis, he shows that it promotes a social system actively encouraging mediocrity and threatened by signs of originality or iconoclasm. Some of Friedenberg's basic assumptions about education in America are shared by Mario Savio in "An End to History." In this essay, Savio—leader of Berkeley's Free Speech Movement, which many consider the opening salvo in the battle for "student power" now sweeping campuses all over the country—discusses some of the reasons for the students' confrontation with university authorities. The charges he made in 1964 are often echoed today: that administration officials, acting as the agents of society at large, are running a custodial system and trying to coerce students into niches within "a moral and intellectual wasteland." An historical background for the revolt of Savio and others of the New Left is provided by Jack Newfield in "The Beat Generation and the Un-Generation," an essay that describes the social atmosphere of the fifties that provoked the student protest of the sixties. Newfield's comments are directly pertinent to the idea of a "generation gap": he suggests that young people become engaged in politics and reform because of the moral laxity of their elders.

Of all the problems young people today confront directly, possibly the most Kafkaesque is the Selective Service system, whose entire political and moral basis is being questioned as never before, mainly by those whose lives it has the power to control. In "The Psychological Effects of the Draft," an excerpt from an exhaustive pamphlet by the American Friends Service Committee, a strong case is made against enforced military service. The military is also the subject of "We Couldn't Swing with It: The 'Intrepid Four,'" in which Robert Stone examines the characters and motives of four young men who deserted from the aircraft carrier U.S.S. Intrepid in protest against the war in Vietnam and are now living as exiles in Europe. Stone's essay raises questions not only about guilt and responsibility, but also about the passage from citizen to outlaw. In this it is similar to "Prison Diary," in which Lawrence Ferlinghetti, a poet laureate of the Beat Generation, tells why he went to jail for his anti-war convictions.

The short story in this section is Philip Roth's "The Conversion of the Jews," a tragi-comic account of a boy's coming of age in a world that is annoyed by his probing questions and tries to silence him by molding his personality to fit its needs.

BRUNO BETTELHEIM

Joey: A "Mechanical Boy"

Joey, when we began our work with him, was a mechanical boy. He functioned as if by remote control, run by machines of his own powerfully creative fantasy. Not only did he himself believe that he was a machine but, more remarkably, he created this impression in others. Even while he performed actions that are intrinsically human, they never appeared to be other than machine-started and executed. On the other hand, when the machine was not working we had to concentrate on recollecting his presence, for he seemed not to exist. A human body that functions as if it were a machine and a machine that duplicates human functions are equally fascinating and frightening. Perhaps they are so uncanny because they remind us that the human body can operate without a human spirit, that body can exist without soul. And Joey was a child who had been robbed of his humanity.

Not every child who possesses a fantasy world is possessed by it. Normal children may retreat into realms of imaginary glory or magic powers, but they are easily recalled from these excursions. Disturbed children are not always able to make the return trip; they remain withdrawn, prisoners of the inner world of delusion and fantasy. In many ways Joey presented a classic example of this state of infantile autism.

At the Sonia Shankman Orthogenic School of the University of Chicago it is our function to provide a therapeutic environment in which such children may start life over again. I have previously described in this magazine the rehabilitation of another of our patients ["Schizophrenic Art: A Case Study"; *Scientific American*, April, 1952]. This time I shall concentrate upon the illness, rather than the treatment. In any age, when the individual has escaped into a delusional world, he has usually fashioned it from bits and pieces of the world at hand. Joey, in his time and world, chose the machine and froze himself in its image. His story has a general relevance to the understanding of emotional development in a machine age.

Joey's delusion is not uncommon among schizophrenic children today. He wanted to be rid of his unbearable humanity, to become completely automatic. He so nearly succeeded in attaining his goal that he could almost convince others, as well as himself, of his mechanical character. The descriptions of autistic children in the literature take for their point of departure and comparison the normal or abnormal human being. To do justice to Joey I would have to compare him simultaneously to a most inept infant and a highly complex piece of machinery. Often we had to force ourselves by a conscious act of will to realize that Joey was a child. Again and again his acting-out of his delusions froze our own ability to respond as human beings.

During Joey's first weeks with us we would watch absorbedly as this at once fragile-looking and imperious nine-year-old went about his mechanical existence. Entering the dining room, for example, he would string an imaginary wire from his "energy source"—an imaginary electric outlet—to the table. There he "insulated" himself with paper napkins and finally plugged himself in. Only then could Joey eat, for he firmly believed that the "current" ran his ingestive apparatus. So skillful was the pantomime that one had to look twice to be sure there was neither wire nor outlet nor plug. Children and members of our staff spontaneously avoided stepping on the "wires" for fear of interrupting what seemed the source of his very life.

For long periods of time, when his "machinery" was idle, he would sit so quietly that he would disappear from the focus of the most conscientious observation. Yet in the next moment he might be "working" and the center of our captivated attention. Many times a day he would turn himself on and shift noisily through a sequence of higher and higher gears until he "exploded," screaming "Crash, crash!" and hurling items from his ever present apparatus—radio tubes, light bulbs, even motors or, lacking these, any handy breakable object. (Joey had an astonishing knack for snatching bulbs and tubes unobserved.) As soon as the object thrown had shattered, he would cease his screaming and wild jumping and retire to mute, motionless nonexistence.

Our maids, inured to difficult children, were exceptionally attentive to Joey; they were apparently moved by his extreme infantile fragility, so strangely coupled with megalomaniacal superiority. Occasionally some of the apparatus he fixed to his bed to "live him" during his sleep would fall down in disarray. This machinery he contrived from masking tape, cardboard, wire and other paraphernalia: Usually the maids would pick up such things and leave them on a table for the children to find, or disregard them entirely. But Joey's machine they carefully restored: "Joey must have the carburetor so he can breathe." Similarly they were on the alert to pick up and preserve the motors that ran him during the day and the exhaust pipes through which he exhaled.

How had Joey become a human machine? From intensive interviews with his parents we learned that the process had begun even before birth. Schizophrenia often results from parental rejection, sometimes combined ambivalently with love. Joey, on the other hand, had been completely ignored.

"I never knew I was pregnant," his mother said, meaning that she had already excluded Joey from her consciousness. His birth, she said, "did not make any difference." Joey's father, a rootless draftee in the wartime civilian army, was equally unready for parenthood. So, of course, are many young couples. Fortunately most such parents lose their indifference upon the baby's birth. But not Joey's parents. "I did not want to see or nurse him," his mother declared. "I had no feeling of actual dislike—I simply didn't want to take care of him." For the first three months of his life Joey "cried most of the time." A colicky baby, he was kept on a rigid four-hour feeding schedule, was not touched unless necessary and was never cuddled or played with. The mother, preoccupied with herself, usually left Joey alone in the crib or playpen during the day. The father discharged his frustrations by punishing Joey when the child cried at night.

Soon the father left for overseas duty, and the mother took Joey, now a year and a half old, to live with her at her parents' home. On his arrival the grandparents noticed that ominous changes had occurred in the child. Strong and healthy at birth, he had become frail and irritable; a responsive baby, he had become remote and inaccessible. When he began to master speech, he talked only to himself. At an early date he became preoccupied with machinery, including an old electric fan which he could take apart and put together again with surprising deftness.

Joey's mother impressed us with a fey quality that expressed her insecurity, her detachment from the world and her low physical vitality. We were struck especially by her total indifference as she talked about Joey. This seemed much more remarkable than the actual mistakes she made in handling him. Certainly he was left to cry for hours when hungry, because she fed him on a rigid schedule; he was toilet-trained with great rigidity so that he would give no trouble. These things happen to many children. But Joey's existence never registered with his mother. In her recollections he was fused at one moment with one event or person; at another, with something or somebody else. When she told us about his birth and infancy, it was as if she were talking about some vague acquaintance, and soon her thoughts would wander off to another person or to herself.

When Joey was not yet four, his nursery school suggested that he enter a special school for disturbed children. At the new school his autism was immediately recognized. During his three years there he experienced a slow improvement. Unfortunately a subsequent two years in a parochial school destroyed this progress. He began to develop compulsive defenses, which he called his "preventions." He could not drink, for example, except through elaborate piping systems built of straws. Liquids had to be "pumped" into him, in his fantasy, or he could not suck. Eventually his behavior became so upsetting that he could not be kept in the parochial school. At home things did not improve. Three months before entering the Orthogenic School he made a serious attempt at suicide.

To us Joey's pathological behavior seemed the external expression of an overwhelming effort to remain almost nonexistent as a person. For weeks Joey's only reply when addressed was "Bam." Unless he thus neutralized whatever we said, there would be an explosion, for Joey plainly wished to close off every form of contact not mediated by machinery. Even when he was bathed he rocked back and forth with mute, engine-like regularity, flooding the bathroom. If he stopped rocking, he did this like a machine too; suddenly he went completely rigid. Only once, after months of being lifted from his bath and carried to bed, did a small expression of puzzled pleasure appear on his face as he said very softly: "They even carry you to your bed here."

For a long time after he began to talk he would never refer to anyone by name, but only as "that person" or "the little person" or "the big person." He was unable to designate by its true name anything to which he attached feelings. Nor could he name his anxieties except through neologisms or word contaminations. For a long time he spoke about "master paintings" and "a master painting room" (i.e., masturbating and masturbating room). One of his machines, the "criticizer," prevented him from "saying words which have unpleasant feelings." Yet he gave personal names to the tubes and motors in his collection of machinery. Moreover, these dead things had feelings; the tubes bled when hurt and sometimes got sick. He consistently maintained this reversal between animate and inanimate objects.

In Joey's machine world everything, on pain of instant destruction, obeyed inhibitory laws much more stringent than those of physics. When we came to know him better, it was plain that in his moments of silent withdrawal, with his machine switched off, Joey was absorbed in pondering the compulsive laws of his private universe. His preoccupation with machinery made it difficult to establish even practical contacts with him. If he wanted to do something with a counselor, such as play with a toy that had caught his vague attention, he could not do so: "I'd like this very much, but first I have to turn off the machine." But by the time he had fulfilled all the requirements of his preventions, he had lost interest. When a toy was offered to him, he could not touch it because his motors and his tubes did not leave him a hand free. Even certain colors were dangerous and had to be strictly avoided in toys and clothing, because "some colors turn off the current, and I can't touch them because I can't live without the current."

Joey was convinced that machines were better than people. Once when he bumped into one of the pipes on our jungle gym he kicked it so violently that his teacher had to restrain him to keep him from injuring himself. When she explained that the pipe was much harder than his foot, Joey replied: "That proves it. Machines are better than the body. They don't break; they're much harder and stronger." If he lost or forgot something, it merely proved that his brain ought to be thrown away and replaced by machinery. If he spilled something, his arm should be broken and twisted off because it did not work properly. When his head or arm failed to work as it should, he tried to punish it by hitting it. Even Joey's feelings were mechanical. Much later in his therapy, when he had formed a timid attachment to another child and had been rebuffed, Joey cried: "He broke my feelings."

Gradually we began to understand what had seemed to be contradictory in Joey's behavior—why he held on to the motors and tubes, then suddenly destroyed them in a fury, then set out immediately and urgently to equip himself with new and larger tubes. Joey had created these machines to run his body and mind because it was too painful to be human. But again and again he became dissatisfied with their failure to meet his need and rebellious at the way they frustrated his will. In a recurrent frenzy he "exploded" his light bulbs and tubes, and for a moment became a human being—for one crowning instant he came alive. But as soon as he had asserted his dominance through the self-created explosion, he felt his life ebbing away. To keep on existing he had immediately to restore his machines and replenish the electricity that supplied his life energy.

What deep-seated fears and needs underlay Joey's delusional system? We were long in finding out, for Joey's preventions effectively concealed the secret of his autistic behavior. In the meantime we dealt with his peripheral problems one by one.

During his first year with us Joey's most trying problem was toilet behavior. This surprised us, for Joey's personality was not "anal" in the Freudian sense; his original personality damage had antedated the period of his toilet-training. Rigid and early toilet-training, however, had certainly contributed to his anxieties. It was our effort to help Joey with this problem that led to his first recognition of us as human beings.

Going to the toilet, like everything else in Joey's life, was surrounded by elaborate preventions. We had to accompany him; he had to take off all his clothes; he could only squat, not sit, on the toilet seat; he had to touch the wall with one hand, in which he also clutched frantically the vacuum tubes that powered his elimination. He was terrified lest his whole body be sucked down.

To counteract this fear we gave him a metal wastebasket in lieu of a toilet. Eventually, when eliminating into the wastebasket, he no longer needed to take off all his clothes, nor to hold on to the wall. He still needed the tubes and motors which, he believed, moved his bowels for him. But here again the all-important machinery was itself a source of new terrors. In Joey's world the gadgets had to move their bowels, too. He was terribly concerned that they should, but since they were so much more powerful than men, he was also terrified that if his tubes moved their bowels, their feces would fill all of space and leave him no room to live. He was thus always caught in some fearful contradiction.

Our readiness to accept his toilet habits, which obviously entailed some hardship for his counselors, gave Joey the confidence to express his obsessions in drawings. Drawing these fantasies was a first step toward letting us in, however distantly, to what concerned him most deeply. It was the first step in a year-long process of externalizing his anal preoccupations. As a result he began seeing feces everywhere; the whole world became to him a mire of excrement. At the same time he began to eliminate freely wherever he happened to be. But with this release from his infantile imprisonment in compulsive rules, the toilet and the whole process of elimination became less dangerous. Thus far it had been beyond Joey's comprehension that anybody could possibly move his bowels without mechanical aid. Now Joey took a further step forward; defecation became the first physiological process he could perform without the help of vacuum tubes. It must not be thought that he was proud of this ability. Taking pride in an achievement presupposes that one accomplishes it of one's own free will. He still did not feel himself an autonomous person who could do things on his own. To Joey defecation still seemed enslaved to some incomprehensible but utterly binding cosmic law, perhaps the law his parents had imposed on him when he was being toilet-trained.

It was not simply that his parents had subjected him to rigid, early training. Many children are so trained. But in most cases the parents have a deep emotional investment in the child's performance. The child's response in turn makes training an occasion for interaction between them and for the building of genuine relationships. Joey's parents had no emotional investment in him. His obedience gave them no satisfaction and won him no affection or approval. As a toilet-trained child he saved his mother labor, just as household machines saved her labor. As a machine he was not loved for his performance, nor could he love himself.

So it had been with all other aspects of Joey's existence with his parents. Their reactions to his eating or noneating, sleeping or wakening, urinating or defecating, being dressed or undressed, washed or bathed did not flow from any unitary interest in him, deeply embedded in their personalities. By treating him mechanically his parents made him a machine. The various functions of life—even the parts of his body—bore no integrating relationship to one another or to any sense of self that was acknowledged and confirmed by others. Though he had acquired mastery over some functions, such as toilet-training and speech, he had acquired them separately and kept them isolated from each other. Toilet-training had thus not gained him a pleasant feeling of body mastery; speech had not led to communication of thought or feeling. On the contrary, each achievement only steered him away from self-mastery and integration. Toilet-training had enslaved him. Speech left him talking in neologisms that obstructed his and our ability to relate to each other. In Joey's development the normal process of growth had been made to run backward. Whatever he had learned put him not at the end of his infantile development toward integration but, on the contrary, farther behind than he was at its very beginning. Had we understood this sooner, his first years with us would have been less baffling.

It is unlikely that Joey's calamity could befall a child in any time and culture but our own. He suffered no physical deprivation; he starved for human contact. Just to be taken care of is not enough for relating. It is a necessary but not a sufficient condition. At the extreme where utter scarcity reigns, the forming of relationships is certainly hampered. But our society of mechanized plenty often makes for equal difficulties in a child's learning to relate. Where parents can provide the simple creature-comforts for their children only at the cost of significant effort, it is likely that they will feel pleasure in being able to provide for them; it is this, the parents' pleasure, that gives children a sense of personal worth and sets the process of relating in motion. But if comfort is so readily available that the parents feel no particular pleasure in winning it for their children, then the children cannot develop the feeling of being worthwhile around the satisfaction of their basic needs. Of course parents and children can and do develop relationships around other situations. But matters are then no longer so simple and direct. The child must be on the receiving end of care and concern given with pleasure and without the exaction of return if he is to feel loved and worthy of respect and consideration. This feeling gives him the ability to trust; he can entrust his well-being to persons to whom he is so important. Out of such trust the child learns to form close and stable relationships.

For Joey relationship with his parents was empty of pleasure in comfort-giving as in all other situations. His was an extreme instance of a plight that sends many schizophrenic children to our clinics and hospitals. Many months passed before he could relate to us; his despair that anybody could like him made contact impossible.

When Joey could finally trust us enough to let himself become more infantile, he began to play at being a papoose. There was a corresponding change in his fantasies. He drew endless pictures of himself as an electrical papoose. Totally enclosed, suspended in empty space, he is run by unknown, unseen powers through wireless electricity. . . .

As we eventually came to understand, the heart of Joey's delusional system was the artificial, mechanical womb he had created and into which he had locked himself. In his papoose fantasies lay the wish to be entirely reborn in a womb. His new experiences in the school suggested that life, after all, might be worth living. Now he was searching for a way to be reborn in a better way. Since machines were better than men, what was more natural than to try rebirth through them? This was the deeper meaning of his electrical papoose.

As Joey made progress, his pictures of himself became more dominant in his drawings. Though still machine-operated, he has grown in self-importance. . . . Another great step forward is represented in

. . . [another picture]. Now he has acquired hands that do something, and he has had the courage to make a picture of the machine that runs him. Later still the papose became a person, rather than a robot encased in glass.

Eventually Joey began to create an imaginary family at the school: the "Carr" family. Why the Carr family? In the car he was enclosed as he had been in his papoose, but at least the car was not stationary; it could move. More important, in a car one was not only driven but also could drive. The Carr family was Joey's way of exploring the possibility of leaving the school, of living with a good family in a safe, protecting car. . . .

Joey at last broke through his prison. In this brief account it has not been possible to trace the painfully slow process of his first true relations with other human beings. Suffice it to say that he ceased to be a mechanical boy and became a human child. This newborn child was, however, nearly 12 years old. To recover the lost time is a tremendous task. That work has occupied Joey and us ever since. Sometimes he sets to it with a will; at other times the difficulty of real life makes him regret that he ever came out of his shell. But he has never wanted to return to his mechanical life.

One last detail and this fragment of Joey's story has been told. When Joey was 12, he made a float for our Memorial Day parade. It carried the slogan: "Feelings are more important than anything under the sun." Feelings, Joey had learned, are what make for humanity; their absence, for a mechanical existence. With this knowledge Joey entered the human condition.

EDGAR Z. FRIEDENBERG

The Modern High School: A Profile

Not far from Los Angeles, though rather nearer to Boston, may be located the town of Milgrim, in which Milgrim High School is clearly the most costly and impressive structure. Milgrim is not a suburb. Although it is only fifty miles from a large and dishonorable city and a part of its conurbation, comparatively few Milgrimites commute to the city for work. Milgrim is an agricultural village which has outgrown its nervous system; its accustomed modes of social inte-

The Modern High School: A Profile. © Copyright 1963, 1965 by Edgar Z. Fried-enberg. Originally appeared in *Commentary*. Another version appears in *Coming of Age in America: Growth and Acquiescence* by Edgar Z. Friedenberg. Reprinted by permission of Random House, Inc.

gration have not yet even begun to relate its present, recently acquired inhabitants to one another. So, though it is not a suburb, Milgrim is not a community either.

Milgrim's recent, fulminating growth is largely attributable to the rapid development of light industry in the outer suburbs, with a resulting demand for skilled labor. But within the past few years, further economic development has created a steady demand for labor that is not so skilled. In an area that is by no means known for its racial tolerance or political liberalism, Milgrim has acquired, through no wish of its own, a sizable Negro and Puerto Rican minority. On the shabby outskirts of town, a number of groceries label themselves Spanish-American. The advanced class in Spanish at Milgrim High School makes a joyful noise—about the only one to be heard.

Estimates of the proportion of the student body at Milgrim who are, in the ethnocentric language of demography, non-white, vary enormously. Some students who are clearly middle-class and of pinkish-gray color sometimes speak as if they themselves were a besieged minority. Most responsible staff members produce estimates of from twelve to thirty per cent. Observations in the corridors and lunchrooms favor the lower figure. They also establish clearly that the non-whites are orderly and well behaved, though somewhat more forceful in their movements and manner of speech than their light-skinned colleagues.

What is Milgrim High like? It is a big, expensive building, on spacious but barren grounds. Every door is at the end of a corridor; there is no reception area, no public space in which one can adjust to the transition from the outside world. Between class periods the corridors are tumultuously crowded; during them they are empty. But at both times they are guarded by teachers and students on patrol duty. Patrol duty does not consist primarily in the policing of congested throngs of moving students, or the guarding of property from damage. Its principal function is the checking of corridor passes. Between classes, no student may walk down the corridor without a form, signed by a teacher, telling where he is coming from, where he is going, and the time, to the minute, during which the pass is valid. A student caught in the corridor without such a pass is sent or taken to the office; there a detention slip is made out against him, and he is required to remain after school for two or three hours. He may do his homework during this time, but he may not leave his seat or talk.

There is no physical freedom whatever at Milgrim. During class breaks, the lavatories are kept locked, so that a student must not only obtain a pass but find the custodian and induce him to open the facility. Indeed Milgrim High's most memorable arrangements are its corridor passes and its johns; they dominate social interaction. "Good morning, Mr. Smith," an attractive girl will say pleasantly to one of her teachers in the corridor. "Linda, do you have a pass to be in your locker after the bell rings?" is his greeting in reply. There are more classifications of washrooms than there must have been in the Confederate Navy. The common sort, marked just "Boys" and "Girls," are generally locked. Then there are some marked, "Teachers, Men" and "Teachers, Women," unlocked. Near the auditorium are two others marked simply, "Men" and "Women," which are intended primarily for the public when the auditorium is being used for some function. During the school day cardboard signs saying "Adults Only" are placed on these doors. Girding up my maturity, I used this men's room during my stay at Milgrim. Usually it was empty; but once, as soon as the door clicked behind me, a teacher who had been concealed in the cubicle began jumping up and down to peer over his partition and verify my adulthood.

He was not a voyeur; he was checking on smoking. At most public high schools, students are forbidden to smoke, and this is probably the most common source of friction with authorities. It focuses, naturally, on the washrooms which are the only place students can go where teachers are not supposed to be. Milgrim, for a time, was more liberal than most; last year its administration designated an area behind the school where seniors might smoke during their lunch period. But, as a number of students explained to me during interviews, some of these seniors had "abused the privilege" by lighting up before they got into the area, and the privilege had been withdrawn. No student, however, questioned that smoking was a privilege rather than a right.

The concept of privilege is important at Milgrim. Teachers go to the head of the chow line at lunch; whenever I would attempt quietly to stand in line the teacher on hall duty would remonstrate with me. He was right, probably; I was fouling up an entire informal social system by my ostentation. Students on hall patrol also were allowed to come to the head of the line; so were seniors. Much of the behavior that Milgrim depends on to keep it going is motivated by the reward of getting a government-surplus peanut butter or tuna fish sandwich without standing in line.

The luncheon itself is a major learning experience, which must make quite an impression over four years' time. There are two large cafeterias which are used as study halls during the periods before and after the middle of the day. The food, by and large, is good, and more tempting than the menu. The atmosphere is not quite that of a prison, because the students are permitted to talk quietly, under the frowning scrutiny of teachers standing around on duty, during their meal—they are not supposed to talk while standing in line, though this rule is only sporadically enforced. Standing in line takes about a third of their lunch period, and leaves plenty of time for them to eat what is provided them. They may not, in any case, leave the room when they have finished, any more than they could leave a class. Toward the end of the period a steel gate is swung down across the corridor, dividing the wing holding the cafeterias, guidance offices, administrative offices, and auditorium from the rest of the building. Then the first buzzer sounds, and the students sweep out of the cafeteria and press silently forward to the gate. A few minutes later a second buzzer sounds, the gate is opened, and the students file out to their classrooms.

During the meal itself the atmosphere varies in response to chance events and the personality of the teachers assigned supervisory duty; this is especially true in the corridor where the next sitting is waiting in line. The norm is a not unpleasant chatter; but about one teacher in four is an embittered martinet, snarling, whining, continually ordering the students to stand closer to the wall and threatening them with detention or suspension for real or fancied insolence. On other occasions, verbal altercations break out between students in the cafeteria or in line and the *student* hall patrolmen. In one of these that I witnessed, the accused student, a handsome, aggressive-looking young man, defended himself in the informal but explicit language of working-class hostility. This roused the teacher on duty from his former passivity. He walked over toward the boy, and silently but with a glare of contempt, beckoned him from the room with a crooked finger and led him along the corridor to the administrative office: the tall boy rigid in silent protest, the teacher, balding and stoop-shouldered in a wrinkled suit, shambling ahead of him. The youth, I later learned, was suspended for a day. At some lunch periods all this is drowned out by Mantovani-type pop records played over the public address system.

What adults generally, I think, fail to grasp even though they may actually know it, is that there is no refuge or respite from this: no coffee break, no taking ten for a smoke, no room like the teachers' room, however poor, where the youngsters can get away from adults. High schools don't have club rooms; they have organized gym and recreation. A student cannot go to the library when he wants a book; on certain days his schedule provides a forty-five minute library period. "Don't let anybody leave early," a guidance counselor urged during a group-testing session at Hartsburgh, an apparently more permissive school that I also visited. "There really isn't any place for them to go." Most of us are as nervous by the age of five as we will ever be, and adolescence adds to the strain; but one thing a high-school student learns is that he can expect no provision for his need to give in to his feelings, or swing out in his own style, or creep off and pull himself together.

The little things shock most. High-school students—and not just, or even particularly, at Milgrim—have a prisoner's sense of time. They don't know what time it is outside. The research which occasioned my presence at Milgrim, Hartsburgh, and the other schools in my study required me to interview each of twenty-five to thirty students at each school three times. My first appointment with each student was set up by his guidance counselor; I would make the next appointment directly with the student and issue him the passes he needed to keep it. The student has no *open* time at his own disposal; he has to select the period he can miss with least loss to himself. Students well-adapted to the school usually pick study halls; poorer or more troublesome students pick the times of their most disagreeable classes; both avoid cutting classes in which the teacher is likely to respond vindictively to their absence. Most students, when asked when they would like to come for their next interview, replied, "I can come any time." When I pointed out to them that there must, after all, be some times that would be more convenient for them than others, they would say, "Well tomorrow, fourth period" or whatever. But hardly any of them knew when this would be in clock time. High-school classes emphasize the importance of punctuality by beginning at regular but uneven times like 10:43 and 11:27, which are, indeed, hard to remember; and the students did not know when this was.

How typical is all this? The elements of the composition—the passes, the tight scheduling, the reliance on threats of detention or suspension as modes of social control are nearly universal. The usurpation of any possible *area* of student initiative, physical or mental, is about as universal. Milgrim forbids boys to wear trousers that end more than six inches above the floor, and has personnel fully capable of measuring them. But most high schools have some kind of dress regulation; I know of none that accepts and relies on the tastes of students.

There are differences, to be sure, in tone; and these matter. They greatly affect the impact of the place on students. Take, for comparison and contrast, Hartsburgh High. Not fifteen miles from Milgrim, Hartsburgh is an utterly different community. It is larger, more compact, and more suburban; more of a place. Hartsburgh High is much more dominantly middle class and there are few Negroes in the high school there.

First impressions of Hartsburgh High are almost bound to be favorable. The building, like Milgrim, is new; unlike Milgrim's, it is handsome. External walls are mostly glass, which gives a feeling of light, air, and space. At Hartsburgh there is none of the snarling, overt hostility that taints the atmosphere at Milgrim. There are no raucous buzzers; no bells of any kind. Instead, there are little blinker lights arranged like the Mexican flag. The green light blinks and the period is over; the white light signals a warning; when the red light blinks it is time to be in your classroom. Dress regulations exist but are less rigorous than at Milgrim. Every Wednesday, however, is dress-up day; boys are expected to wear ties and jackets or jacket-sweaters, the girls wear dresses rather than skirts and sweaters. The reason is that on Wednesday the school day ends with an extra hour of required assembly and, as the students explain, there are often outside visitors for whom they are expected to look their best.

Students at Hartsburgh seem much more relaxed than at Milgrim. In the grounds outside the main entrance, during lunch period, there is occasional horseplay. For ten minutes during one noon hour I watched three boys enacting a mutual fantasy. One was the audience who only sat and laughed, one the aggressor, and the third—a pleasant, inarticulate varsity basketball player named Paul—was the self-appointed victim. The two protagonists were portraying in pantomime old, silent-movie-type fights in slow motion. The boy I did not know would slowly swing at Paul, who would sink twisting to the ground with grimaces of anguish; then the whole sequence would be repeated with variations, though the two boys never switched roles. In my interviews with Paul I had never solved the problems arising from the fact that he was eloquent only with his arms and torso movements, which were lost on the tape recorder, and it was a real pleasure to watch him in his own medium. This was a pleasure Milgrim would never have afforded me. Similarly, in the corridors at Hartsburgh I would occasionally come upon couples holding hands or occasionally rather more, though it distressed me that they always broke guiltily apart as soon as they saw me or any adult. One of my subjects, who was waiting for his interview, was dancing a little jig by himself in the corridor when I got to him. This was all rather reassuring.

It was also contrary to policy. There is a regulation against couples holding hands and they are punished if caught by the kind of teacher who hates sexuality in the young. The air and space also, subtly, turn out to be illusions if you try to use them. Hartsburgh High is built around a large, landscaped courtyard with little walks and benches. I made the mistake of trying to conduct an interview on one of these benches. When it was over we could not get back into the building except by disturbing a class, for the doors onto this inviting oasis can only be opened from inside, and nobody ever goes there. Since the courtyard is completely enclosed by the high-school building, this arrangement affords no additional protection from intruders; it merely shuts off a possible place for relaxation. The beautiful glass windows do not open enough to permit a body to squirm through and, consequently, do not open enough to ventilate the rooms, in which there are no individual controls for the fiercely effective radiators. Room temperature at Hartsburgh is a matter of high policy.

Teachers do not hide in the washrooms at Hartsburgh; but the principal recently issued a letter warning that any student caught in the vicinity of the school with "tobacco products" would be subject to suspension; students were directed to have their parents sign the letter as written acknowledgment that they were aware of the regulation and return it to school. Staff, of course, are permitted to smoke. At Hartsburgh a former teacher, promoted to assistant principal, serves as a full-time disciplinarian, but students are not dragged to his office by infuriated teachers, as sometimes happens at Milgrim. Instead, during the first period, two students from the school Citizenship Corps go quietly from classroom to classroom with a list, handing out summonses.

Along with having a less rancorous and choleric atmosphere than Milgrim, Hartsburgh seems to have more teachers who like teaching and like kids. But the fundamental pattern is still one of control, distrust, and punishment. The observable differences—and they are striking—are the result almost entirely, I believe, of *structural* and demographic factors and occur despite very similar administrative purposes. Neither principal respects adolescents at all or his staff very much. Both are preoccupied with good public relations as they understand them. Both are inflexible, highly authoritarian men. But their situations are different.

At Milgrim there is a strong and imaginative district superintendent, who is oriented toward the national educational scene. He likes to have projects, particularly in research and guidance. Guidance officers report through their chairman directly to him, not to the building principal; and the guidance staff is competent, tough, and completely professional. When wrangles occur over the welfare of a student they are likely to be open, with the principal and the guidance director as antagonists; both avoid such encounters if possible, and neither can count on the support of the district office; but when an outside force—like an outraged parent—precipitates a conflict, it is fought out. At Hartsburgh, the district superintendent is primarily interested in running a tight ship with no problems. To this end, he backs the authority of the principal whenever this might be challenged. The guidance office is vestigial and concerned primarily with college placement and public relations in the sense of inducing students to behave in socially acceptable ways with a minimum of fuss.

In these quite different contexts, demographic differences in the student bodies have crucial consequences. At Milgrim, the working-class students are not dominant—they have not got quite enough self-confidence or nearly enough social savvy to be—but they are close enough to it to be a real threat to the nice, college-bound youngsters who set the tone in their elementary and junior high school and who expect to go on dominating the high school. These view the rapid influx of lower-status students as a rising wave that can engulf them, while the newcomers, many of whom are recent migrants or high-school transfers from the city, can remember schools in which they felt more at home.

The result is both to split and to polarize student feeling about the school, its administration, and other students. Nobody likes Milgrim High. But the middle-class students feel that what has ruined it is the lower-class students, and that the punitive constraint with which the school is run is necessary to keep them in line. In some cases these students approach paranoia: one girl—commenting on a mythical high school described in one of our semi-projective research instruments—said, "Well, it says here that the majority of the students are Negro—about a third" (the actual statement is "about a fifth").

The working-class students are hard-pressed; but being hard-pressed they are often fairly realistic about their position. If the Citizenship Corps that functions so smoothly and smugly at Hartsburgh were to be installed at Milgrim, those who actually turned people in and got them in trouble would pretty certainly receive some after-school instruction in the way social classes differ in values and in the propensity for non-verbal self-expression. At Milgrim, the working-class kids know where they stand and stand there. They are exceptionally easy to interview because the interviewer need not be compulsively non-directive. Once they sense that they are respected, they respond enthusiastically and with great courtesy. But they do not alter their position to give the interviewer what they think he wants, or become notably anxious at disagreeing with him. They are very concrete in handling experience and are not given to generalization. Most of them seem to have liked their elementary school, and they share the general American respect for education down to the last cliché—but then one will add, as an afterthought, not bothering even to be contemptuous, "Of course, you can't respect *this* school." They deal with their situation there in correspondingly concrete terms. Both schools had student courts last year, for example, and Hartsburgh still does, though few students not in the Citizenship Corps pay much attention to it. Student traffic corpsmen give out tickets for corridor offenses, and these culprits are brought before an elected student judge with an administrative official of the school present as adviser. But Milgrim had a student court last year that quickly became notorious. The "hoody element" got control of it, and since most of the defendants were their buddies, they were either acquitted or discharged on pleas of insanity. The court was disbanded.

The struggle at Milgrim is therefore pretty open, though none of the protagonists see it as a struggle for freedom or could define its issues in terms of principles. The upper-status students merely assent to the way the school is run, much as middle-class white Southerners assent to what the sheriff's office does, while the lower-status students move, or get pushed, from one embroilment to the next without ever quite realizing that what is happening to them is part of a general social pattern. At Hartsburgh the few lower-status students can easily be ignored rather than feared by their middle-class compeers who set the tone. They are not sufficiently numerous or aggressive to threaten the middle-class youngsters or their folkways; but, for the same reason, they do not force the middle-class youngsters to make common cause with the administration. The administration, like forces of law and order generally in the United States, is accepted without deference as a part of the way things are and work. Americans rarely expect authority to be either intelligent or forthright; it looks out for its own interests as best it can. Reformers and troublemakers only make it nervous and therefore worse; the best thing is to take advantage of it when it can help you and at other times to go on living your own life and let it try to stop you.

This is what the Hartsburgh students usually do, and, on the whole, the results are pleasant. The youngsters, being to some degree ivy, do not constantly remind the teachers, as the Milgrim students do, that their jobs have no connection with academic scholarship. Many of the teachers, for their part, act and sound like college instructors, do as competent a job, and enjoy some of the same satisfactions. The whole operation moves smoothly. Both Milgrim and Hartsburgh are valid examples—though of very different aspects—of American democracy in action. And in neither could a student learn as much about civil liberty as a Missouri mule knows at birth.

What is learned in high school, or for that matter anywhere at all, depends far less on what is taught than on what one actually experiences in the place. The quality of instruction in high school varies from sheer rot to imaginative and highly skilled teaching. But classroom content is often handled at a creditable level and is not in itself the source of the major difficulty. Both at Milgrim and Hartsburgh, for example, the students felt that they were receiving competent instruction and that this was an undertaking the school tried seriously to handle. I doubt, however, that this makes up for much of the damage to which high-school students are systematically subjected. What is formally taught is just not that important, compared to the constraint and petty humiliation to which the youngsters with few exceptions must submit in order to survive.

The fact that some of the instruction is excellent and a lot of it pretty good *is* important for another reason; it makes the whole process of compulsory schooling less insulting than it otherwise would be by lending it a superficial validity. Society tells the adolescent that he is sent to school in order to learn what he is taught in the classroom. No anthropologist and very few high-school students would accept this as more than a rationalization; but rationalizations, to be at all effective, must be fairly plausible. Just as the draft would be intolerable if the cold war were wholly a piece of power politics or merely an effort to sustain the economy, so compulsory school attendance would be intolerable if what went on in the classrooms were totally inadequate to students' needs and irrelevant to their real intellectual concerns. Much of it is, but enough is not, to provide middle-class students, at least, with an answer when their heart cries out "For Christ's sake, what am I doing here?"

But far more of what is deeply and thoroughly learned in the school is designed to keep the heart from raising awkward, heartfelt issues—if design governs in a thing so subtle. It is learned so thoroughly by attendance at schools like Milgrim or even Hartsburgh that most Americans by the time they are adult cannot really imagine that life could be organized in any other way.

First of all, they learn to assume that the state has the right to compel adolescents to spend six or seven hours a day, five days a week, thirty-six or so weeks a year, in a specific place, in charge of a particular group of persons in whose selection they have no voice, performing tasks about which they have no choice, without remuneration and subject to specialized regulations and sanctions that are applicable to no one else in the community nor to them except in this place. Whether this law is a service or a burden to the young—and, indeed, it is both, in varying degrees—is another issue altogether. As I have noted elsewhere, compulsory school attendance functions as a bill of attainder against a particular age group. The student's position is that of a conscript, who is protected by certain regulations but in no case permitted to use their breach as a cause for terminating his obligation. So the first thing the young learn in school is that there are certain sanctions and restrictions that apply only to them; that they do not participate fully in the freedoms guaranteed by the state, and that *therefore, these freedoms do not really partake of the character of inalienable rights.*

Of course not. The school, as schools continually stress, acts *in loco parentis;* and children may not leave home because their parents are unsatisfactory. What I have pointed out is no more than a special consequence of the fact that students are minors, and minors do not, indeed, share all the rights and privileges—and responsibilities —of citizenship. Very well. However one puts it, we are still discussing the same issue. The high school, then, is where you really learn what it means to be a minor.

For a high school is not a parent. Parents may love their children, hate them, or like most parents, do both in a complex mixture. But they must nevertheless permit a certain intimacy and respond to their children as persons. Homes are not run by regulations, though the parents may think they are, but by a process of continuous and almost entirely unconscious emotional homeostasis, in which each member affects and accommodates to the needs, feelings, fantasy life, and character structure of the others. This may be, and often is, a terribly destructive process; I intend no defense of the family as a social institution. But children grow up in homes or the remnants of homes, are in physical fact dependent on parents, and too intimately related to them to permit their area of freedom to be precisely defined. This is not because they have no rights or are entitled to less respect than adults, but because intimacy conditions freedom and growth in ways too subtle and continuous to be defined as overt acts.

Free societies depend on their members to learn early and thoroughly that public authority is not like that of the family; that it cannot be expected—or trusted—to respond with sensitivity and intimate perception to the needs of individuals but must rely basically, though as humanely as possible, on the impartial application of general formulae. This means that it must be kept functional, specialized, and limited to matters of public policy; the meshes of the law are too coarse to be worn close to the skin. Especially in an open society, where people of very different backgrounds and value systems must function together, it would seem obvious that each must understand that he may not push others further than their common undertaking demands, or impose upon them a manner of life that they feel to be alien.

After the family, the school is the first social institution an individual must deal with—the first place in which he learns to handle himself with strangers. The school establishes the pattern of his subsequent assumptions as to what relations between the individual and society are appropriate and which constitute invasions of privacy and constraints on his spirit—what the British, with exquisite precision, call "taking a liberty." But the American public school evolved as a melting pot, under the assumption that it had not merely the right but the duty to impose a common standard of genteel decency on a polyglot body of immigrants' children and thus insure their assimilation into the better life of the American dream. It accepted, also, the tacit assumption that genteel decency was as far as it could go. If America has generally been governed by the practical man's impatience with other individuals' rights, it has also accepted the practical man's determination to preserve his property by discouraging public extravagance. With its neglect of personal privacy and individual autonomy the school incorporates a considerable measure of Galbraith's "public squalor." The plant may be expensive—for this is capital goods; but little is provided graciously, liberally, simply as an amenity, either to teachers or students, though administrative offices have begun to assume an executive look.

The first thing the student learns, then, is that as a minor, he is subject to peculiar restraints; the second is that these restraints are general, not limited either by custom or by the schools' presumed commitment to the curriculum. High-school administrators are not professional educators in the sense that a physician, an attorney, or a tax accountant are professionals. They do not, that is, think of themselves as practitioners of a specialized instructional craft, who derive their authority from its requirements. They are specialists in keeping an essentially political enterprise from being strangled by conflicting community attitudes and pressures. They are problem-oriented, and the feelings and needs for growth of their captive and unenfranchised clientele are the least of their problems; for the status of the "teen-ager" in the community is so low that even if he rebels, the school is not blamed for the conditions against which he is rebelling. He is simply a truant or a juvenile delinquent; at worst the school has "failed to reach him." What high-school personnel become specialists in, ultimately, is the *control* of large groups of students even at catastrophic expense to their opportunity to learn. These controls are not exercised primarily to facilitate instruction, and particularly, they are in no way limited to matters bearing on instruction. At several schools in our sample boys had been ordered—sometimes on the complaint of teachers—to shave off beards. One of these boys had played football for the school; he was told that, although the school had no legal authority to require him to shave, he would be barred from the banquet honoring the team unless he complied. Dress regulations are another case in point.

Of course these are petty restrictions, enforced by petty penalties. American high schools are not concentration camps. But I am not complaining about their severity; what disturbs me is what they teach their students concerning the proper relationship of the individual to society, and in this respect the fact that the restrictions and penalties are unimportant in themselves makes matters worse. Gross invasions are more easily recognized for what they are; petty restrictions are only resisted by "troublemakers." What matters in the end is that the school does not take its own business of education seriously enough to mind it.

The effects on the students are manifold. The concepts of dignity and privacy, notably deficient in American adults folkways, are not permitted to develop here. The school's assumption of custodial control of students implies that power and authority are indistinguishable. If the school's authority is not limited to matters pertaining to education, it cannot be derived from its educational responsibilities. It is a naked, empirical fact, to be accepted or controverted according to the possibilities of the moment. In such a world, power counts more than legitimacy; if you don't have power, it is naïve to think you have rights that must be respected. . . . Wise up. High school students experience regulation only as control, not as protection; they know, for example, that the principal will generally uphold the teacher in any conflict with a student, regardless of the merits of the case. Translated into the high-school idiom, *suaviter in modo, fortiter in re* becomes "If you get caught, it's just your ass."

Students do not often resent this; that is the tragedy. All weakness tends to corrupt, and impotence corrupts absolutely. Identifying, as the weak must, with the more powerful and frustrating of the forces that impinge upon them, they accept the school as the way life is and close their minds against the anxiety of perceiving alternatives. Many students like high school; others loathe and fear it. But even the latter do not object to it on principle; the school effectively obstructs their learning of the principles on which objection might be based; though these are among the principles that, we boast, distinguish us from totalitarian societies.

Yet, finally, the consequence of continuing through adolescence to submit to diffuse authority that is not derived from the task at hand—as a doctor's orders or the training regulations of an athletic coach, for example, usually are—is more serious than political incom-

petence or weakness of character. There is a general arrest of development. An essential part of growing up is learning that, though differences of power among men lead to brutal consequences, all men are
peers; none is omnipotent, none derives his potency from magic, but
only from his specific competence and function. The policeman represents the majesty of the state, but this does not mean that he can
put you in jail; it means, precisely, that he cannot—at least not for
long. Any person or agency responsible for handling throngs of young
people—especially if he does not like them or is afraid of them—is
tempted to claim diffuse authority and snare the youngster in the
trailing remnants of childhood emotion which always remain to trip
him. Schools succumb to this temptation, and control pupils by
reinvoking the sensations of childhood punishment, which remain
effective because they were originally selected, with great unconscious guile, to dramatize the child's weakness in the face of authority. "If you act like a bunch of spoiled brats, we'll treat you like
a bunch of spoiled brats," is a favorite dictum of sergeants, and school
personnel, when their charges begin to show an awkward capacity
for independence.

Thus the high school is permitted to infantilize adolescence; in
fact, it is encouraged to by the widespread hostility to "teen-agers"
and the anxiety about their conduct found throughout our society. It
does not allow much maturation to occur during the years when most
maturation would naturally occur. Maturity, to be sure, is not conspicuously characteristic of American adult life, and would almost
certainly be a threat to the economy. So perhaps in this, as in much
else, the high school is simply the faithful servant of the community.

There are two important ways in which it can render such service.
The first of these is through its impact on individuals: on their values,
their conception of their personal worth, their patterns of anxiety,
and on their mastery and ease in the world—which determine so
much of what they think of as their fate. The second function of the
school is Darwinian; its biases, though their impact is always on individual youngsters, operate systematically to mold entire social
groups. These biases endorse and support the values and patterns
of behavior of certain segments of the population, providing their
members with the credentials and shibboleths needed for the next
stages of their journey, while they instill in others a sense of inferiority and warn the rest of society against them as troublesome and un-
trustworthy. In this way the school contributes simultaneously to so-

cial mobility and to social stratification. It helps see to it that the kind of people who get ahead are the kind who will support the social system it represents, while those who might, through intent or merely by their being, subvert it, are left behind as a salutary moral lesson.

MARIO SAVIO

An End to History

Last summer I went to Mississippi to join the struggle there for civil
rights. This fall I am engaged in another phase of the same struggle,
this time in Berkeley. The two battlefields may seem quite different
to some observers, but this is not the case. The same rights are at
stake in both places—the right to participate as citizens in [a] democratic society and to struggle against the same enemy. In Mississippi,
an autocratic and powerful minority rules, through organized violence,
to suppress the vast, virtually powerless, majority. In California, the

An End to History. From *Humanity*, December 1964. Reprinted by permission
of the author. This essay is the lightly edited transcript of a tape recording made
during the sit-in that climaxed the Free Speech Movement at Berkeley.

privileged minority manipulates the University bureaucracy to suppress the students' political expression. That "respectable" bureaucracy masks the financial plutocrats: that impersonal bureaucracy is the efficient enemy in a "Brave New World."

In our free speech fight at the University of California, we have come up against what may emerge as the greatest problem of our nation—depersonalized, unresponsive bureaucracy. We have encountered the organized status quo in Mississippi, but it is the same in Berkeley. Here in Berkeley we find it impossible usually to meet with anyone but secretaries. Beyond that, we find functionaries who cannot make policy but can only hide behind the rules. We have discovered total lack of response on the part of the true policy makers. To grasp a situation which is truly Kafkaesque, it is necessary to understand the bureaucratic mentality. And we have learned quite a bit about it this fall, more outside the classroom than in.

As bureaucrat, an administrator believes that nothing new happens. He occupies an a-historical point of view. In September, to get the attention of this bureaucracy which had issued arbitrary edicts suppressing student political expression and refused to discuss its action, we held a sit-in on the campus. We sat around a police car and kept it immobilized for over thirty-two hours. At last, the administrative bureaucracy agreed to negotiate. But instead, on the following Monday, we discovered that a committee had been appointed, in accordance with usual regulations, to resolve the dispute. Our attempt to convince any of the administrators that an event had occurred, that something new had happened, failed. They saw this simply as something to be handled by normal University procedures.

The same is true of all bureaucracies. They begin as tools—means to certain legitimate goals—and they end up feeding their own existence. The conception that bureaucrats have is that history has in fact come to an end. No events can occur, now that the Second World War is over, which can change American society substantially. We proceed by standard procedures as we are.

The most crucial problems facing the United States today are the problem of automation and the problem of racial injustice. Most people who will be put out of jobs by machines will not accept an end to events, this historical plateau, as the point beyond which no change occurs. Negroes will not accept an end to history here. All of us must refuse to accept history's final judgment that in America there is no place in society for people whose skins are dark. On campus students are not about to accept it as fact that the University has ceased evolving and is in its final state of perfection, that students and faculty are respectively raw material and employees, or that the University is to be autocratically run by unresponsive bureaucrats.

Here is the real contradiction: The bureaucrats hold history as ended. As a result significant parts of the population both on campus and off are dispossessed, and these dispossessed are not about to accept this a-historical point of view. It is out of this that the conflict has occurred with the University bureaucracy and will continue to occur until that bureaucracy becomes responsive or until it is clear that the University can not function.

The things we are asking for in our civil rights protests have a deceptively quaint ring. We are asking for the due process of law. We are asking for our actions to be judged by committees of our peers. We are asking that regulations ought to be considered as arrived at legitimately only from the consensus of the governed. These phrases are all pretty old, but they are not being taken seriously in America today, nor are they being taken seriously on the Berkeley campus.

I have just come from a meeting with the Dean of Students. She notified us that she was aware of certain violations of University regulations by certain organizations. University Friends of SNCC, which I represent, was one of these. We tried to draw from her some statement on these great principles—consent of the governed, jury of one's peers, due process. The best she could do was to evade or to present the administration party line. It is very hard to make any contact with the human being who is behind these organizations.

The university is the place where people begin seriously to question the conditions of their existence and raise the issue of whether they can be committed to the society they have been born into. After a long period of apathy during the fifties, students have begun not only to question, but, having arrived at answers, to act on those answers. This is part of a growing understanding among many people in America that history has not ended, that a better society is possible, and that it is worth dying for.

This free speech fight points up a fascinating aspect of contemporary campus life. Students are permitted to talk all they want so long as their speech has no consequences.

One conception of the university, suggested by a classical Christian formulation, is that it be in the world but not of the world. The conception of Clark Kerr by contrast is that the university is part and parcel of this particular stage in the history of American society; it stands to serve the needs of American industry; it is a factory that turns out a certain product needed by industry or government. Because speech does often have consequences which might alter this perversion of higher education, the university must put itself in a position of censorship. It can permit two kinds of speech: speech which encourages continuation of the status quo, and speech which advocates changes in it so radical as to be irrelevant in the foreseeable future. Someone may advocate radical change in all aspects of American society, and this I am sure he can do with impunity. But if someone advocates sit-ins to bring about changes in discriminatory hiring practices, this can not be permitted because it goes against the status quo of which the university is a part. And that is how the fight began here.

The administration of the Berkeley campus has admitted that external, extra-legal groups have pressured the University not to permit students on campus to organize picket lines, not to permit on campus any speech with consequences. And the bureaucracy went along. Speech with consequences, speech in the area of civil rights, speech which some might regard as illegal, must stop.

Many students here at the University, many people in society, are wandering aimlessly about. Strangers in their own lives, there is no place for them. They are people who have not learned to compromise, who for example have come to the University to learn to question, to grow, to learn—all the standard things that sound like clichés because no one takes them seriously. And they find at one point or another that for them to become part of society, to become lawyers, ministers, business men, or people in government, very often they must compromise those principles which were most dear to them. They must suppress the most creative impulses that they have; this is a prior condition for being part of the system. The university is well structured, well tooled, to turn out people with all the sharp edges worn off—the well-rounded person. The university is well equipped to produce that sort of person, and this means that the best among the people who enter must for four years wander aimlessly much of the time questioning why they are on campus at all, doubting whether there is any point in what they are doing, and looking toward a very bleak existence afterward in a game in which all of the rules have been made up—rules which one can not really amend.

It is a bleak scene, but it is all a lot of us have to look forward to. Society provides no challenge. American society in the standard conception it has of itself is simply no longer exciting. The most exciting things going on in America today are movements to change America. America is becoming ever more the utopia of sterilized, automated contentment. The "futures" and "careers" for which American students now prepare are for the most part intellectual and moral wastelands. This chrome-plated consumers' paradise would have us grow up to be well-behaved children. But an important minority of men and women coming to the front today have shown that they will die rather than be standardized, replaceable, and irrelevant.

JACK NEWFIELD

The Beat Generation
and the
Un-Generation

*The employers will love this generation. They aren't going to press many
grievances. They are going to be easy to handle. There aren't going to be
any riots.*

CLARK KERR, 1959

A time-capsule representative of the generation reaching adulthood
during the 1950's would have consisted of a subpoena, a blacklist,
a television tube, a gray flannel suit, a copy of *Time* magazine with

The Beat Generation and the Un-Generation. From *A Prophetic Minority* by
Jack Newfield. Copyright © 1966 by Jack Newfield. Reprinted by permission of
The New American Library, Inc., New York.

Herman Wouk on the cover, a Lawrence Welk album, an "I like Ike" button, and a blank sheet of paper.

It was a decade during which a senator from Mississippi was able to bully the greatest newspaper in the world; a President's favorite reading was pulp cowboy novels; a Gallup Poll showed that 58 percent of all college students listed *Mad* as their favorite magazine; and an ex-socialist wrote a book called *The End of Ideology*. It was a time when potential poets read Jack Kerouac and potential radicals ran for student council.

It was a decade during which McCarthyism was the most vital political movement in the land, and liberalism, after two decades of creative exertion, had reached a point of pessimistic exhaustion. Many of the older liberal architects of the New Deal and the CIO were comfortably ensconced in labor bureaucracies and academic hierarchies. In the argot of the fight game, the liberals weren't hungry anymore.

McCarthyism had put the liberals on the defensive, making them wonder who had lost China and who had promoted Peress. Moreover, the liberals' idea bank was empty. The New Deal had used up all their intellectual capital, and now only slogans were left to cope with the new post-World War II problems of the anti-colonial revolution, the Cold War, nuclear proliferation, and technology and automation.

At the same time radicalism was at its absolute nadir. The Socialist Party was a shell. The cumulative blows of the Korean War, the Rosenbergs' conviction, the Smith Act trials, the Hungarian revolt, and the revelations about Stalin at the 20th Soviet Party Congress wrecked the Communist Party and its apparatus. In 1957 the Labor Youth League, the CP's youth arm, voted to dissolve.

Radicals were driven out of public life and liberals bullied into silence and conformity. *Time* magazine hailed the reconciliation between capitalist America and its intellectuals. The country seemed to be dozing in an easy chair after a great meal, belching intermittently to prove it was not quite asleep.

In its issue of March 9, 1957, at the height of the Silence, *The Nation* devoted an entire issue to reports from sixteen college campuses documenting the extraordinary apathy that afflicted the young. Stanley Kunitz, the poet and English professor at Queens College, wrote:

However, I must add that when a liberal or speculative voice is heard in the classroom, it is more likely than not to be the professor's, despite whatever caution the years might have taught him. As for the students, they matriculate cautious, wanting above all—so well conditioned are they by the prevailing social climate—to buy security for themselves in the full knowledge that the price is conformity. "Why should we go out on a limb about anything?" one of them remarked in class. "We know what happened to those who did." Another expressed a measure of gratitude towards Senator McCarthy for having taught his generation a valuable lesson: "to keep its mouth shut."

Poet Karl Shapiro, writing from the University of Nebraska, the crucible of the Norris-LaFollette Progressivism, commented:

Passivity is the last word we expect to use in connection with a generation of students, but that's the only word that applies to the American university student of the last few years.

Perhaps the sharpest evocation of the dead feeling of the 1950's came in an article that appeared in an obscure periodical called *Assay*, published by the University of Washington. It was written by a co-ed named Dorothy Kosobud Doe, and it said in part:

What we all lack who are under 30, is some guiding passion, some moral vision if you will. We are unable to wind the loose threads of our experience into some larger pattern, and we know it. We write to please this authority or that professor while the universe skids about under our feet. We profess to disbelieve everything partially because, at heart, we do not yet believe in ourselves. What we are facing is a process of re-education, of self-discovery—a painful process, but without it no human being has understood the reason for his short walk across eternity . . . if our revolt seems mild, it is because we have not found anything to promote; deep in the dreams of ourselves in our relation to others, we realize with Yeats that there's more enterprise in walking naked.

Why the 1950's did not provide rebellious, sensitive souls like Dorothy with "some guiding passion" or "anything to promote" is a mystery. Why the New Left didn't emerge then, when there was a virulent right wing that threatened to become a majority, when there was a series of economic recessions, when there were atrocities like the lynchings of Emmett Till and Mack Charles Parker, and when there was an unthawed Cold War, is an enigma of history. That the New Radicalism flowered *after* the death rattle of McCarthyism and during a period of remarkable prosperity contradicts most theories about the nature of social discontent and rebellion.

My own suspicion is that rebellion explodes not when repression is at its worst, but when it begins to ebb, when the possibility of something better is dimly glimpsed. Both the American and the Hungarian revolutions took place when conditions were beginning to improve. The same is true of the birth of the New Left here. It happened after Khrushchev's visit to America and after the liberal victories in the 1958 congressional elections.

The election of John Kennedy in 1960 probably hastened the flowering of the New Radicalism. In that election the nation chose vitality over torpor, adventure over caution, hope over passivity; and this decision liberated energies bottled up for a decade. If Nixon had won in 1960, I think the earliest protests would have been crushed in a McCarthyite paroxysm and the New Left aborted. Kennedy provided a friendly umbrella for the New Left to grow under, and held up a vision of social idealism, represented by the Peace Corps, which led students to take the logical next step—into SNCC and SDS.

My own undergraduate experience at Hunter College in the Bronx was foreshadowed by a sign I saw during my freshman semester (1956) on the bulletin board in the office of the student newspaper, the *Hunter Arrow*. The sign read bluntly, "Conform or Die."

Hunter was lucky enough during the McCarthy plague to have a liberal Catholic president, Dr. George N. Shuster. But the college had neither the radical tradition of CCNY, Antioch, or Berkeley, nor the rich intellectual tradition of Harvard, Chicago, or Michigan. The students, mostly lower middle class and Jewish, reflected their families and their times. They were fearful and conformist. During my later terms on the *Arrow* we officially banned the use of the word "apathy" because it had been so overworked in shrill editorials of exhortation.

Few of the three thousand undergraduates joined any of the myriad campus clubs and organizations, a lesson absorbed from the "don't sign and don't join" McCarthy experience. We all remembered the State Department employee McCarthy pilloried because of editorials he had written for the *Columbia Spectator* and petitions he had signed twenty-five years before. When speakers like Norman Thomas came to the campus they addressed seventy-five students and hundreds of vacant auditorium seats. At Hunter, politics meant running for student council on an innocuous platform, and dissent meant a vague, emotional yearning for Adlai Stevenson. The life pattern today's campus rebels recoil from in disgust, my classmates deified: marry well and early, don't be a troublemaker, start a career in daddy's business or in a large corporation, and save up for a split-level home in the lily-white suburbs.

The vast majority of my classmates just sat through four years. They didn't challenge any authority, take any risks, or ask any questions. They just memorized "the given," not even complaining when instructors turned them into mindless tape recorders, demanding they recite rather than reason. They seemed genuinely content with the world, and interested only in being rewarded with a painless niche in it. They signed loyalty oaths without complaint in order to receive college loans. When the administration suggested stringent dress regulations on the campus, the student council meekly voted to ratify this infringement on their liberties. When a maverick political science instructor was denied tenure and left, no one protested.[1] Most of my classmates became teachers, accountants, press agents, housewives, and salesmen.

No public question seemed to touch Hunter's class of '60; not McCarthyism, not Dulles' brinksmanship, not pollution of the atmosphere by nuclear testing, not even the nascent integration movement. They were worse than a Silent Generation or an Un-committed Generation—they were an Un-generation.

They were an Un-generation in the sense that nothing positive distinguished them or set them apart. They were bereft of passions, of dreams, of gods. Even their small, conventional expectations were squeezed out of the same label-less tube. If any single characteristic bound them together it was withdrawal. Not the experimental, alienated withdrawal of the Beats, but a timid, unfeeling withdrawal. They withdrew from conflict and emotion into a false, protective, "cool" detachment. They took up the pose of the jazz buff who dug the "cool jazz" of Brubeck and Getz. They carried around paperbacks by clinical and unfeeling novelists like William Golding and the latest example of *The New Yorker* school of bloodless, overde-

---

[1] By 1961, however, attitudes had changed. Eighty-five percent of the Hunter student body supported a strike against the City University speaker ban, which denied Communists, black nationalists, and others the right to speak on campuses.

tailed fiction. And their *Zeitgeist*—J. D. Salinger—stood for a total withdrawal from reality into the womb of childhood, innocence, and mystical Zen. Most of my contemporaries even managed to sustain their withdrawal beyond graduation, drifting off to Europe or going on to take meaningless graduate courses.

There were, I suspect, deeper reasons for the Un-generation's withdrawal than the intimidation by McCarthyism and the collapse of an energizing liberalism. One such reason seems to have been the instructive image of a passive President who withdrew from the world's problems. Just as John Kennedy's celebrated vigor ignited the country's spirit in 1960, I think Eisenhower's inability to deal with segregation, Laos, Eastern Europe, the economy, McCarthy, and the rest created a sense of futility in the country at large.

A second underlying cause of the Silence was the often-forgotten fact that American youth has never been particularly political in the way that Latin American, Asian, and European youth have. There was no dramatic upsurge of youthful radicalism accompanying the Progressive movement, the Populists, the abolitionists, or the American Revolution itself. American youth has no tradition of vanguard radicalism. One of the more subtle inspirations to the New Left was, I think, the catalytic role students played in 1960 in overthrowing the reactionary regimes of Menderes in Turkey and Syngman Rhee in Korea.

The last of the deeper reasons for the Silence was probably the traditional banality of the American campus and student-government politics. Until quite recently campus politics were insulated from "outside issues" like war, civil rights, and poverty; they have been a substitute for, rather than a supplement to, the substantive national politics of the country. Indicatively, the FSM had at its core the notion of replacing real issues in the real world for the vacuity of campus politics. Also, I suspect that the traditional style of campus sandbox politics tended to reinforce the feeling of helplessness and futility in coping with the adult world of complex, worldly issues. Campus politics were constructed to prepare Joe College to become a docile Organization Man.

The psychopath is a rebel without a cause, an agitator without a slogan, a revolutionary without a program: in other words his rebelliousness is aimed to achieve goals satisfactory to himself alone; he is incapable of exertions for the sake of others.

DR. ROBERT LINDNER

It was a bone-chilling November night during my junior year at Hunter. The college auditorium was packed tight for a debate on "Is There a Beat Generation?" The combatants were British novelist Kingsley Amis; James Wechsler, the liberal hero of my youth; anthropologist Ashley Montague; and the alleged "King of the Beats," novelist Jack Kerouac. From the start it was clear that much of the leotard and beard-freckled mob (mostly non-Hunter types) had come to cheer the King of the Beats, look over Amis as a possible Angry Young Man, and scorn the committed liberalism of Wechsler as a delusion for squares and do-gooders.

But Kerouac disappointed his disciples. Gulping brandy compulsively, dragging poet Allen Ginsberg out of the wings like a donkey, reciting doggerel about Harpo Marx and clowning with Wechsler's hat, Kerouac seemed more in harmony with the clown spirit of his "beloved Harpo" than with the merchandised image of the creative, adventuristic, iconoclastic Beats.

When asked from the audience to "define the Beat Generation," Kerouac belched drunkenly, "Being Beat goes back to my ancestors, to the rebellious, the weird, the mad. To Laurel and Hardy, to Popeye; to Lamont Cranston, the Shadow, with his insane heh-heh-heh laugh. . . ."

Wechsler, the optimistic liberal, could only respond to Kerouac's premature Camp by sputtering, "I think what you are doing is to try to destroy anybody's instinct to care about this world. . . . There is no valor in the Beats' flight and irresponsibility."

Wechsler, of course, was right, and the irrational, impotent dissent of Kerouac that night at Hunter was a fairly accurate example of the Beat Generation. The Beats were not political or effective, and except for Ginsberg and William Burroughs, not very creative. They were the children of futility. They withdrew from society into an anti-social subculture, instead of challenging and trying to change the society. But with the traditional voices of dissent mute, the Beat Generation became the only option for those in opposition. The Beats may have been rebels without a cause, but theirs was the only rebellion in town.

The Beat Generation was partly a small literary faction that centered around an in-group of friends. Kerouac, who according to critic Seymour Krim "single-handedly created the Beat Generation," was the leader. The more gifted followers included Allen Ginsberg, the Jewish-radical-mystical-homosexual from Paterson, New Jersey; Gregory Corso, whom critic Robert Mazzocco once labeled, "The Shelley of the Mafia"; and William Burroughs, junkie, petty criminal, and dark genius out of the millionaire Burroughs adding-machine family and Harvard, '36.

The Beat movement was also a sociological phenomenon; an underground subsociety that developed about 1953, was mythicized by the Beat novelists and poets, and quickly spawned colonies in North Beach, San Francisco; Venice West, Los Angeles; Greenwich Village, New York; and outposts in Mexico City, Paris, and Tangiers. Its full-timers ranged from dreamy teen-agers on the bum to maladjusted Korean war veterans to jazzmen, criminals, and peyote-inspired poets. Each weekend its ranks would be swollen with Bronx boys picking up Brooklyn girls on MacDougal Street in the Village. At its periphery Beat just meant sloppy dress, inter-racial dating and poetry read to jazz backgrounds. At its vortex it meant criminality, mainline drug addiction, and mental instability. Lawrence Lipton, the Beats' Boswell, wrote: "One of the things which distinguish the holy barbarians [the Beats] from the respectable poets is their insistence on the non-rational as a way of knowing and a therapy to overcome squareness."

Allen Ginsberg, who saw "the best minds of my generation destroyed by madness," once spent eight months in a mental institution. Later he dedicated his brilliant work, *Howl*, to the institutionalized Carl Solomon. Seymour Krim wrote a chilling essay, "The Insanity Bit," after he "flipped out." And Kerouac was discharged from the Navy as a "schizoid personality."

A study of the San Francisco Beat enclave by psychiatrist Dr. Francis Rigney in the late 1950's showed 60 percent "were so psychotic or crippled by tensions, anxiety and neurosis as to be nonfunctional in the competitive world." In contrast, the several studies released so far made of the student radicals at Berkeley show them to be stable, serious, and of above-average intelligence. The point is that the Beats had to "cop out" of the Rat Race because they couldn't perform; the New Left chooses to reject a society it could easily be successful in.

The Beat Generation was anything but a revolutionary thrust to create a new society. It was as hostile to politics as it was to police and employment agencies. I recall asking one of Hunter's few authentic Beats to join the 1959 Youth March for Integrated Schools, and his laconic response, "You're too enthusiastic, man. Cool it."

The closest the Beats came to politics was to write bad poetry against the Bomb. But even this was more in the nature of self-justification for their own immediate savoring of all experience than a moral or political outcry against the shadow of genocide. Paul Goodman, generally sympathetic to the Beat impulse, pointed out in *Growing Up Absurd* that the Beats were no more against nuclear warfare than "mothers with families or squares who have common sense." And critic George Dennison, in putting down a Beat poem about the Bomb, observed, "The poet seems miffed that people pay attention to the atom bomb instead of to him."

Perhaps because the Beats—as writers and participants—didn't threaten anybody politically, the Beat Generation ended up as a Madison Avenue and Hollywood gimmick. The beatnik joined the plump suburban matron and the jowly business tycoon as a stock cartoon figure; slouched, bearded, and mumbling, "Like, man. . . ." A New York entrepreneur went into business renting out "real live beatniks" at twenty-five dollars per evening, plus carfare. *Playboy Magazine* had a "Beat Playmate of the Month." Hollywood ground out a Grade Z epic called *The Beat Generation* and an artless adaptation of Kerouac's novel, *The Subterraneans*. And the July, 1959, issue of *The Saturday Evening Post* featured a short story by Harriet Frank called, "Beauty and the Beatnik," whose hero declaims, "Let's face it. I'm a beatnik, through and through. James Jones, Jack Kerouac. They're Dun and Bradstreet compared to me. I'm a real bum."

Still, despite their absurdity and ultimate commercialization, many of the values of the Beats have been absorbed into the broader stream of the New Left. The Beats seem to be a greater influence on the New Radicals than are the 1930's Left.

On many campuses today hipster and bohemian types serve as a sort of *lumpen* proletariat, an easily available army of bodies, ready to participate in any demonstration. But they are generally not the creative and stable leaders of movements; rather the undisciplined followers who get interviewed by cynical television reporters. SNCC's Texas-born Casey Hayden has a point when she says, "The beatniks were—and are—just the Movement without altruism and energy. They are alienated by exactly the same things we are, but they just can't act on their discontent in an effective political way."

Nevertheless, the Beats' mysticism, anarchy, anti-intellectualism, sexual and drug experimentation, hostility to middle-class values, and idealization of the Negro and of voluntary poverty all have clear parallels in the New Left. Moreover, there is a broad area of overlap between the Beats' creative expressions and the cultural tastes of the New Left. Individuals like Bob Dylan, Paul Krassner, and Allen Ginsberg serve as bridges between the two traditions. And within the New Left there is considerable liking for writers like Norman Mailer and Jean Genet; musical rebels like the Beatles and the half-rock'n'-roll, half-pornographic Fugs; and for underground film-makers like Kenneth Anger. Both movements represent a rebellion against Puritanism, hypocrisy, repression, and commercialism. Only the Beats were apolitical, self-indulgent, and a bit mad, while the New Left has a moral vision of a new society and is trying to create it with social activism.

More than anything else, the Beat Generation was a portent, the first wind of a new storm, a coded signal that America's youth was starting to gag on conformity, materialism, and silence. By the end of the 1950's there were not only the subcultures of Beats, but the irreverent satire of Lenny Bruce and Mort Sahl, the stirrings of SANE, Martin Luther King's local protests against segregation, and the slow growth of dissident publications like *I. F. Stone's Weekly*, *The Village Voice*, and *The Realist*.

This subtle new mood, which was to spawn the sit-in movement in 1960, was clearly perceived by Arthur Schlesinger, Jr., in a prophetic essay penned late in 1959 and called, "The New Mood in Politics." Perhaps thinking already of John Kennedy's bid for the Presidency, he wrote:

> At periodic moments in our history, our country has paused on the threshold of a new epoch in our national life, unable for a moment to open the door, but aware that it must advance if it is to preserve its national vitality and identity. One feels that we are approaching such a moment now. . . .
>
> The beginning of a new political epoch is like the breaking of a dam. Problems which have collected in the years of indifference, values

which have suffered neglect, energies which have been denied employ-ment—all suddenly tumble as in a hopeless, swirling flood onto an arid plain. . . .

The Beat Generation was the first trickle of the angry flood that is now promising to wash away so many of America's false to-tems, and cleanse so many of its rotted institutions.

AMERICAN FRIENDS
SERVICE COMMITTEE

The Psychological Effects of the Draft

Any attempt to assess the psychological effects of conscription is complicated by this question: How does one differentiate between the effect of the draft and the effect of the armed forces and war? It is impossible to examine the psychological effects of compulsory service without a context, and the context must, of course, be that of the military establishment. As we shall attempt to show, conscription has profound effects upon the individual, upon his family, and upon society.

The Psychological Effects of the Draft. From *The Draft?* A report prepared for the Peace Education Division of the American Friends Service Committee. Copyright © 1968 by Hill and Wang, Inc. Reprinted by permission of Hill and Wang, Inc.

THE EFFECTS ON THE INDIVIDUAL

The draft usurps the individual's opportunity to choose his own future and assigns that right to government officials. This is a serious enough deprivation for the individual, but the folly of it is magnified when we reflect that the institution of conscription casts aside voluntary choice in favor of an extremely inefficient system that unquestionably mismatches a high percentage of individuals.

Certain people are eminently more suited than others to life in the armed forces. The authoritarian personality as identified by Adorno et al. combines the traits of conventionalism and conformity with a submissive, uncritical deference to superiors, a tendency to overassertion toward underlings, and a punitive, rejecting attitude toward those who violate conventional values; he opposes the subjective, the imaginative, and the tender-minded. His thinking is superstitious, stereotyped, and rigid; he exaggerates assertion of strength and toughness; he has a generalized hostility and a relative lack of personal regard for others. The authoritarian personality has a tendency to attribute evil intent and actions to other groups, particularly minorities; he shows an exaggerated interest in and vigilance against sexual activity on the part of others, coupled with unconscious self-doubts about sexual adequacy.[1]

Whether an authoritarian personality can be determined with certainty by psychological testing is a matter of some professional difference of opinion; however, clinical observation does seem to identify individuals who combine many, if not all, of these personality traits. People with these traits fit quite well in the armed forces. The draft, however, instead of allowing authoritarian persons, by their own decision, to choose the military where they will fit and be psychologically comfortable while others choose civilian life, forces all types of draftees into the military milieu, a setting that welcomes the confirmed authoritarians, seduces the latent authoritarians, and makes the large remainder miserable.

A major evil of the draft is that it takes certain decisions out of the hands of individuals and places men in military life where they must submit to being continually manipulated. As Adorno et al. pointed

[1] T. W. Adorno et al., The Authoritarian Personality (New York: Harper & Bros., 1950).

out, for our democratic way of life to flourish "there must be an increase in people's capacity to see themselves and to be themselves.
This cannot be achieved by the manipulation of people however
well grounded in modern psychology the devices of manipulation
might be. . . ." [2] An example of the kind of manipulation indulged
in by the armed forces is the manner in which recruitment literature
plays upon the need of men, particularly with authoritarian personality tendencies, to assure themselves of their masculinity. The following are excerpts from "The Mark of a Man," a recruiting pamphlet
for the army (italics ours throughout) :

> An "action guy" can't just wait for things to happen—he makes them
> happen. Routine plugging along just isn't for him. He's *too much of*
> *a man* for that. His mind and muscles thrive on the challenge of ac-
> tion! *If you are this kind of man you can prove it to the world* in a
> way that really counts . . . as a modern combat soldier.
> A countdown on the launching pad is an experience no *real man*
> can forget.
> You'll meet *regular men* who really know the score and you'll
> proudly wear the *Mark of a Man* as one of the action guys of the com-
> bat arms.[3]

The appeal of the armed forces recruiters to the masculinity
theme is psychologically effective in getting men to sign up. Concern
about masculinity also plays a role during training. In a group of
navy frogmen trainees studied psychologically, the 25 per cent who
successfully completed the grueling training showed evidence of fear
of women and doubts about their own sexual adequacy. The author
of the report comments ". . . it is quite possible that their unconscious motivation to complete the course was based on a need to
prove their masculinity coupled with a fear of involvement with
women." [4] These men were also less successful than their fellow
trainees in coping with anxiety by verbal expression; they were "action
men" in the words of the recruiting pamphlet cited. These characteristics have also been found in a disproportionately large number
of paratroopers, among whom some observers have reported a high

[2] *Ibid.*
[3] "The Mark of a Man." U.S. Government Printing Office, 1963: 690248.
[4] D. W. Heyder and H. S. Wambach, "Sexuality and Affect in Frogmen," *Arch.*
General Psychiatry, September 1964, Vol. 11, No. 3, pp. 286–289.

160AMERICAN FRIENDS SERVICE COMMITTEE

incidence of acting out socially destructive behavior apparently related to efforts to prove masculinity.

The recruiting approach, by appealing to masculinity, not only exploits a psychological need but also strengthens the popular fallacy that the armed forces will "make a man of him," a fallacy that is subscribed to by many law enforcement officials and parents dealing with disturbed youth. The advent of nuclear weapons and advanced military technology, however, has rendered this concept even more ridiculous. The amount of positive character formation involved in releasing napalm or bombs on a distant civilian population must be minimal, while the carrying out of a task without moral commitment or even against personal conviction is psychologically destructive of a man as an independent rational being.

The following is a description without apology by military psychiatrists of the basic training of an airman:

> Basic training is designed to orient individuals to a new way of life and to establish new identities for them. Adaptation to and development of a sense of identification with the military are the goals of basic training. To accomplish this the basic trainee initially experiences an increasing depreciation of self-esteem as a result of his inadequacy to achieve the standards of basic training. However, in the attempt to adapt to the psychical and psychological stresses, he begins to reconstitute his scale of values by fusing some of his old values with a newly acquired set. A critical element in the introduction of this orientation . . . is the . . . leadership of the training instructors, which clearly raises the suggestibility of the airmen and encourages them to accept a new viewpoint. . . . Earlier training in the postponement of gratification, in the toleration of negative feelings of hostility, fear and anxiety and in the acceptance of authority (arbitrary) is critical for preparing individuals to adjust to the stress of basic training.[5]

Depreciation of self-esteem, reduction to a state of relatively helpless suggestibility, and then rescue by identification with military superiors, and reliance on early training in the acceptance of arbitrary authority are all parts of a carefully engineered process in basic military training; but these negative factors in the development of a socially responsible human being are essential for military life.

[5] A. Kiev and M. B. Giffen, "Some Observations on Airmen Who Break Down During Basic Training," *American Journal of Psychiatry*, August 1965, Vol. 122, No. 2, pp. 184–188.

Another description of the process of basic military training follows:

The basic training period was, therefore, not one of gradual inculcation of the Army mores but one of intensive shock treatment. The new recruit, a lone individual, is helplessly insecure in the bewildering newness and complexity of his environment. Also he is a man; he must show that he is tough enough to "take it." . . . With personal insecurity on the one hand and the motivation to "see it through" on the other he is malleable to the discipline, which consists of a fatiguing physical ordeal and continued repetition of acts until they become semi-automatic, in an atmosphere dominated by fear. . . .[6]

Some of the elements of this process bear remarkable resemblance to the techniques of "brain washing" as reported from prisoner-of-war camps. The fact that our military is willing to exploit the psychological helplessness of the new soldier in this manner is an indictment, not only of the draft, but of the entire war system.

If one selects such military training for oneself, the personality characteristics, overt or latent, which have led one to accept it may also assist one to endure it and to adapt it to one's psychological needs; it is quite another thing to undergo this same military training under compulsion. Though the draftee may endure the training, its psychological effect upon him may be quite destructive. In fact, as Dubin states,

The very nature of military administration and command is predicated on the implicit assumption that the rank and file of soldiers will be either indifferent or non-job oriented. Accordingly we find of all forms of administration the military is the most mechanical, the most highly structured, and most impersonal and indifferent to personal variability.[7]

Once drafted, and totally submerged in military ways and having lost his identity as a civilian, the draftee may be relatively free from

[6] S. A. Stouffer et al., The American Soldier: Adjustment During Army Life, Vol. 1, Studies in Social Psychology in World War II (Princeton, N.J.: Princeton University Press, 1949).
[7] R. Dubin, The World of Work: Industrial Society and Human Relations (Englewood Cliffs, N.J.: Prentice-Hall, 1958), p. 259.

conflict and uncertainties but this freedom is accompanied by a greater narrowness or perhaps rigidity of identity and a greater dependence upon external definition and support. This mold, while it may make for relative absence of discomfort, cramps personality growth and expansion.

There are other negative effects of "service" with the armed forces on the part of the men who are acting against their will. The conscript in peacetime, for example, often fails to experience the stabilizing influence of close interpersonal relationships with his peers in that he avoids full commitment to friends in the armed forces because of probable transfer or rotation of assignment.

The sense of inexorability of the draft aggravates feelings of personal helplessness and undermines the young person's sense of his own responsibility to society. Often, for example, behavioral excesses are occasioned by a feeling that "If they are going to 'get me' soon anyway, why should I place strict curbs on my behavior now?" At the same time the uncertainty of the timing of the draft call prevents taking the usual defensive measures against feelings of insecurity, such as planning, building, and saving.

Depression is a prominent psychiatric problem in peacetime overseas troops. An army psychiatrist states, "An important determinant in these reactions was the feeling of being passively forced into an intolerable situation which they felt helpless to alter." [8]

Conscription is part of a whole system that subordinates the individual to the group. Even army psychiatrists are forced to accept and condone this because it is pragmatically necessary: "Success in therapy is largely determined by the degree with which the psychiatrist identifies with the needs of the combat group, as opposed to his participation with the desires of the individual." [9] Worse than this, conscription prostitutes all the finer traits of man—duty, loyalty, sense of responsibility, etc.—placing them in the service of an unworthy cause—aggression against his fellow men. This is a severe contradiction which requires us to live with many fictions in order to maintain reason. Such fictions include the idea that our enemy is not really "people," that God is on our side, etc.

[8] R. F. Yazmajian, "Depression in Peacetime Overseas Troops," Psychiatric Quarterly, Vol. 38, 1964, pp. 504–511.

[9] A. J. Glass, "Psychotherapy in the Combat Zone," American Journal of Psychiatry, April 1954, Vol. 110, No. 10, pp. 725–731.

How much personality change is possible in late adolescence and early adulthood, i.e., the years when men are drafted? It has been argued that the armed forces do not make young men any more or less military or aggressive or authoritarian than they were destined to be anyway because their personalities were already largely formed by the time they were six or so. Sanford points out that the individual between the ages of seventeen and twenty-two does have the potential for change in at least five different ways: stabilizing of the ego identity, deepening of interests, freedom in personal relations, humanizing of values, and general development and strengthening of the ego.[10]

Conscription interferes seriously with all of these modes of growth. For example, stabilizing of ego identity requires "being placed in social roles that require new responses, having to make decisions concerning what roles one is going to take, learning from experience that some roles are suited and others not suited to one's interests and needs." The draftee is hardly in a position to profit from such circumstances. He is given little opportunity to develop freedom in personal relationships, since he is required to relate to his peers and others according to a very limited, inflexible series of authoritarian patterns. Sensitive values are discounted in a dehumanized milieu which encourages the authoritarian, punitive portions of his conscience at the expense of its more generous aspects. His opportunities to grow by successful decision-making are few since most decisions are made for him.

Although one need not fear that the military can create authoritarian personalities out of the men who are least oriented in that direction, the military does furnish a setting in which latent authoritarian traits are reinforced and in which humaneness, imagination, tolerance, and human brotherhood are discouraged. The armed forces give opportunity for some to achieve a kind of success and recognition in an authoritarian setting. Especially vulnerable are great numbers of the culturally deprived young men who before entering the military have had little chance for success and recognition. Therefore, those who find any success and satisfaction in military life are likely to incorporate within their personalities some of the authoritarian atmosphere that attended that success.

[10] R. N. Sanford, *Self and Society* (New York: Atherton Press, 1966), pp. 274ff.

In summary, not only does the draft interfere with positive personality growth, it tends to foster the development of authoritarian personality traits.

Studies made by the army's Mental Health Consultation Services and by the U.S. Disciplinary Barracks have shown that among the "problem group" of soldiers (stockade prisoners, disciplinary barracks prisoners, AWOL's) there is a disproportionately higher percentage of Regular Army men as opposed to draftees. Military medical studies also suggest that there may be a slightly higher incidence of psychiatric disorder among men who enlisted (RA). However, it is also the impression of military psychiatrists that among the group identified as excellent soldiers there is also a disproportionately higher percentage of Regular Army men. This seems to say that while the armed forces attract some marginally adjusted individuals, many of them have or develop traits, even some psychopathic traits, that make them proficient fighters (as in the case of the frogmen and paratroopers). In fact, Marshall says

> Company by company we found in our work that there were men who had been consistently bad actors in the training period, marked by faults of laziness, unruliness and disorderliness, who just as consistently became lions on the battlefield, with all of the virtues of sustained aggressiveness, warm obedience and thoughtfully planned action.[11]

The draftees tend to be those who comply with the authoritarian system without causing it trouble.

The basic injury to personality caused by military conscription is the injury caused by militarism. Conscription seems to compound the evil, but similar damage is done to personality by military life whether it is entered by voluntary enlistment or by conscription.

THE EFFECTS OF THE FAMILY

Much less is written and understood about the effect of military conscription on the family than one might expect. This seems to be

[11] S. L. A. Marshall, *Men Against Fire* (New York: William Morrow, 1961). See Chapter V, "Fire as the Cure." [Quotations from *Men Against Fire* are reprinted here by permission of the publisher. Copyright, 1947, by S. L. A. Marshall.]

related to the fact that less is known about the effect of the father-child relationship than about the mother-child relationship. The main reasons for this may be that: (1) mothers are more involved and perhaps more concerned than are fathers with child-rearing, and (2) mothers are more available for interview.

Ackerman states:

> The psychological implications of military service are many, for the military takes over some of the protective and educational functions of parents in preparing young males for adulthood. At the same time it may create certain conflicts in the adolescent, divided allegiance between parental authority and the authority of the military, conflict between standards of the family and the standards of the peer group in the military unit, which may involve a temporary renunciation of personal responsibility for sexual aggression and for violence. There may also arise conflict over the necessity for automatic and uncritical obedience to superior officers and the surrender of individual responsibility to the dictates of the military . . . it is certain, however, that changes in the character of the adolescent male result from this societally imposed period of transition. . . . Eventually the adolescent returns from the military to his civilian community and feels the full impact of the conflict of values that dominate it, all too often ill prepared to deal with its problems.
>
> The feminine half of the adolescent community, although not directly involved in compulsory military service, reacts to its influence on the males. If the serviceman, feeling the urge to live while he can, fast and furiously, indulges himself totally in the appetites of the body, the girl responds. If as soon as he gets by the hurdle of the military he turns cautious and seeks out a safe niche in the community, a steady job, a home, a car, she responds. She too is out to get what she can, particularly the security of marriage, home, and a respected place in the community. But today's young woman cannot easily trust herself to the man. He may be gone tomorrow.[12]

Except for physicians and dentists fathers have not been drafted since World War II, but many draftees have become husbands and fathers while in the armed forces. These men affect the emotional health of their children in at least two ways: first by their relationship with the mother, and second with the child himself. Bartemeier summarizes the effect via the mother as follows:

[12] N. W. Ackerman, The Psychodynamics of Family Life (New York: Basic Books, 1958), pp. 213ff.

While it is true that a woman's attitude toward pregnancy, childbirth and motherhood has been definitely molded and determined by her relationship with her own parents and siblings, it is equally true that her emotional needs in her relationship with her husband are of major importance for her sense of well-being. How adequately or inadequately his relationship with her satisfies these needs determines very importantly how well or poorly she functions as a mother to their children.

To give consistently to her child the love he needs, a woman needs the consistent love of her husband and the certainty of his love for their child . . . she may not be aware of any [of her] antagonistic feelings, but the infant may sense them through her tenseness, through her lack of customary gentleness, through awkward movements which are frightening to an infant, or through the cessation of her breast milk.[13]

We might add that not only does the young mother need to know that her husband loves her and that he loves their child; both mother and child need his actual presence.

Young families face many insecurities because of the draft. Research would be in order concerning the effect of the draft on the age at which young people marry, but in any case it is probably safe to say that the draft does produce some young and hasty marriages founded on shaky motivation and anxiety about immediate separation or separation at a frighteningly uncertain time. The young man who is draft eligible faces the frustration of having his occupational choice limited since employers are unwilling to hire him for the better-paying job. There is also anxiety and conflict among young married students over the demands of family life and the necessity of maintaining grades high enough to avoid being drafted. Once drafted, "hostility which is suppressed by the draftee rather than expressed to officers or NCO's because of possible consequences is often released to his wife, much to her surprise and chagrin." [14]

While many of these destructive psychological effects on the family are the result of the military system itself, the added anxiety of the uncertainty of the draft adds a further dimension to the disruption

[13] L. Bartemeier, "The Contribution of the Father to the Mental Health of the Family," *American Journal of Psychiatry*, October 1953, Vol. 110, No. 4, p. 277–280.

[14] E. S. Uyeki, "Draftee Behavior in the Cold-War Army," *Social Problems*, Vol. 8, 1960, pp. 151–158.

of family life and therefore of the personalities and emotional health of the next generation. It is our children who must have the chance to work the miracle. It is they who must carve out a world that has meaning and value; we deny them the chance if we damage the family matrix for their growth.

THE EFFECTS ON SOCIETY

All the psychological effects on the individual and his family, as members of society, have their inevitable influence on society itself. It is especially damaging to a society when its officials engage in the immorality of manipulating personalities and thereby set the interests of the state over and against the needs of the individual.

Men have a natural aversion to killing men. As S. L. A. Marshall, a military historian, has pointed out: "The fear of aggression has been expressed to him so strongly and absorbed by him so deeply and pervadingly—practically with his mother's milk—that it is part of the normal man's emotional makeup. This is his great handicap when he enters combat. It stays his trigger finger. . . ." Marshall's World War II studies showed that on the average, even in a heavy engagement, fewer than 25 per cent of the riflemen in actual front-line combat fired their weapons at all. "The best showing that could be made by the most spirited and aggressive companies was that one man in four had made at least some use of his fire power."

To the field commander this is an intolerable state of affairs, one that leads even a relatively humane military observer like Marshall to write:

> The fundamental problem is how to build up fire volume and develop more willing firers. One cannot deny that looseness of fire at times creates a certain hazard for troops. But this problem must be viewed in proportion; we cannot afford to miss the forest for the sake of a few trees. Though it is hard on the nerves at the time, so far as the end result is concerned it is better by far to have a company of green, trigger-happy soldiers than a company that lacks the will to use its weapons.[15]

As Marshall also states, it seems reasonable to believe that

[15] Marshall, *op. cit.*, pp. 78, 82.

If resistance to the idea of firing can be overcome for a period, it can be defeated permanently. Once the plunge is made, the water seems less forbidding. As with every other duty in life, it is made easier by virtue of the fact that a man may say to himself: "I have done it once, I can do it again."

But what happens when the army succeeds in overcoming man's natural aversion to killing? Marshall cites the following incident from an actual June 1944 battle in Normandy:

At the foot of the hill an enemy machine gun opened fire on the patrol but the bullets went high. The men broke and "ran like dogs." Millsaps (their Lieutenant) and a sergeant beat them back with physical violence. After they were again collected, Millsaps lost almost an hour, alternately bullying and pleading with them before they would go forward.

At last they charged the enemy, closing within hand-grappling distance. The slaughter began with grenade, bayonet and bullet. Some of the patrol were killed and some wounded. But all now acted as if oblivious to danger. The slaughter once started could not be stopped. Millsaps tried to regain control but his men paid no heed. Having slaughtered every German in sight they ran on into the barns of the French farmhouses where they killed the hogs, cows and sheep. The orgy ended when the last beast was dead.[16]

In February 1967, a young American soldier returned from Vietnam was tried and acquitted after shooting to death his wife and another man in a rage. He had told police, "It was just like in Vietnam —everything went red."

What connection exists between these two incidents and the effect of the draft on society is uncertain. Certainly both episodes are unusual, but no matter what the incidence of crimes of violence among veterans is, it seems logical that that incidence must be increased by the draft because the draft increases the total number of men trained to overcome their natural aversion to killing.

It is interesting that the panel of thirty-two physicians, psychologists, and nationally known psychiatrists, convened by Governor John Connally to make a report on the "Texas sniper," murderer of sixteen people, recommended that a massive, nation-wide study be made to determine whether there is a growing tendency toward violence in the U.S. Dr. Dana L. Farnsworth, director of health service

[16] *Ibid.*, p. 183.

at Harvard University and spokesman for the group, said, "I am concerned in that it appears there is an increasing tendency toward violence. We would like to know what the reasons are."[17] Significantly, the committee suggested that combat-trained soldiers should be given training to de-emphasize violence before they are returned to civilian life.

Disturbing phenomena in addition to crimes of violence also seem to increase as veterans return, according to Waller:

> Military experience also weakens the taboos which protect property and hedge about sexual indulgence . . . veterans are frequently restless and highly mobile, and thus they tend to drift away from the local communities which would either hold them in line or make allowances for their behavior. For these reasons many veterans become criminals. . . .
>
> Even in the most favorable cases, however, it seems probable that the veteran's anger does not disappear altogether. Instead, the residues of resentment are redirected into different channels, usually into channels of class, race, and religious antagonism. Whomever a man would naturally hate, he hates a little more because he has been a soldier.[18]

Waller gives as an example the Ku Klux Klan which was founded in 1865 by Civil War veterans and which still has a strong appeal to veterans who have absorbed the authoritarianism of the military system.

One serious effect of the draft on society is that it creates a class of veterans who did not have the benefit of stable models for independent adulthood during a critical phase of development. This is especially true as the draft tends to focus on the nineteen-year-old:

> Especially will the strain of transition be marked in those younger men who entered the army at age 18 or 19; they were still adolescents when inducted. They have come of age within the army and have no remembered experience of adulthood in civilian society. From a paternalistic school system, they have come straight into the paternalism of the army, substituting one cloister for another. Lacking the earlier experience of adjustment in adulthood, they will have fewer memories to give them bearing in the quest for stability.[19]

---

[17] *New York Times*, September 9, 1966.

[18] W. Waller, *The Veteran Comes Back* (New York: Dryden Press, 1944).

[19] R. A. Nisbet, "The Coming Problem of Assimilation," *American Journal of Sociology*, Vol. L, No. 4, January 1945, pp. 261ff.

Society desperately needs persons with a sense of responsibility, but the armed forces produce in the soldier the habit of thinking of himself as the dependent cog in a gigantic mechanism. "The average soldier diminishes as a self-directing person and becomes more and more an entity governed by exterior compulsions. Personal irresponsibility becomes in mounting degree the theme of his social existence." [20]

Last, conscription, or the acquisition of military manpower, is like the stockpiling of military material, possession of which is a strong psychological impetus toward its use in war. The use of men and weapons is seen then as justification for their possession, particularly if they are expensive. Justification may require the maintenance of an atmosphere of fear and suspicion by the support of the "bogey man" fantasy, for example, of an "international conspiracy."

Since the psychological effects of military conscription upon the individual, the family, and society are highly negative, it seems appropriate to ask why the draft, despite its evils, receives so much support from so many and why there are so few, relatively speaking, who succeed in resisting it. Representative Thomas B. Curtis, Missouri, points to the persistence of the old attitude: "If I had to serve in the Army, then everybody else should have to also." [21] He points out that this attitude is "not in tune with technological and demographic changes that have reduced the need for raw manpower while making more of it available." However, proponents of the draft, he says, are intent on realizing their own past experience in the younger generation. The World War II "days of heroics and sacrifice are fondly remembered and the horrors and follies of those experiences are erased by time."

The Group for the Advancement of Psychiatry, a group of prominent psychiatrists, suggests that

As the individual feels more alienated in mass society, he finds it more and more difficult to place himself in opposition to the huge pressures of the Organization. Fear of losing occupational security or of attacks on one's integrity, loyalty, or family are more than people

[20] Ibid.
[21] T. B. Curtis, "Conscription and Commitment," Playboy, February 1967, pp. 89ff.

can bear. As a defense against such fears and conflicts, one feels great relief in joining the party, the organization, or the club, and in becoming only an inconspicuous particle in the larger scheme.[22]

Erich Fromm sees this problem as an escape from freedom: "The frightened individual seeks for somebody or something to tie himself to; he cannot bear to be his own individual self any longer, and he tries frantically to get rid of it and to feel security again by the elimination of this burden; the self." [23]

The draft places the young man who seeks to oppose it in a serious psychological squeeze. He must be strong enough to withstand not only his own internal doubts, if any, about his course of action, but also the probability of direct public censure. Society does, in fact, deal sternly with some of those who refuse to register for the draft. For example, a study of draft resisters in prison during World War II showed that despite their excellent previous records, the members of one of the religious groups (Jehovah's Witnesses) were meted out comparatively severe sentences, the median being 4.4. years.[24] This was almost two years higher than the median sentence imposed on psychopathic prisoners or confirmed criminals.

Any institution that persists despite obsolescence must have some psychological support as well as its more material justification. Why have so many submitted to the draft? Perhaps because of the reasons already outlined. Perhaps because they desire an "escape from freedom" into the security of a life where the burden of making decisions has been removed. Perhaps because of its appeal to "manliness," although clearly it requires far more courage to refuse. Perhaps because the military system represents control of and at the same time a legitimatized channeling of the expression of aggression.

The psychological costs of the draft to individuals, families, and society itself are so great that, if we persist in the draft as our way of protecting our present way of life, we will destroy from within what we are attempting to protect. It seems essential that society,

[22] Group for the Advancement of Psychiatry, *Psychiatric Aspects of the Prevention of Nuclear War*, GAP Report No. 57, 1954, p. 253.

[23] E. Fromm, *Escape from Freedom* (New York: Rinehart, 1941).

[24] M. J. Pescor, "A Study of Selective Service Law Violators," *American Journal of Psychiatry*, March 1949, Vol. 163, pp. 642–652.

for the protection of its future, abandon conscription. Society desperately needs a generation of men of good will, men as free as possible of prejudice and aggression. The draft is systematically destroying our hope for such a generation.

ROBERT STONE

We Couldn't Swing with It: The "Intrepid Four"

The four young men sit around a casually furnished room, sipping wine. The eaves of the ancient house, the cobbled streets below are deeply covered with snow. On the apartment walls are poster pictures of Bertrand Russell, Groucho Marx, and W. C. Fields. A Beatles record is on the machine.

"One thing really got to me," one of the young men says, turning the music down. "I picked up a *Fortune* magazine, and it said that in 1966 the five hundred major American companies had their biggest year. That was a year of war, that biggest year. And we're supposed to be a peace-loving society, we're supposed to be pursuing peace. But the biggest companies make their biggest profits when there's a war on."

"At the expense of American soldiers," a second young man says. He has a small trimmed goatee and a necklace of beads. "And at the expense of the Vietnamese." His speech is soft, Southern.

A third youth lights a cigarette and smiles bitterly. He is dark-eyed, intense. "Did you read *his* State of the Union Message? I mean that was the epitome of all the damn hypocrisy about the war, the same hypocrisy that's all over everything in the States. *He* uses words like Freedom and Democracy and Justice—the words are cool, they sound great. Everybody knows what those words mean, right? If people just sit back and listen and they don't know anything about what's going on, it all sounds real nice. But if you just look around, man, at the war and at the way things are in the States now, you can't do anything but throw that damn piece of paper down. The hypocrisy of it slaps you right in the face."

"It ain't any cowboy can throw words around like that, though," the Southerner says. "He must have some staff. I mean they must be real cool, that staff he's got."

"I can't read the magazines anymore," the fourth says. "I can't read any of it. Johnson, Romney, Reagan—It's too sickening."

"I don't know," the dark youth says. "What's it gonna take to wake the eight-to-five deadheads up? You get a feeling watching it," he goes on, "a feeling of—what's the word?—of when you see something happening and you've got to do something to make it stop. But, like, you're just one person against a whole system. And you think, what can I do?"

The names of the four young men are Craig Anderson, Richard Bailey, John Barilla, and Michael Lindner. Until October 23, 1967, they were Airmen of the United States Navy, serving aboard the giant aircraft carrier U.S.S. *Intrepid* in the waters off North Vietnam. On that day, while their ship was in port near Yokohama, Japan, they deserted, subsequently destroying their identification cards and their uniforms. The act of desertion, all four affirm, was intended as an act of nonviolent protest against their country's intervention in Vietnam.

The events that followed their action have since entered the literature of the cold war. To the propaganda mills of the Communist world, their lonely gesture was a gift to be exploited; to American apologists, a shameful, embarrassing piece of willfulness to be explained away into inconsequence.

Yet for all the exploitation and explanation, Americans are confronted with a disturbing fact. Four of their young countrymen from quite average backgrounds, who differed little from millions of their contemporaries at home, chose to invite prison, exile, and disgrace for themselves and their families in order to disassociate themselves from a war which their society declared to be a crusade. Like so many other incidents of the Vietnam War, it is unfamiliar, confusing, disheartening to most Americans. We cannot help wondering what moved these young men, what view of the world led them into a public act of defiance. For those concerned with exploring the values, the moral responses, the alienation of a sizable proportion of American youth today, their story is worth examining.

Bailey, Barilla, and Lindner were members of the ship's company, assigned to duty on the flight deck as part of a catapult crew. Anderson was an Airman serving with VA-145, a jet fighter-bomber squadron.

They came to know each other in the course of the *Intrepid*'s long voyage from Norfolk, Virginia, to the Tonkin Gulf. By the time the ship had settled into its tense wartime routine, launching daily sorties against the cities and factories of North Vietnam, they were part of a group of crewmen of about their own age (all were under twenty-one) who met regularly after working hours to listen to rock music, occasionally to smoke pot (a pastime which has become hardly less common among young servicemen in the war zone than it is among university students), and above all, to engage in long nightly bull sessions.

The topics they talked about were the usual concerns of their age group, girls, cars, music—meaning the Beatles, Ravi Shankar, and especially Bob Dylan—and, of course, the war. Quite a few among the *Intrepid*'s crewmen, particularly the younger ones, had become aware that the action in which they were engaged was regarded as a moral wrong in quarters to which they looked for a sort of inspiration. One of the four deserters recalls listening to the chaplain's evening prayer and thinking of the Dylan anti-war ballad "God on Our Side."

"The ship was pretty much of a cross section of American society," John Barilla says, "at least of young guys. There were maybe 20 percent who thought the war was absolutely right and felt a lot about it and maybe about the same who had questions in their minds. The rest I don't think thought much about it. They were just doing like they were told."

Barilla, twenty years old, comes from Baltimore. His father is a rigger with Bethlehem Steel; his two brothers work for a supermarket chain. When he left high school in Baltimore, he spent a few months wandering in Florida indulging his hobby of skin diving. Why did he join the Navy?

"I accepted military service just like all the other kids I went to high school with did. I had the same choice they had, college or the service. I didn't think college was my forte—there wasn't any academic subject I was really interested in, and I wasn't out to make a million dollars. Going into the service after high school is traditional in the society, at least where I come from. You don't fight it.

"You go along with anything until something happens that opens your eyes. You know, when you're young you tend to be a romanticist about things. It takes you a while to find out the difference between the way things are supposed to be and the way they really are. You go along accepting things for no other reason than that you're born into the system. I didn't think much about the military system, the war system, before I went in. Every once in a while it would occur to me—what a waste of time it is, what a waste of lives. But when I got out there and I was in it, part of it, the hypocrisy of the whole deal got to me—I couldn't dodge it.

"Every day we were out there getting the planes off, the pilots went out and dropped their bombs on those people, and every night at prayer time the chaplain told them how when they were up there doing the bombing they were close to God. I'll admit that chaplain looked like he was dead a lot of the time.

"But a time came when it was either go on swinging with the system or do something about it. And for us, the only thing to do about it was desert."

Michael Lindner, nineteen, is slightly built, bespectacled, cool of speech. If he had done his time and come home, he thinks, he would have gone on to college. He comes from Mount Pocono, Pennsylvania; his upbringing was Lutheran, and his parents, he says without sarcasm, are "righteous Christians." His father is employed as a technician at the Tobyhana, Pennsylvania, army depot where he works with radioactive matter.

Lindner also joined the Navy to fulfill his national service obligation. He had been in for only nine months when he deserted in Japan.

"There were bombs everywhere," Lindner tells it now. "They were stowed in every available space. You saw them when you went to chow, and you saw them the first thing in the morning. You couldn't get away from the sight of them. Sometimes you could go out on deck and see explosions on the coast, mountains burning, tremendous fires going up. You think, we're killing an awful lot of people over there. And how do they know the difference between a Communist and a farmer?

"It was just being out there with all the time to think that did it. None of us found the Navy unbearable or anything. I mean, we were doing fine—we had hot meals and hot showers. We didn't have it anything like the troops on the line or the Vietnamese. But once we'd thought about it a lot and talked it over, we couldn't see things in the old ways, we couldn't go on swinging with it."

Richard Bailey, also nineteen, had written poetry while in high school in Jacksonville, Florida, and continued to write some in the Navy. When he joined in the desertion, he left unread the last fifty pages of Crime and Punishment. ("I'll get back to it when I get some time.")

Bailey's father is the Jacksonville branch manager of a national insurance company and a commander in the naval reserve. Bailey joined the Navy after graduation; he had not done particularly well in high school. When he signed up, he says, he had not considered the "moral aspects" of the war.

"When the time came," he says, "it was as easy for me as walking out of a room. It wasn't that the Navy was so bad—the Navy's just an extension of the society. But at a certain point while we were in Tonkin Gulf, the whole scene became intolerable. It's one thing to go along with a war when it doesn't touch you, but it's something else when you're part of it every day.

"Let's say we're supposed to be fighting for the American presence in Asia—well, just look at Subic Bay in the Philippines. There's an American presence there—it's five-year-old kids pimping for their sisters, bumming cigarettes in the street. I've talked to guys who've been in Saigon, and it's the same.

"One of the Marines I talked to aboard the Intrepid was in combat in Vietnam; he talked about how it was. Those guys are told to shoot anything that moves—don't trust anybody—even a little kid can kill you! No one fighting over there regards the Vietnamese as human. But that's not their fault. They haven't got the time.

"But what the hell are we supposed to be saving those people from that's any worse than what we're giving them?"

Craig Anderson, a tall, extremely quiet-spoken Californian, was almost twenty-one when he went over, eldest of the four and the only one whose attitudes toward American society and the war were set before his entry into service.

The son of a widowed secretary in San Jose, Anderson had spent a year at West Valley College, majoring in law enforcement.

"I wanted to see what the prospective police-types were like," he says.

Living within fifty miles of San Francisco, Anderson had spent some time on the fringes of the "hippie scene" in the Haight-Ashbury section there. He seems to have been more an observer than a participant in the action; he is not, in manner or speech, a hippie type.

"I joined the Navy because I thought—incorrectly, as it turned out—that the Navy would be the easiest service to get a discharge from. I didn't intend to fulfill my so-called military obligation. I felt I rejected American society on the basis of conditions in the United States, and the military in my view is just a sick extension of a sick social structure. When I was in boot camp, I stated my position to a psychiatrist there, and I was recommended for discharge. The recommendation was overruled.

"So my position wasn't something that just popped up, or came to me in the Tonkin Gulf. Out there, I felt as though I'd become a cog in the machinery, completely helpless. But feeling as I did, and having the time to think that I had, I decided that I was going to have to do something. I met Mike Lindner while we were both on mess cook duty, and later I met John and Dick Bailey. We discovered that we had essentially the same ideas about a lot of things, but we didn't find out how much we thought alike until we'd been out in the gulf for quite a while."

Lindner, Bailey, and Barilla agree that Anderson had the "most to lose" of all of them. While the other three still had years to do in the Navy, Anderson had only another month of service in Vietnamese waters and only six months more in the Navy. As the eldest, the most convinced in his rejection of America and the war, did he persuade them?

No, the others say.

"The situation was intolerable for all of us. Remember we worked on the flight deck. I don't even remember who brought up the idea of deserting first. We decided on it together."

During the long weeks in the Gulf of Tonkin, with the ship operating on wartime routine, all four had brushes with their immediate superiors.

"We'd stay up late at night, drinking coffee, bullshitting," John Barilla says. "Sometimes we'd talk and listen to music all night, we'd go nights without sleeping. Not only the four of us, but a bunch of guys who more or less thought the way we did and were interested in what we were interested in. We talked about what we did before we went in, about our girls, about the war.

"We pissed a lot of people off, of course. Sometimes when we went into a crew's lounge, the oldtimers, the lifers, would get up and walk out. We were all a little wigged out, I think. Like I'd sit on the mess deck at night and tell fortunes.

"There was a lot of grass being blown on the *Intrepid*, and they'd have locker inspections all the time to look for it. Now and then they'd find some in some cat's locker and he'd go up to the Man. Naturally, they suspected us. We'd be sitting around listening to Ravi Shankar, and the masters-at-arms would come in and roust us. *You know* what Ravi Shankar did to their minds. But they never caught us with grass. Sure, we burned some sometimes, no more than plenty of other people aboard who didn't mind the war at all.

"I got on to their shit list, of course. They were bugged at me because I went to Electronic Technician School and decided I didn't want to be an E.T., that was one thing. And they didn't like my friends—I'd get lectures, warning, you know. They'd give me very simple boring jobs as punishment, like watching fuel gauges. They knew we were staying up late, listening to music and like that, so one day I was sent up to the Air Boss [the Senior Flight Officer], and that man showed me pictures of what happened to people who got in accidents on the flight deck. I asked them if they had pictures of what happened to people who had napalm dropped on them.

"Sometimes they argued with me. They didn't want trouble, they

wanted you to think like they did. I told this First Class that I was
for life, and that I wasn't going to be for death, for killing people.
The First Class got very shook, he said, no, he was for life—he was
for defending the freedom of the people in Vietnam. But I don't
think he really believed that himself. He wanted to feel good about
it, but he couldn't."

Richard Bailey, a middle-class white boy from Florida, ran afoul
of the race issue, which he says is one of his special concerns.

"One of the things I want to get with," Bailey says, "is soul music,
the whole soul thing. I had a few friends among the Negro guys
aboard. I used to hang with them sometimes to listen to music and
just talk about how it is.

"One day a petty officer in my division took me aside and said,
'In this division we don't hang around with niggers.' "

There was a vogue aboard the *Intrepid* for carved belt buckles;
sailors would chisel into their fatigue belts monograms, pictures, or
names of girls, varieties of tattoo art. Shortly after the carrier took up
Station Yankee, Michael Lindner chiseled into his buckle the en-
circled, inverted Y which the international peace movement takes as
a symbol.

He was promptly ordered to efface it. "It's not Navy," his superiors
informed him—which was true enough.

"It was just a reaction to all the jive going on," Lindner says.

Anderson, the committed pacifist, refused to work on the flight
deck at all. With him, as with the others, the authorities aboard employed a cautious reasonableness.

"I had a long talk with one of the division petty officers," he says.
"I told him what I thought about the war and that I wasn't going
to work on the planes. When he left, he looked like he was ready to
cry."

Presumably in the interest of not rocking the boat, Anderson's
superiors assigned him below-decks as the squadron's compartment
cleaner, in which capacity he wielded nothing more lethal than
Clorox.

But when the *Intrepid* steamed north from its combat station for
liberty calls on Hong Kong and Japan, Anderson, Bailey, Barilla, and
Lindner had "pretty much decided to desert."

"We thought about doing it in Hong Kong," Barilla says, "but
we figured that wasn't a good idea. It meant that even if we could
get away from the American military—which we didn't think was very

likely—there wouldn't be anyplace for us to run to except Red China. And you can dig we didn't want any part of those people."

In Japan, they decided that the day had come. On the afternoon of October 23, when liberty commenced for the nonduty sections, the four presented their liberty cards to the officer of the deck, saluted the colors, and walked out of the lives they had lived for nineteen and twenty years. (Two other sailors who had intended to go with them decided against it at the last minute.)

"We meant it as a gesture of protest against the war," Anderson said. "We knew that we didn't have much of a chance to stay free in a country as saturated with the American military presence as Japan. You could say we expected to be apprehended. For myself, I didn't look forward to fifteen years in a federal prison. But I was ready to do it as an act against war."

As soon as they were able to change into their civilian clothes, they destroyed their military identity cards and their uniforms. In military jurisprudence, these actions define the difference between desertion and absence without leave, a much less serious offense. Once they destroyed their uniforms, there was no chance for them to "cop a plea" and plead guilty to the lesser offense at a court-martial.

"We went up to Tokyo, and we told every Japanese person that talked to us that we were American sailors and we deserted because of the war. We thought the S.P.'s were coming any minute," Richard Bailey tells it.

"But a funny thing happened. In all our wandering around coming on to people, we didn't meet a single Japanese person that wasn't against the war. Everybody—everybody that we spoke to—was for us. We had no idea that people in Japan felt that way. We assumed they were as brainwashed as Americans, because they've got a pro-U.S. government that supports the war. But we weren't especially trying to contact peace groups. We were just trying to talk to as many people as we could."

One of the people that the boys talked to put them in touch with representatives of Bahrein, a youth-oriented, Marxist-influenced peace group which American authorities regard as Communist-run. In the meantime, the alarm had gone off. With Shore Patrol and Military Police searching the streets of Tokyo for them, the four gave a taped interview to a Japanese television producer who had sought them out. The brief interview, shown later on U.S. and Canadian television, was the first look that Americans at home got of the "Intrepid Four." Like most of the subsequent media interviews given out by the four, it was not counted impressive. They have tended to "freeze" decidedly when faced with cameras and microphones.

After the interview, American military authorities intensified their search. But while the Armed Forces Police canvassed the customary haunts of deserters, the beer joints and geisha houses along Japan's many "Fleet Streets," the four were being passed from house to house, sleeping each night at the home of a different sympathizer. A great many people in Tokyo, Japanese of quite varying political allegiances, and even some Americans, assisted in their concealment.

After several days, a member of Bahrein brought the boys into contact with the Russian Embassy in Tokyo, and at that point they entered into the overripe world of international intrigue and propaganda. Their story became, for a while, part of the literature of the cold war.

The involvement of Soviet diplomacy in this act of desertion brought a kind of comfort to the orthodox evangelists of both East and West. For the Russians, the propaganda points to be scored were obvious—the boys were true international proletarians, who refused to fight their Red brothers in an imperialistic war.

U.S. spokesmen were in a position to explain events in terms of Soviet intrigue—these men were "defectors," "turncoats," pawns of the Comintern apparat.

As it happened, neither side drew the sustenance expected from subsequent events; the Russians, in terms of their investment, might have reason to feel particularly shortchanged.

"There was only one thing we wanted at that point," Barilla says, "and that was passage to a neutral country. We decided on Sweden; what we'd heard about it made it seem like the right place. Now, we couldn't get there by way of the United States, that was sure. We couldn't go by way of Vietnam. We weren't going to walk into Red China. When we were put in touch with the Russians, we decided to ask them for passage through."

"A lot of people have the idea from the press," Anderson says, "that we defected to the Soviet Union and then changed our minds. But there wasn't any question of that. We made it clear to the Russians from the beginning that we only wanted safe conduct. We aren't politicians, we aren't Marxists. We had no desire to change from one war-geared society to another war-geared society."

*

Through the offices of Bahrein, the four sailors spoke with a Russian official at the Soviet Embassy. They were told that a Russian freighter would be taking on cargo in Yokohama within a few days. The official then presented them with visitor's passes which would enable them to board the vessel.

"That was it," says Richard Bailey. "They gave us the passes and let us go at that. It was like the rest was up to us. We went aboard and cooled it, and when we were sure we were outside Japanese territorial waters, we turned ourselves over to the Russian captain. He looked pretty shook. I don't know whether he was surprised or not." The ship, the S.S. *Baikal*, took them to the port of Nahodka on the Soviet Pacific Coast. There they were met by functionaries they understood to be representatives of the Soviet Red Cross.

"The people that met us at Nahodka were the weirdest people I've ever seen in my life. I mean, we didn't know anything about Russia, we didn't have any idea of what to expect; and these cats really freaked us. They sent us by train to another city where we were supposed to get an aircraft for Moscow, and they were all right along. If they offered you a cigarette or tea or vodka, you couldn't tell them no. They wouldn't hear no. You had to take it. They were like an American movie idea of Russian agents, you know?

"The aircraft was like a flying houseboat. When we were taxiing into takeoff I couldn't believe the thing would ever get off the ground. And inside, it was divided into compartments like a European train. The flight to Moscow took over twelve hours; we just sat up straight in our upholstered seats with these weird guys in the compartment with us. I'll never forget the smell of Russian cigarettes. They really stink."

The boys were lodged in a Moscow apartment. Delegations from the officially sponsored Soviet peace organizations visited them. There were official receptions and guided tours of the city and its surroundings.

A few days after their arrival, Moscow radio and television broadcast interviews with them, together with their statements. According to Craig Anderson, they were not coached or fed material, no effort was made by Russian broadcasters to bring their position into line with Communist policy. They feel that Radio Moscow treated them more impartially than the Western media to whom they later gave interviews.

Very shortly, however, the Byzantine-cum-Victorian splendor of their Moscow suite, the huge vodka-laced meals, the piety and occasional evasiveness of their guides began to rankle their cool adolescent sensibilities.

"They were so straight, you couldn't believe it," Bailey relates. "And at that point we'd already done our thing, we didn't give a damn. We started putting them on a lot."

Statues and images of Lenin abounded in the streets of Moscow. "Who's that?" the boys would ask innocently. They asked the question fifty times a day.

"Lenin," they were told solemnly each time and Lenin's place in history was patiently re-explained to them.

"John Lennon?" (Ho, ho. Hollow laughter and stylized handshakes exchanged among the four. Simmering silence from the guide.)

"John? No, no. Not John. Nicolai—" and so forth.

"What kind of car is that?" Mike Lindner, mild teen-aged car freak, would inquire.

"That is a Volga."

"And what kind of car is that?"

"That is a Volga."

They inquired regularly about the make of passing cars. The cars always turned out to be Volgas. If the Soviet authorities in charge of this curious state visit experienced a flash of identification with the officers of U.S.S. *Intrepid*, they did not betray it.

"We were breaking their minds," Barilla says, "but they kept cool. They were extremely up tight. We began to want them to do something human, break a little—but they never did."

Mike Lindner occasionally pressed his embarrassed translators into service on his forays to pick up girls on the boulevards. Dick Bailey took to breaking down the formal rigor of haute cuisine with such un-kulturny practices as spooning shrimp into his soup.

"I admit it was sort of stupid," he says. "But we kept feeling like we had to do something to loosen up the atmosphere."

John Barilla attended the Bolshoi Ballet wearing mismatching shoes, his jacket inside out, puffing furiously from a Russian cigarette in imitation of a Central European villain from a silent movie. He caused his hosts even more embarrassment by raising unpleasant questions. Why did they put writers in jail? How long did they put them in jail for? What had they written?

"We never got to see Lenin's tomb," Barilla says. "I guess they were afraid to take us there."

They were, however, taken for a flying tour of several Soviet regions, including the Caucasian Republics (on the tours they were generally not exposed to the "masses"), and presented with $500 each as a parting gift from the Soviet Peace Union.

"We had a pretty good relationship with a few people there," Bailey recalls. "Some of the writers we talked to were nice guys. One of the official cats was all right too. Just before we left we'd been giving him a hard time and he sort of shrugged his shoulders and said, 'I don't know—I'm just a simple Communist.' The people who we had something going with were sorry to see us go, I think, and we were sort of sorry to leave them. They got a little emotional at the airport. You know, Russians are like that."

Had anyone there tried to persuade them to remain in the Soviet Union?

They laugh the question away. No, they say, the subject never came up. It had been understood from the start that their destination was Sweden.

"If we stayed there, we'd have been in jail in six months," John Barilla says. "It was a good feeling to go aboard that SAS jet for Stockholm. You know, a normal-type aircraft with a cool-looking stewardess, all that—"

Once in Sweden, they were looked after and lodged by a number of sympathetic Swedish intellectuals. They decided to split up to avoid forming what they called "an American enclave." Bailey and Lindner settled finally at the home of one of Sweden's leading actors, Gösta Eckmann. Eckmann and his wife, an attractive Ethiopian girl adopted in infancy and reared in Sweden, have a beautiful suburban house in the fir forest that surrounds Stockholm.

Anderson and Barilla took up residence at the Jakobsberg Folk School, an institution famous throughout Scandinavia for its experimental methods in adult education and sociological research.

After a week or two of seeming hesitation, the Swedish Foreign Ministry announced that the "Intrepid Four" were being granted permission to settle in the country. The decision was consistent with Sweden's traditional attitude toward fugitives from military justice and seems to have satisfied public and press opinion there. If there are any sections of the Swedish public who support America's Vietnam position, they are not in evidence.

Before the four arrived from Russia, two U.S. servicemen had already sought and received asylum in Sweden, and during the past winter the number of deserters has increased. Over twenty servicemen, mainly soldiers stationed in West Germany, have settled in and around Stockholm after deserting—nominally at least—over the war in Vietnam.

Many of the deserters there now have committed themselves to the violent destruction of the society they rejected. The more militant are in close touch with an ultraleft student organization which calls itself the NLF, after the National Liberation Front of Vietnam. Although the four sailors from the *Intrepid* have cordial relations with their fellow deserters, their brand of radicalism, inchoate and half-formed as it may be, is quite a different thing from that of NLF.

Craig Anderson spoke for all four when he told the Swedish Broadcasting Company that he and his friends rejected both the American and Soviet systems and all other systems "based on war."

"What we believe in," he said, "is reconciliation. We believe that what's poisoning the world now is ignorance. The force of ignorance is still so strong that man isn't ready to live in the technological society he's built for himself. The only thing worth doing is to try and work the ignorance out of both sides."

Bailey, who speaks occasionally of visiting India, has been reading Spofford Sibley's book *The Quiet Battle*, a work on the power of nonviolence. The book was given him by a Swedish pacifist family with whom he stayed on his arrival, and he intends now to read as much as he can on the application of "positive nonviolence" to social concerns. His desertion as well as that of his friends was a moral act, he says, not a political one.

The pacifist attitude, to which each of the "Intrepid Four" subscribes—perhaps an echo of the so-called "love revolution" among college-aged youth in America—is their principal expressed motivation. The answer, as in Bob Dylan's song, is blowing in the wind.

If they have not reasoned out the implications of this dream, they have yet held to it in the course of their wanderings with considerable strong-mindedness. Undoubtedly, they could have assured themselves a more cordial reception in Moscow and among the young revolutionaries of Stockholm if they had professed militancy of a less idealistic sort.

All four agree that the war is not over for them; they intend to engage what they conceive as the forces of war in their own way. They talk about the possibility of a "supermovement," but they were disappointed by the small response they received from pacifists in the States.

Life in Stockholm is not unpleasant for twenty-year-olds. The loveliness and liberality of Swedish girls are well known (although Mike Lindner says that he and his friends haven't formed any close feminine attachments yet. "They took us around to a lot of parties, and we were kind of a curiosity. We have to wait until things settle to get anything human going"). In the streets of the Old City, there are discotheques and poster shops displaying the latest groove from San Francisco. Stockholm has hookahs and mandalas and hash. (The Animals were in town while I was there; Jimi Hendrix was due.)

Eric Hammerquist, headmaster of the Jakobsberg Folk School, expects them to do well. "They will be very busy here," he says. "If they learn the language sufficiently they may be in a position to go on to a university. They are quite intelligent."

A quietly jovial man, the very image of a Northern scholar, Hammerquist makes no secret of his delight in giving aid and comfort to opponents of the Vietnam War. "I think we may advertise abroad," he says dryly. "Special Summer Courses for American deserters. We may pose our prettiest girls in posters that say 'I Want You,' like Uncle Sam."

But exile, after all, must be lived by the day. What about the price, one asks, the forsaking of home, of parents?

They speak soberly about their families and about the hopelessness of making them understand. There is no rancor in what they say, only regret. They take comfort in a letter written them by an American pacifist woman who told them that it is the turn of their generation to provide answers.

Anderson, Bailey, and Lindner have all had mail from home—it expressed, for the most part, anxiety and incomprehension.

John Barilla has not heard a word from his parents since the day he went over the hill.

They express no regret over the loss of America.

Anderson says he misses San Francisco sometimes—"that's it."

Dick Bailey tells of hearing a record of Frank Sinatra's, "Strangers in the Night," in a restaurant; it made him miss nights in Florida, he says. "But then you think of the States and how everything is supposed to be that great and then you think—what? What is there really? Shit, the rewards aren't that great."

I saw the "Intrepid Four" for the last time at a party attended by students and faculty of the Folk School. It was, as they say, a wild scene—the students, a mixed bag of radicals, sociologists, and delinquents, were reacting to their beer in the customary Swedish fashion. The Rolling Stones were on the machine, there was dancing, a roaring fire against the subzero cold outside; the girls were gorgeous.

The sailors had skillfully separated girls from the general doings and were holding a semiprivate gathering of their own in Anderson and Barilla's living quarters.

They were using a drinking glass as an ashtray because the student in the room adjoining theirs had broken their ashtray earlier to prove a revolutionary point. A dedicated revolutionary, their neighbor had also broken the huge windows of the United States Embassy during an anti-war demonstration.

"He wanted to know what our position was," Barilla told me. "He doesn't pick up on nonviolence. I told him—all right, I'm a nihilist. He said, OK, if you're a nihilist then I can do anything I like. So he stepped on the ashtray."

Barilla smiled warily. "We'll do it our way, if we can," he said. "We didn't change the world by what we did, but it was a nonviolent act. It accomplished something. I mean, we don't pretend to know all the answers."

LAWRENCE FERLINGHETTI

Prison Diary

Santa Rita Rehabilitation Center, January 4, 1968—what are we doing here in this dank tank? Probing the limits of legitimate political
dissent in this unenlightened country? Nonviolent gesture of block-
ing the entrance to war at Oakland Army Induction Center hereby
judged beyond that limit. Rehabilitate us, please . . . First rough
impressions of anybody's first time in jail: suddenly realizing what
"incarcerated" really means. Paranoid fear of the unknown, fear of
not knowing what's going to happen to your body, fear of getting
thrown in The Hole. . . . Routine of being booked, fingerprinted,

Prison Diary. From *Ramparts*, March 1968. Originally titled "Santa Rita Journal."
Reprinted by permission of the author.

mugged, shunted from bullpen to bullpen itself a shock for any "first offender." . . . Naive vestigial illusions about the inherent goodness of man fly out the barred window. . . . From Oakland jail, shunted through a series of sealed boxes, the first on wheels—long gray bus, windows blinded, 50 inmates behind locked grate, the freeway where yesterday we rode free now visible only through holes in grate. . . . Prison sighted half hour later on a forlorn plain at Pleasanton. . . . Barbed wire fences and watchtowers. Poor man's concentration camp? . . . Shunted through another series of holding cells, several more hours of not knowing one's immediate fate, just as likely you'll be put in "Graystone" maximum security pen as in General Compound. . . . I take the easier way out: I don't refuse to shave or work. Reforming the prison system is another issue. Rather have a pen than a beard (and so keep this journal). Pen mightier than beard. Opportunity to infiltrate general prison population with non-violent ideas? Another naive liberal illusion!

The prison is about two-thirds black, and the other third is Mexican, Pachuco and white North American. They've got their own problems and their own enemies, and they've no use for "nonviolence." The jungle is full of felons and, as for the war, most of them have the attitudes of their jailers and think what we're doing in Vietnam is great, violence being one way of life they fully understand. This sure deflates the myth promoted by Our President equating anti-war demonstrations with "crime in the streets" and with ghetto wars. If there were any blacks busted this time at the Oakland Induction Center, I didn't see them. (And if I were black, in Oakland, I'd stay away too). . . .

January 5—There's not a political prisoner in my barracks. The most "uncooperative" of the demonstrators are in Graystone, two in a cell or in The Hole on bread and skimmed milk. A larger group is in Compound 8 with no privileges and a meal-and-a-half a day. A little incident happened today when they were marching back from the mess hall. The last in the line suddenly went limp and sat down in the middle of the Compound street. He was a kid of about 20 with medium-long hair he'd refused to cut. One officer ran up to him and tried to make him get up. He would not. The officer made a signal and four other officers wearing black leather gloves came at the double up the center of the street from the gate. They had no guns or night sticks. Each took an arm or a leg of the boy and started dragging him. He was a big kid, and they couldn't get his tail off the ground. They got him out of sight in a hurry. When I got back to barracks, someone had an Oakland Tribune with a photo of four Marines carrying a dead Marine buddy away from a Vietnam battlefield in the same style. . . .

January 6—I told them I had printing experience, and they put me stencilling pants! "Santa Rita" in pure white on every pair. "Gives us something to aim at!" the deputy told me, laughing, sighting his fingers at the stencil marks. Very funny. Holy prison, named for a Spanish saint. . . . Goya should have seen a place like this. He did, he did. Goya faces in the morning chowline, a thousand of them sticking out of blue denims, out of Goya's "Disasters of War." These are the disasters of peace. Down rows and rows of long wooden tables, half of skid row mixed with Oakland ghettos and the backwash of various nearby penitentiaries, long-term cons now here hung up on short-term crimes—petty boosters, bad check artists, child molesters, free-way, drag-racers, car thieves, armed robbers, mail frauds, sex-freaks, winos, hypes, pushers, you name it. And political prisoners. . . . Sit swine-like at the trough, gobbling the chow from metal trays. Great place to keep from getting too refined; dig these myriad beat faces. . . . Here comes "Orfeo"—very handsome young Negro dude with a fine great black beard. Walked out of a Genet prison novel. Just stood there smiling like a black angel without wings when they told him to shave or get thrown in The Hole. They came back later and took him away. Now he shows up again in the mess hall, looking as wild and gentle as ever. I believe he is truly mad and they know it. I don't believe he understood anything they told him. They let him keep his beard. He'll fly away over the rooftops one day, to a shack on a hillside above Rio and live with a beautiful mulatto and tend goats, blowing a wreathed horn. And the horn full of grass. . . .

Another face in the gallery across the table from me: enormous ragged gray head, with hogshead snout, on a 200-pound body in ragged jeans. Great hams of white hands. But the face, the face: white stubble from shaggy hair to throat, rum-pot eyes. Small pig-eyes, but not mean looking. Just dumb and staring. This is what has become of "The Man with the Hoe." Long, heavy jaw with great, protruding rows of white teeth. Grunted and snuffled as he slurped his pancakes. When he called for the coffee pitcher, his voice came out in a thin squeal. Man, what have you done to this man? Man, who made you

like that? Man, has Mother ever seen you, seen what has become of
you? Man, you still alive inside? (I hear your stentor breath.) Man,
are you to be born again? Live again, love again? Man. Who is there
to redeem you. Fidel Castro? The true revolutionary, Fidel said, is
one whose first concern is the *redemption* of mankind. . . . Faces
fallen out of wombs somewhere, long ago. Now rolled down streets
and come to rest among writhing bodies in a painting by Bosch, Gar-
den of Paradise. . . . Feed and shuffle out, doubles of models Goya
used in a Toledo madhouse. "By Graystone's foetid walls." . . .
One doesn't eat here to consume food; one eats to consume time.
And time is life. . . .

January 7—Sunday in the Compound, and "religious services":
let them explain away the existence of evil here. The older one gets,
the more one learns to believe in the very real existence of evil. This
place proves it. The making of criminals. The redemption of mankind? The rehabilitation of man? They put 19-year-old Judith Bloom-
berg and Joan Baez on bread and milk for three days. (On the men's
side, Gary Lisman fasted for 12 days.) These kids are the greatest.
They are busted for disturbing the "peace" and are hauled away. They
plead *nolo contendere*. They do not wish to contend. They are telling
their elders they can have it. They are telling the Establishment that
they want nothing to do with its power structure and refuse even to
dispute the legal terms of that evil. . . . As long as there are guns,
they will shoot, telescopically. . . . At the weekly movie tonight, the
inmates spy Joan Baez through a crack in the curtain hiding the bal-
cony where the women prisoners sit. A hundred felons turn and raise
their hands in the Peace Sign and shout, "We love you, Joan!"

January 8—The Enormous Room of my barracks: a black inmate
is reading "Synanon" (the place is full of junkies). He doesn't realize what an elite place Synanon may be. Diedrich, the founder, must
have read Hermann Hesse's *Magister Ludi* (the Bead Game) and
seized upon the conception of an elite world-within-a-world depicted
by Hesse in Germany—Castallia being the name of the German intellectual elite created to govern society, with its own special *esprit
de corps*, its own hierarchy, its own pecking order—a self-contained
world of its own—Synanon also having developed its own cadre of
first leaders framed on the wall, approval and status in its society dependent on length of residence, etc., the drug user rejected by the

outside straight world here able to reject that society himself in favor of Synanon's own hierarchy: the Bead Game on its own level. And the prison system with its own Bead Game. . . . Shigeyoshi Murao comes to see me during visiting hours and tells me it looks just like the prisoner of war camps they kept Nisei in during World War Two.

January 9—Obscenity: violation of the Penal Code: today in the Commissary line when I tried to exchange a word with Dr. Lee Rather (a political prisoner), Officer Dykes hollered at me: "Get your fucking ass out of here, you motherfucker!"

January 10—Back in the barracks, the sealed life goes on. We are on some blind ship, all portholes sealed. Siren sounds and loudspeaker barks. Up for the count. Then down again, felon shipmates stretched in their bunks, staring at the overhead. . . . You spend a lot of time staring at nothing in a place like this. Great place to develop the Tragic Sense of Life. "Lucy in the Sky with Diamonds" comes over the barracks radio, and I picture myself in a boat on a river, where newspaper taxis await on the shore, waiting to take me away. . . .

January 11—Awakened at exactly three a.m. by a guard with a flashlight and told to get up and stand by my bunk. "You're going to court today." From three to eight a.m. I wait in a bullpen with over 50 other inmates going to court. The cell is 20' by 15', and over half the inmates have to stand up all that time. I talk to one black felon who has been gotten up like this three days in a row, and if he wants to fight his case this is the way he can do it. . . . Life goes on at Santa Rita. Or death. . . . I got the Santa Rita blues. . . .

Afterthoughts and vituperations: Really realize how a hole like this literally makes criminals: 18-year-old first-offender thrown in for disturbing society's deep sleep now making his first hard connection with hard drugs (they are shooting it up in the john!) and enforced homosexuality (bend over, buddy!). . . .
Guards with hard-edge voices careful not to show any human feelings for inmates, on the watch for the slightest lack of obsequiousness on the part of prisoners, now and then goading them a bit with a choice obscenity . . . a slip of the tongue in return, and you're in The Hole with your tongue hanging out. . . .

Plus mail officers with German names withholding mail and books at will, first class letters opened and censored. . . . Working in the mailroom I note two books (sent directly to an inmate from City Lights Bookstore) withheld: Debray's *Revolution in the Revolution?* and *Black Power.* . . . Burn, baby, burn—but in here, baby, it's you who'll be burning. . . . Later, when I am loose, I send *Gandhi on Non-Violence* to an inmate felon, and it comes back stamped "Unacceptable."

Unhappy Dehabilitation Center, man-made excrescence befouling the once-beautiful landscape in the shadow of distant Mount Diablo: Devil's mount!

If only revolution can blot out such scenes, let there be revolution; but not a revolution of hate leading in the end to just another super-state. . . .

PHILIP ROTH

The Conversion
of the Jews

"You're a real one for opening your mouth in the first place," Itzie
said. "What do you open your mouth all the time for?"

"I didn't bring it up, Itz, I didn't," Ozzie said.

"What do you care about Jesus Christ for anyway?"

"I didn't bring up Jesus Christ. He did. I didn't even know what
he was talking about. Jesus is historical, he kept saying. Jesus is historical." Ozzie mimicked the monumental voice of Rabbi Binder.

"Jesus was a person that lived like you and me," Ozzie continued. "That's what Binder said—"

"Yeah? . . . So what! What do I give two cents whether he lived
or not. And what do you gotta open your mouth!" Itzie Lieberman favored closed-mouthedness, especially when it came to Ozzie Freedman's questions. Mrs. Freedman had to see Rabbi Binder twice before about Ozzie's questions and this Wednesday at four-thirty would
be the third time. Itzie preferred to keep *his* mother in the kitchen;
he settled for behind-the-back subtleties such as gestures, faces, snarls
and other less delicate barnyard noises.

"He was a real person, Jesus, but he wasn't like God, and we don't
believe he is God." Slowly, Ozzie was explaining Rabbi Binder's position to Itzie, who had been absent from Hebrew School the previous afternoon.

"The Catholics," Itzie said helpfully, "they believe in Jesus Christ,
that he's God." Itzie Lieberman used "the Catholics" in its broad-
east sense—to include the Protestants.

Ozzie received Itzie's remark with a tiny head bob, as though it
were a footnote, and went on. "His mother was Mary, and his father probably was Joseph," Ozzie said. "But the New Testament says
his real father was God."

"His *real* father?"

"Yeah," Ozzie said, "that's the big thing, his father's supposed to
be God."

"Bull."

"That's what Rabbi Binder says, that it's impossible—"

"Sure it's impossible. That stuff's all bull. To have a baby you
gotta get laid," Itzie theologized. "Mary hadda get laid."

"That's what Binder says: 'The only way a woman can have a
baby is to have intercourse with a man.' "

"He said *that*, Ozz?" For a moment it appeared that Itzie had
put the theological question aside. "He said that, intercourse?" A little curled smile shaped itself in the lower half of Itzie's face like a
pink mustache. "What you guys do, Ozz, you laugh or something?"

"I raised my hand."

"Yeah? Whatja say?"

"That's when I asked the question."

Itzie's face lit up. "Whatja ask about—intercourse?"

"No, I asked the question about God, how if He could create the heaven and earth in six days, and make all the animals and the fish and the light in six days—the light especially, that's what always gets me, that He could make the light. Making fish and animals, that's pretty good—"

"That's damn good." Itzie's appreciation was honest but unimaginative: it was as though God had just pitched a one-hitter.

"But making light . . . I mean when you think about it, it's really something," Ozzie said. "Anyway, I asked Binder if He could make all that in six days, and He could *pick* the six days He wanted right out of nowhere, why couldn't He let a woman have a baby without having intercourse."

"You said intercourse, Ozz, to Binder?"

"Yeah."

"Right in class?"

"Yeah."

Itzie smacked the side of his head.

"I mean, no kidding around," Ozzie said, "that'd really be nothing. After all that other stuff, that'd practically be nothing."

Itzie considered a moment. "What'd Binder say?"

"He started all over again explaining how Jesus was historical and how he lived like you and me but he wasn't God. So I said I understood that. What I wanted to know was *different*."

What Ozzie wanted to know was always different. The first time he had wanted to know how Rabbi Binder could call the Jews "The Chosen People" if the Declaration of Independence claimed all men to be created equal. Rabbi Binder tried to distinguish for him between political equality and spiritual legitimacy, but what Ozzie wanted to know, he insisted vehemently, was different. That was the first time his mother had to come.

Then there was the plane crash. Fifty-eight people had been killed in a plane crash at La Guardia. In studying a casualty list in the newspaper his mother had discovered among the list of those dead eight Jewish names (his grandmother had nine but she counted Miller as a Jewish name); because of the eight she said the plane crash was "a tragedy." During free-discussion time on Wednesday Ozzie had brought to Rabbi Binder's attention this matter of "some of his relations" always picking out the Jewish names. Rabbi Binder had begun to explain cultural unity and some other things when Ozzie stood up at his seat and said that what he wanted to know was dif-

ferent. Rabbi Binder insisted that he sit down and it was then that
Ozzie shouted that he wished all fifty-eight were Jews. That was the
second time his mother came.

"And he kept explaining about Jesus being historical, and so I
kept asking him. No kidding, Itz, he was trying to make me look stupid."

"So what he finally do?"

"Finally he starts screaming that I was deliberately simple-minded
and a wise guy, and that my mother had to come, and this was the
last time. And that I'd never get bar-mitzvahed if he could help it.
Then, Itz, then he starts talking in that voice like a statue, real slow
and deep, and he says that I better think over what I said about the
Lord. He told me to go to his office and think it over." Ozzie leaned
his body towards Itzie. "Itz, I thought it over for a solid hour, and
now I'm convinced God could do it."

Ozzie had planned to confess his latest transgression to his
mother as soon as she came home from work. But it was a Friday
night in November and already dark, and when Mrs. Freedman came
through the door she tossed off her coat, kissed Ozzie quickly on the
face, and went to the kitchen table to light the three yellow candles,
two for the Sabbath and one for Ozzie's father.

When his mother lit the candles she would move her two arms
slowly towards her, dragging them through the air, as though persuad-
ing people whose minds were half made up. And her eyes would
get glassy with tears. Even when his father was alive Ozzie remembered that her eyes had gotten glassy, so it didn't have anything to
do with his dying. It had something to do with lighting the candles.

As she touched the flaming match to the unlit wick of a Sabbath
candle, the phone rang, and Ozzie, standing only a foot from it,
plucked it off the receiver and held it muffled to his chest. When his
mother lit candles Ozzie felt there should be no noise; even breathing,
if you could manage it, should be softened. Ozzie pressed the phone
to his breast and watched his mother dragging whatever she was dragging, and he felt his own eyes get glassy. His mother was a round,
tired, gray-haired penguin of a woman whose gray skin had begun to
feel the tug of gravity and the weight of her own history. Even when
she was dressed up she didn't look like a chosen person. But when she
lit candles she looked like something better; like a woman who knew
momentarily that God could do anything.

After a few mysterious minutes she was finished. Ozzie hung up the phone and walked to the kitchen table where she was beginning to lay the two places for the four-course Sabbath meal. He told her that she would have to see Rabbi Binder next Wednesday at four-thirty, and then he told her why. For the first time in their life together she hit Ozzie across the face with her hand.

All through the chopped liver and chicken soup part of the dinner Ozzie cried; he didn't have any appetite for the rest.

On Wednesday, in the largest of the three basement classrooms of the synagogue, Rabbi Marvin Binder, a tall, handsome, broad-shouldered man of thirty with thick strong-fibered black hair, removed his watch from his pocket and saw that it was four o'clock. At the rear of the room Yakov Blotnik, the seventy-one-year-old custodian, slowly polished the large window, mumbling to himself, unaware that it was four o'clock or six o'clock, Monday or Wednesday. To most of the students Yakov Blotnik's mumbling, along with his brown curly beard, scythe nose, and two heel-trailing black cats, made of him an object of wonder, a foreigner, a relic, towards whom they were alternately fearful and disrespectful. To Ozzie the mumbling had always seemed a monotonous, curious prayer; what made it curious was that old Blotnik had been mumbling so steadily for so many years, Ozzie suspected he had memorized the prayers and forgotten all about God.

"It is now free-discussion time," Rabbi Binder said. "Feel free to talk about any Jewish matter at all—religion, family, politics, sports—"

There was silence. It was a gusty, clouded November afternoon and it did not seem as though there ever was or could be a thing called baseball. So nobody this week said a word about that hero from the past, Hank Greenberg—which limited free discussion considerably.

And the soul-battering Ozzie Freedman had just received from Rabbi Binder had imposed its limitation. When it was Ozzie's turn to read aloud from the Hebrew book the rabbi had asked him petulantly why he didn't read more rapidly. He was showing no progress. Ozzie said he could read faster but that if he did he was sure not to understand what he was reading. Nevertheless, at the rabbi's repeated suggestion Ozzie tried, and showed a great talent, but in the midst of a long passage he stopped short and said he didn't understand a word he was reading, and started in again at a drag-footed pace. Then came the soul-battering.

Consequently when free-discussion time rolled around none of the students felt too free. The rabbi's invitation was answered only by the mumbling of feeble old Blotnik.

"Isn't there anything at all you would like to discuss?" Rabbi Binder asked again, looking at his watch. "No questions or comments?"

There was a small grumble from the third row. The rabbi requested that Ozzie rise and give the rest of the class the advantage of his thought.

Ozzie rose. "I forget it now," he said, and sat down in his place. Rabbi Binder advanced a seat towards Ozzie and poised himself on the edge of the desk. It was Itzie's desk and the rabbi's frame only a dagger's-length away from his face snapped him to sitting attention.

"Stand up again, Oscar," Rabbi Binder said calmly, "and try to assemble your thoughts."

Ozzie stood up. All his classmates turned in their seats and watched as he gave an unconvincing scratch to his forehead.

"I can't assemble any," he announced, and plunked himself down.

"Stand up!" Rabbi Binder advanced from Itzie's desk to the one directly in front of Ozzie; when the rabbinical back was turned Itzie gave it five-fingers off the tip of his nose, causing a small titter in the room. Rabbi Binder was too absorbed in squelching Ozzie's nonsense once and for all to bother with titters. "Stand up, Oscar. What's your question about?"

Ozzie pulled a word out of the air. It was the handiest word. "Religion."

"Oh, now you remember?"

"Yes."

"What is it?"

Trapped, Ozzie blurted the first thing that came to him. "Why can't He make anything He wants to make!"

As Rabbi Binder prepared an answer, a final answer, Itzie, ten feet behind him, raised one finger on his left hand, gestured it meaningfully towards the rabbi's back, and brought the house down.

Binder twisted quickly to see what had happened and in the midst of the commotion Ozzie shouted into the rabbi's back what he couldn't have shouted to his face. It was a loud, toneless sound that had the timbre of something stored inside for about six days.

"You don't know! You don't know anything about God!"
The rabbi spun back towards Ozzie. "What?"
"You don't know—you don't—"
"Apologize, Oscar, apologize!" It was a threat.
"You don't—"
Rabbi Binder's hand flicked out at Ozzie's cheek. Perhaps it had only been meant to clamp the boy's mouth shut, but Ozzie ducked and the palm caught him squarely on the nose.

The blood came in a short, red spurt on to Ozzie's shirt front.

The next moment was all confusion. Ozzie screamed, "You bastard, you bastard!" and broke for the classroom door. Rabbi Binder lurched a step backwards, as though his own blood had started flowing violently in the opposite direction, then gave a clumsy lurch forward and bolted out the door after Ozzie. The class followed after the rabbi's huge blue-suited back, and before old Blotnik could turn from his window, the room was empty and everyone was headed full speed up the three flights leading to the roof.

If one should compare the light of day to the life of man: sunrise to birth; sunset—the dropping down over the edge—to death; then as Ozzie Freedman wiggled through the trapdoor of the synagogue roof, his feet kicking backwards bronco-style at Rabbi Binder's outstretched arms—at that moment the day was fifty years old. As a rule, fifty or fifty-five reflects accurately the age of late afternoons in November, for it is in that month, during those hours, that one's awareness of light seems no longer a matter of seeing, but of hearing: light begins clicking away. In fact, as Ozzie locked shut the trapdoor in the rabbi's face, the sharp click of the bolt into the lock might momentarily have been mistaken for the sound of the heavier gray that had just throbbed through the sky.

With all his weight Ozzie kneeled on the locked door; any instant he was certain that Rabbi Binder's shoulder would fling it open, splintering the wood into shrapnel and catapulting his body into the sky. But the door did not move and below him he heard only the rumble of feet, first loud then dim, like thunder rolling away.

A question shot through his brain. "Can this be *me*?" For a thirteen-year-old who had just labeled his religious leader a bastard, twice, it was not an improper question. Louder and louder the question came to him—"Is it me? Is it me?"—until he discovered himself no longer kneeling, but racing crazily towards the edge of the roof,

his eyes crying, his throat screaming, and his arms flying everywhich-
way as though not his own.

"Is it me? Is it me ME ME ME ME! It has to be me—but is it!"

It is the question a thief must ask himself the night he jimmies
open his first window, and it is said to be the question with which
bridegrooms quiz themselves before the altar.

In the few wild seconds it took Ozzie's body to propel him to
the edge of the roof, his self-examination began to grow fuzzy. Gazing down at the street, he became confused as to the problem beneath the question: was it, is-it-me-who-called-Binder-a-bastard? or,
is-it-me-prancing-around-on-the-roof? However, the scene below settled all, for there is an instant in any action when whether it is you
or somebody else is academic. The thief crams the money in his
pockets and scoots out the window. The bridegroom signs the hotel register for two. And the boy on the roof finds a streetful of people gaping at him, necks stretched backwards, faces up, as though he
were the ceiling of the Hayden Planetarium. Suddenly you know
it's you.

"Oscar! Oscar Freedman!" A voice rose from the center of the
crowd, a voice that, could it have been seen, would have looked like
the writing on scroll. "Oscar Freedman, get down from there. Immediately!" Rabbi Binder was pointing one arm stiffly up at him;
and at the end of that arm, one finger aimed menacingly. It was the
attitude of a dictator, but one—the eyes confessed all—whose personal valet had spit neatly in his face.

Ozzie didn't answer. Only for a blink's length did he look towards
Rabbi Binder. Instead his eyes began to fit together the world beneath him, to sort out people from places, friends from enemies, participants from spectators. In little jagged starlike clusters his friends
stood around Rabbi Binder, who was still pointing. The topmost
point on a star compounded not of angels but of five adolescent boys
was Itzie. What a world it was, with those stars below, Rabbi Binder
below . . . Ozzie, who a moment earlier hadn't been able to control
his own body, started to feel the meaning of the word control: he
felt Peace and he felt Power.

"Oscar Freedman, I'll give you three to come down."

Few dictators give their subjects three to do anything; but, as always, Rabbi Binder only looked dictatorial.

"Are you ready, Oscar?"

Ozzie nodded his head yes, although he had no intention in the world—the lower one or the celestial one he'd just entered—of coming down even if Rabbi Binder should give him a million.

"All right then," said Rabbi Binder. He ran a hand through his black Samson hair as though it were the gesture prescribed for uttering the first digit. Then, with his other hand cutting a circle out of the small piece of sky around him, he spoke. "One!"

There was no thunder. On the contrary, at that moment, as though "one" was the cue for which he had been waiting, the world's least thunderous person appeared on the synagogue steps. He did not so much come out the synagogue door as lean out, onto the darkening air. He clutched at the doorknob with one hand and looked up at the roof.

"Oy!"

Yakov Blotnik's old mind hobbled slowly, as if on crutches, and though he couldn't decide precisely what the boy was doing on the roof, he knew it wasn't good—that is, it wasn't-good-for-the-Jews. For Yakov Blotnik life had fractionated itself simply: things were either good-for-the-Jews or no-good-for-the-Jews.

He smacked his free hand to his in-sucked cheek, gently. "Oy, Gut!" And then quickly as he was able, he jacked down his head and surveyed the street. There was Rabbi Binder (like a man at an auction with only three dollars in his pocket, he had just delivered a shaky "Two!"); there were the students, and that was all. So far it-wasn't-so-bad-for-the-Jews. But the boy had to come down immediately, before anybody saw. The problem: how to get the boy off the roof?

Anbody who has ever had a cat on the roof knows how to get him down. You call the fire department. Or first you call the operator and you ask her for the fire department. And the next thing there is great jamming of brakes and clanging of bells and shouting of instructions. And then the cat is off the roof. You do the same thing to get a boy off the roof.

That is, you do the same thing if you are Yakov Blotnik and you once had a cat on the roof.

When the engines, all four of them, arrived, Rabbi Binder had four times given Ozzie the count of three. The big hook-and-ladder swung around the corner and one of the firemen leaped from it, plunging headlong towards the yellow fire hydrant in front of the synagogue. With a huge wrench he began to unscrew the top nozzle. Rabbi Binder raced over to him and pulled at his shoulder.

"There's no fire . . ."

The fireman mumbled back over his shoulder and, heatedly, continued working at the nozzle.

"But there's no fire, there's no fire . . ." Binder shouted. When the fireman mumbled again, the rabbi grasped his face with both his hands and pointed it up at the roof.

To Ozzie it looked as though Rabbi Binder was trying to tug the fireman's head out of his body, like a cork from a bottle. He had to giggle at the picture they made: it was a family portrait—rabbi in black skullcap, fireman in red fire hat, and the little yellow hydrant squatting beside like a kid brother, bareheaded. From the edge of the roof Ozzie waved at the portrait, a one-handed, flapping, mocking wave; in doing it his right foot slipped from under him. Rabbi Binder covered his eyes with his hands.

Firemen work fast. Before Ozzie had even regained his balance, a big, round, yellowed net was being held on the synagogue lawn. The firemen who held it looked up at Ozzie with stern, feelingless faces.

One of the firemen turned his head towards Rabbi Binder. "What, is the kid nuts or something?"

Rabbi Binder unpeeled his hands from his eyes, slowly, painfully, as if they were tape. Then he checked: nothing on the sidewalk, no dents in the net.

"Is he gonna jump, or what?" the fireman shouted.

In a voice not at all like a statue, Rabbi Binder finally answered, "Yes, yes, I think so . . . He's been threatening to . . ."

Threatening to? Why, the reason he was on the roof, Ozzie remembered, was to get away; he hadn't even thought about jumping. He had just run to get away, and the truth was that he hadn't really headed for the roof as much as he'd been chased there.

"What's his name, the kid?"

"Freedman," Rabbi Binder answered. "Oscar Freedman."

The fireman looked up at Ozzie. "What is it with you, Oscar? You gonna jump, or what?"

Ozzie did not answer. Frankly, the question had just arisen.

"Look, Oscar, if you're gonna jump, jump—and if you're not gonna jump, don't jump. But don't waste our time, willya?"

Ozzie looked at the fireman and then at Rabbi Binder. He wanted to see Rabbi Binder cover his eyes one more time.

"I'm going to jump."

And then he scampered around the edge of the roof to the corner, where there was no net below, and he flapped his arms at his sides, swishing the air and smacking his palms to his trousers on the downbeat. He began screaming like some kind of engine, "Wheeeee . . . wheeeeee," and leaning way out over the edge with the upper half of his body. The firemen whipped around to cover the ground with the net. Rabbi Binder mumbled a few words to Somebody and covered his eyes. Everything happened quickly, jerkily, as in a silent movie. The crowd, which had arrived with the fire engines, gave out a long, Fourth-of-July fireworks oooh-aahhh. In the excitement no one had paid the crowd much heed, except, of course, Yakov Blotnik, who swung from the doorknob counting heads. "Fier und tsvansik . . . finf und tsvantsik . . . Oy, Gut!" It wasn't like this with the cat.

Rabbi Binder peeked through his fingers, checked the sidewalk and net. Empty. But there was Ozzie racing to the other corner. The firemen raced with him but were unable to keep up. Whenever Ozzie wanted to he might jump and splatter himself upon the sidewalk, and by the time the firemen scooted to the spot all they could do with their net would be to cover the mess.

"Wheeeee . . . wheeeee . . ."

"Hey, Oscar," the winded fireman yelled, "What the hell is this, a game or something?"

"Wheeeee . . . wheeeee . . ."

"Hey, Oscar—"

But he was off now to the other corner, flapping his wings fiercely. Rabbi Binder couldn't take it any longer—the fire engines from nowhere, the screaming suicidal boy, the net. He fell to his knees, exhausted, and with his hands curled together in front of his chest like a little dome, he pleaded, "Oscar, stop it, Oscar. Don't jump, Oscar. Please come down . . . Please don't jump."

And further back in the crowd a single voice, a single young voice, shouted a lone word to the boy on the roof.

"Jump!"

It was Itzie. Ozzie momentarily stopped flapping.

"Go ahead, Ozz—jump!" Itzie broke off his point of the star and courageously, with the inspiration not of a wise-guy but of a disciple, stood alone. "Jump, Ozz, jump!"

Still on his knees, his hands still curled, Rabbi Binder twisted his body back. He looked at Itzie, then, agonizingly, back to Ozzie.

"OSCAR, DON'T JUMP! PLEASE, DON'T JUMP . . . please please . . ."

"Jump!" This time it wasn't Itzie but another point of the star. By the time Mrs. Freedman arrived to keep her four-thirty appointment with Rabbi Binder, the whole little upside down heaven was shouting and pleading for Ozzie to jump, and Rabbi Binder no longer was pleading with him not to jump, but was crying into the dome of his hands.

Understandably Mrs. Freedman couldn't figure out what her son was doing on the roof. So she asked.

"Ozzie, my Ozzie, what are you doing? My Ozzie, what is it?"

Ozzie stopped wheeeeeeing and slowed his arms down to a cruising flap, the kind birds use in soft winds, but he did not answer. He stood against the low, clouded, darkening sky—light clicked down swiftly now, as on a small gear—flapping softly and gazing down at the small bundle of a woman who was his mother.

"What are you doing, Ozzie?" She turned towards the kneeling Rabbi Binder and rushed so close that only a paper-thickness of dusk lay between her stomach and his shoulders.

"What is my baby doing?"

Rabbi Binder gaped up at her but he too was mute. All that moved was the dome of his hands; it shook back and forth like a weak pulse.

"Rabbi, get him down! He'll kill himself. Get him down, my only baby . . ."

"I can't," Rabbi Binder said, "I can't . . ." and he turned his handsome head towards the crowd of boys behind him. "It's them. Listen to them."

And for the first time Mrs. Freedman saw the crowd of boys, and she heard what they were yelling.

"He's doing it for them. He won't listen to me. It's them." Rabbi Binder spoke like one in a trance.

"For them?"

"Yes."

"Why for them?"

"They want him to . . ."

Mrs. Freedman raised her two arms upward as though she were conducting the sky. "For them he's doing it!" And then in a gesture older than pyramids, older than prophets and floods, her arms came slapping down to her sides. "A martyr I have. Look!" She tilted her head to the roof. Ozzie was still flapping softly. "My martyr."

"Oscar, come down, *please*," Rabbi Binder groaned.

In a startlingly even voice Mrs. Freedman called to the boy on the roof. "Ozzie, come down, Ozzie. Don't be a martyr, my baby."

As though it were a litany, Rabbi Binder repeated her words. "Don't be a martyr, my baby. Don't be a martyr."

"Gawhead, Ozz—*be* a Martin!" It was Itzie. "Be a Martin, be a Martin," and all the voices joined in singing for a Martindom, whatever *it* was. "Be a Martin, be a Martin . . ."

Somehow when you're on a roof the darker it gets the less you can hear. All Ozzie knew was that two groups wanted two new things: his friends were spirited and musical about what they wanted; his mother and the rabbi were even-toned, chanting, about what they didn't want. The rabbi's voice was without tears now and so was his mother's.

The big net stared up at Ozzie like a sightless eye. The big, clouded sky pushed down. From beneath it looked like a gray corrugated board. Suddenly, looking up into that unsympathetic sky, Ozzie realized all the strangeness of what these people, his friends, were asking: they wanted him to jump, to kill himself; they were singing about it now—it made them that happy. And there was an even greater strangeness: Rabbi Binder was on his knees, trembling. If there was a question to be asked now it was not "Is it me?" but rather "Is it us? . . . Is it us?"

Being on the roof, it turned out, was a serious thing. If he jumped would the singing become dancing? Would it? What would jumping stop? Yearningly, Ozzie wished he could rip open the sky, plunge his hands through, and pull out the sun; and on the sun, like a coin, would be stamped JUMP or DON'T JUMP.

Ozzie's knees rocked and sagged a little under him as though they were setting him for a dive. His arms tightened, stiffened, froze, from shoulders to fingernails. He felt as if each part of his body were going to vote as to whether he should kill himself or not—and each part as though it were independent of *him*.

The light took an unexpected click down and the new darkness, like a gag, hushed the friends singing for this and the mother and rabbi chanting for that.

Ozzie stopped counting votes, and in a curiously high voice, like one who wasn't prepared for speech, he spoke.

"Mamma?"

"Yes, Oscar."

"Mamma, get down on your knees, like Rabbi Binder."

"Oscar—"

"Get down on your knees," he said, "or I'll jump."

Ozzie heard a whimper, then a quick rustling, and when he looked down where his mother had stood he saw the top of a head and beneath that a circle of dress. She was kneeling beside Rabbi Binder.

He spoke again. "Everybody kneel." There was the sound of everybody kneeling.

Ozzie looked around. With one hand he pointed towards the synagogue entrance. "Make *him* kneel."

There was a noise, not of kneeling, but of body-and-cloth stretching. Ozzie could hear Rabbi Binder saying in a gruff whisper, ". . . or he'll *kill* himself," and when next he looked there was Yakov Blotnik off the doorknob and for the first time in his life upon his knees in the Gentile posture of prayer.

As for the firemen—it is not as difficult as one might imagine to hold a net taut while you are kneeling.

Ozzie looked around again; and then he called to Rabbi Binder.

"Rabbi?"

"Yes, Oscar."

"Rabbi Binder, do you believe in God?"

"Yes."

"Do you believe God can do Anything?" Ozzie leaned his head out into the darkness. "Anything?"

"Oscar, I think—"

"Tell me you believe God can do Anything."

There was a second's hesitation. Then: "God can do Anything."

"Tell me you believe God can make a child without intercourse."

"He can."

"Tell me!"

"God," Rabbi Binder admitted, "can make a child without intercourse."

"Mamma, you tell me."

"God can make a child without intercourse," his mother said.

"Make *him* tell me." There was no doubt who *him* was.

In a few moments Ozzie heard an old comical voice say something to the increasing darkness about God.

Next, Ozzie made everybody say it. And then he made them all say they believed in Jesus Christ—first one at a time, then all together.

When the catechizing was through it was the beginning of evening. From the street it sounded as if the boy on the roof might have sighed.

"Ozzie?" A woman's voice dared to speak. "You'll come down now?"

There was no answer, but the woman waited, and when a voice finally did speak it was thin and crying, and exhausted as that of an old man who has just finished pulling the bells.

"Mamma, don't you see—you shouldn't hit me. He shouldn't hit me. You shouldn't hit me about God, Mamma. You should never hit anybody about God—"

"Ozzie, please come down now."

"Promise me, promise me you'll never hit anybody about God."

He had asked only his mother, but for some reason everyone kneeling in the street promised he would never hit anybody about God.

Once again there was silence.

"I can come down now, Mamma," the boy on the roof finally said. He turned his head both ways as though checking the traffic lights. "Now I can come down . . ."

And he did, right into the center of the yellow net that glowed in the evening's edge like an overgrown halo.

culture
and
anarchy

The essays in this section discuss some of the contradictions in traditional institutions which make them purveyors of both culture and anarchy —often simultaneously. In "The University as Employment Agency," noted historian Henry Steele Commager writes of the university with a point of view quite different from Mario Savio's in "An End to History," although he arrives at surprisingly similar conclusions. Commager criticizes universities for being more responsive to the needs and desires of governmental agencies such as the CIA and private corporations such as Dow Chemicals than to what he terms "the moral passion" of their students. His essay shows that by protecting what seem to be cultural investments in such products as espionage and na-palm, higher education provokes outrage and rebellion in students who feel that these commodities are malignant. Commager also raises some interesting questions about the position of education in modern society and its increasing dependence on government.

Another institution that is held up to a bright light in this section is the police. In "The Brutality," Ed Cray documents instances of what he terms "police violence"; he asks whether or not this brutality is sanctioned by American society's attitude toward law and order.

Violence in a wider social context is also the subject of Tom Wolfe's essay "Porno-violence." In an imaginative criticism of Americans' fixation with "the pornography of violence," Wolfe describes the tendency of the mass media to encourage a taste for the bizarre and the bloody. Then, in a related essay, Hunter S. Thompson discusses one phenomenon of the Hell's Angels. In "The Motorcycle Gangs: Losers and Outsiders," he shows how these feared cyclists are less threats to culture than outcasts who are excluded from society in the way of the poor and other minori-ties; he also suggests that they are the creation of such institutions as law enforcement agencies and newspapers with a taste for the baroque.

The remaining pieces in this section provide a change of pace. Frank-lin Russell's "A Madness of Nature" describes the spawning habits of the capelin, a small fish that seems to go temporarily insane when it comes ashore to lay its eggs. The author—himself a naturalist—uses the capelin as a metaphor for societies that become obsessed with their own prosperity and begin to destroy themselves with random, unthinking motion.

The last two essays are about topics that figure prominently in contemporary America's fantasies about itself: drugs and sex. In "The
Marihuana Problem—Myth or Reality?", Dr. Alfred R. Lindesmith's
broad scientific inquiry into the use of marijuana, there is a brief history
of how this drug was validated as a bona fide social "menace" and some
insight into what the real problems in its use are. Then, in "Sex and
Secularization," Harvey Cox attacks the false, dehumanizing images of
sexuality that exist today and shows how they are the outgrowths of
principles deeply embedded in our culture.

The short story with which this section ends, "Joe, the Vanishing
American" by Harvey Swados, is about work, one young worker in particular. It shows how jobs can become meaningless and how lives are
drastically changed when they do.

HENRY STEELE COMMAGER

The University as Employment Agency

From Harvard Yard to Madison and Berkeley, students are taking
into their own hands and hearts, what university administrators have
failed to take into their hands or their minds: the problem of the
obligation of the university to private corporations and to government. Students are protesting and, where protests are ineffective,
demonstrating against the practice of lending the facilities of the
university to recruitment of students by corporations and the military. Sometimes their protest takes the form of forcibly banning recruiters from university facilities, thus exposing them to the wrath

The University as Employment Agency. From *The New Republic*, February 24,
1968. Reprinted by permission of the author.

of deans and presidents who, unwilling to face the central issue of on-campus recruitment, embrace with enthusiasm the marginal issue of bad manners.

For the explosion of this controversy on campus, the university authorities have only themselves to blame for not formulating any policy which could stand the test of logical scrutiny. Most of them are still sullenly taking refuge in precedent, or involving irrelevant arguments of "freedom of information." Student demonstrations against recruitment are, then, a monument to the absence of foresight and of imagination in university administrators, and an excess of imagination in students. All who are concerned with the academic enterprise will agree that an excess of imagination and of moral passion in the young is to be preferred to the absence of either in their elders.

The basic principle which should govern the relations of the university to recruiters is that which should govern all other activities of the academy. The university is not an employment agency; it is not an adjunct of corporations; it is not an instrument of government. Wherever feasible the university should make available its facilities to legitimate educational enterprises. It is under no obligation whatsoever to make its facilities available to what is not educational.

Guided by this simple principle the university can deal with the awkward problem of recruiting with reasonable consistency and fairness. There are and will be exceptions and borderline cases—as Supreme Court opinions testify daily—exceptions and borderline cases in the interpretation of the Constitution and the Bill of Rights. So far, however, none of these borderline cases has caused any difficulties. Students have not protested against recruitment by the Peace Corps, or Head Start, or the United Nations, and it is unlikely that they will. The organizations whose recruiting has precipitated the crisis throughout the academic world are not borderline cases. By no stretch of the imagination can it be alleged that Dow Chemical Company, the Marines or the CIA are educational enterprises, or that they contribute to the educational enterprise. Dow Chemical is a business corporation; its business is to make money, and it recruits students at universities because that is one of the ways it hopes to make money. No university is under any obligation whatever to help Dow Chemical make money. The Marines and the Navy, admirable as they no doubt are, are not educational enterprises. Their business is to fight. The university is an interested party in this enterprise, just as it is an interested party in tax collecting or in the maintenance of law and order, but it is under no more obligation to lend its facilities to the Marines and the Navy than it is to lend them to the Department of the Treasury or the Department of Justice.

But, it is asserted, every student has a right to hear what these, and other, organizations have to say. So they have, and a university which sought to deny them this right would be derelict in its duty to its students, and to its own character. The argument is, however, wholly irrelevant to the situation which confronts us. Every student has a right to a great many things that the university is not obliged to provide. He has a right to read all newspapers, all magazines and all books, but the university is not obliged to provide him with all newspapers, magazines and books. It subscribes to *The New York Times* and *Foreign Affairs*, not to *Playboy*. Any student who wants to read that can buy it at the local newsstand, but anyone who argued that the principle of free access to information required the university library to subscribe to all publications would be regarded as bereft of his senses. So any student who wants to hear what Dow Chemical or the CIA wants to say could, without serious inconvenience, visit them off-campus. Dow Chemical, like all corporations, can rent space in local office buildings just as it buys space in local newspapers. The Marines and the CIA can use the local post office to conduct interviews. Except at a very few colleges, so remote from civilization that there are neither stores nor offices nor post offices available, no student (and no recruiter) will be seriously inconvenienced if universities adopt the common-sense rule of confining the use of their facilities to purposes incontrovertibly educational.

Balanced against what is merely ingrained habit, or, at the most, inconvenience to a few students of walking a few blocks to an office building or post office, are two considerations of importance. First is the principle (if it rises to the dignity of that), that the college should not throw open its facilities indiscriminately to all comers— business, religious, fraternal, political, military—for if it did, it would find those facilities swamped. It must and in fact it does, even now, discriminate. Even those who defend most ardently the "right" of students to interview Dow Chemical are not prepared to provide facilities for the Rotary, the Lions and the Kiwanis, the Elks and the Masons and the Woodmen of the World, the Baptists, the Mormons and the Jehovah's Witnesses, and so on *ad infinitum*. The only sound basis for discrimination is educational. The second principle is more fundamental. When the university is called upon to weigh the conflicting claims of those who plead habit or convenience, against those who plead deep moral convictions—moral convictions which are shared by a large segment of our society and are therefore neither eccentric nor perverse—it should not hesitate to tip the balance on the side of moral convictions. Certainly it is unworthy of the academy to drift—or to allow itself to be maneuvered into—a position where out of stubbornness, out of thoughtlessness, out of inertia, it flouts the legitimate moral sentiments of its students and its faculty. To argue that some students may entertain moral convictions about seeing recruiters on-campus rather than off-campus is frivolous, for it ascribes moral significance to what is a mere matter of personal convenience.

Some institutions, prepared to concede that they are not under any obligation to provide facilities for recruiting to private corporations, do insist, or at least assert, that they have some kind of moral obligation to cooperate with government, especially at a time of crisis and war. Therefore, they add, even though government has ample facilities already available to it in federal, state and local government buildings, the university should stand ready to lend its premises to government recruiters. This is a plausible argument when used selectively, but not persuasive when applied indiscriminately.

Time and again in the past, the university has acknowledged an obligation to cooperate with state and national government—and keep in mind that what we are considering here is not any legal obligation to obey the law, but a voluntary cooperation which is beyond the obligation of the law. Does it follow from past and current practice, that the university has an obligation to cooperate with every branch, every department, every bureau of government for any and all purposes?

Such a conclusion is untenable, and universities have already rejected it. Few universities are prepared to make available to snooping committees of legislatures, or even to the FBI, the names of members of all student organizations. Many have refused to provide draft boards with records of student grades. No self-respecting university now would cooperate with un-American acitivities committees, state or national, in investigating professors. Nor are universities under obligation to lend their facilities indiscriminately to the enforcement of laws. The laws of Massachusetts (and until recently of Connecticut) made use of contraceptives by anyone, single or married, a misdemeanor; it is scarcely conceivable that any university in that state, public or private, would entertain a request from state law enforcement agencies to help discover and bring to justice members of faculty or student body who violate these laws. Nor do universities yield, generally, to the plea of convenience. If students want information on taxes, they expect to go to the local tax authorities, or perhaps to a bank; if they want information on voting they go to the town hall; if they want to take out a driver's license, they go to the local police. The universities are not expected to provide these services for the students, or even to provide the facilities where these particular government agencies can give out "information."

Even when it comes to carrying on scientific research, which is clearly educational in character, universities do not casually or indiscriminately make available their offices and laboratories or libraries, but select what is valuable to *them*, and then draw up contracts which carefully safeguard the right of the university to supervise the research, protect scholars and avoid secrecy, and which provide, too, for compensation for the use of academic facilities.

Does the university then have the right—the moral right, for the legal is clearly beyond dispute—to decide with which governmental activities it will cooperate? Does it have the right to say Yes to the Peace Corps, but No to the Marines; Yes to the Smithsonian Institution, but No to the CIA?

Let us consider—because it is the most controversial of them all —the obligation of the university to the CIA.

The readiness of the university to lend its facilities, and its good name, to the CIA is the most notorious example of the fix in which it finds itself when it blindly follows the principle of the Open Door to all government agencies. For the CIA is, by definition, subversive of the academy. Its business is subversion at home as well as abroad, and by giving it a free hand and ample money, the Congress has endorsed this function. It has, by its own admission, subverted universities, scholars, student organizations, research, publications, even churches and philanthropic institutions. Its whole character is at war with what the university stands for. It loves secrecy, but the university flourishes only in the light. It takes refuge in anonymity, but the university must know the credentials of those to whom it gives its confidence. It is chauvinistic, but the university is by its nature cosmopolitan and international. It works not to find and certainly not to proclaim truth, but the major purpose of the university is to extend the frontiers of truth.

Clearly the university is under no obligation to collaborate with the CIA simply because it is a government agency. This conclusion has not only the sanction of centuries of the history of universities; it has legal sanction as well. For to the argument that the university should not look beyond the official credentials of an agency of the government—an argument advanced with considerable earnestness by those who wish to avoid the moral issue—we must consider the counterargument of the legal principle adopted by the United States at the time of the Nuremberg War Crimes trials. The official American position, submitted by Supreme Court Justice Robert Jackson, was quite simply that no citizen is bound to accept as legal and valid every act of his government, nor can he avoid responsibility for his conduct by placing responsibility on the government. This position was accepted by the Tribunal, and under it men like Albert Speer, Minister of Munitions, were found guilty. It is not necessary to argue that the CIA is violating international law; it is enough to recognize the validity of the principle that institutions, such as universities, are not precluded from inquiring into the credentials of such branches of the government as make demands upon them.

Whatever we may think about the larger place of the CIA in the scheme of national defense, we can scarcely avoid the conclusion that it is degrading for the university to lend its facilities, and a reputation painfully won over a period of 800 years, to cooperate in its own subversion. It is degrading for it to extend the hand of fellowship to those who are engaged in perverting its character.

Even those who are prepared to concede in principle the right of students to oppose corporate or military recruiting on campus, deplore the manner in which they have asserted, or demonstrated, that right. Almost everywhere student demonstrations have been accompanied by bad manners, and in some places by force and violence. Now it is very wrong for the young to display discourtesy in these situations, and quite intolerable for them to resort to violence, even the somewhat negative violence of refusing access to a recruiting-office room. Clearly the young should model themselves here on those who are older and wiser, model themselves on the spokesmen and representatives of our nation, on whom rests ultimate responsibility for the maintenance of an orderly society. What a pity they do not follow the example, in their protests, of distinguished statesmen like Senators Russell Long and John Stennis, who think all dissenters should be jailed; of presidential candidate George Wallace who thinks they should be shot; or of Rep. Mendel Rivers of South Carolina who thinks the proper response to flag burning is burning the Bill of Rights. What a pity they do not model themselves on official defenders of law and order like the police of Watts, Cleveland, Detroit, Newark and Philadelphia, or the US Marshals in Washington. How distressing they do not conform to the models of that military who try so hard to enlist them, "General-Bomb-Them-Back-to-the-Stone-Age" LeMay, for example, or the Air Force officers who habitually fly over Communist China in violation of international law. How much wiser they would be if they studied the conduct of the CIA whose interests their deans so sedulously protect, and who have never been known to resort to violence, and who conduct their operations in some 60 countries throughout the globe with the nicest regard to the legal amenities. How it would improve their characters if instead of milling about the campus in futile demonstrations they resorted to their libraries and read how their government eschewed violence and championed law at the time of the Bay of Pigs invasion of Cuba, or of the intervention by Marines in Guatemala and Santo Domingo. How much wiser they would be if they studied the Kellogg-Briand Peace Pact, or the Charter of the United Nations and reflected on their own government's faithfulness in their commitment to these renunciations of war. But we should remember that students are young, and that they have not had the training and experience which has made their rulers such models of moderation and of reason.

On this whole matter of discourtesy and violence that so often accompanies demonstrations it is relevant to recall what the Rev. Samuel J. May—he was uncle to the Little Women—wrote to his friend the Rev. William Ellery Channing about the demonstrations of abolitionists against slavery:

> You must not expect those who have left to take up this great cause [of abolition] that they will plead it in all that seemliness of phrase which the scholars . . . might use. But the scholars and the clergy and the statesmen had done nothing. We abolitionists are what we

are—babes, sucklings, obscure men, silly women, publicans, sinners, and we shall manage the matter we have taken in hand just as might be expected of such persons as we are. It is unbecoming in abler men who stood by, and would do nothing, to complain of us because we manage this matter no better.

To this Dr. Channing answered in words that apply to demonstrators against the Vietnam war as against the abolitionists: "The great interests of humanity do not lose their claims on us because sometimes injudiciously maintained."

Indeed they do not. Yet more and more those in authority, in the academy as in government, are avoiding moral issues and taking refuge in questions of conduct or of manners. Instead of falling back on the familiar principle, "I disagree with what you say but shall defend to the death your right to say it," they substitute, "I may agree with you, but I disapprove profoundly of the manner in which you say it."

What is this silence that has fallen on the leadership of the university—presidents, deans, boards of trustees and regents alike? The leaders of the religious community have spoken out boldly enough— heads of great theological seminaries, distinguished theologians and clergymen. The scientific community has taken a strong stand on the moral issues of the war and of nuclear weapons, Nobel Prize winners, heads of great scientific organizations. The rank and file of the academic community, teachers, scholars, students, have seen that here are moral issues that must be faced, and have wrestled with them. But from Cambridge to Berkeley, from Madison to Baton Rouge, not a single president of a great university has taken a public stand on what is the greatest moral issue of our time.

Are they silent because they are bemused by the notion that with their position they take a vow of moral continence? They did not so reason in the past—not at the time of the two World Wars, not during discussions of the League of Nations, or of communism. Is it because they fear that if they spoke out like independent men, they would somehow "commit" their institutions? If so they are mistaken in fact and logic. No president can commit his university, which consists of faculty and students, to a moral position, or a political. No one supposes that a senator who speaks out somehow commits the United States Senate, or that a judge who speaks his mind commits the Supreme Court, or even that a business executive can commit his corporation and his stockholders to political positions. Why should presidents or deans indulge in the vanity of supposing that they can somehow commit great universities? Yet here they stand numbed by timidity, taking refuge from the obligation to confront great moral questions by escaping into the easy activity of applying petty disciplinary measures to students who embarrass them.

If presidents, deans, trustees and regents are unwilling or unable to protect and exalt the dignity of the university, they should be grateful to students who have remembered it and exalted it. If universities have refused to face the major moral issues of our day they should rejoice that they have, somehow, helped to produce students who are neither paralyzed nor timid, who are sensitive to moral issues and prepared to respond to them, however convulsively.

On this matter of recruitment, as on the larger issues of the relation of the academy to the moral problems which glare upon us from every quarter of the horizon, this generation of university presidents, so respectable, so cautious, may yet hear from their own students that immortal taunt of Henri IV: "Go hang yourself, brave Crillon; we fought at Arques and you were not there."

ED CRAY

The Brutality

The rookie patrolman described the attitude of fellow officers on the force of a Midwestern city:

> They [veteran police officers] feel that it's okay to rough a man up in the case of sex crimes. One of the older men advised me that if the courts didn't punish a man, we should. . . . They feel definitely, for example, in extreme cases like rape, that if a man is guilty he ought to be punished even if you could not get any evidence on him. My feeling is that all the men on the force feel that way, at least from what they have told me.[1]

[1] William A. Westley, "Violence and the Police," *American Journal of Sociology*, LIX (1953), p. 38.

The Brutality. Reprinted by permission of Coward-McCann, Inc., from *The Big Blue Line: Police Power vs. Human Rights* by Ed Cray. Copyright © 1967 by Ed Cray.

Private punishment is meted out not only to sex criminals, but also to any group the police dislike—Muslims in Los Angeles, beatniks in various cities, Hell's Angels motorcyclists throughout California, homosexuals in almost every major city where they congregate, civil rights demonstrators in Chester, Pennsylvania, and peace demonstrators in Washington, D.C. At the moment they encounter the police, none of these people need be breaking the law to incite the police to violence; they merely need be members of a visible minority, usually without influence, and distasteful to the law enforcement officers.

Specific individuals are also singled out for special attention. These are the people who have continually confounded the police by beating the charges placed against them, by standing up to the police, or by refusing to accord the police the respect the officers insist is their due. Like the proscribed groups, these individuals need not be committing a crime to merit a working over. Simply crossing paths with a policeman in foul humor is enough.

The group that police feel deserves the harshest punishment is composed of suspects charged with assaulting or murdering a police officer. No group is more likely to show up in court marked by bruises received in a fall or while attempting to escape.

Salvatore Burrone was arrested on the night of November 1, 1961, and taken to Boston's Joy Street police station to be booked on armed robbery and assault with intent to murder a police officer. Burrone was placed in a cell, then was joined by a second prisoner who stated under oath:

> As the detective was putting me in, he said, "Get in there with that (swearword)" and punched Burrone on the side of the head, knocking him down. While Burrone was on the floor, this detective . . . kicked him in the side. I helped Burrone up onto the bunk in the cell and he said to Burrone, "You will never shoot another cop, you (swearword)."

Three hours after he was first arrested, Burrone was placed in a second cell with another prisoner who later stated in an affidavit:

> I took one look and I said: "Man, what hit you? A freight train?" He said that the police beat up on him all night in station number three. He could just barely walk, so I helped him into his bunk as he could not seem to do it himself. He was moaning and calling for the doctor. I yelled for the guard and the guard took him to the hospital at the jail.

In the jail hospital, Burrone was bleeding from both ears, his face was bruised and swollen, both wrists had been rubbed raw by handcuffs clamped on too tightly, and one leg had been bruised by a kick. Burrone told both a doctor and a nurse he had started spitting up blood after he was punched, kicked, and hit in the stomach with nightsticks.

Burrone confessed twice, once in a lineup and once in the hospital. Five weeks later, at his preliminary hearing, he pleaded guilty on the advice of counsel, even though the earlier confessions were not introduced as evidence. On June 29, 1965, an appellate judge ruled that Burrone "was severely beaten as he alleges at the Joy Street police station but that the confession given by him to the police was not used against him due to his pleas of guilty to each indictment."

Salvatore Burrone's case was anything but unusual. His court-appointed attorney for the appeal noted, "Whenever a police officer is shot or killed [in Boston], the suspect is invariably beaten," then added, "A judge told me, 'Whenever a policeman has been assaulted, I wonder how badly the suspect is.' " [2]

The attitude of supervising officers who might put an abrupt halt to this private punishment remains as complaisant as it was twenty-five years ago. In 1941, after three escaped convicts who had killed a prison guard at Sing Sing had been recaptured, they were:

> knocked to the ground by a Sing Sing prison guard and struck by an Ossining policeman. Pictures taken by William Stahl, a *Daily Mirror* photographer, leave no doubt of the reception which was tendered to Riordan and McGale at the headquarters despite the presence of numerous reporters and photographers. . . . The atmosphere at Ossining headquarters was admitted by Arthur W. Mead, Ossining police lieutenant in charge, on cross-examination:
> Q. And it was perfectly all right with you to have these prisoners beaten and knocked around, wasn't it?
> A. Perfectly all right for them to be knocked down, yes, sir.
> Q. And beaten? Is that right? It was in accordance with your wishes?
> A. Not wishes.
> Q. But you were satisfied?

[2] Interview with Ronald Chisholm, Massachusetts Defenders Committee, November 5, 1965. The Burrone case is drawn from petitioner's brief and supporting affidavits and the "Findings, Rulings and Order" of Justice Paul C. Reardon of the Supreme Judicial Court of Massachusetts in *Burrone v. Massachusetts*, No. 63450 Law, decided June 29, 1965.

A. Yes, sir.[3]

In 1962, New York City police were hunting the suspected slayers of two detectives killed during a Brooklyn holdup. On May 21, three days after the double murder, police picked up twenty-seven-year-old Richard Melville, identified as a petty gambler and friend of the suspected killers.

At the 66th Precinct House, Melville testified in court, his arms were twisted behind his back, and he was beaten by two lieutenants and three plainsclothesmen about the head and genitals. Stripped naked, he was forced to lie face down on a bed in a secluded room in the station house and was repeatedly struck with both a wooden stick and rubber hose. In a grisly reminder of the Gestapo, he told the court that lighted cigarettes were applied to his bare back.

Melville told police what they wanted to know: one of the suspects had confessed the double murder to him and had asked for a place to hide.

In the subsequent trial of the two men, Melville stated under cross-examination that he was testifying only as a result of the beating he had received at the police station. The suspects were convicted, and the conviction was sustained by New York's Court of Appeals. That court on March 11, 1965, condemned what it termed "the shocking and reprehensible" treatment of Melville in the station house.[4]

Two years later New York City Police Private Henry Walburger was shot by an armed bandit who was holding two partially disrobed women at gunpoint in their apartment. The next day the killer's court-appointed attorney charged that his client had been escorted

[3] U.S. v. Jackson, 257 F. 2d 7, 11 (1958); certiorari denied, 78 S. Ct. 1152 (1958).

[4] See The New York Times, February 9, 1966, for a summary of the Melville case, and the decision in State v. Portelli and Rosenberg, New York Court of Appeals, March 11, 1965. Eleven months after the court's condemnation of the officers, the police department was still investigating the station house beating. The files of the ACLU of Southern California contain a statement by a victim of a similar burning—a cigarette stubbed out on an arrestee's back—at the hands of a Los Angeles Sheriff's deputy. Joseph Fichter, with the collaboration of Brian Jordan, "Police Handling of Arrestees, a Research Study of Police Arrests in New Orleans" (New Orleans, March, 1964), p. 50, quotes a judge: "I was recently going through the —— District, and I saw a Negro spread out on the floor with several officers over him. There was something like mud on the Negro's arm, and when I looked closer I could see it was cigar ashes where they had been burning the man."

to the police station by "20 or 30 police officers," that no part of his
body was unbruised, and that as the suspect was being led to the
booking desk, a plainclothesman kicked him in the groin. "I not
only saw it," the attorney said, "I heard it." [5]

It is not only the cop killer whom police believe merits the private punishment of law enforcement officers avenging their own.
Those who *assault* police—either to resist arrest or to defend themselves—may also be punished by vengeful officers.

The seven jailers, all members of the Los Angeles Sheriff's Department, woke the three prisoners shortly after midnight on January
23, 1966, and hustled them through the darkened halls of the jail to
a recreation room, there to settle accounts for two brother officers
whom the three prisoners had sent to the hospital a week before.

The prisoners, each awaiting trial on two counts of felonious
assault, had been arrested after a melee at a private party, but not
before the two deputies sent to quell the disturbance had been injured.

The beating in the darkened recreation room of the jail lasted
only a short while, each of the seven deputies using his fists while
the three prisoners were shoved from man to man. None of the three
offered any resistance; none was injured more than "superficially,"
the sheriff later told reporters.

Apparently none of the jailers knew the two injured deputies
other than casually. It was enough that members of the department
had been injured and their assailants remained unpunished. The
seven were dismissed from the department four days later.[6]

Police do not reserve physical punishment for those who have
committed the graver crimes of murdering or assaulting a peace officer. Any arrestee who flouts the authority of police or makes their
task even slightly more difficult than usual may be punished for his
untoward conduct. The physical brutality has not even the slightest

[5] The Staten Island (New York) *Advance*, July 28, 1964; see also UPI photograph No. NXP 1434336, July 27, 1964, taken of the alleged killer as he was
being booked. His chin is swathed in bandages, his lips appear swollen, his right
cheek is cut and bleeding, and blood shows on his chin and through the bandage.
Private Walburger's death was appropriately noted by some as epitomizing the
highest ideals of police service. Walburger and his murderer were whites; the
women the officer was defending were Negroes.
[6] Los Angeles *Times*, January 27, 28, 1966.

of law enforcement motives—even the illegal means to a justifiable end such as the coercion of a confession from a guilty suspect. It is simply, in and of itself, private punishment by law enforcement officers.

Alton Snell made the mistake of trying to resist the three sheriff's officers who placed him under arrest on Labor Day, 1965, in Altadena, California.

> I asked them, "What are you going to arrest me for?" And one of them said, "Are you going peaceful? Or are we going to have to take you?" So I said, "What are you going to arrest me for? What have I done?" They kept asking, "Are you going peaceful? Or are we going to have to take you?" And then they attacked me and tried to strong-arm me. So that's when I attacked them back. I tried to hit back, but they grabbed my legs out from under me and knocked me down. They put the handcuffs on my right wrist and pulled my arm so far that it hurt my chest. . . . Then they put the other handcuff on me very tight. The scars from the handcuffs are still visible today [six weeks later]. Then they helped me up and took me to the car. . . .
> They stopped the car in the parking lot behind the sheriff's station. The officer who had first approached me got out of the driver's seat and came around to the right rear door where I was sitting. The other officer, who was sitting next to me, got out and came around too. The first officer opened the door and hit me in the mouth with his fist. They both snatched me out of the car and the first officer just kept beating on me. He hit me in the mouth and in the stomach and the other officer held me up. . . .[7]

Brutality, especially in jailhouses, is not an isolated incident. A West Virginia newspaper editorialized: "We have seen blood in the [Raleigh County] jail elevator so many times that we are forced to believe that prisoners are 'roughed up' in the elevator—where there can be no witnesses." In the Seattle city jail a former civilian employee of the police department stated under oath he witnessed "a dozen or more assaults" during a fifteen-month period. In New Orleans one out of five people arrested complained he was slapped, pushed around, punched, or thoroughly beaten. A Boston attorney estimates that between one-fourth and one-sixth of Negroes arrested

[7] "Statement of Mr. Alton R. Snell, 2062 El Sereno, Pasadena, California, taken November 21, 1965, by William D. Hunnell" (available from the ACLU, Pasadena Chapter, Box 133, Pasadena, California), pp. 2–3. Snell's statement was made under penalty of perjury.

in that city are "roughed up" by police, a figure comparable to that of New Orleans.[8]

If the victims complain, it becomes a question of accepting the unsupported word of a "criminal" against the corroborative statements of any number of police officers who cross one another's *t's* and dot one another's *i's*. Only rarely will the victim gain any satisfaction, no matter how implausible the story the police tell.

In at least one case, officers investigating a complaint of police brutality were told that an arrestee in a station house not only attacked a police officer, but suffered a fall to boot. A lieutenant on the Philadelphia force reported, "Three officers had to hold Wise to restrain him. I tried to calm him down by talking to him. I ordered the officers to release him. Upon being released, Wise threw himself at the officers. They side-stepped, and he fell on the floor."

After a second altercation in the cell block, allegedly because he attempted to escape, Wise was taken to the hospital to be treated for a fractured jaw and a gash on his forehead. The Philadelphia Police Advisory Board recommended that Ellis Wise's assailant be suspended from the force for thirty days after a hearing in February, 1964.[9]

The falling phenomenon assumes proportions of truly epic implausibility when the accident results in the death of a prisoner. In Newark, New Jersey, civil rights organizations were quick to question the death of Benjamin Bryant, arrested on June 15, 1964, as a suspect in an ice-pick slaying. According to police, Bryant became "dizzy" during an interrogation at police headquarters and fell against a filing cabinet. He died in a hospital of head injuries three weeks later.[10]

---

[8] The Beckley (West Virginia) *Raleigh-Register*, August 7, 1964; "Affidavit of Richard J. Variot," dated October 19, 1964, in the files of the ACLU of Washington; Fichter, *op. cit.*, p. 49; Alan Gartner, "The Police and the Community: Police Practices and Minority Groups" (Unpublished Florina Lasker Fellowship paper on Civil Liberties and Civil Rights, Brandeis University, 1964), p. 8.

[9] "Sixth Annual Report of the Police Advisory Board, City of Philadelphia, Dec. 31, 1964," Exhibit C, p. 1; "Memorandum to the Police Commissioner from Commanding Officer—Community Relations Division, Nov. 22, 1963," on "Ill Treatment of [*sic*] Policeman, PCR No. 63-058, Re: Ellis Wise."

[10] The New York *Herald-Tribune*, August, 1, 1964. The author's files contain fourteen haphazardly gathered news stories from seven newspapers reporting the deaths of prisoners held in custody. Three were the result of falls, officials announced. Seven were from injuries to the skull; one was from an untreated spinal fracture. Only two could be attributed firmly to disease rather than to physical

In departments where ranking officers have made clear their disapproval of physical mistreatment of suspects, the brutality is removed from the privacy of the station house to the quiet of deserted streets. The explanation of a fall or an attack on a police officer becomes "resisting arrest." As much as the arrestee may deny the charge, he is inevitably confronted with the letter-perfect testimony of two policemen, who recite, with infinite detail, his attack on them when all they had done was politely ask him his name and business.

Most such assaults on the streets or in the back seat of police cars are unobserved. Rare is the eyewitness in the ghetto who doesn't fear retaliation because he spoke out; rarer still is the witness, like Mrs. Emma Louise Hall, who is merely an observer, unimplicated in the arrest or assault:

> On Saturday, Aug. 21, 1965, at approximately 4:25 P.M., I was sitting in my living room in front of a picture window looking out into the street. I saw a police car drive up. I stood up to see better because I was worried that the passenger in the police car might be my son, who was not home at the time. They parked against the curb directly in front of my house, approximately 20 feet from the window through which I was looking. I saw the driver of the vehicle get out of the police car and walk around to the rear door on the curb side. The passenger officer, who had red hair, also got out of the front seat on the curb side. They opened the door, and a Negro, who was between 20 and 30 years of age, wearing a stingey-brim hat and orange shirt and dark pants, riding in the back seat of the police car got out on the curb beside the police car. I couldn't hear them talking, nor did my three children, Carole, 17; Terri Lynne, 12; and Christopher Duane, 9, who also saw the entire incident. After they stood there for just a few seconds, I saw the red-haired officer and the driver frisk the Negro. Then the red-haired officer hit the Negro in the stomach. The Negro did not swing nor did he make a threatening motion. The Negro doubled over, and the two officers shoved the Negro to the easement between the sidewalk and the curb stone. The Negro lay on his stomach, and the red-haired officer—who was the most [sic] aggressive of the two—grabbed the Negro's head and began slamming it against the packed dirt of the easement. The other officer tried to hold the

---

injury. On May 27, 1966, radio commentator Edward P. Morgan (ABC network) reported the death of a Negro woman, arrested as a drunk in Durham, North Carolina, who died of a cerebral hemorrhage. A second death was narrowly averted in that city when a nurse suggested to two policemen that the man they were arresting as a drunk "or something" might be a diabetic. He was.

Negro's body in place. The police fell to their knees beside the Negro and handcuffed him with his hands behind his back very roughly. He did not try to fight back at any time. After the Negro was handcuffed, the red-haired officer hit him two more times with his fist.

When the two policemen realized they had been seen not only by the Hall family, but also by the passengers in a passing car, they ordered the Negro back into the police car. Grinning, the red-haired officer brushed off his clothes, walked around to the driver's side of the squad car, and nonchalantly got in. They drove off, confident that the witnesses would not wish to become involved, and would not report the beating.[11]

At certain times and with certain individuals, the police feel no special constraints and will openly, even insolently, brutalize arrestees. Their victims must be of a class or group with little prestige in the community or be openly antagonistic to the views of the majority; they must merit some police attention prior to their arrests; and the officers involved must share the prevalent, or what they believe is the prevalent, community opinion about the group.

These conditions usually apply in Southern states resisting racial integration. Reports of brutality during police attempts to throttle civil rights demonstrations are frequent and well documented. But civil rights demonstrations and demonstrators in the North have also encountered the hostility of law enforcement officers.

Six weeks of almost nightly demonstrations had taxed the resources and nerves of the eighty-man police force of Chester, Pennsylvania. By April 24, 1964, the patience of the city police and the state troopers called in to control the street marches and sit-ins had all but disappeared. Whatever their own states of mind, police were certain that their strict handling of the demonstrators was supported by the city's power structure, which remained unmoved by the grievances of the Negro community. A commission appointed by Governor William Scranton later reported:

> This attitude was to some extent reflected in the methods adopted by the police to repress the demonstrations. An overworked police force, with no real training in dealing with civil rights demonstrations or

---

[11] "Police Malpractice and the Watts Riot, a Report by the American Civil Liberties Union of Southern California" (October, 1965), pp. 18–19. Mrs. Hall was able to furnish the number of the police car to identify the officer further.

crowd control, was instructed to enforce the law strictly in order to show that the acts of civil disobedience were not an acceptable way to gain the desired results.

On three separate nights, police violence "seems to have been used to inculcate fear and confusion in the demonstrators and their sympathizers." In at least seven cases, law enforcement officers used excessive force "without much distinction as to whether a particular person had or had not given provocation to warrant its use."

Herman Dawson had driven to the police station to disperse demonstrators gathered there on the night of April 22, 1964. Dawson claims that state troopers poured out of the station and began hitting the car in which he was riding with their nightsticks and striking at him through the open window. Pulled from the vehicle, he was struck by a cluster of officers as he stood beside the car, he told investigators. Police claim Dawson resisted arrest, swung at and kicked police officers, and had to be forcibly subdued.

Dawson broke free of the police and ran up the street. Before he had gone more than a few feet, he either tripped or fell. As many as twelve policemen and state troopers circled him as he lay on the sidewalk, repeatedly slamming their nightsticks against his body. One of five witnesses, a reporter for a local paper, described the beating as so frenzied that the officers were even hitting one another.

When the reporter shouted, "Stop it!" to the police, he was arrested by an auxiliary policeman, a city employee deputized to beef up the inadequate force.

Dawson was treated for multiple contusions of his scalp, right wrist, and right thigh in a hospital emergency room and was then admitted to the hospital for treatment of brain concussion, a fractured jaw, lacerations on his upper lip, and a dislocated jaw. He spent eleven days in the hospital.

Bing Williams had been a spectator that same night at the demonstration in front of the police station until a police sergeant announced over a bullhorn that demonstrators and spectators alike risked arrest if they remained.

Williams walked to a friend's car parked nearby; as he entered the parking lot, he saw people run past him in wild flight. Just as he reached for the door handle, he was hit from behind on the head, he said. He fell against the car as more than a dozen policemen and a state trooper swung at him with their nightsticks. He was ordered to get up and run, but when he tried to stand, he was knocked down again. He lost consciousness; when he came to, he was in the hospital.

Williams was eventually treated for a fractured wrist and a laceration on his scalp, which required twenty stitches to close. None of the police officers who appeared before the governor's commission could explain how Williams had come to be injured.

The Bull Moose—Two nights later, while dispersing demonstrators and spectators, a state trooper was struck in the chest by a brick thrown from the crowd. At least three troopers saw the man who threw the brick duck into a neighborhood tavern, the crowded Bull Moose.

A large number of police and state troopers followed the suspect into the bar. When they discovered that they could not identify the assailant, a detective ordered the bar closed. In their hurry to get out of the building, police said, some of the patrons may have been injured, but no one was struck, either inside the Bull Moose or on the sidewalk in front of the building.

Three patrons and the bartender, in addition to other witnesses, testified that they either were struck by police nightsticks or saw others hit. Leroy Thomas was one of the "niggers" ordered out; he said he was hit five or six times on the head inside the Bull Moose and again on the spine as he stumbled out. Ten stitches were taken in the hospital to close cuts on his head and over his eye. He was not arrested.

Benjamin Hawkins was in the bar when the law enforcement officers entered. Knocked to the floor, he was kicked, he said, then hit again by a nightstick on the sidewalk. The second blow spun Hawkins into a parked car, his right hand smashing through a headlight. His wife took him to the hospital, where he was treated for multiple lacerations and contusions and where the tip of his right ring finger was amputated. After six days in the hospital, Hawkins was discharged. He was not arrested either.

A third patron of the Bull Moose, John Scott, was searched inside the bar and then, while he held his hands in the air, was hit on the head. Leaving the building, he was hit two more times by nightsticks.

The governor's commission concluded:

[The preponderance of evidence supported] the belief that after the state troopers had entered the bar they struck several patrons with their batons, and struck some of the patrons again as they left the building. . . . From the evidence before it, the commission believes no justification was shown for hitting any person inside the Bull Moose. [The state trooper's] assailant was not identified, the patrons in the Bull Moose were in a state of confusion, did not affront the police, and offered little, if any, resistance to them.

In all, the commission found that officers had used excessive force in at least seven of fifteen incidents which it investigated. Despite this finding, neither the governor nor responsible city authorities had taken steps to discipline the offending officers by June, 1965. Chester Mayor James H. Gorbey summed up his attitude three months after the riots at a state convention of the Fraternal Order of Police: "You can't enforce the law with pillows." The convention in turn passed a resolution thanking the mayor for "fighting charges of police brutality stemming from civil rights demonstrations this Spring in Chester." [12]

As unpopular as the Chester civil rights demonstrators were, the Assembly of Unrepresented People protesting the war in Vietnam was even less likely to be praised by Washington, D.C., police. After a group of these protesters elected to stage a sit-in on the street in front of the Capitol on August 9, 1965, police began making mass arrests.

By the time police had broken up the demonstration and momentarily restored the public peace, 365 persons were in custody, and at least 42 had either witnessed or claimed to have been victimized by excessive police force.

Washington police could not plead a lack of experience with demonstrations to explain the injuries to those arrested. It is a rare day in the Capitol that some individual or group does not parade in front of the White House or the Capitol to dramatize a plea for the redress of grievances, real or imagined.

And only a year before the Metropolitan Police Department had handled the massive March on Washington for Jobs and Freedom and its horde of 200,000 without a hitch. But by August, 1963, the

[12] The Chester cases were drawn from "Report of the Commission Appointed by the Governor to Investigate Charges of Excessive Use of Force by Police in Chester, Pennsylvania," Thomas W. Pomeroy, Jr., chairman (Scranton, Pennsylvania, Governor's Office, November, 1964), pp. 70–104; S-1–S-35; the Allentown (Pennsylvania) Call-Chronicle, July 23, 1964; ACLU of Pennsylvania, Civil Liberties Record (June, 1965), p. 1. Three civil suits for damages have been filed as an outgrowth of the Chester demonstrations.

civil rights movement had become almost respectable in official circles, and the well-organized march was to be joined by some of the nation's prominent celebrities.

The Assembly of Unrepresented People enjoyed no such protective mantle. Their cause was unpopular, and the police apparently felt little constraint in their manner of handling the nonviolent, noncooperative arrestees.

According to later statements, the members of the *ad hoc* assembly were deliberately kicked as they sat upon the ground; dragged by the ear or by the legs when they went limp, or passively noncooperative; hit with billy clubs if they did not move fast enough to suit arresting officers; thrown into overcrowded, closed paddy wagons to sit under a 90-degree sun for as long as ninety minutes; and deliberately beaten in some cases when the all-seeing television cameras were busy elsewhere.[13]

The peace demonstrators' experience in supposedly enlightened Washington was similar to that of Eric Weinberger in Brownsville, Tennessee, on August 6, 1963. Weinberger, the organizer and the only white in a civil rights demonstration stopped by police, was attacked by a surly crowd of white spectators. Hit in the eye, Weinberger was knocked down. Police then loosed their dogs, and he was bitten on the face and hip. As Weinberger was dragged off by police, six officers struck at him or poked him with electric cattle prods. Either accidentally or deliberately, Weinberger was sprayed with tear gas at close range. The gas ate through his clothing and raised large blisters across his back. He was finally released on $1,500 bail. His attackers were not arrested.[14]

Eric Weinberger not only was the victim of excessive force used

[13] The author has in his files signed statements from 43 demonstrators describing their treatment at the hands of police and a fourteen-page, generally corroborative statement by Frederic Solomon, M.D., who was one of a 4-man team that made a medical inspection of the crowded jails on the night of August 9, 1965. See also Andrew Glass' article in the New York *Herald-Tribune*, August 10, 1965; Glass was mistakenly arrested and was penned in one of the overcrowded paddy wagons. On March 5, 1966, a similar case was reported in New York City. Members of the Brooklyn chapter of the DuBois Club were attacked by as many as 150 persons while policemen allegedly looked the other way. The New York Civil Liberties Union complained to the police department, noting, "It appears that on Saturday the police in Brooklyn stood by and failed to protect the members of the DuBois Club from physical abuse and then arrested those who were attacked rather than the attackers."—*The New York Times*, March 8, 1966.

[14] The St. Louis *Post-Dispatch*, August 30, 1963; *Polaris Action Bulletin*, No. 44 (August 19, 1963), p. 1; *Liberation* (Summer, 1963).

by police to effect a quesionable arrest but was also attacked by
people who enjoyed the unofficial blessing of law enforcement officers for the assault. This complacent willingness to look the other
way is an unofficial sanction of lynch law. The "lawbreaker" is punished by his fellow citizens with the tacit approval of the men sworn
to uphold the law. A lawless group is permitted to preempt the lawless officer as judge, jury, and executioner.

.   .   .

TOM WOLFE

Porno-violence

Keeps His Mom-in-law in Chains, meet Kills Son and Feeds Corpse to Pigs. Pleased to meet you. Teenager Twists Off Corpse's Head . . . To Get Gold Teeth, meet Strangles Girl Friend, then Chops Her to Pieces. Likewise, I'm sure. Nurse's Aide Sees Fingers Chopped Off in Meat Grinder, meet. . . .

In ten years of journalism I have covered more conventions than

Porno-violence. First published in Esquire magazine, July 1967. Originally titled "(Intermission) Pause, Now, and Consider Some Tentative Conclusions About the Meaning of This Mass Perversion Called Porno-violence: What It Is and Where It Comes From and Who Put the Hair on the Walls." Reprinted by permission of Tom Wolfe, c/o Marvin Josephson Associates, Inc. Copyright © 1967 Esquire, Inc.

I care to remember. Podiatrists, theosophists, Professional Budget Finance dentists, oyster farmers, mathematicians, truckers, dry cleaners, stamp collectors, Esperantists, nudists and newspaper editors—I have seen them all, together, in vast assemblies, sloughing through the wall-to-wall of a thousand hotel lobbies (the nudists excepted) in their shimmering grey-metal suits and Nicey Short Collar white shirts with white Plasti-Coat name cards on their chests, and I have sat through their speeches and seminars (the nudists included) and attentively endured ear baths such as you wouldn't believe. And yet some of the truly instructive conventions of our times I seem to have missed altogether. One, for example, I only heard about from one of the many anonymous men who have labored in . . . a curious field. This was a convention of the stringers for *The National Enquirer*.

The Enquirer is a weekly newspaper that is probably known by sight to millions more than know it by name. In fact, no one who ever came face-to-face with *The Enquirer* on a newsstand in its wildest days is likely to have forgotten the sight: a tabloid with great inky shocks of type all over the front page saying something on the order of *Gouges Out Wife's Eyes to Make Her Ugly, Dad Hurls Hot Grease in Daughter's Face, Wife Commits Suicide After 2 Years of Poisoning Fails to Kill Husband. . . .*

The stories themselves were supplied largely by stringers, i.e., correspondents, from all over the country, the world, for that matter, mostly copy editors and reporters on local newspapers. Every so often they would come upon a story, usually via the police beat, that was so grotesque the local sheet would discard it or run it in a highly glossed form rather than offend or perplex its readers. The stringers would preserve them for *The Enquirer*, which always rewarded them well and respectfully.

In fact, one year *The Enquirer* convened and feted them at a hotel in Manhattan. It was a success in every way. The only awkward moment was at the outset when the stringers all pulled in. None of them knew each other. Their hosts got around the problem by introducing them by the stories they had supplied. The introductions, I am told, went like this:

"Harry, I want you to meet Frank here. Frank did that story, you remember that story, *Midget Murderer Throws Girl Off Cliff After She Refuses To Dance With Him*."

"Pleased to meet you. That was some story."

"And Harry did the one about *I Spent Three Days Trapped at Bottom of Forty-foot-deep Mine Shaft and Was Saved by a Swarm of Flies.*"

"Likewise, I'm sure."

And *Midget Murderer Throws Girl Off Cliff* shakes hands with *I Spent Three Days Trapped at Bottom of Forty-foot-deep Mine Shaft,* and *Buries Her Baby Alive* shakes hands with *Boy, Twelve, Strangles Two-year-old Girl,* and *Kills Son and Feeds Corpse to Pigs* shakes hands with *He Strangles Old Woman and Smears Corpse with Syrup, Ketchup and Oatmeal* . . . and. . . .

. . . There was a great deal of esprit about the whole thing. These men were, in fact, the avant-garde of a new genre that since then has become institutionalized throughout the nation without anyone knowing its proper name. I speak of the new pornography, the pornography of violence.

Pornography comes from the Greek word *porne,* meaning harlot, and pornography is literally the depiction of the acts of harlots. In the new pornography, the theme is not sex. The new pornography depicts practitioners acting out another, murkier drive: people staving teeth in, ripping guts open, blowing brains out and getting even with all those bastards. . . .

The success of *The Enquirer* prompted many imitators to enter the field, *Midnight, The Star Chronicle, The National Insider, Inside News, The National Close-up, The National Tattler, The National Examiner.* A truly competitive free press evolved, and soon a reader could go to the newspaper of his choice for *Kill the Retarded! (Won't You Join My Movement?)* and *Unfaithful Wife? Burn Her Bed!, Harem Master's Mistress Chops Him with Machete, Babe Bites Off Boy's Tongue,* and *Cuts Buddy's Face to Pieces for Stealing His Business and Fiancée.*

And yet the last time I surveyed the Violence press, I noticed a curious thing. These pioneering journals seem to have pulled back. They seem to be regressing to what is by now the Redi-Mix staple of literate Americans, plain old lust-o-lech sex. *Ecstasy and Me (By Hedy Lamarr),* says *The National Enquirer. I Run A Sex Art Gallery,* says *The National Insider.* What has happened, I think, is something that has happened to avant-gardes in many fields, from William Morris and the Craftsmen to the Bauhaus group. Namely, their discoveries have been preempted by the Establishment and so thoroughly dissolved into the mainstream they no longer look original.

Robert Harrison, the former publisher of *Confidential*, and later publisher of the aforementioned *Inside News*, was perhaps the first person to see it coming. I was interviewing Harrison early in January of 1964 for a story in *Esquire* about six weeks after the assassination of President Kennedy, and we were in a cab in the West Fifties in Manhattan, at a stoplight, by a newsstand, and Harrison suddenly pointed at the newsstand and said, "Look at that. They're doing the same thing *The Enquirer* does."

There on the stand was a row of slick-paper, magazine-size publications, known in the trade as one-shots, with titles like *Four Days That Shook the World, Death of a President, An American Tragedy* or just *John Fitzgerald Kennedy* (1921-1963). "You want to know why people buy those things?" said Harrison. "People buy those things to see a man get his head blown off."

And, of course, he was right. Only now the publishers were in many cases the pillars of the American press. Invariably, these "special coverages" of the assassination bore introductions piously commemorating the fallen President, exhorting the American people to strength and unity in a time of crisis, urging greater vigilance and safeguards for the new President, and even raising the nice metaphysical question of collective guilt in "an age of violence."

In the three and a half years since then, of course, there has been an incessant replay, with every recoverable clinical detail, of those less than five seconds in which a man got his head blown off. And throughout this deluge of words, pictures and film frames, I have been intrigued with one thing. The point of view, the vantage point, is almost never that of the victim, riding in the Presidential Lincoln Continental. What you get is . . . the view from Oswald's rifle. You can step right up here and look point-blank right through the very hairline cross in Lee Harvey Oswald's Optics Ordinance four-power Japanese telescopic sight and watch, frame by frame by frame by frame by frame, as that man there's head comes apart. Just a little History there before your very eyes.

The television networks have schooled us in the view from Oswald's rifle and made it seem a normal pastime. The TV viewpoint is nearly always that of the man who is going to strike. The last time I watched *Gunsmoke*, which was not known as a very violent Western in TV terms, the action went like this: The Wellington agents and the stagecoach driver pull guns on the badlands gang leader's daughter and Kitty, the heart-of-gold saloonkeeper, and kidnap them. Then the badlands gang shoots two Wellington agents. Then they tie up five more and talk about shooting them. Then they desist because they might not be able to get a hotel room in the next town if the word got around. Then one badlands gang gunslinger attempts to rape Kitty while the gang leader's younger daughter looks on. Then Kitty resists, so he slugs her one in the jaw. Then the gang leader slugs him. Then the gang leader slugs Kitty. Then Kitty throws hot stew in a gang member's face and hits him over the back of the head with a revolver. Then he knocks her down with a rock. Then the gang sticks up a bank. Here comes the sheriff, Matt Dillon. He shoots a gang member and breaks it up. Then the gang leader shoots the guy who was guarding his daughter and the woman. Then the sheriff shoots the gang leader. The final exploding bullets signal The End.

It is not the accumulated slayings and bone-crushings that make this porno-violence, however. What makes it porno-violence is that in almost every case the camera angle, therefore the viewer, is with the gun, the fist, the rock. The pornography of violence has no point of view in the old sense that novels do. You do not live the action through the hero's eyes. You live with the aggressor, whoever he may be. One moment you are the hero. The next, you are the villain. No matter whose side you may be on consciously, you are in fact with the muscle, and it is you who disintegrate all comers, villains, lawmen, women, anybody. On the rare occasions in which the gun is emptied into the camera—i.e., into your face—the effect is so startling that the pornography of violence all but loses its fantasy charm. There are not nearly so many masochists as sadists among those little devils whispering into your ears.

In fact, sex—"sadomasochism"—is only a part of the pornography of violence. Violence is much more wrapped up, simply, with status. Volence is the simple, ultimate solution for problems of status competition, just as gambling is the simple, ultimate solution for economic competition. The old pornography was the fantasy of easy sexual delights in a world where sex was kept unavailable. The new pornography is the fantasy of easy triumph in a world where status competition has become so complicated and frustrating.

Already the old pornography is losing its kick because of overexposure. In the late Thirties, Nathanael West published his last and best-regarded novel, *The Day of the Locust,* and it was a terrible flop commercially, and his publisher said if he ever published another book about Hollywood it would "have to be *My Thirty-nine Ways*

of Making Love by Hedy Lamarr." *Ecstasy and Me* is not quite that
. . . but maybe it is. I stopped counting. I know her account begins:
"The men in my life have ranged from a classic case history of impotence, to a whip-brandishing sadist who enjoyed sex only after he
tied my arms behind me with the sash of his robe. There was another man who took his pleasure with a girl in my own bed, while he
thought I was asleep in it."

Yawns all around. The sin itself is wearing out. Pornography cannot exist without certified taboo to violate. And today Lust, like the
rest of the Seven Deadly Sins—Pride, Sloth, Envy, Greed, Anger
and Gluttony—is becoming a rather minor vice. The Seven Deadly
Sins, after all, are only sins against the self. Theologically, the idea of
Lust—well, the idea is that if you seduce some poor girl from Akron,
it is not a sin because you are ruining her, but because you are wasting your time and your energies and damaging your own spirit. This
goes back to the old work ethic, when the idea was to keep every
able-bodied man's shoulder to the wheel. In an age of riches for all,
the ethic becomes more nearly: Let him do anything he pleases, as
long as he doesn't get in my way. And if he does get in my way, or
even if he doesn't . . . well . . . we have *new* fantasies for that.
Put hair on the walls.

Hair on the Walls is the invisible subtitle of Truman Capote's
book, *In Cold Blood.* The book is neither a who-done-it nor a will-
they-be-caught, since the answers to both questions are known from
the outset. It does ask why-did-they-do-it, but the answer is soon as
clear as it is going to be. Instead, the book's suspense is based largely
on a totally new idea in detective stories: the promise of gory details,
and the withholding of them until the end. Early in the game one
of the two murderers, Dick, starts promising to put "plenty of hair
on them-those walls" with a shotgun. So read on, gentle readers, and
on and on; you are led up to the moment before the crime on page
60—yet the specifics, what happened, the gory details, are kept out
of sight, in grisly dangle, until page 244.

But Dick and Perry, Capote's killers, are only a couple of lower-
class bums. With James Bond the new pornography has already
reached dead center, the bureaucratic middle class. The appeal of
Bond has been explained as the appeal of the lone man who can solve
enormously complicated, even world problems through his own
bravery and initiative. But Bond is not a lone man at all, of course.
He is not the Lone Ranger. He is much easier to identify than that.

He is a salaried functionary in a bureaucracy. He is a sport, but a believable one; not a millionaire, but a bureaucrat on expense account. He is not even a high-level bureaucrat. He is an operative. This point is carefully and repeatedly made by having his superiors dress him down for violations of standard operating procedure. Bond, like the Lone Ranger, solves problems with guns and fists. When it is over, however, the Lone Ranger leaves a silver bullet. Bond, like the rest of us, fills out a report in triplicate.

Marshall McLuhan says we are in a period in which it will become harder and harder to stimulate lust through words and pictures—i.e., the old pornography. In an age of electronic circuitry, he says, people crave tactile, all-involving experiences. The same thing may very well happen to the new pornography of violence. Even such able craftsmen as Truman Capote, Ian Fleming, NBC and CBS may not suffice. Fortunately, there are historical models to rescue us from this frustration. In the latter days of the Roman Empire, the Emperor Commodus became jealous of the celebrity of the great gladiators. He took to the arena himself, with his sword, and began dispatching suitably screened cripples and hobbled fighters. Audience participation became so popular that soon various *illuminati* of the Commodus set, various boys and girls of the year, were out there, suited up, gaily cutting a sequence of dwarves and feebles down to short ribs. Ah, swinging generations, what new delights await?

HUNTER S. THOMPSON

The Motorcycle Gangs: Losers and Outsiders

Last Labor Day weekend newspapers all over California gave front-page reports of a heinous gang rape in the moonlit sand dunes near the town of Seaside on the Monterey Peninsula. Two girls, aged 14 and 15, were allegedly taken from their dates by a gang of filthy, frenzied, boozed-up motorcycle hoodlums called "Hell's Angels," and dragged off to be "repeatedly assaulted."

A deputy sheriff, summoned by one of the erstwhile dates, said he "arrived at the beach and saw a huge bonfire surrounded by cyclists of both sexes. Then the two sobbing, near-hysterical girls staggered

The Motorcycle Gangs: Losers and Outsiders. From *The Nation*, May 17, 1965. Reprinted by permission of the publisher.

out of the darkness, begging for help. One was completely nude and the other had on only a torn sweater."

Some 300 Hell's Angels were gathered in the Seaside-Monterey area at the time, having convened, they said, for the purpose of raising funds among themselves to send the body of a former member, killed in an accident, back to his mother in North Carolina. One of the Angels, hip enough to falsely identify himself as "Frenchy of San Bernardino," told a local reporter who came out to meet the cyclists: "We chose Monterey because we get treated good here; most other places we get thrown out of town."

But Frenchy spoke too soon. The Angels weren't on the peninsula twenty-four hours before four of them were in jail for rape, and the rest of the troop was being escorted to the county line by a large police contingent. Several were quoted, somewhat derisively, as saying: "That rape charge against our guys is phony and it won't stick."

It turned out to be true, but that was another story and certainly no headliner. The difference between the Hell's Angels in the papers and the Hell's Angels for real is enough to make a man wonder what newsprint is for. It also raises a question as to who are the real hell's angels.

Ever since World War II, California has been strangely plagued by wild men on motorcycles. They usually travel in groups of ten to thirty, booming along the highways and stopping here and there to get drunk and raise hell. In 1947, hundreds of them ran amok in the town of Hollister, an hour's fast drive south of San Francisco, and got enough press notices to inspire a film called *The Wild One*, starring Marlon Brando. The film had a massive effect on thousands of young California motorcycle buffs; in many ways, it was their version of *The Sun Also Rises*.

The California climate is perfect for motorcycles, as well as surfboards, swimming pools and convertibles. Most of the cyclists are harmless weekend types, members of the American Motorcycle Association, and no more dangerous than skiers or skin divers. But a few belong to what the others call "outlaw clubs," and these are the ones who—especially on weekends and holidays—are likely to turn up almost anywhere in the state, looking for action. Despite everything the psychiatrists and Freudian casuists have to say about them, they are tough, mean and potentially as dangerous as packs of wild boar. When push comes to shove, any leather fetishes or inadequacy feelings that may be involved are entirely beside the point, as anyone who has ever tangled with these boys will sadly testify. When you get in an argument with a group of outlaw motorcyclists, you can generally count your chances of emerging unmaimed by the number of heavy-handed allies you can muster in the time it takes to smash a beer bottle. In this league, sportsmanship is for old liberals and young fools. "I smashed his face," one of them said to me of a man he'd never seen until the swinging started. "He got wise. He called me a punk. He must have been stupid."

The most notorious of these outlaw groups is the Hell's Angels, supposedly headquartered in San Bernardino, just east of Los Angeles, and with branches all over the state. As a result of the infamous "Labor Day gang rape," the Attorney General of California has recently issued an official report on the Hell's Angels. According to the report, they are easily identified:

> The emblem of the Hell's Angels, termed "colors," consists of an embroidered patch of a winged skull wearing a motorcycle helmet. Just below the wing of the emblem are the letters "MC." Over this is a band bearing the words "Hell's Angels." Below the emblem is another patch bearing the local chapter name, which is usually an abbreviation for the city or locality. These patches are sewn on the back of a usually sleeveless denim jacket. In addition, members have been observed wearing various types of Luftwaffe insignia and reproductions of German iron crosses.[1] Many affect beards and their hair is usually long and unkempt. Some wear a single earring in a pierced ear lobe. Frequently they have been observed to wear metal belts made of a length of polished motorcycle drive chain which can be unhooked and used as a flexible bludgeon. . . . Probably the most universal common denominator in identification of Hell's Angels is their generally filthy condition. Investigating officers consistently report these people, both club members and their female associates, seem badly in need of a bath. Fingerprints are a very effective means of identification because a high percentage of Hell's Angels have criminal records.
>
> In addition to the patches on the back of Hell's Angels jackets, the "One Percenters" wear a patch reading "1%-er." Another badge worn by some members bears the number "13." It is reported to represent the 13th letter of the alphabet, "M," which in turn stands for marijuana and indicates the wearer thereof is a user of the drug.

The Attorney General's report was colorful, interesting, heavily biased and consistently alarming—just the sort of thing, in fact, to

---

[1] Purely for decorative and shock effect. The Hell's Angels are apolitical and no more racist than other ignorant young thugs.

make a clanging good article for a national news magazine. Which it did; both barrels. *Newsweek* led with a left hook titled "The Wild Ones," *Time* crossed with a right, inevitably titled "The Wilder Ones." The Hell's Angels, cursing the implications of this new attack, retreated to the bar of the De Pau Hotel near the San Francisco waterfront and planned a weekend beach party. I showed them the articles. Hell's Angels do not normally read the news magazines. "I'd go nuts if I read that stuff all the time," said one. "It's all bullshit."

Newsweek was relatively circumspect. It offered local color, flashy quotes and "evidence" carefully attributed to the official report but unaccountably said the report accused the Hell's Angels of homosexuality, whereas the report said just the opposite. *Time* leaped into the fray with a flurry of blood, booze and semen-flecked wordage that amounted, in the end, to a classic of supercharged hokum: 'Drug-induced stupors . . . no act is too degrading . . . swap girls, drugs and motorcycles with equal abandon . . . stealing forays . . . then ride off again to seek some new nadir in sordid behavior. . . .'"

Where does all this leave the Hell's Angels and the thousands of shuddering Californians (according to *Time*) who are worried sick about them? Are these outlaws really going to be busted, routed and cooled, as the news magazines implied? Are California highways any safer as a result of this published uproar? Can honest merchants once again walk the streets in peace? The answer is that nothing has changed except that a few people calling themselves Hell's Angels have a new sense of identity and importance.

After two weeks of intensive dealing with the Hell's Angels phenomenon, both in print and in person, I'm convinced the net result of the general howl and publicity has been to obscure and avoid the real issues by invoking a savage conspiracy of bogymen and conning the public into thinking all will be "business as usual" once this fearsome snake is scotched, as it surely will be by hard and ready minions of the Establishment.

Meanwhile, according to Attorney General Thomas C. Lynch's own figures, California's true crime picture makes the Hell's Angels look like a gang of petty jack rollers. The police count 463 Hell's Angels: 205 around Los Angeles and 233 in the San Francisco-Oakland area. I don't know about L.A. but the real figures for the Bay Area are thirty or so in Oakland and exactly eleven—with one facing expulsion—in San Francisco. This disparity makes it hard to accept other police statistics. The dubious package also shows convictions on 1,023 misdemeanor counts and 151 felonies—primarily vehicle theft, burglary and assault. This is for all years and all alleged members.

California's overall figures for 1963 list 1,116 homicides, 12,448 aggravated assaults, 6,257 sex offenses, and 24,532 burglaries. In 1962, the state listed 4,121 traffic deaths, up from 3,839 in 1961. Drug arrest figures for 1964 showed a 101 per cent increase in juvenile marijuana arrests over 1963, and a recent back-page story in the *San Francisco Examiner* said, "The venereal disease rate among [the city's] teen-agers from 15-19 has more than doubled in the past four years." Even allowing for the annual population jump, juvenile arrests in all categories are rising by 10 per cent or more each year.

Against this background, would it make any difference to the safety and peace of mind of the average Californian if every motorcycle outlaw in the state (all 901, according to the police) were garroted within twenty-four hours? This is not to say that a group like the Hell's Angels has no meaning. The generally bizarre flavor of their offenses and their insistence on identifying themselves make good copy, but usually overwhelm—in print, at least—the unnerving truth that they represent, in colorful microcosm, what is quietly and anonymously growing all around us every day of the week.

"We're bastards to the world and they're bastards to us," one of the Oakland Angels told a *Newsweek* reporter. "When you walk into a place where people can see you, you want to look as repulsive and repugnant as possible. We are complete social outcasts—outsiders against society."

A lot of this is a pose, but anyone who believes that's all it is has been on thin ice since the death of Jay Gatsby. The vast majority of motorcycle outlaws are uneducated, unskilled men between 20 and 30, and most have no credentials except a police record. So at the root of their sad stance is a lot more than a wistful yearning for acceptance in a world they never made; their real motivation is an instinctive certainty as to what the score really is. They are out of the ball game and they know it—and that is their meaning; for unlike most losers in today's society, the Hell's Angels not only know but spitefully proclaim exactly where they stand.

I went to one of their meetings recently, and half-way through the night I thought of Joe Hill on his way to face a Utah firing squad and saying his final words: "Don't mourn, organize." It is safe to say that no Hell's Angel has ever heard of Joe Hill or would know a Wobbly from a Bushmaster, but nevertheless they are somehow related. The I.W.W. had serious plans for running the world, while the Hell's Angels mean only to defy the world's machinery. But instead of losing quietly, one by one, they have banded together with a mindless kind of loyalty and moved outside the framework, for good or ill. There is nothing particularly romantic or admirable about it; that's just the way it is, strength in unity. They don't mind telling you that running fast and loud on their customized Harley 74s gives them a power and a purpose that nothing else seems to offer.

Beyond that, their position as self-proclaimed outlaws elicits a certain popular appeal, however reluctant. That is especially true in the West and even in California where the outlaw tradition is still honored. The unarticulated link between the Hell's Angels and the millions of losers and outsiders who don't wear any colors is the key to their notoriety and the ambivalent reactions they inspire. There are several other keys, having to do with politicians, policemen and journalists, but for this we have to go back to Monterey and the Labor Day "gang rape."

Politicians, like editors and cops, are very keen on outrage stories, and state Senator Fred S. Farr of Monterey County is no exception. He is a leading light of the Carmel-Pebble Beach set and no friend of hoodlums anywhere, especially gang rapists who invade his constituency. Senator Farr demanded an immediate investigation of the Hell's Angels and others of their ilk—Commancheros, Stray Satans, Iron Horsemen, Rattlers (a Negro club), and Booze Fighters— whose lack of status caused them all to be lumped together as "other disreputables." In the cut-off world of big bikes, long runs and classy rumbles, this new, state-sanctioned stratification made the Hell's Angels very big. They were, after all, Number One. Like John Dillinger.

Attorney General Lynch, then new in his job, moved quickly to mount an investigation of sorts. He sent questionnaires to more than 100 sheriffs, district attorneys and police chiefs, asking for information on the Hell's Angels and those "other disreputables." He also asked for suggestions as to how the law might deal with them.

Six months went by before all the replies were condensed into the fifteen-page report that made new outrage headlines when it was released to the press. (The Hell's Angels also got a copy; one of them

stole mine.) As a historical document, it read like a plot synopsis of
Mickey Spillane's worst dreams. But in the matter of solutions it
was vague, reminiscent in some ways of Madame Nhu's proposals for
dealing with the Vietcong. The state was going to centralize information on these thugs, urge more vigorous prosecution, put them
all under surveillance whenever possible, etc.

A careful reader got the impression that even if the Hell's Angels
had acted out this script—eighteen crimes were specified and dozens
of others implied—very little would or could be done about it, and
that indeed Mr. Lynch was well aware he'd been put, for political
reasons, on a pretty weak scent. There was plenty of mad action, senseless destruction, orgies, brawls, perversions and a strange
parade of "innocent victims" that, even on paper and in careful police language, was enough to tax the credulity of the dullest police reporter. Any bundle of information off police blotters is bound to
reflect a special viewpoint, and parts of the Attorney General's report
are actually humorous, if only for the language. Here is an excerpt:

> On November 4, 1961, a San Francisco resident driving through
> Rodeo, possibly under the influence of alcohol, struck a motorcycle
> belonging to a Hell's Angel parked outside a bar. A group of Angels
> pursued the vehicle, pulled the driver from the car and attempted to
> demolish the rather expensive vehicle. The bartender claimed he had
> seen nothing, but a cocktail waitress in the bar furnished identification
> to the officers concerning some of those responsible for the assault.
> The next day it was reported to officers that a member of the Hell's
> Angels gang had threatened the life of this waitress as well as another
> woman waitress. A male witness who definitely identified five partici-
> pants in the assault including the president of the Vallejo Hell's
> Angels and the Vallejo "Road Rats" advised officers that because of
> his fear of retaliation by club members he would refuse to testify to
> the facts he had previously furnished.

That is a representative item in the section of the report titled
"Hoodlum Activities." First, it occurred in a small town—Rodeo is
on San Pablo Bay just north of Oakland—where the Angels had
stopped at a bar without causing any trouble until some offense was
committed against them. In this case, a driver whom even the police
admit was "possibly" drunk hit one of their motorcycles. The same
kind of accident happens every day all over the nation, but when it
involves outlaw motorcyclists it is something else again. Instead of
settling the thing with an exchange of insurance information or, at

the very worst, an argument with a few blows, the Hell's Angels beat the driver and "attempted to demolish the vehicle." I asked one of them if the police exaggerated this aspect, and he said no, they had done the natural thing: smashed headlights, kicked in doors, broken windows and torn various components off the engine.

Of all their habits and predilections that society finds alarming, this departure from the time-honored concept of "an eye for an eye" is the one that most frightens people. The Hell's Angels try not to do anything halfway, and anyone who deals in extremes is bound to cause trouble, whether he means to or not. This, along with a belief in total retaliation for any offense or insult, is what makes the Hell's Angels unmanageable for the police and morbidly fascinating to the general public. Their claim that they "don't start trouble" is probably true more often than not, but their idea of "provocation" is dangerously broad, and their biggest problem is that nobody else seems to understand it. Even dealing with them personally, on the friendliest terms, you can sense their hair-trigger readiness to retaliate.

This is a public thing, and not at all true among themselves. In a meeting, their conversation is totally frank and open. They speak to and about one another with an honesty that more civilized people couldn't bear. At the meeting I attended (and before they realized I was a journalist) one Angel was being publicly evaluated; some members wanted him out of the club and others wanted to keep him in. It sounded like a group-therapy clinic in progress—not exactly what I expected to find when just before midnight I walked into the bar of the De Pau in one of the bleakest neighborhoods in San Francisco, near Hunters Point. By the time I parted company with them —at 6:30 the next morning after an all-night drinking bout in my apartment—I had been impressed by a lot of things, but no one thing about them was as consistently obvious as their group loyalty. This is an admirable quality, but it is also one of the things that gets them in trouble: a fellow Angel is *always right* when dealing with outsiders. And this sort of reasoning makes a group of "offended" Hell's Angels nearly impossible to deal with.

Here is another incident from the Attorney General's report:

On September 19, 1964, a large group of Hell's Angels and "Satan's Slaves" converged on a bar in South Gate (Los Angeles County), parking their motorcycles and cars in the street in such a fashion as to block one-half of the roadway. They told officers that three members of the club had recently been asked to stay out of the bar and that they had come to tear it down. Upon their approach the bar owner locked the doors and turned off the lights and no entrance was made, but the group did demolish a cement block fence. On arrival of the police, members of the club were lying on the sidewalk and in the street. They were asked to leave the city, which they did reluctantly. As they left, several were heard to say that they would be back and tear down the bar.

Here again is the ethic of total retaliation. If you're "asked to stay out" of a bar, you don't just punch the owner—you come back with your army and destroy the whole edifice. Similar incidents—along with a number of vague rape complaints—make up the bulk of the report. Eighteen incidents in four years, and none except the rape charges are more serious than cases of assault on citizens who, for their own reasons, had become involved with the Hell's Angels prior to the violence. I could find no cases of unwarranted attacks on wholly innocent victims. There are a few borderline cases, wherein victims of physical attacks seemed innocent, according to police and press reports, but later refused to testify for fear of "retaliation." The report asserts very strongly that Hell's Angels are difficult to prosecute and convict because they make a habit of threatening and intimidating witnesses. That is probably true to a certain extent, but in many cases victims have refused to testify because they were engaged in some legally dubious activity at the time of the attack.

In two of the most widely publicized incidents the prosecution would have fared better if their witnesses and victims *had* been intimidated into silence. One of these was the Monterey "gang rape," and the other a "rape" in Clovis, near Fresno in the Central Valley. In the latter, a 36-year-old widow and mother of five children claimed she'd been yanked out of a bar where she was having a quiet beer with another woman, then carried to an abandoned shack behind the bar and raped repeatedly for two and a half hours by fifteen or twenty Hell's Angels and finally robbed of $150. That's how the story appeared in the San Francisco newspapers the next day, and it was kept alive for a few more days by the woman's claims that she was getting phone calls threatening her life if she testified against her assailants.

Then, four days after the crime, the victim was arrested on charges of "sexual perversion." The true story emerged, said the Clovis chief of police, when the woman was "confronted by witnesses. Our investigation shows she was not raped," said the chief. "She participated in lewd acts in the tavern with at least three Hell's Angels before the owners ordered them out. She encouraged their advances in the tavern, then led them to an abandoned house in the rear. . . . She was not robbed but, according to a woman who accompanied her, had left her house early in the evening with $5 to go bar-hopping." That incident did not appear in the Attorney General's report.

But it was impossible not to mention the Monterey "gang rape," because it was the reason for the whole subject to become official. Page one of the report—which *Time's* editors apparently skipped—says that the Monterey case was dropped because ". . . further investigation raised questions as to whether forcible rape had been committed or if the identifications made by victims were valid." Charges were dismissed on September 25, with the concurrence of a grand jury. The deputy District Attorney said "a doctor examined the girls and found no evidence" to support the charges. "Besides that, one girl refused to testify," he explained, "and the other was given a lie-detector test and found to be wholly unreliable."

This, in effect, was what the Hell's Angels had been saying all along. Here is their version of what happened, as told by several who were there:

> One girl was white and pregnant, the other was colored, and they were with five colored studs. They hung around our bar—Nick's Place on Del Monte Avenue—for about three hours Saturday night, drinking and talking with our riders, then they came out to the beach with us—them and their five boy friends. Everybody was standing around the fire, drinking wine, and some of the guys were talking to them —hustling 'em, naturally—and soon somebody asked the two chicks if they wanted to be turned on—you know, did they want to smoke some pot? They said yeah, and then they walked off with some of the guys to the dunes. The spade went with a few guys and then she wanted to quit, but the pregnant one was really hot to trot; the first four or five guys she was really dragging into her arms, but after that she cooled off, too. By this time, though, one of their boy friends had got scared and gone for the cops—and that's all it was.

But not quite all. After that there were Senator Farr and Tom Lynch and a hundred cops and dozens of newspaper stories and articles in the national news magazines—and even this article, which is a direct result of the Monterey "gang rape."

When the much-quoted report was released, the local press—primarily the *San Francisco Chronicle*, which had earlier done a long and fairly objective series on the Hell's Angels—made a point of saying the Monterey charges against the Hell's Angels had been dropped for lack of evidence. *Newsweek* was careful not to mention Monterey at all, but *The New York Times* referred to it as "the alleged gang rape" which, however, left no doubt in a reader's mind that something savage had occurred.

It remained for *Time*, though, to flatly ignore the fact that the Monterey rape charges had been dismissed. Its article leaned heavily on the hairiest and least factual sections of the report, and ignored the rest. It said, for instance, that the Hell's Angels' initiation rite "demands that any new member bring a woman or girl [called a 'sheep'] who is willing to submit to sexual intercourse with each member of the club." That is untrue, although, as one Angel explained, "Now and then you get a woman who likes to cover the crowd, and hell, I'm no prude. People don't like to think women go for that stuff, but a lot of them do."

We were talking across a pool table about the rash of publicity and how it had affected the Angels' activities. I was trying to explain to him that the bulk of the press in this country has such a vested interest in the *status quo* that it can't afford to do much honest probing at the roots, for fear of what they might find.

"Oh, I don't know," he said. "Of course I don't like to read all this bullshit because it brings the heat down on us, but since we got famous we've had more rich fags and sex-hungry women come looking for us than we ever had before. Hell, these days we have more action than we can handle."

FRANKLIN RUSSELL

A Madness of Nature

Beyond the northern beach, a gray swell rolls in from Greenland and runs softly along the shore. The horizon is lost in a world of gray, and gulls glide, spectral in the livid air. Watching, I am enveloped in the sullen waiting time and feel the silence, drawn out long and thin. I wait for the sea to reveal a part of itself.

A capelin is perhaps the best-hunted creature on earth. It is not more than five inches long, about the size of a young herring, and undistinguished in appearance, except that when it is freshly caught, it is the color of mercury. As the capelin dies, its silvery scales

A Madness of Nature. From *New American Review* #2, 1968. Reprinted by permission of John Cushman Associates, Inc. Copyright © 1968 Franklin Russell.

tarnish and the glitter goes out like a light, ending a small allegory about nature, a spectacle of victims, victors, and an imperative of existence. Its death illuminates a dark process of biology in which there are shadows of other, more complex lives.

The capelin are born to be eaten. They transform oceanic plankton into flesh which is then hunted greedily by almost every sea creature that swims or flies. Their only protection is fecundity. One capelin survives to adulthood from every ten thousand eggs laid, and yet a single school may stir square miles of sea.

In mid-June, the capelin gather offshore. They can be seen everywhere and at all times in history, symbols of summer and fertility, of Providence and danger. I see them along the shores of Greenland, Iceland, Norway, and near Spitsbergen. I follow them across the northern coast of Russia. Chill air, gray seas, the northern silence are the capelin's world in Alaska, in the Aleutians, around Hudson Bay, and along the northeastern shores of North America. But the capelin of the Newfoundland coast are the most visible. Here, they spawn on the beaches rather than in deep water offshore, and I have come to see their rush for eternity.

They gather a thousand feet offshore, coalescing into groups of a hundred thousand to break the water's surface with bright chuckling sounds. They gather, and grow. Soon they are in the millions, with other millions swimming up from the offshore deeps. They gather, now in the billions, so densely packed together in places that the sea shimmers silver for miles and flows, serpentine, with the swelling body of a single, composite creature.

The fish do, in fact, possess a common sense of purpose. Nothing can redirect their imperative to breed. I once swam among them and saw them parting reluctantly ahead of me, felt their bodies flicking against my hands. Looking back, I saw them closing in, filling up the space created by my passage. The passive fish tolerated me, in their anticipation of what they were about to do.

At this time of the year they are so engrossed that they barely react when a host of creatures advances to kill them. Beneath and beyond them, codfish pour up out of the deep. They overtake the capelin, eat them, plunge their sleek, dark bodies recklessly into shallow water. Some have swum so rapidly from such depths that their swim bladders are distended by the sudden drop in water pressure. The cod are gigantic by comparison with the capelin. Many weigh one hundred pounds or more, and will not be sated until they have eaten scores of capelin each. The water writhes with movement and foam where cod, headlong in pursuit, drive themselves clear out of the sea and fall back with staccato slaps.

The attack of the codfish is a brutal opening to a ritual, and a contradiction in their character. Normally, they are sedentary feeders on the sea floor. Now, however, they are possessed. Their jaws rip and tear; the water darkens with capelin blood: the shredded pieces of flesh hang suspended or rise to the surface.

Now a group of seabirds, the parrotlike puffins, clumsy in flight, turn over the capelin, their grotesque, axlike beaks probing from side to side as they watch the upper layers of the massacre. They are joined by new formations of birds until several thousand puffins are circling. They are silent, and there is no way of knowing how they were summoned from their nesting burrows on an island that is out of sight. They glide down to the water—stub-winged cargo planes—land awkwardly, taxi with fluttering wings and stamping paddle feet, then dive.

At the same time, the sea view moves with new invasions of seabirds. Each bird pumps forward with an urgency that suggests it has received the same stimulus as the cod. The gulls that breed on cliffs along a southern bay come first, gracefully light of wing, with raucous voice as they cry out their anticipation. Beneath them, flying flat, direct, silent, come murres, black-bodied, short-tailed, close relatives of the puffins. The murres land and dive without ceremony. Well offshore, as though waiting confirmation of the feast, shearwaters from Tristan da Cunha turn long, pointed wings across the troughs of waves and cackle like poultry.

The birds converge, and lose their identity in the mass thickening on the water. Small gulls—the kittiwakes, delicate in flight—screech and drop and rise and screech and drop like snowflakes on the sea. They fall among even smaller birds, lighter than they, which dangle their feet and hover at the water's surface, almost walking on water as they seek tiny pieces of shredded flesh. These are the ocean-flying petrels, the Mother Carey's chickens of mariners' legends, which rarely come within sight of land. All order is lost in the shrieking tumult of the hundreds of thousands of birds.

Underwater, the hunters meet among their prey. The puffins and murres dive below the capelin and attack, driving for the surface. The cod attack at mid-depth. The gulls smother the surface and press the capelin back among the submarine hunters. The murres and puffins fly underwater, their beating wings turning them rapidly back and forth. They meet the cod, flail wings in desperate haste, are caught, crushed, and swallowed. Now seabirds as well as capelin become the hunted. Puffin and murre tangle wings. Silver walls of capelin flicker, part, re-form. Some seabirds surface abruptly, broken wings dangling. Others, with a leg or legs torn off, fly frantically, crash, skitter in shock across the water.

I see the capelin hunters spread across the sea, but also remember them in time. Each year the hunters are different because many of them depend on a fortuitous meeting with their prey. A group of small whales collides with the capelin, and in a flurry of movement they eat several tons of them. Salmon throw themselves among the capelin with the same abandon as the codfish, and in the melee become easy victims for a score of seals that kill dozens of them, then turn to the capelin and gorge themselves nearly stuporous. They rise, well beyond the tumult of the seabirds, their black heads jutting like rocks from the swell, to lie with distended bellies and doze away their feast. Capelin boil up around them for a moment but now the animals ignore them.

The capelin are hosts in a ceremony so ancient that a multitude of species have adapted to seeking a separate share of the host's bounty. The riotous collision of cod, seal, whale, and seabird obscures the smaller guests at the feast. Near the shore wait small brown fish —the cunner—one of the most voracious species. Soon they will be fighting among themselves for pieces of flesh as the capelin begin their run for the beach, or when the survivors of the spawning reel back into deep water, with the dead and dying falling to the bottom. If the water is calm and the sun bright, the cunner can be seen in two fathoms, ripping capelin corpses to pieces and scattering translucent scales like silver leaves in a wind of the sea.

Closer inshore, at the wave line, the flounder wait. They know the capelin are coming and their role is also predetermined. They cruise rapidly under the purling water in uncharacteristic excitement. They are not interested in capelin flesh. They want capelin eggs, and they will gorge as soon as spawning starts.

Now, the most voracious of all the hunters appear. Fishing vessels come up over the horizon. They brought the Portuguese of the fifteenth century, who anchored offshore, dropped their boats, and rowed ashore to take the capelin with handnets, on beaches never before walked by white men. They brought Spaniards and Dutchmen, Englishmen and Irish, from the sixteenth to the twentieth centuries. Americans, Nova Scotians, Gloucestermen, schoonermen, bankermen, longliner captains have participated in the ritual. All of them knew that fresh capelin is the finest bait when it is skillfully used, and can attract a fortune in codfish flesh, hooked on the submarine banks to the south.

But presently, these hunters are Newfoundlanders. They bring their schooners flying inshore like great brown-and-white birds, a hundred, two hundred, three hundred sail. They heel through the screaming seabirds, luff, anchor, and drop their dories with the same precision of movement of the other figures in the ritual. In an hour, three thousand men are at work from the boats. They work as the codfish work, with a frenzy that knots forearms and sends nets spilling over the sterns to encircle the capelin. They lift a thousand tons of capelin out of the sea, yet they do not measurably diminish the number of fish.

Meanwhile, landbound hunters wait for the fish to come within range of their lead-weighted handnets. Women, children, and old people crowd the beach with the able-bodied men. The old people have ancestral memories of capelin bounty. In the seventeenth and eighteenth centuries, when food was often short, only the big capelin harvest stood between them and starvation during the winter.

Many of the shore people are farmers who use the capelin for fertilizer as well as for food. Capelin corpses, spread to rot over thin northern soils, draw obedient crops of potatoes and cabbages out of the ground, and these, mixed with salted capelin flesh, become winter meals.

The children, who remember dried capelin as their candy, share the excitement of waiting. They chase one another up and down the beach and play with their own nets and fishing rods. Some are already asleep because they awoke before dawn to rouse the village, as they do every capelin morning, with the cry: "They've a-come, they've a-come!"

At the top of the beach, old women lie asleep or sit watching the seabirds squabbling and the dorymen rowing. They are Aunt Sadie and Little Nell and Bessie Blue and Mother Taunton, old ladies from several centuries. They know the capelin can save children in hard winters when the inshore cod fishery fails. They get up at two o'clock in the morning when the capelin are running, to walk miles to the nearest capelin beach. They net a barrel of fish, then roll the barrel, which weighs perhaps a hundred pounds, back home. They have finished spreading the fish on their gardens, or salting them, before the first of their grandchildren awakes.

They have clear memories of catching capelin in winter, when the sea freezes close inshore and the tide cracks the ice in places. Then millions of capelin, resting out the winter, rise in the cracks. An old woman with a good net can take tons of passive fish out of the water for as long as her strength lasts and for as far as her net reaches.

A cry rises from the beach: "Here they come!"

The ritual must be played out, according to habit. The dorymen and the seabirds, the rampaging cod and cunner cannot touch or turn the purpose of the capelin. At a moment, its genesis unknown, they start for the shore. From the top of some nearby cliffs I watch and marvel at the precision of their behavior. The capelin cease to be a great, formless mass offshore. They split into groups that the Newfoundlanders call wads—rippling gray lines, five to fifty feet wide—and run for the shore like advancing infantry lines. One by one, they peel away from their surviving comrades and advance, thirty to forty wads at a time.

Each wad has its discipline. The fish prepare to mate. Each male capelin seeks a female, darting from one fish to another. When he finds one, he presses against her side. Another male, perhaps two males, press against her other side. The males urge the female on toward the beach. Some are struck down by diving seabirds but others take their places. Cod dash among them and smash their sexual formations; they re-form immediately. Cunner rise and rip at them; flounder dart beneath them toward the beach.

The first wad runs into beach wavelets, and a hundred nets hit the water together; a silver avalanche of fish spills out on the beach. In each breaking wavelet the capelin maintain their formations, two or three males pressed tightly against their female until they are all flung up on the beach. There, to the whispering sound of tiny fins and tails vibrating, the female convulsively digs into the sand, which is still moving in the wake of the retreating wave. As she goes down, she extrudes up to fifty thousand eggs, and the males expel their milt.

The children shout; their bare feet fly over the spawning fish; the nets soar; sea boots grind down; the fish spill out; gulls run in the shallows under the children's feet; the flounder gorge. A codfish, two feet long, leaps out of the shallows and hits the beach. An old man scoops it up. The wads keep coming. The air is filled with birds. The dorymen shout and laugh.

The flood of eggs becomes visible. The sand glistens, then is greasy with eggs. They pile in driftlines that writhe back and forth in each wave. The female capelin wriggle into masses of eggs. The shallows are permeated with eggs. The capelin breathe eggs. Their mouths fill with eggs. Their stomachs are choked with eggs. The wads keep pouring onward, feeding the disaster on the beach.

Down come the boots and the nets, and the capelin die, mouths open and oozing eggs. The spawning is a fiasco. The tide has turned. Instead of spawning on the shore with the assurance of rising water behind them, each wad strikes ashore in retreating water. Millions are stranded but the wads keep coming.

In the background, diminished by the quantity of fish, other players gasp and pant at their nets. Barrels stack high on the beach. Horses whinny, driven hard up the bank at the back of the beach. Carts laden with barrels weave away. Carts bringing empty barrels bounce and roar down. The wads are still coming. Men use shovels to lift dead and dying fish from driftlines that are now two and three feet high. The easterly wind is freshening. The wavelets become waves. The capelin are flung up on the beach without a chance to spawn. They bounce and twist and the water flees beneath them.

It is twilight, then dark; torches now spot the beach, the offshore dories, and the schooners. The waves grow solidly and pile the capelin higher. The men shovel the heaps into pyramids, then reluctantly leave the beach. Heavy rain blots out beach and sea.

I remain to watch the blow piling up the sea. At the lowest point of the tide, it is driving waves high up on the beach, roiling the sand, digging up the partially buried eggs, and carrying them out to sea. By dawn most of the eggs are gone. The capelin have disappeared. The seabirds, the schooners, the cod, flounder, cunner, seals, whales have gone. Nothing remains except the marks of human feet, the cart tracks on the high part of the beach, the odd pyramid of dead fish. The feast is done.

The empty arena of the beach suggests a riddle. If the capelin were so perfectly adapted to spawn on a rising tide, to master the task of burying eggs in running sand between waves, to *know* when the tide was rising, why did they continue spawning after the tide turned? Was that, by the ancient rules of the ritual, intentional? If it was, then it indicated a lethal error of adaptation that did not jibe with the great numbers of capelin.

I wonder, then, if the weak died and the strong survived, but dismiss the notion after recalling the indiscriminate nature of all capelin deaths. There was no Darwinian selection for death of the stupid or the inexperienced. Men slaughtered billions, this year and last year and for three hundred years before, but the capelin never felt this pin-pricking on their colossal corporate bodies. Their spawning was a disaster for reasons well beyond the influence of men.

A nineteenth-century observer, after seeing a capelin-spawning, recorded his amazement at "the astonishing *prosperity* of these creatures, cast so wilfully away. . . ." It was in the end, and indeed throughout the entire ritual, the sheer numbers of capelin that scored the memory. The *prosperity* of the capelin preceded the disaster but then, it seemed, created it. Prosperity was not beneficial or an assurance of survival. The meaning of the ritual was slowly growing into sense. Prosperity unhinges the capelin. Prosperity, abundance, success, drive them on. They become transformed and throw themselves forward blindly. . . .

I turn from the beach, warm and secure, and take a blind step forward.

ALFRED R. LINDESMITH

The Marihuana Problem— Myth or Reality?

The primary fact about marihuana which ought to be taken into account by legislators but is not, is that it is not a habit-forming drug. By this is meant that the regular use of marihuana does not produce tolerance, and its abrupt cessation does not lead to withdrawal distress. As a consequence the problem of controlling or regulating its use is sharply different from that presented by the genuine drugs of addiction, i.e., the opiates such as heroin and morphine and their synthetic equivalents. Nevertheless, by federal legislation in 1951 and

The Marihuana Problem—Myth or Reality? From *The Addict and the Law* by Alfred R. Lindesmith. Copyright © 1965 by Indiana University Press. Reprinted by permission of the publisher.

1956, the increased penalties imposed on opiate users and peddlers were also applied to the users and distributors of marihuana. This extension was made casually with little discussion or investigation and with no apparent appreciation that the use of marihuana is something almost totally different from the use of heroin.

EFFECTS OF SMOKING MARIHUANA

Marihuana is ordinarily used in this country by smoking. The effects it produces are experienced as exhilaration, loss of inhibitions, a changed sense of time, and other psychological effects which have sometimes been described and extravagantly praised by those who have experienced them. These effects are in a general way comparable to the stimulating effects produced by alcohol in the sense that they are intoxicating, although they differ qualitatively from those of alcohol.

Intrinsically, however, marihuana is less dangerous and less harmful to the human body than is alcohol. It is, for example, not habit-forming, whereas alcohol is. While the alcoholic commonly substitutes alcohol for food, marihuana sharply stimulates the appetite. Chronic alcoholism is associated with various psychotic conditions and diseases such as Korsakoff's psychosis and cirrhosis of the liver. In comparison, the smoking of marihuana produces relatively trivial physical effects, although it does appear that immoderate use of the more concentrated products of the hemp plant also produce deleterious bodily effects. Such effects, however, are not conspicuous among American reefer smokers, probably because of the relatively small quantities of the essential drug that are ingested from the poor quality marihuana ordinarily consumed in this country. The American marihuana smoker who inadvertently uses too much when he switches, let us say, to the more potent ganja plant raised in Mexico and the West Indies is likely to experience nothing more alarming than going to sleep and waking up hungry.

USE OF MARIHUANA IN OTHER COUNTRIES

Marihuana consists of the dried and crumbled stems, leaves, and seed pods of a plant known as Indian hemp or *Cannabis sativa.*

These materials are often mixed with tobacco and in the United States
are ordinarily smoked. In many other parts of the world a special
type of hemp plant of unusual potency, known commonly as *ganja*,
is used in a similar manner or it may be brewed and drunk as ganja
tea—a common practice in the West Indies, where this drink is
prized for its alleged therapeutic efficacy. In India the uncultivated
hemp plant is smoked as marihuana is here and is also drunk. It is
known there as *bhang*. The essential drug of the hemp plant is *cannabis indica* or *cannabinol* and it, of course, can be taken in this form.
This essential drug is derived primarily from the resin of the female
hemp plant. This concentrated hemp resin is commonly known as
hashish and is immensely more powerful than either ganja or marihuana. The comparison of hashish and marihuana is like that between
pure alcohol and beer. Lurid accounts of the psychological effects
and dangers of hemp are often based upon observations made by
and upon hashish users. The mixture smoked as marihuana ordinarily
contains very small quantities of the drug and its effects are correspondingly less spectacular, less dangerous, and less harmful than those
of hashish.[1]

The medical use of *cannabis indica* has declined in Western medicine but it is still extensively used in the Ayurvedic and Unani systems of indigenous medicine in India. In various parts of the world
folk beliefs attribute great therapeutic and even divine virtues to the
drug. In Jamaica it is known to many persons of the lower classes as
"the wisdom weed" and it is alleged that it stimulates good qualities
in the person who uses it and brings him closer to God. The use of
ganja there is supported by references to various Biblical passages
which recommend the "herbs of the field." The same passages, inci-
dentally, are taken by the devotes of peyote (a cactus containing
mescaline) to refer to that plant. A back-to-Africa protest cult in
Jamaica, known as the Ras Tafari, has adopted ganja as a symbol of
the movement and its members sometimes refer to themselves as the
"herb men." In defiance of the Government, members of this cult,
and others who are simply impressed by the fact that ganja is a more
profitable crop than any other, grow and harvest the plant and use
some of it themselves. Ganja tea is regarded as a prime ameliorative
agent in the folk treatment of many diseases including asthma, tu-

[1] For general discussions of marihuana see: Robert P. Walton, *Marihuana: America's New Drug Problem* (Philadelphia: Lippincott, 1938), and Norman Taylor,
Flight from Reality (New York: Duell, Sloan and Pearce, 1949).

berculosis, venereal disease, and many others, especially all types of respiratory ailments. Ganja cigarettes are extensively used by the workers in the sugar cane fields and some foremen of the sugar producing companies state that, were it not for ganja, they would have difficulty finding workingmen to harvest their crops.[2]

On the book jacket of Professor Robert P. Walton's 1938 book entitled, *Marihuana: America's New Drug Problem*, Frederick T. Merrill and Mr. Anslinger are quoted.[3] The latter observed: "It is a new peril—in some ways the worst we have met, and it concerns us all." Merrill was even more emphatic and alarmed: "If the abuse of this narcotic drug is not stamped out at once, the cost in crime waves, wasted human lives, and insanity will be enormous." Quoting Walton, Merrill notes that marihuana often produces "uncontrollable irritability and violent rages, which in most advanced forms cause assault and murder." He continues: "Amnesia often occurs, and the mania is frequently so acute that the heavy smoker becomes temporarily insane. Most authorities agree that permanent insanity can result from continual over-indulgence." Marihuana has had no noticeable effect in increasing the population of our mental institutions and whatever crimes of violence it may instigate are as nothing when compared to those that are linked with the use of alcohol.

Norman Taylor notes that the hemp plant, called *Cannabis sativa* by Linnaeus in the eighteenth century, probably originated in Central Asia or in China, where it was described in a book on pharmacy written by one Shen Nung nearly three thousand years before the birth of Christ.[4] The euphoric potential of the resinous female plant was known then and troubled Chinese moralists, who called it the "Liberator of Sin." Nung, however, recommended the medicine from this plant for "female weakness, gout, rheumatism, malaria, beri-beri, constipation and absent-mindedness." From China the use of hemp spread westward to India, to the Middle East, and along both sides of the Mediterranean, and ultimately reached Europe and the Western hemisphere. Nowhere has its use been eradicated, even after thousands of years of effort in some instances. Recent publica-

---

[2] From observations and interviews with Jamaicans by the writer during a visit to that island.

[3] [Merrill wrote a book on *Japan and the Opium Menace* (1942). Harry J. Anslinger was U.S. Commissioner of Narcotics from 1930 to 1962. P. C.]

[4] N. Taylor, *Flight from Reality*, p. 27.

tions of the United Nations comment on the apparent continued spread of the practice.

The evil reputation of hemp was enhanced when, during the eleventh century, it became linked with a cult headed by one Hasan which initiated a new political tactic of secret assassination to cleanse the Moslem world of false prophets. Hasan's full name was Hashishin and he was called the Old Man of the Mountain. The terms *hashish* and *assassin* are linked with the name of *Hasan* and his cult.

USE BY LOWER CLASSES

It is possible that the bad reputation of marihuana and other forms of this drug reflects in part the bias of upper classes against an indulgence of the lower strata. Since hemp grows luxuriantly without cultivation in many parts of the world, it is available to many of its devotees at extremely low cost—in India, for example, at about one-twentieth the price of good quality whiskey in 1894, when the English carried out an extensive inquiry into the subject.[5] Denunciations of the weed come characteristically from persons of those classes which prefer whiskey, rum, gin, and other alcoholic beverages and who do not themselves use marihuana. Such persons, overlooking the well-known effects of alcohol, commonly deplore the effects of hemp upon the lower classes and often believe that it produces murder, rape, violence, and insanity.

Despite the prevalence of these beliefs among the drinkers of rum and whiskey and the upper classes generally, impartial investigations invariably have shown no such results. The moderate use of hemp, according to the Indian Hemp Drug Commission in 1894, does not produce significant mental or moral injuries, does not lead to disease, nor does it necessarily or even usually lead to excess any more than alcohol does. Excess, the Commission said, is confined to the idle and dissipated.[6] Many years later in New York City similar conclusions were stated on the basis of experimental study and from an

[5] *Report of the Indian Hemp Drug Commission* (7 vols.; Simla, India, 1894), cited by N. Taylor, *Flight from Reality*, p. 34.

[6] N. Taylor, *Flight from Reality*, pp. 34–35.

examination of violent crimes committed in that city over a period of years.[7]

In Jamaica, where the lower classes regard the drug with favor, persons of high social status commonly assert that ganja is a potent cause of much of the personal violence which is relatively frequent there among the working classes. This is staunchly denied by the ganja users, who contend that the effects are usually in the opposite direction but admit that ganja may bring out the evil in some persons who are already evil. Police examination of violent crimes in Jamaica suggest that ganja has little connection with them and that they arise rather from sexual jealousy and the highly informal manner in which sexual matters are arranged on that island among the simpler people of the lower classes.

MARIHUANA AND ALCOHOL

In general, virtually all of the charges that are made against marihuana tend to shrink or dissolve entirely when they are closely examined by impartial investigators. The present tendency of the rank-and-file policeman, despite the enormous penalties attached to handling marihuana, is to regard it as a minor problem hardly deserving serious attention except for those who handle the weed in large amounts for mercenary purposes or who promote its use among the uninitiated.

Ironically, the accusations that are leveled at marihuana are all applicable to alcohol, as has been demonstrated by innumerable investigations. These studies indicate that much murder, rape, and homicide is committed by persons under the influence. The special psychoses and ailments of alcoholics are numerous and well delineated in countless scientific and literary productions. The menace of the drinking driver of automobiles is well understood by all and is more or less accepted as one of the inevitable hazards of life in the modern world. It is well known, too, that the manufacturers of alcoholic beverages advertise their products and seek to enlarge their markets and that the use of alcohol spreads from those who already

[7] *The Marihuana Problem in the City of New York: Sociological, Medical, Psychological and Pharmacological Studies* by the Mayor's Committee on Marihuana, George B. Wallace, Chairman (Lancaster, Pa.: Jaques Cattell Press, 1945).

have the practice to those who do not. Why, then, so much excitement about marihuana? It is said that marihuana sometimes causes girls and women to lose their virtue and innocence, but the role of alcohol in this respect is infinitely more important. It seems inconsistent, therefore, that while the decision to drink or not to drink is viewed as a personal moral decision, the use of marihuana should be viewed as a heinous crime subject to long prison sentences.

Among those who have never used hemp or seen it used by others the belief is often found that marihuana acts as a sexual stimulant or aphrodisiac. Actually its effects, like those of opiates, are in exactly the opposite direction, tending to cause the user to lose interest in the opposite sex. Users more frequently than not report the absence of ideas of sex or say that Venus herself could not tempt them when they are under the influence of this drug.

THE EFFECTS OF ANTI-MARIHUANA LEGISLATION

In 1937 the Congress passed a Marihuana Tax Act, modeled after the Harrison Act. It was designed to curb the use of marihuana by the use of the federal police power, and like the Harrison Act imposed penalties upon both buyers and sellers. This Act was the result of a publicity campaign staged by the Federal Bureau of Narcotics under Mr. Anslinger's direction and leadership. The bill was passed with little discussion after brief hearings on the ground that marihuana was a highly dangerous drug inciting its users to commit crimes of violence and often leading to insanity.[8]

The beliefs concerning marihuana which led to this legislation may be represented in a pure and extreme form by turning to the writing of a hyperactive reformer and alarmist of the period, Earle Albert Rowell.[9] He claimed in 1939 that he had spent fourteen years

---

[8] See *Taxation of Marihuana:* Hearings before the Committee on Ways and Means, U.S. House of Representatives, 75th Cong., 1st sess., April and May, 1937 (hereafter called *House Marihuana Hearings, 1937*); and *Taxation of Marihuana:* Hearings before a Subcommittee of the Committee on Finance, U.S. Senate, 75th Cong., 1st sess., on H.R. 6906 (hereafter called *Senate Marihuana Hearings, 1937*).

[9] Earle Albert Rowell and Robert Rowell, *On the Trail of Marihuana, the Weed of Madness* (Mountain View, Cal.: Pacific Press Publishing Association, 1939). See also Earle Albert Rowell, *Dope: Adventures of David Dare* (Nashville, Tenn.: Southern Publishing Association, 1937).

campaigning against this weed, delivering more than four thousand lectures in forty states and personally pulling up and destroying many flourishing hemp fields. Mr. Rowell's zealous opposition to marihuana was only slightly less intense than his disapproval of alcohol and tobacco. The use of tobacco, he correctly observed, invariably precedes the smoking of the deadly reefer. Mr. Rowell came into disfavor with the Bureau of Narcotics around 1938 and this agency spent considerable energy and manpower in an attempt to silence and discredit him. This may have been because of Mr. Rowell's view that opiate addiction is a disease or perhaps because of his repeated allegations that the police were not sufficiently diligent in destroying marihuana.

Mr. Rowell summarized the effects of marihuana as follows:

> We know that marihuana—
> 1. Destroys will power, making a jellyfish of the user. He cannot say no.
> 2. Eliminates the line between right and wrong, and substitutes one's own warped desires or the base suggestions of others as the standard of right.
> 3. Above all, causes crimes; fills the victim with an irrepressible urge to violence.
> 4. Incites to revolting immoralities, including rape and murder.
> 5. Causes many accidents both industrial and automobile.
> 6. Ruins careers forever.
> 7. Causes insanity as its speciality.
> 8. *Either in self-defense or as a means of revenue, users make smokers of others, thus perpetuating evil.* [Italics in original.] [10]

In 1939 when Rowell published his book, marihuana was regarded as a relatively new drug menace in the United States. Mr. Rowell thought that he had already detected an increase of the population of mental hospitals because of it:

> Asylums and mental hospitals in this country are beginning to see and feel the influence of marihuana, and are awaking to its deleterious effects on the brain. As we traveled through the various states, superintendents of these institutions told us of cases of insanity resulting from marihuana.[11]

---

[10] E. A. Rowell and R. Rowell, *On the Trail of Marihuana*, p. 33.
[11] *Ibid.*, p. 51.

"The baleful mental effects of marihuana," he said, "begin soon after the first reefer is smoked. . . ."[12]

When Mr. Anslinger appeared before the Senate subcommittee which was investigating the illicit drug traffic in 1955 under the guidance of Senator Price Daniel, there were only a few offhand discussions of marihuana. Mr. Anslinger observed that the Bureau in its national survey was "trying to keep away from the marihuana addict, because he is not a true addict." The real problem, he said, was the heroin addict. Senator Daniel thereupon remarked:

> Now, do I understand it from you that, while we are discussing marihuana, the real danger there is that the use of marihuana leads many people eventually to the use of heroin, and the drugs that do cause complete addiction; is that true? [13]

Mr. Anslinger agreed:

> That is the great problem and our great concern about the use of marihuana, that eventually if used over a long period, it does lead to heroin addiction.[14]

Senators Welker and Daniel pursued the subject, and Mr. Anslinger, when prompted, agreed that marihuana was dangerous. Senator Welker finally asked this question:

> Is it or is it not a fact that the marihuana user has been responsible for many of our most sadistic, terrible crimes in this nation, such as sex slayings, sadistic slayings, and matters of that kind?

Mr. Anslinger hedged:

> There have been instances of that, Senator. We have had some rather tragic occurrences by users of marihuana. It does not follow that all crime can be traced to marihuana. There have been many brutal crimes traced to marihuana, but I would not say that it is a controlling factor in the commission of crimes.[15]

[12] Ibid.
[13] Daniel Subcommittee Hearings, Part 5, 1955, p. 16.
[14] Ibid.
[15] Ibid., p. 18.

Eighteen years earlier, in 1937, the year in which the federal anti-marihuana law was passed, Mr. Anslinger had presented a very different picture of marihuana. Prior to 1937 Mr. Anslinger and the Bureau of Narcotics had spearheaded a propaganda campaign against marihuana on the ground that it produced an immense amount of violent crime such as rape, mayhem, and murder, and that many traffic accidents could be attributed to it. During the 1937 hearings before a House subcommittee, Representative John Dingell of Michigan asked Mr. Anslinger: "I am just wondering whether the marihuana addict graduates into a heroin, an opium, or a cocaine user."

Mr. Anslinger replied: "No, sir; I have not heard of a case of that kind. I think it is an entirely different class. The marihuana addict does not go in that direction." [16]

A few months later in the same year, before a Senate subcommittee which was considering the antimarihuana law which the Bureau of Narcotics had asked for, Mr. Anslinger commented: "There is an entirely new class of people using marihuana. The opium user is around 35 to 40 years old. These users are 20 years old and know nothing of heroin or morphine." [17]

The theme stated by the Commissioner of Narcotics in 1955, that the main threat in marihuana is that it leads to the use of heroin, is now ordinarily cited as the principal justification for applying to it the same severe penalties that are applied in the case of heroin. Reformer Rowell in 1939 was more logical and consistent than either the Senators or the Commissioner when he emphasized that cigarette smoking invariably preceded reefer smoking. Mr. Rowell told of a shrewd gangster whom he engaged in what now appears as a prophetic discussion of the prospects of the dope industry.[18]

The gangster remarked: "Marihuana is the coming thing."

"But," I protested in surprise, "marihuana is not a habit-forming drug like morphine or heroin; and, besides, it's too cheap to bother with."

He laughed. "You don't understand. Laws are being passed now by various states against it, and soon Uncle Sam will put a ban on it. The price will then go up, and that will make it profitable for us to handle."

[16] House Marihuana Hearings, 1937, p. 24.

[17] Senate Marihuana Hearings, 1937, pp. 14–15.

[18] E. A. Rowell and R. Rowell, On the Trail of Marihuana, pp. 69–74.

The gangster, according to Mr. Rowell, then commented on the shrewd manner in which the tobacco companies had popularized cigarettes among the soldiers of the First World War and on the enormous increase in cigarette consumption by young persons. He grew eloquent: "Every cigarette smoker is a prospect for the dope ring via the marihuana road. Millions of boys and girls now smoke. Think of the unlimited new market!"

Mr. Rowell got the idea and commented as follows to his readers:

Slowly, insidiously, for over three hundred years, Lady Nicotine was setting the stage for a grand climax. The long years of tobacco using were but an introduction and training for marihuana use. Tobacco, which was first smoked in a pipe, then as a cigar, and at last as a cigarette, demanded more and more of itself until its supposed pleasures palled, and some of the tobacco victims looked about for something stronger. Tobacco was no longer potent enough.

Mr. Rowell was not optimistic about the future:

Marihuana will continue to be a problem for both police and educators, because it is so easy to grow, to manufacture, and to peddle, and is such a quick source of easy money. The plant can be grown anywhere; it can be harvested secretly, prepared in twenty-four hours without a penny of investment for equipment; and every cigarette user is a prospect. As our laws are enforced and the weed becomes scarcer, the price will rise, and greater profit accrue to venturesome and successful peddlers. Whereas now it is usually peddled by lone wolves, as soon as the weed becomes scarcer and the price rises, organized crime will step in and establish a monopoly.[19]

While Mr. Rowell, in the manner of reforming alarmists, exaggerated the evil with which he was preoccupied, the above appraisal of the effects of the Marihuana Tax Act has been reasonably well borne out by subsequent events. Certainly it was a more realistic assessment of the law's effects than any that were made by the legislators who passed the bill or by the officials who promoted it. Mr. Rowell was also completely right in pointing out that virtually every marihuana smoker graduated to this practice from cigarette smoking. His gangster informant was correct in his calculation that state and federal laws prohibiting marihuana would make the weed more

[19] *Ibid.*, pp. 88–89.

expensive and more profitable for peddlers to handle, and also correctly foresaw that with the same merchants handling both marihuana and heroin it would become a simple matter for marihuana users to switch from the less to the more dangerous drug, as they have done.

In the United States during the nineteenth century, and the early decades of the twentieth, addiction to opiates frequently developed from the abuse of alcohol. This still occurs to some extent and is frequently reported from other parts of the world, for morphine provides a potent means of relieving the alcoholic hangover. An American doctor once advocated as a cure of alcoholism that alcohol addicts be deliberately addicted to morphine, arguing with considerable plausibility that of the two habits the latter was obviously the lesser evil.[20] Moreover, he practiced what he preached and recommended his technique with considerable enthusiasm for use by others.

The truth of the matter, of course, is that very few cigarette smokers go on to marihuana, very few marihuana users go on to heroin, and very few alcohol users graduate to the use of heroin. Since some barbiturate and amphetamine users progress to heroin it should be added that it is also only a very small proportion who do. If all of these substances were to be prohibited because they are sometimes involved in the progression toward heroin addiction there is little doubt that the illicit traffic in marihuana and heroin would be expanded to include the other offending substances and that the movement from less to more serious habits would be greatly facilitated.

No one, of course, recommends the use of marihuana nor does anyone deny that there are evil effects and consequences associated with using it. The fact that the use of marihuana is outlawed, for example, means that it is often obtained through association with unsavory types, often used in an underworld environment, and the user takes the risk of criminal prosecution. It is also undeniable that marihuana intoxication may sometimes lead to automobile accidents and to irresponsible or criminal acts. The controversy with respect to marihuana is solely concerning the relative prevalence or frequency of such results in comparison to similar consequences following from the use of alcoholic beverages. All empirical investigations indicate that alcohol constitutes a far greater social danger than does marihuana.

[20] J. R. Black, "Advantages of Substituting the Morphia Habit for the Incurably Alcoholic," *Cincinnati Lancet-Clinic*, XXII, n.s. (1889), Part I, 537–41.

MAYOR LAGUARDIA'S COMMITTEE ON MARIHUANA

Mayor LaGuardia's Committee on Marihuana, on the basis of a close examination of the matter in New York City, stressed the relative triviality of the effects of marihuana use in a report published in 1945.[21] In the July 1943 issue of the *Military Surgeon*, the editor, Colonel J. M. Phalen, commented as follows in an editorial on "The Marihuana Bugaboo":

> The smoking of the leaves, flowers and seeds of *Cannabis sativa* is no more harmful than the smoking of tobacco or mullein or sumac leaves. . . . The legislation in relation to marihuana was ill-advised . . . it branded as a menace and a crime a matter of trivial importance. . . . It is hoped that no witch hunt will be instituted in the military service over a problem that does not exist.[22]

Similar statements have been made by many other competent investigators and observers.

On the other hand, as has been pointed out, a sharply divergent view has been presented by law enforcement officials, particularly by the Federal Bureau of Narcotics, and also by many individual writers. The sharp divergence of views among the scientifically oriented evidently depends upon the manner in which the research is done. Investigators who rely on the opinions of high echelon officials, who have no direct acquaintance with the use of marihuana and who base their opinions on anecdotes rather than actual statistical data, usually reach the conclusion that marihuana is a highly dangerous drug which produces much violent crime and insanity. These conclusions, as we have suggested, may be a reflection of upper-class hostility toward an unfamiliar lower-class indulgence. More critical and skeptical investigators, who look for basic statistical evidence, invariably fail to find it and end up writing debunking articles for which they are roundly abused by the moralists.

It is often felt that, even if the dangers of marihuana are exaggerated, these exaggerations and misstatements should be allowed to stand so that they may frighten adolescents away from the drug. The implication that adolescents are influenced to any appreciable degree

---

[21] *The Marihuana Problem in the City of New York.*
[22] Cited by N. Taylor, *Flight from Reality*, p. 36.

by articles appearing in scientific journals is probably absurd. Those who use marihuana probably come to do so on the basis of personal associations and direct observations of their own.

The deliberate circulation of false information is self-defeating in that the adventurous, experimentally inclined youth can quickly discover for himself, by trying the weed or talking to those who have smoked it, that much of the officially circulated view is false. He is then prepared to believe that everything he has been told about narcotics is equally wrong.

When Mayor LaGuardia's Committee on Marihuana made its report, it was strongly attacked by those committed to a belief in the marihuana menace. The *Journal of the American Medical Association* in 1943 published a letter from Mr. Anslinger in which he criticized an article by Drs. Allentuck and Bowman on findings derived from the New York study in which they had participated.[23] There were rumors that the New York marihuana study was to be suppressed, but after considerable delay, it was ultimately released in 1945. On April 28, 1945, the *Journal of the American Medical Association* editorially assailed the report, using language and arguments of a type not ordinarily found in learned journals:

> For many years medical scientists have considered cannabis a dangerous drug. Nevertheless, a book called "Marihuana Problems" by the New York City Mayor's Committee on Marihuana submits an analysis by seventeen doctors of tests on 77 prisoners and, on this narrow and thoroughly unscientific foundation, draws sweeping and inadequate conclusions which minimize the harmfulness of marihuana. Already the book has done harm. One investigator has described some tearful parents who brought their 16 year old son to a physician after he had been detected in the act of smoking marihuana. A noticeable mental deterioration had been evident for some time even to their lay minds. The boy said he had read an account of the LaGuardia Committee report and that this was his justification for using marihuana. He read in *Down Beat*, a musical journal, an analysis of this report under the caption "Light Up, Gates, Report Finds Tea a Good Kick."
> A criminal lawyer for marihuana drug peddlers has already used the LaGuardia report as a basis to have defendants set free by the court. . . .
> The book states unqualifiedly to the public that the use of this narcotic does not lead to physical, mental or moral degeneration and that

[23] *J.A.M.A.*, 121, No. 3 (Jan. 16, 1943), 212–13.

permanent deleterious effects from its continued use were not observed on 77 prisoners. This statement has already done great damage to the cause of law enforcement. Public officials will do well to disregard this unscientific, uncritical study, and continue to regard marihuana as a menace wherever it is purveyed.[24]

Despite the fact that this editorial continues to be cited and reproduced to discredit the New York study, the conclusions of the report enjoy considerable status and are undoubtedly far closer to the realities of the situation than is the view represented by the A.M.A. editorial. Indeed, if one judges the law enforcement agencies by their actions rather than their words, it appears that even the police, to a considerable extent, have swung over to the viewpoint of the Mayor's Committee.

MARIHUANA ARRESTS

After 1951 the budget and field force of the Federal Bureau of Narcotics were substantially enlarged. Nevertheless, the number of marihuana arrests has steadily declined and by 1960 it was close to the vanishing point, with only 169 such cases. In previous years the numbers of federal marihuana violations were reported as follows: [25]

1952	1,288
1954	508
1956	403
1958	179

Of the 169 federal marihuana violations reported in 1960, 88 occurred in California, 16 in Maryland, and 13 in Kentucky. No other state had as many as ten, and no violations were reported from 28 states. We have already noted that the Bureau does not bother to count marihuana users in its national survey of addiction and does not regard marihuana as an addicting drug. The above figures on enforcement suggest that, at the federal level at least, the marihuana laws are being largely ignored since it is not claimed that the use of marihuana is diminishing.

[24] *J.A.M.A.*, 127, No. 17 (April 28, 1945), 1129.
[25] From the annual reports of the Bureau of Narcotics for the years indicated. In 1962 the number of marihuana cases was 242. (*Traffic in Opium and Other Dangerous Drugs*, 1962, p. 62.)

Statistics on marihuana prosecutions as such are extremely difficult to obtain and data that are available are very unreliable and incomplete. The Federal Narcotics Bureau presented to the Daniel Subcommittee a summary of marihuana prosecutions for the year 1954, giving both federal and nonfederal cases. It is not claimed that the

Marihuana Arrests—Federal and Local by States—1954[26]

State	Arrests Federal	Arrests Local	State	Arrests Federal	Arrests Local
Alabama	2	6	New Hampshire	0	0
Arizona	25	4	New Jersey	5	26
Arkansas	2	0	New Mexico	23	10
California	51	1,101	New York	5	407
Colorado	28	1	North Carolina	0	0
Connecticut	2	6	North Dakota	0	0
Delaware	0	1	Ohio	25	23
District of			Oklahoma	2	13
Columbia	3	17	Oregon	1	8
Florida	4	30	Pennsylvania	3	50
Georgia	4	1	Rhode Island	0	0
Idaho	0	2	South Carolina	4	0
Illinois	13	327	South Dakota	0	0
Indiana	0	14	Tennessee	11	1
Iowa	0	8	Texas	325	612
Kansas	2	0	Utah	4	0
Kentucky	39	8	Vermont	0	0
Louisiana	17	105	Virginia	0	1
Maine	0	0	Washington	22	10
Maryland	2	30	West Virginia	0	0
Massachusetts	5	1	Wisconsin	0	47
Michigan	30	270	Wyoming	4	0
Minnesota	0	5	Alaska	5	0
Mississippi	0	1	Hawaii	14	23
Missouri	9	15			
Montana	0	6	Totals	713	3,205
Nebraska	1	13			
Nevada	16	2	Grand Total		3,918

[26] *Daniel Subcommittee Hearings*, 1955, pp. 267–71, exhibit 7. Note the unexplained discrepancy between the federal total given here and that of the preceding citation.

latter are complete; they are merely figures from some of the main cities in the indicated states.

From this table it will be seen that 3,263 of the total of 3,918 arrests were made in the six states of California, Texas, Illinois, Michigan, New York, and Louisiana. These states are, in one way or another, centers of the marihuana traffic. High arrest rates in California, Texas, and Louisana no doubt arise from the fact that considerable quantities of marihuana are smuggled into the country there from Mexico and the Caribbean area. The rates in Illinois, Michigan, and New York reflect mainly police activity in the three large cities of Detroit, Chicago, and New York, all of them narcotics distribution centers. Heroin arrests are also highest in the states of California, New York, Illinois, and Michigan, while Texas and Louisana are farther down on the list.

The penalty provisions applicable to marihuana users under state and federal law are about the same as those applied to heroin users. These penalties are entirely disproportionate to the seriousness of the offending behavior and lead to gross injustice and undesirable social consequences. For example, it is well known that many jazz musicians and other generally inoffensive persons use or have used marihuana. To send these persons to jail is absurd and harmful and serves no conceivable useful purpose. The moderate or occasional marihuana user is not a significant social menace. Jails and prisons, chronically overcrowded, should be used for those who present a genuine threat to life and property. The absurdity is compounded when an occasional judge, ignorant of the nature of marihuana, sends a marihuana user to prison to cure him of his nonexistent addiction. The writer was once in court when a middle-aged Negro defendant appeared before the judge charged with having used and had in his possession one marihuana cigarette during the noon hour at the place where he had worked for a number of years. This man had no previous criminal record and this fact was stated before the court. Nevertheless, a two-year sentence was imposed to "dry up his habit."

The President's Advisory Commission which reported on narcotic and drug abuse in 1963 took cognizance of the relatively trivial nature of the marihuana evil by suggesting that all mandatory sentences be eliminated for crimes involving it and that judges be granted full discretionary power in dealing with offenders.[27] These sugges-

[27] *Final Report:* The President's Advisory Commission on Narcotic and Drug Abuse, p. 42.

tions are excessively timid and not entirely logical, for there is no good reason why a mere user of marihuana should be subjected to a jail sentence at all. The marihuana user probably ought to be dealt with by the law along the same lines that are used with persons who drink alcohol.

If it is deemed in the public interest to punish smokers of marihuana, such punishments should ordinarily consist of fines only, up to some maximum of perhaps $500.00, depending upon the offense and the defendant's ability to pay. These fines might be scaled down or eliminated entirely for persons who provided information concerning their source of supply. Police efforts should be focused primarily on the traffic rather than on the user. Persons driving automobiles under the influence of the drug might be fined and deprived of their driving licenses for a period of time. Crimes which could be shown to the satisfaction of a court of law to be linked with the use of marihuana ought to be dealt with about the way that crimes arising from the use of alcohol are handled.

Laws such as this, with penalties of a reasonable nature, would probably be more effective than those now in effect because they would be more enforceable and more in accord with the nature of the problem being dealt with. They would have the effect of reducing the discrepancy that now exists between the laws as written and the laws as they are actually enforced. A more matter-of-fact and realistic handling of the marihuana problem would also probably reduce the aura of sensationalism which now surrounds the subject and diminish the illicit glamor which is now attached to the hemp plant.

It is argued by some that the marihuana industry should be brought under control by legalization, taxation, licensing, and other devices like those used to control alcohol—and to exploit it as a source of revenue. Advocates of this view might well argue that there should be no unfair discrimination among vices; that if the greater evil of alcohol use is legal, the lesser one of marihuana smoking should be so as well. Since the smoking of marihuana will undoubtedly continue regardless of legislation against it, it can also be argued that it would be better to accept the inevitable than to wage war for a lost cause.

In opposition to this extremely permissive position, the more conservative reformer can call attention to the fact that, outside of a few Asian and African countries, the use of this substance is everywhere disapproved of and subject to legal restrictions. It is possible that legal sanctions exercise some deterrent effect and that without them the use of this drug might spread even more rapidly and assume more virulent forms. Should the use of marihuana become anywhere nearly as widespread as that of alcohol it might be too late to talk of effective restrictions since the users would command too many votes. A legal marihuana or ganja industry which advertised its product and sought to improve it through research and experimentation would be a distinct embarrassment to the nation as a whole as well as being a direct economic threat to the alcoholic beverage industries and possibly to the tobacco industry. A final and decisive argument seems to be that public opinion is not likely in the foreseeable future to accept indulgence in marihuana as an equivalent of, or substitute for, indulgence in alcohol.

The long history of the use of marihuana, the spread of the practice throughout the world in the face of determined and sometimes fanatical opposition, and the persistence of the practice once it is established—all suggest that the smoking of marihuana will continue in the United States for some time to come. The practical question seems to be one of minimizing and controlling the practice while avoiding the extreme tactics of prohibitionists. A comprehensive, impartial public inquiry into the matter, based on the assumption that marihuana is *not* the same as heroin, might help to bring about a more sober and rational approach to an indulgence which merits some concern but which is far less serious than is presently suggested by the harsh inflexibility of current laws.

HARVEY COX

Sex and Secularization

No aspect of human life seethes with so many unexorcised demons as does sex. No human activity is so hexed by superstition, so haunted by residual tribal lore, and so harassed by socially induced fear. Within the breast of urban-secular man, a toe-to-toe struggle still rages between his savage and his bourgeois forebears. Like everything else, the images of sex which informed tribal and town society are expiring along with the eras in which they arose. The erosion of traditional values and the disappearance of accepted modes of behavior have

Sex and Secularization. Reprinted with permission of The Macmillan Company from *The Secular City: Secularization and Urbanization in Theological Perspective* by Harvey Cox. Copyright © Harvey Cox 1965.

left contemporary man free, but somewhat rudderless. Abhorring a vacuum, the mass media have rushed in to supply a new code and a new set of behavioral prototypes. They appeal to the unexorcised demons. Nowhere is the persistence of mythical and metalogical denizens more obvious than in sex, and the shamans of sales do their best to nourish them. Nowhere is the humanization of life more frustrated. Nowhere is a clear word of exorcism more needed.

How is the humanization of sex impeded? First it is thwarted by the parading of cultural-identity images for the sexually dispossessed, to make money. These images become the tyrant gods of the secular society, undercutting its liberation from religion and transforming it into a kind of neotribal culture. Second, the authentic secularization of sex is checkmated by an anxious clinging to the sexual standards of the town, an era so recent and yet so different from ours that simply to transplant its sexual ethos into our situation is to invite hypocrisy of the worst degree.[1]

Let us look first at the spurious sexual models conjured up for our anxious society by the sorcerers of the mass media and the advertising guild. Like all pagan deities, these come in pairs—the god and his consort. For our purposes they are best symbolized by The Playboy and Miss America, the Adonis and Aphrodite of a leisure-consumer society which still seems unready to venture into full postreligious maturity and freedom. The Playboy and Miss America represent The Boy and The Girl. They incorporate a vision of life. They function as religious phenomena and should be exorcised and exposed.

THE RESIDUE OF TRIBALISM

Let us begin with Miss America. In the first century B.C., Lucretius wrote this description of the pageant of Cybele:

> Adorned with emblem and crown . . . she is carried in awe-inspiring state. Tight-stretched tambourines and hollow cymbals thunder all round to the stroke of open hands, hollow pipes stir with Phrygian strain. . . . . She rides in procession through great cities and mutely enriches mortals with a blessing not expressed in words. They strew

[1] [This second aspect of Cox's argument, constituting the second part of his chapter, is not included here. P. C.]

all her path with brass and silver, presenting her with bounteous alms, and scatter over her a snow-shower of roses.[2]

Now compare this with the annual twentieth-century Miss America pageant in Atlantic City, New Jersey. Spotlights probe the dimness like votive tapers, banks of flowers exude their varied aromas, the orchestra blends feminine strings and regal trumpets. There is a hushed moment of tortured suspense, a drumroll, then the climax—a young woman with carefully prescribed anatomical proportions and exemplary "personality" parades serenely with scepter and crown to her throne. At TV sets across the nation throats tighten and eyes moisten. "There she goes, Miss America—" sings the crooner. "There she goes, your ideal." A new queen in America's emerging cult of The Girl has been crowned.

Is it merely illusory or anachronistic to discern in the multiplying pageants of the Miss America, Miss Universe, Miss College Queen type a residuum of the cults of the pre-Christian fertility goddesses? Perhaps, but students of the history of religions have become less prone in recent years to dismiss the possibility that the cultural behavior of modern man may be significantly illuminated by studying it in the perspective of the mythologies of bygone ages. After all, did not Freud initiate a revolution in social science by utilizing the venerable myth of Oedipus to help make sense out of the strange behavior of his Viennese contemporaries? Contemporary man carries with him, like his appendix and his fingernails, vestiges of his tribal and pagan past.

In light of this fertile combination of insights from modern social science and the history of religions, it is no longer possible to see in the Miss America pageant merely an over-publicized prank foisted on us by the advertising industry. It certainly is this, but it is also much more. It represents the mass cultic celebration, complete with a rich variety of ancient ritual embellishments, of the growing place of The Girl in the collective soul of America.

This young woman—though she is no doubt totally ignorant of the fact—symbolizes something beyond herself. She symbolizes The Girl, the primal image, the One behind the many. Just as the Virgin

[2] This is quoted from Lucretius ii, 608f. in T. R. Glover, *The Conflict of Religions in the Early Roman Empire* (Boston: Beacon, 1960), p. 20. It was originally published in 1909 by Methuen & Co. Ltd.

appears in many guises—as our Lady of Lourdes or of Fatima or of Guadalupe—but is always recognizably the Virgin, so with The Girl.

The Girl is also the omnipresent icon of consumer society. Selling beer, she is folksy and jolly. Selling gems, she is chic and distant. But behind her various theophanies she remains recognizably The Girl. In Miss America's glowingly healthy smile, her openly sexual but officially virginal figure, and in the name-brand gadgets around her, she personifies the stunted aspirations and ambivalent fears of her culture. "There she goes, your ideal."

Miss America stands in a long line of queens going back to Isis, Ceres, and Aphrodite. Everything from the elaborate sexual taboos surrounding her person to the symbolic gifts at her coronation hints at her ancient ancestry. But the real proof comes when we find that the function served by The Girl in our culture is just as much a "religious" one as that served by Cybele in hers. The functions are identical—to provide a secure personal "identity" for initiates and to sanctify a particular value structure.

Let us look first at the way in which The Girl confers a kind of identity on her initiates. Simone de Beauvoir says in *The Second Sex* that "no one is *born* a woman." [3] One is merely born a female, and *"becomes* a woman" according to the models and meanings provided by the civilization. During the classical Christian centuries, it might be argued, the Virgin Mary served in part as this model. With the Reformation and especially with the Puritans, the place of Mary within the symbol system of the Protestant countries was reduced or eliminated. There are those who claim that this excision constituted an excess of zeal that greatly impoverished Western culture, an impoverishment from which it has never recovered. Some would even claim that the alleged failure of American novelists to produce a single great heroine (we have no Phaedra, no Anna Karenina) stems from this self-imposed lack of a central feminine ideal.

Without entering into this fascinating discussion, we can certainly be sure that, even within modern American Roman Catholicism, the Virgin Mary provides an identity image for few American girls. Where then do they look for the "model" Simone de Beauvoir convincingly contends they need? For most, the prototype of femininity seen in their mothers, their friends, and in the multitudinous

[3] Simone de Beauvoir, *The Second Sex* (New York: Knopf, 1958; London: Cape), p. 41.

images to which they are exposed on the mass media is what we have called The Girl.

In his significant monograph *Identity and the Life Cycle*, Erik Erikson reminds us that the child's identity is not modeled simply on the parent but on the parent's "super-ego." [4] Thus in seeking to forge her own identity the young girl is led beyond her mother to her mother's ideal image, and it is here that what Freud called "the ideologies of the superego . . . the traditions of the race and the people" become formative. It is here also that The Girl functions, conferring identity on those for whom she is—perhaps never completely consciously—the tangible incarnation of womanhood.

To describe the mechanics of this complex psychological process by which the fledgling American girl participates in the life of The Girl and thus attains a woman's identity would require a thorough description of American adolescence. There is little doubt, however, that such an analysis would reveal certain striking parallels to the "savage" practices by which initiates in the mystery cults shared in the magical life of their god.

For those inured to the process, the tortuous nightly fetish by which the young American female pulls her hair into tight bunches secured by metal clips may bear little resemblance to the incisions made on their arms by certain African tribesmen to make them resemble their totem, the tiger. But to an anthropologist comparing two ways of attempting to resemble the holy one, the only difference might appear to be that with the Africans the torture is over after initiation, while with the American it has to be repeated every night, a luxury only a culture with abundant leisure can afford.

In turning now to an examination of the second function of The Girl—supporting and portraying a value system—a comparison with the role of the Virgin in the twelfth and thirteenth centuries may be helpful. Just as the Virgin exhibited and sustained the ideals of the age that fashioned Chartres Cathedral, as Henry Adams saw, so The Girl symbolizes the values and aspirations of a consumer society. (She is crowned not in the political capital, remember, but in Atlantic City or Miami Beach, centers associated with leisure and consumption.) And she is not entirely incapable of exploitation. If men sometimes sought to buy with gold the Virgin's blessings on their questionable causes, so The Girl now dispenses her charismatic fa-

[4] Erik Erikson, *Identity and the Life Cycle* (New York: International University Press, 1959).

vor on watches, refrigerators, and razor blades—for a price. Though The Girl has built no cathedrals, without her the colossal edifice of mass persuasion would crumble. Her sharply stylized face and figure beckon us from every magazine and TV channel, luring us toward the beatific vision of a consumer's paradise.

The Girl is *not* the Virgin. In fact she is a kind of anti-Madonna. She reverses most of the values traditionally associated with the Virgin—poverty, humility, sacrifice. In startling contrast, particularly, to the biblical portrait of Mary in Luke 1:46-55, The Girl has nothing to do with filling the hungry with "good things," hawking instead an endless proliferation of trivia on TV spot commercials. The Girl exalts the mighty, extols the rich, and brings nothing to the hungry but added despair. So The Girl does buttress and bring into personal focus a value system, such as it is. In both social and psychological terms, The Girl, whether or not she is really a goddess, certainly acts that way.

Perhaps the most ironic element in the rise of the cult of The Girl is that Protestantism has almost completely failed to notice it, while Roman Catholics have at least given some evidence of sensing its significance. In some places, for instance, Catholics are forbidden to participate in beauty pageants, a ruling not entirely inspired by prudery. It is ironic that Protestants have traditionally been most opposed to lady cults while Catholics have managed to assimilate more than one at various points in history.

If we are correct in assuming that The Girl *functions* in many ways as a goddess, then the cult of The Girl demands careful Protestant theological criticism. Anything that functions, even in part, as a god when it is in fact not God, is an idol. When the Reformers and their Puritan offspring criticized the cult of Mary it was not because they were anti-feminist. They opposed anything—man, woman, or beast (or dogma or institution)—that usurped in the slightest the prerogatives that belonged alone to God Almighty. As Max Weber has insisted, when the prophets of Israel railed against fertility cults, they had nothing against fertility. It is not against sexuality but against a cult that protest is needed. Not, as it were, against the beauty but against the pageant.

Thus the Protestant objection to the present cult of The Girl must be based on the realization that The Girl is an *idol*. She functions as the source of value, the giver of personal identity. But the values she mediates and the identity she confers are both spurious.

Like every idol she is ultimately a creation of our own hands and cannot save us. The values she represents as ultimate satisfactions—mechanical comfort, sexual success, unencumbered leisure—have no ultimacy. They lead only to endless upward mobility, competitive consumption, and anxious cynicism. The devilish social insecurities from which she promises to deliver us are, alas, still there, even after we have purified our breaths, our skins, and our armpits by applying her sacred oils. She is a merciless goddess who draws us farther and farther into the net of accelerated ordeals of obeisance. As the queen of commodities in an expanding economy, the fulfillment she promises must always remain just beyond the tips of our fingers.

Why has Protestantism kept its attention obsessively fastened on the development of Mariolatry in Catholicism and not noticed the sinister rise of this vampirelike cult of The Girl in our society? Unfortunately, it is due to the continuing incapacity of theological critics to recognize the religious significance of cultural phenomena outside the formal religious system itself. But the rise of this new cult reminds us that the work of the reformer is never done. Man's mind is indeed—as Luther said—a factory busy making idols. The Girl is a far more pervasive and destructive influence than the Virgin, and it is to her and her omnipresent altars that we should be directing our criticism.

Besides sanctifying a set of phony values, The Girl compounds her noxiousness by maiming her victims in a Procrustean bed of uniformity. This is the empty "identity" she panders. Take the Miss America pageant, for example. Are these virtually indistinguishable specimens of white, middle-class postadolescence really the best we can do? Do they not mirror the ethos of a mass-production society, in which genuine individualism somehow mars the clean, precision-tooled effect? Like their sisters, the finely calibrated Rockettes, these meticulously measured and pretested "beauties" lined up on the Boardwalk bear an ominous similarity to the faceless retinues of goose-steppers and the interchangeable mass exercisers of explicitly totalitarian societies. In short, *who* says this is beauty?

The caricature becomes complete in the Miss Universe contest, when Miss Rhodesia is a blonde, Miss South Africa is white, and Oriental girls with a totally different tradition of feminine beauty are forced to display their thighs and appear in spike heels and Catalina swim suits. Miss Universe is as universal as an American adman's stereotype of what beauty should be.

The truth is that The Girl can*not* bestow the identity she promises. She forces her initiates to torture themselves with starvation diets and beauty-parlor ordeals, but still cannot deliver the satisfactions she holds out. She is young, but what happens when her followers, despite added hours in the boudoir, can no longer appear young? She is happy and smiling and loved. What happens when, despite all the potions and incantations, her disciples still feel the human pangs of rejection and loneliness? Or what about all the girls whose statistics, or "personality" (or color) do not match the authoritative "ideal"?

After all, it is God—not The Girl—who is God. He is the center and source of value. He liberates men and women from the bland uniformity of cultural deities so that they may feast on the luxurious diversity of life He has provided. The identity He confers frees men from all pseudo-identities to be themselves, to fulfill their human destinies regardless whether their faces or figures match some predetermined abstract "ideal." As His gift, sex is freed from both fertility cults and commercial exploitation to become the thoroughly human thing He intended. And since it is one of the last items we have left that is neither prepackaged nor standardized, let us not sacrifice it too hastily on the omnivorous altar of Cybele.

The Playboy, illustrated by the monthly magazine of that name, does for the boys what Miss America does for the girls. Despite accusations to the contrary, the immense popularity of this magazine is not solely attributable to pin-up girls. For sheer nudity its pictorial art cannot compete with such would-be competitors as *Dude* and *Escapade*. *Playboy* appeals to a highly mobile, increasingly affluent group of young readers, mostly between eighteen and thirty, who want much more from their drugstore reading than bosoms and thighs. They need a total image of what it means to be a man. And Mr. Hefner's *Playboy* has no hesitation in telling them.

Why should such a need arise? David Riesman has argued that the responsibility for character formation in our society has shifted from the family to the peer group and to the mass-media peer-group surrogates.[5] Things are changing so rapidly that one who is equipped by his family with inflexible, highly internalized values becomes unable to deal with the accelerated pace of change and with the varying

[5] David Riesman, *The Lonely Crowd* (New Haven: Yale University Press, 1950; Harmondsworth, Middlesex: Penguin).

contexts in which he is called upon to function. This is especially true in the area of consumer values toward which the "other-directed person" is increasingly oriented.

Within the confusing plethora of mass media signals and peer-group values, *Playboy* fills a special need. For the insecure young man with newly acquired free time and money who still feels uncertain about his consumer skills, *Playboy* supplies a comprehensive and authoritative guidebook to this forbidding new world to which he now has access. It tells him not only who to be; it tells him *how* to be it, and even provides consolation outlets for those who secretly feel that they have not quite made it.

In supplying for the other-directed consumer of leisure both the normative identity image and the means for achieving it, *Playboy* relies on a careful integration of copy and advertising material. The comic book that appeals to a younger generation with an analogous problem skillfully intersperses illustrations of incredibly muscled men and excessively mammalian women with advertisements for body-building gimmicks and foam-rubber brassière supplements. Thus the thin-chested comic-book readers of both sexes are thoughtfully supplied with both the ends and the means for attaining a spurious brand of maturity. *Playboy* merely continues the comic-book tactic for the next age group. Since within every identity crisis, whether in teens or twenties, there is usually a sexual-identity problem, *Playboy* speaks to those who desperately want to know what it means to be a man, and more specifically a *male*, in today's world.

Both the image of man and the means for its attainment exhibit a remarkable consistency in *Playboy*. The skilled consumer is cool and unruffled. He savors sports cars, liquor, high fidelity, and book-club selections with a casual, unhurried aplomb. Though he must certainly *have* and *use* the latest consumption item, he must not permit himself to get too attached to it. The style will change and he must always be ready to adjust. His persistent anxiety that he may mix a drink incorrectly, enjoy a jazz group that is passé, or wear last year's necktie style is comforted by an authoritative tone in *Playboy* beside which papal encyclicals sound irresolute.

"Don't hesitate," he is told, "this assertive, self-assured weskit is what every man of taste wants for the fall season." Lingering doubts about his masculinity are extirpated by the firm assurance that "real men demand this ruggedly masculine smoke" (cigar ad). Though "the ladies will swoon for you, no matter what they promise, don't give them a puff. This cigar is for men only." A fur-lined canvas field jacket is described as "the most masculine thing since the cave man." What to be and how to be it are both made unambiguously clear.

Since being a male necessitates some kind of relationship to females, *Playboy* fearlessly confronts this problem too, and solves it by the consistent application of the same formula. Sex becomes one of the items of leisure activity that the knowledgeable consumer of leisure handles with his characteristic skill and detachment. The girl becomes a desirable—indeed an indispensable—"Playboy accessory."

In a question-answering column entitled "The Playboy Adviser," queries about smoking equipment (how to break in a meerschaum pipe), cocktail preparation (how to mix a Yellow Fever), and whether or not to wear suspenders with a vest alternate with questions about what to do with girls who complicate the cardinal principle of casualness either by suggesting marriage or by some other impulsive gesture toward a permanent relationship. The infallible answer from the oracle never varies: sex must be contained, at all costs, within the entertainment-recreation area. Don't let her get "serious."

After all, the most famous feature of the magazine is its monthly fold-out photo of a *play*mate. She is the symbol par excellence of recreational sex. When playtime is over, the playmate's function ceases, so she must be made to understand the rules of the game. As the crew-cut young man in a *Playboy* cartoon says to the rumpled and disarrayed girl he is passionately embracing, "Why speak of love at a time like this?"

The magazine's fiction purveys the same kind of severely departmentalized sex. Although the editors have recently dressed up the *Playboy* contents with contributions by Hemingway, Bemelmans, and even a Chekhov translation, the regular run of stories relies on a repetitious and predictable formula. A successful young man, either single or somewhat less than ideally married—a figure with whom readers have no difficulty identifying—encounters a gorgeous and seductive woman who makes no demands on him except sex. She is the prose duplication of the cool-eyed but hot-blooded playmate of the fold-out.

Drawing heavily on the fantasy life of all young Americans, the writers utilize for their stereotyped heroines the hero's schoolteacher, his secretary, an old girl friend, or the girl who brings her car into the

garage where he works. The happy issue is always a casual but satis-
fying sexual experience with no entangling alliances whatever. Unlike the women he knows in real life, the Playboy reader's fictional
girl friends know their place and ask for nothing more. They present
no danger of permanent involvement. Like any good accessory, they
are detachable and disposable.

Many of the advertisements reinforce the sex-accessory identification in another way—by attributing female characteristics to the
items they sell. Thus a full-page ad for the MG assures us that this
car is not only "the smoothest pleasure machine" on the road and
that having one is a "love-affair," but most important, "you drive it
—it doesn't drive you." The ad ends with the equivocal question
"Is it a date?" [6]

Playboy insists that its message is one of liberation. Its gospel
frees us from captivity to the puritanical "hatpin brigade." It solemnly crusades for "frankness" and publishes scores of letters con-
gratulating it for its unblushing "candor." Yet the whole phenomenon of which Playboy is only a part vividly illustrates the awful fact
of a new kind of tyranny.

Those liberated by technology and increased prosperity to new
worlds of leisure now become the anxious slaves of dictatorial taste-
makers. Obsequiously waiting for the latest signal on what is cool
and what is awkward, they are paralyzed by the fear that they may
hear pronounced on them that dread sentence occasionally intoned
by "The Playboy Adviser": "You goofed!" Leisure is thus swallowed
up in apprehensive competitiveness, its liberating potential transformed into a self-destructive compulsion to consume only what is
à la mode. Playboy mediates the Word of the most high into one section of the consumer world, but it is a word of bondage, not of freedom.

Nor will Playboy's synthetic doctrine of man stand the test of
scrutiny. Psychoanalysts constantly remind us how deep-seated sexuality is in the human being. But if they didn't remind us, we would
soon discover it ourselves anyway. Much as the human male might
like to terminate his relationship with a woman as he would snap
off the stereo, or store her for special purposes like a camel's-hair jacket,

---

[6] This whole fusing of sex and machine symbols in contemporary mass media was
once brilliantly explored by Marshall McLuhan in The Mechanical Bride, now
out of print.

it really can't be done. And anyone with a modicum of experience with women knows it can't be done. Perhaps this is the reason *Playboy*'s readership drops off so sharply after the age of thirty.

Playboy really feeds on the existence of a repressed fear of involvement with women, which for various reasons is still present in many otherwise adult Americans. So *Playboy*'s version of sexuality grows increasingly irrelevant as authentic sexual maturity is achieved.

The male identity crisis to which *Playboy* speaks has at its roots a deep-set fear of sex, a fear that is uncomfortably combined with fascination. *Playboy* strives to resolve this antinomy by reducing the proportions of sexuality, its power and its passion, to a packageable consumption item. Thus in *Playboy*'s iconography the nude woman symbolizes total sexual accessibility but demands nothing from the observer. "You drive—it doesn't drive you." The terror of sex, which cannot be separated from its ecstasy, is dissolved. But this futile attempt to reduce the *mysterium tremendum* of the sexual fails to solve the problem of being a man. For sexuality is the basic form of all human relationship, and therein lies its terror and its power.

.   .   .

HARVEY SWADOS

Joe, the Vanishing American

If Walter had not been so desperately anxious to go away to college he might never have been able to stick it out those first few weeks at the factory. His father, once district sales manager for a bankrupt sewing-machine concern, had come down in the world and was now a continually uneasy clerk in the branch office of a usury outfit called the Friendly Finance Corporation; his mother, who had borne Walter late in life, clung jealously to the fading prestige conferred on her by her many beneficences on behalf of the Ladies' Guild.

Joe, the Vanishing American. From *On the Line* by Harvey Swados, published by Atlantic-Little, Brown and Co., 1957. Reprinted by permission of Robert Lantz.

Walter had never done anything harder than shovel the neighbors' snowy driveways and sell magazines to reluctant relatives. But the night of his graduation from high school his father grunted in a choked voice that there was no money to send him to college. Walter swore to himself that he would get a college education if he had to rob a bank. At the commencement exercise a classmate had told him that you could get a job at the new auto assembly plant if you said on your application that you had worked as a garage mechanic. While his parents rocked creakily, proud but miserable, on the porch glider, Walter mounted the narrow steps to his little room and sat down at his desk. If he could work steadily at the plant for a year he ought to be able to save several thousand dollars even after contributing his share of the household expenses. Without saying a word to his parents, he went to the plant the following morning and filled out an application blank. Three days later he received a telegram asking him to report for work at six-thirty A.M.

When he returned, gray and exhausted, from his first long day in the body shop to which he had been assigned, Walter found his mother sitting in the parlor and sobbing into a handkerchief. She raised her eyes at the slamming of the door and stared at him in horror.

"Look at you!" she cried, and immediately Walter knew that her first shock was at the way he *looked*, not at how he must have *felt*. Nevertheless Walter felt it his filial duty to explain that he would not have to march past the neighbors in greasy coveralls, but could wear sport clothes to work and change at the plant; furthermore, he hinted, when his mother was preparing his sandwiches for the next day's lunch, he could just as easily carry them in a little paper sack as in a metal lunchbox.

His father, keeping them company in the kitchen, took a different tack, and even blustered a little about the advantages of working for a huge corporation.

"I don't see why Walter couldn't have started with something more pleasant," his mother said plaintively, smoothing mayonnaise across white bread. "In an office he could at least use his brains."

"Don't kid yourself," her husband replied. "There's no shame attached to factory work any more. Besides, Walter has a darned good chance to advance if he shows them the stuff he's got."

Implicit in all this was his parents' fear that Walter had started down a dead-end street, and their own shame at not having been able to send him away to college. Anxious not to inflame their feelings, Walter refrained from defending his decision; even if he were only to point out that he would be making big money, it would be a direct insult to his father, who at fifty-nine was making only five dollars a week more than his son. So he put the case negatively.

"There's just no place else around," he said, "that would pay me anything like what I'm going to be making at the auto plant."

"The boy is right, mother," his father said decisively, much to Walter's satisfaction. "You're doing the smart thing, Walter."

Thus challenged at home, Walter had no alternative but to grit his teeth and swear to himself that nothing would make him quit until he had reached his goal. Like a groggy but game boxer, he measured out his future not with the end of the fight in view, for that would have been too far away, but rather in terms of more immediate accomplishments: his first automatic nickel raise at the end of four weeks, his second automatic nickel raise at the end of eight weeks, his acceptance as a permanent employee at the end of ninety days, and most of all his listing as a metal-finisher, which would mean that he would be in the highest-paid group in the plant and that he would be recognized as a skilled worker, a man who had made the grade.

His surroundings meant nothing to Walter, who had not expected that the factory would look like an art gallery; but the work, and the conditions under which he had to do it, were a nightmare of endless horror from which Walter sometimes thought, stumbling wearily out of the plant after ten hours of unremitting anguish, he would one day awaken with a scream. It was not simply that the idea of working on an endless succession of auto bodies as they came slowly but ineluctably rolling down the assembly line like so many faceless steel robots was both monotonous and stupefying, or that the heavy work of finding bumps and dents in them, knocking them out and filing them down, was in itself too exhausting.

No, it was the strain of having to work both fast and accurately, with the foreman standing over him and glaring through his thick-lensed glasses, that made Walter dread the beginning of each day. Under the best of conditions, he figured, he had three and a half minutes to complete his metal-finishing work from the time he started a job on his line to the time it reached the platform and was swung off on hooks toward the bonderizing booth. If he began at the very beginning, as soon as the inspector had indicated bad spots with a stump of chalk, circling hollows and x-ing high spots, he could finish

before the job reached the final inspector at the far end of the line—
unless the dents were too deep or too numerous, in which case he
was still madly pounding and filing, squatting and straining with the
sweat running down his temples and his cheekbones while the solder-
flower worked next to him in a tangle of rubber hose, melting lead
and a blazing gun with a flame so hot that it scorched dry the running sweat on his face, and the final inspector stood over him, im-
perturbably chalking newly discovered hollows and pimples in the in-
furiating metal. Then he would straighten up from his hopeless effort
and with a despairing glance at the impassive pick-up man, who had
to finish what he had left undone, he would hurry back down the
line, praying to dear God that the next car—he did every third one—
would be in fairly decent condition.

Worst of all were the times when he would hear a piercing whistle
and would look up from the damnable dent at which he had been
rapping blindly with the point of his file, to see Buster the foreman all
the way past the platform, waving angrily with his cigar. Hurrying
from his unfinished work to his punishment, Walter would try to
steel himself against what he knew was coming, but it was no use.

"You call yourself a metal man?" Buster would ask, stuffing the
cigar between his teeth with an angry snap. "You want to get metal-
finisher's pay and you let a job like that go through?" His eyes glinting with rage behind his thick spectacles, Buster would gesticulate at
one of Walter's cars, freshly speckled with chalk marks as it swung
in the air. "Get going on it!"

And Walter would hurl himself at the job, dashing the sweat from
his brow with the back of his gloved hand and filing away in a clumsy
fury.

By the time he had somehow or other repaired what he had left
undone, he would find on hastening back to the line that he was far
behind once again in his regular work, so far behind that it might
take him the better part of an hour to gradually work his way back
on the line to where he really belonged, safe for the moment from
shouted complaints.

Inevitably the men around him had suggestions as to how Walter might better his condition. Of the two other metal-finishers who
worked on the line with him, one was a dour, fattish man, a leader
in the opposition of the local union and disgusted because it did nothing to provide security for probationary employees like Walter.

"I'll tell you something else. There's countries where a bright young hard-working fellow like you, that wants to go to college, doesn't have to waste the best years of his life in factory work just to save the money for college fees. He gets sent right through school and the government foots the bills. All he has to do is show that he's got the stuff and his future is secure."

Walter allowed that this sounded fine, although "having the stuff" sounded uncomfortably like his father's eulogies of life in America, but he could not see what practical good it did him here and now— unless he was supposed to get satisfaction from the bitterness of knowing that in mysterious other countries his opposite numbers were better off than he.

The third metal-finisher, a lean efficient sardonic man, had been listening silently to this talk of free college careers. He put his wiry hand inside his open-necked khaki shirt, scratched the coarse curling hair below his throat, and laughed aloud.

"What's the matter?" asked his fattish colleague suspiciously.

"You think your propaganda's going to change this boy's ideas about the other side of the world when everything here tells him he's got it so good?" He tapped the fat man on the shoulder with the butt end of his file as patronizingly as if he were patting him on the head. "Even if he has to suffer for his education in a way that shouldn't be necessary, he's free. He can blunder around and maybe even learn something that isn't listed in the college catalogues. These poor kids you want him to envy, they may be getting their college for nothing, but they're paying a higher price for it than this fellow ever will. And the sad part is that most of them probably don't even know what the price is." And he turned back to his work without giving the fat man a chance to reply.

Fortunately for the three of them, the fat metal-finisher was transferred. He was only replaced, however, by an intense worker with two vertical wrinkles between his brows, who watched Walter's ineffectual work with growing impatience. At last he could stand it no more.

"In this game, kid, the knack of it is in the speed. The speed," he said fiercely, "and the way you concentrate on the job. If you're going to fumble around and just bitch about your mistakes, you'll be a long time getting straightened out." He greeted his own badly dented job, rolling toward them, with a smile of genuine pleasure.

"Size it up quick, pick out the worst dents, and get going on them right away. Leave the high spots for last—the pick-up men don't mind doing them."

The third man, the gray-haired cynic whom everyone liked but no one seemed to know, had been listening quietly, with a strange, mild grin on his long and youthful face. He put a stick of chewing gum in his mouth, ruminated for a moment, and said: "What you really want is for him to enjoy his work, Orrin. Might be more practical if you'd get down and actually show him how to do it. Here, hold on a minute, Walter."

Walter had been squatting on his haunches before the wheelhousing of his job, blindly pounding with a hammer at his hidden screwdriver, trying hopelessly to punch a hole underneath so that with the screwdriver he could dig out a deep dent as the others did, trying so hopelessly that as he smashed the hammer against his left hand, missing the butt end of the screwdriver, he had to squeeze his eyes to keep the tears from starting forth.

"Give me that screwdriver."

Handing up the tool to the laconic man, Walter noticed for the first time that he bore an unusual tattoo, faded like an old flag, on his right forearm: an American eagle, claws gripping his wrist, beak opened triumphantly at the elbow—you could almost hear it screaming. Without a word the man took the screwdriver and swiftly pressed it to a grinding wheel, fashioning a beveled point.

"Try it now."

Walter stuck the screwdriver under the car, rapped at it smartly several times—bang! it was through and resting against the outer skin of the car, just at the very dent. Gratefully, he turned to the gray-haired man, but he was gone, like a mirage.

There was something mirage-like about him, anyway. He drove to to and from work alone, he never engaged in small talk, he never hung around with a group at lunch hour or before work, he kept a paper book in the hip pocket of his khaki trousers, and always when he was not concentrating on his own work, when he was watching Walter or listening to the others handing him advice, he had that mocking irreligious smile on his long narrow youthful face. What was more, his cold blue eye seemed always to be on Walter, sizing him up, watching not so much his work, as everyone else did, but his temperament and his personality. It made him uncomfortable.

Gradually Walter began to sort out the other men around him, the ones who had more common reality in their talk and their tastes. Most companionable of them all was Kevin, the former rural school teacher, now an immigrant hook-man. His accent was so delightful, his turns of speech so happy, that Walter engaged the towering red-head in conversation at every opportunity.

"Hey, Kevin," he shouted at him one day, "how old were those kids you taught in County Kerry?"

"Ah, Walter," Kevin sighed, showing his long white teeth as he spoke, "they weren't *all* such children. If you were to see some of the older girls—quite well-developed, they were. Oh, how shameful if they had known what was passing through their schoolmaster's mind!"

Kevin laughed at the memory, Walter at the picture the big fellow conjured up of countryside lust; he turned around and there was the gray-haired metal-finisher, smiling too, but so coldly you would have thought him a scientist observing a successful experiment. It was chilling, and yet not wholly unpleasant. In a way that he could not define, Walter felt that he was being judged and approved.

This third man, reserved and anonymous as ever, continued to observe him as Walter chatted not only with Kevin and the second metal-finisher, but with all of the other men on their line. Conversation was necessarily shouted and fragmentary, but Walter was astonished at how intimacies could be revealed in the course of a few phrases:

"A man's a fool to get married."

"Grab the overtime while you can. In the auto industry you never know when you'll be laid off."

"Happiest time of my life was when I was in the army."

"Only reason I'm here is because I was too stupid to learn a trade."

"I came here out of curiosity, but my curiosity's all used up."

"My wife says if I quit I'll have a better chance to line up a construction job."

"Walter, don't turn out like those college men who can tell you how to do everything but can't do a damn thing themselves."

The only one to rebuff Walter's friendly overtures was Pop, the seamy-faced little inspector with a rooster's ruff of yellowing white hair that rose and tumbled down over his forehead, and sunken old lips from which depended miraculously a heavy, unlit cigar. Wizened, pale and bloodless, he regarded Walter, for no apparent reason, with bottomless contempt. With a little cap perched sideways on his Niagara of a head like a precarious canoe, and a soft brown cloth knotted about the hand with which he probed Walter's work for defects and omissions, he seemed to Walter like some strange and hateful gnome.

"Kids like you," he said in a dry and rusty monotone, "they come and go. Twenty-three years I'm here, and I seen a million like you. Not steady, not reliable, don't want to learn, just out for fun. You'll never make a metal man."

I don't want to be a metal man, Walter wanted to reply; I just want to make my money and get out of here. But this was, he knew, just what Pop was goading him to say, so he held his tongue. A moment later he was glad that he had, for he was startled to hear the third metal-finisher address him.

"Pop is an exception," he said, bending over Walter's car and scrubbing at it with his sandpaper as he spoke. "By and large there is a democracy of age in the factory. Men who have been here since before you were born fought for a union contract guaranteeing equal treatment for you. Ninety days after you start you get the same wage as a worker who's been on the job nineteen years. A man twice your age will treat you as a working partner and an adult. Where else is that true?"

"Yes," Walter replied angrily, "but Pop—"

"He's got reason to be bitter. Some day I'll tell you why."

He straightened up abruptly and walked away to his own job. But the words he had used reverberated in Walter's mind. Who was he, with his young-old face and his expressions like "democracy of age"? Walter asked, but no one seemed to know. Some said he was a seaman and adventurer, and his big tattoo was pointed to as proof, for he had been heard to state himself that he had acquired it in Lourenço Marques; but others, who had themselves come to the assembly line from rural homesteads, were positive from clues he had let fall that he had formerly been an itinerant farm laborer; and there were even those who swore that he was really an educated man, a kind of college professor amusing himself by slumming among them.

Whoever he was, for the time he had nothing more to say. But Walter felt his presence, for he was always ready to lend a hand, always laconically helpful, always silently observing and listening.

One day the younger inspector at the beginning of the line, blowing genial clouds of illegal pipe smoke, gave Walter some frank and cynical advice.

"Been listening to the bosses talking about you, buddy." He took the pipe from his mouth and formed a fat smoke ring. "Want to know what's wrong with what you're doing?"

"I guess so," said Walter dully.

"You try too hard. You're trying to do a good job—that's the worst thing you can do."

Walter stared in bewilderment at the inspector. "But why?"

"They're interested in pulling production. If you're going to be running up and down the line all day trying to make every job perfect, you're just going to get in people's way. What the bosses will do is, they'll look for an excuse to fire you before your probationary period is up, or else they'll stick you in a routine lower-paying job."

"Then . . ."

"I've been here ten years. Believe me," he drew on his pipe once again and smiled disarmingly, "they're not interested in making good cars, they're interested in making cars. You know what production means? Volume. And you know what they hired you for? To camouflage, not to get rid of every flaw. Hide them so they don't show up after the car's been through paint, so the customer doesn't see them at the dealer's, and you'll get along great."

"Camouflage them how?"

"With your sandpaper. With the grinding wheel. If you hit them up and down and then across, final inspection will never know what's underneath. Make it look good, and confusing. Be a camouflage artist and the bosses'll very seldom bother you."

Walter could not help laughing. "Listen, how could you stand it here for ten years? Every day I think maybe I ought to get out and look for something else."

"For six years," the inspector said pleasantly, "I was like you. This was going to be just temporary until I found something with a real future. It took me six years to realize that I was going to be spending the rest of my life here—it's like breaking in a wild horse, only with a human being it takes longer. I got married, had three kids, now I'm building a home near the plant. So I make the best of it, I take it easy and I have as much fun as I can, and I hate to see a guy like you breaking his back all for nothing."

Bending over his work, Walter raised his file and heard the in-

spector's final shot, lightly enough intended but bearing its own
weight of bitterness and resignation: "You'd be surprised how many
fellows I've heard talking just like you, couldn't stand the work, going to quit any day, and now they're five and ten year men, starting
to think about retirement benefits."

Walter could not clarify in his own mind what it was about the
inspector's attitude that increased his desperation, not until his silent partner eased up to him from nowhere and said quietly, "Kind
of terrified you, didn't he?"

"Not exactly terrified."

"Just the same, it's no fun to be doing time and to be told that
your sentence just might turn out to be indefinite. Then if you've
got a good imagination you can see yourself gradually getting used
to it, even getting to like the routine, so that one day follows another
and the first thing you know the wrinkles are there and the kids
are grown up and you don't know where it's all gone to, your life."

Walter felt himself shuddering. Was it from the blower overhead
that he felt his hot sweat turning cold and drying on his face? He
said, "I suppose you have to be cynical if you're going to stay here."

"Day after day your life becomes a joke without any point, a trick
that you play on yourself from punching in to punching out."

"But that's only if you're an imaginative or a sensitive person."

For the first time, the man's angular face hardened. "Don't you
think somebody like that inspector had his ambitions? Don't you
think he still has his man's pride? Did you ever figure the cost of the
job in terms of what it does to the personality of a clever intelligent
fellow like him? He says if you're going to be trapped you might as
well make the best of it, and by his lights he may be right. Anyway
don't be too quick to blame him—he probably never had the opportunity to save money and go off to college."

No one had ever, not ever in eighteen years, talked to Walter in
such a way. He would never again be able to look at a man like the
inspector without compassion. Even at home in the evening with
his father, whom he could no longer talk to about anything but
baseball or weather (although they both tried clumsily to broach
other more serious topics), Walter found that he was viewing this
desolate man not just as his father but as a man who had his own
miseries; and this, he knew, was a part of growing up that could not
have come about as it had without the influence of his strange friend
in the factory.

More and more as the weeks passed and exhaustion was gradually overcome by vitality, only to be transformed into monotony, Walter came to feel that only this man could explain the real meaning of the assembly line. But he remained aloof, insubstantial as a ghost. The more he held to himself, the more Walter was piqued, and determined to make the ghost speak.

At last one day he ventured to demand: "Say, what does that tattoo of yours stand for, that big bird?"

The man smiled with one side of his mouth. "That old bird is the American eagle." He raised his arm briefly, flexed it, and let it fall to his side. "It's screaming with rage at what's happened to the republic."

"What *has* happened?"

"Where are the guts? Where's the drive? In a place like this a man's life goes down the drain like scummy water."

"But you're working here too," Walter said boldly.

The man shook his head slowly, with such finality that there was something elemental about the gesture. "I'm not a settled-down man, I'm just passing through."

Walter cleared his throat. "I don't even know your name."

"Why should you? Instead of learning names, we refer to the fellow with the bad teeth, or the guy with the blue coveralls. When I work next to a man for months and learn that his wife is being operated on for cancer of the breast and still don't know his name, it tells me something not just about him and me, but about the half-connections that are all the factory allows you in the way of friendships."

"The old-timers are clubby enough, but everybody else claims they're here for a limited time. The place is so big and everything seems so temporary that I suppose we don't feel the need of introducing ourselves."

The older man looked at Walter somberly. "No one who comes here wants to admit that the place has any real connection with his real life. He has to say that he is just putting in his time here, and so no matter how friendly he is by nature he has to think of the people around him as essentially strangers, men whom he can't even trouble to say good-by to when he quits or gets laid off."

"But *your* name—"

"Call me Joe."

Walter pursued him: "Every third guy on the line must be named Joe. Joe what?"

He smiled again, his long Yankee countenance creasing in a cold grin. "Joe, the vanishing American." And he turned his back on Walter and bent to his work as the line resumed its endless progress.

But he was a curious man, a nosey man, and he was there, listening and leering, when Walter found a minute to respond without cursing to a bitter remark of Pop's. Walter turned on him with the anger he had managed to suppress when speaking to the old inspector.

"It's easy for you to stand there and laugh. You think you're better than anybody else in the shop."

Joe hitched up his khaki trousers and replied with deliberate anger, "I never claimed that. I just read a little more and ponder a little more than the average fellow. That's why I don't laugh at them, I feel sorry for them. If I'm a little freer, I've had to make sacrifices for it—no dependents, no ties." He added cryptically, "They punish you one way or they punish you another way."

Walter did not quite understand, but it struck him that these remarks were a prelude to farewell. He asked uneasily, "You're not going to quit?"

"One of these days. Maybe the weather will turn, or I'll hear of something else, or I'll have words with Buster . . ." He added with somewhat more warmth, "But I'll be back—if not here, some place like here. You won't, though. That's why I hope you won't forget what it was like for the people who made the things you'll be buying."

Walter cried indignantly: "How could I? How could I ever forget?" It seemed to him that the thick scurf of silver through which he shuffled as he worked, the glittering waste of lead filings and melted sticks, were so many needles, each carrying its stinging injection of memory—of sweat, exhaustion, harrying, feverish haste, and stupid boredom.

"You forget worse things, don't you? Pain, and even death? You'll think back on the days when you were slaving away to save money for college, and they'll strike you as comical, maybe even romantic."

"God forbid!" Walter laughed. And yet he had suddenly a shivery foretaste of a future beyond the one of which he daydreamed as he worked.

When the siren screamed the end of their nine and a half hours

Walter hurled his file and apron into his tool box and trotted down the aisle toward the time clock. Turning the corner of the body shop office just as its lights were extinguished, he ran headlong into the iron antennae of a fork truck and cried aloud with pain as the metal plate struck his shinbone. Tottering backward, Walter was suddenly gripped by the forearm and pulled erect. He turned gratefully and found himself staring into the eyes of Joe.

Smarting with soreness and embarrassment, Walter demanded aggressively, "I suppose that's what you want me to remember!"

A faint stubble glinted along Joe's narrow cheeks. Graying like his iron hair, it aged him as it grew. He scraped his hand across it wearily and replied quietly, "Never mind the machinery. Remember the men. The men make the machines, and they make their own tragedies too. Once your own life gets easier, you'll take it for granted not only that theirs must be easier too, but that they deserve what they get anyway, that some law of natural selection has put you up where you are and them down where they are."

They had reached the clock bay where they took their place meekly in line, waiting to punch out, shuffling forward every few seconds while they spoke in low voices. Around them a swarm of men surged toward freedom—noisy boys with laughter to spare for the evening, haggard weary men in their forties, surly powerful black men in stained coveralls and scrawny brown men chattering in Spanish, vacant-faced fools with slack jaws and dangling hands, shrewd-eyed men fingering their union contract books, composing their campaign leaflets, and computing their chances of election to positions that would lift them out of the work routine.

"Why do they stay?"

"They're trapped, that's why. They say everybody's supposed to be, one way or another, but it's worse to be stuck here. Spending your life on the production line means counting out the minutes, being grateful that Mondays go fast because you're rested, and hating Tuesdays because the week is so long. It means that you're paying off forever on all the things you've been pressured into buying by getting up every day in order to do something you'd never, never think of doing if it was a matter of choice. It means never having anything to look forward to in all of your working life." Joe took his card from the rack, clicked it in the time clock, and with a wave of his hand was gone.

*

What was happening, as Walter woke daily to the dawn's dull alarm and went from the still house through the newly washed streets to the waiting assembly line, was that his self-pity, so strong that the page blurred before him when he lay in bed reading himself to sleep, was altering into a maturer concern with the fate of others who could not, like himself, set a term to their labor.

He began to question the men on the line with him, one after another, to find out how many of them felt as he did about what they were doing for a living. More sure of himself with every passing hour, he moved up and down the line, demanding, whenever there was a moment, an answer to his insistent question: "Do you think anybody likes coming in here to work?"

"Everybody does one day a week—payday," said the solder-flower.

"Not even the bosses," said the deck-fitter. "Do you think anybody with sense would knock himself out in this dirt and noise if it wasn't for the money?"

And the door-fitter said wryly, "Do you know what this kind of work is? It's colored man's work. Why, even the colored men are smartening up—they turn up their noses at it too, unless they get strapped."

Saddened and bewildered by this last comment, Walter turned away from the man who had made it, and who had punctuated his bitter remark with a series of thunderous blows on a door that he was fitting. Only Orrin, the second metal-finisher, grudgingly admitted that the work was a challenge to him, that the pay was fair, and that there were worse jobs. Behind them all, long-jawed Joe, caught up with his work as usual, stood casually beveling his screwdriver.

"I hear you've been taking a little poll," he said to Walter.

"What's it to you?" Walter asked truculently. He was in no mood to be mocked.

With apparent irrelevance, Joe replied by demanding, "How come you fixed on being an engineer?"

Walter was taken aback. "Why, that's where everybody says the future is."

"That's not reason enough for a fellow to struggle and sweat to get to college. Damn it, doesn't anybody go out and do what he wants to any more? I'm not saying you wouldn't make a good engineer, or that it wouldn't be fine for a change to have some engineers who care as much about people as they do about gadgets. But supposing you find out after you get to college that you want to spend your time learning something useless—are you going to leave yourself open for it?"

"Boy, you sure are free with advice."

Joe looked at him gravely. His long sad jaw had the hint of a smile. "The men on the line like you, Walter. They don't think you're nosey when you ask questions. They think you're one of them, and in a good way you are. Maybe that's why I've got hopes for you."

Walter fought hard against the influence of the older man, whose crabbed and subversive outlook was so foreign to everything Walter had been taught, but he was forced to admit to himself that more and more he was seeing the factory through Joe's cold discerning eyes; and he began to fear that if Joe were ever to leave, the plant would have no real existence other than as a money-producing nightmare. Not only was there no one else really to talk to about it, but Joe had forced Walter to try to formulate his emerging ideas in an adult and comprehensible way.

"The worst thing about the assembly line is what it does to your self-respect," he said to Joe early one morning as they squatted on their haunches, waiting for the starting siren. "It's hard to keep from feeling like a fool when you know that everybody looks down on what you're doing, even the men who are doing it themselves."

Joe hung his hammer and metal spoon from the brass hook at his belt. "The big pitch has always been that we're a practical people, that we've proved to all the impractical European dreamers that production can serve people. But instead people are serving production. Look how frightened, how hysterical the bosses get when the line stops—they can't afford to figure what it costs you to keep it moving—they only know they've got a production quota. Of course when sales resistance starts building up and they put the cork back in themselves, they give you just the opposite story. Who can blame the poor slob in the middle for suspecting that the whole setup is really as nutty as a fruitcake, and for feeling ashamed of himself for being caught up in it?"

"All right," Walter challenged him. "Who's crazy? You, me, the guys around us, or the board of directors?"

"Anybody who gets suckered into believing that there's anything real behind the billboards they put up to get the show on the road, so that he commits himself to buying the billboard pictures by selling his life on the installment plan. I sympathize with any joker who begins to suspect that the whole world is against him, that he's the victim of a huge conspiracy organized to make his car fall apart before it's been paid off. Doesn't life in the factory seem to be deliberately designed to lower your own self-esteem? What happens when you're knocking down a dent? If you rap it too hard from the inside, you have to file it down that much more, and you hate yourself for it. If you don't rap it hard enough you only find out after it's moved on down the line, and then you have to hurry up and wallop it again. In either case you hate yourself instead of hating the car, or the invisible man that started up the line." He laughed briefly in anticipation of what he was about to add. "It's like the man that hits his thumb with a hammer while he's hanging a picture—only here he keeps hitting his thumb because they're moving the wall as fast as the union will let them. Who does he yell at every time that ball peen comes down on his nail? Himself."

"I wonder," Walter said slowly, "how many people actually feel that way."

"More than you can count. It's always safe to figure that if you feel something, the world must be full of people who feel the same way. Every sensible man realizes as he gets older that his feelings aren't unique. After all, that's the basis of the best art: the fact that you recognize yourself in it, and all those inner experiences that you'd thought no one else but you could know."

Walter was willing to recognize that he was not the only one to cringe when Buster called him back on a badly done job, to swear at himself for the mistakes that made him fall behind, to realize how he was being trapped into swearing at himself and deflecting his anger from what he did to the way he did it. But it was hard for him to believe that there were others who felt as intensely as he did, who beat their heads against the bars as he did, who dreamed of sunlight and freedom as he did, even though Joe tried to persuade him that the difference was often one of degree, or of his being able to express his feelings in a way that others couldn't. This was one of the questions that Walter was eager to argue with Joe, who moved from one extreme position to another, always mocking, always challenging him to learn what he stood for and to defend it like a man.

"You know something," Walter burst out impetuously one day, "I don't know what I would have done here without you."

Instead of laughing, or belittling this praise, Joe's face darkened. The next morning he was not on the line.

By the third day of his absence Walter was beginning to feel as though it had all been a dream, as though he were slipping once again into the awful pit of loneliness, exhaustion and self-doubting despair. As a last resort he sought out the men on the line to learn what they thought of Joe.

"He's irresponsible," said Pop.

"He's the kind of guy that just don't care," said the younger inspector. "No wife, no kids, no wonder he can take off three days without worrying about getting a reprimand or getting fired."

"He knows his work," said Orrin grudgingly. "I don't know where he learned it, but he did. Just the same, he takes off. You can't *afford* to take off like that nowadays, not if you want to hold down a job."

On the fourth day he came back. He told no one where he had been. "Am I glad to see you!" Walter exclaimed—but Joe merely indicated, with a cold grin and a turn of his tattooed arm, that from time to time things came up that were more important than the making of automobiles. He did not set to work, but almost immediately was engaged in serious talk with Buster the foreman and with the union shop steward. The two were arguing vigorously, but suddenly Joe cut them off simply by lifting his hand. He said something very briefly, shoved his hands into his pockets, and the discussion was finished.

To Walter's amazement, he came back to the line, picked up his toolbox, and nodded casually to him.

"I just quit, Walter," he said. "Going to hit the road."

"But—"

"You'll make out all right, no matter what you do. I don't even have to wish you good luck."

Then he was off down the aisle, on his way to the tool crib and the plant police and the parking lot and God alone knew where after that, without so much as a handshake or an inclination of his lean frame. Suddenly Walter remembered something: "Hey!" he shouted. But Joe—if he heard him—did not turn around and soon was out of sight.

You never told me about Pop, he wanted to tell Joe, you never answered all the questions I was going to ask you—but even if Joe had not gone for good, Walter would not have known how to say to him all the things that should have been said, the words of gratitude and self-confidence.

When the relief man came a few minutes later to give him a twelve-minute break, he hurried to the bathroom. There, just beyond the big circular sink that could accommodate half a dozen men, he could see out the tilted window to the vast parking lot.

The dull winter light was gloomy and deceptive, and so vague was the air that the dark ranks of massed automobiles were no more than darker blurs against the background of the gray steel fencing and the lowering sky. One of the cars moved, or was it his imagination? But no, the red tail-light dimmed, glowed, dimmed. Joe, the vanishing American, was swinging out of the lot and away from the production line, out of Walter's life and into someone else's, out of the present and into what lay beyond the gate. He was leaving the future to Walter, who now at last could wave his farewell, with his face pressed to the cool window as he watched the little light disappearing from view.

Then he washed the sweat from his face and returned to his work.

a state of the nation

The most urgent and controversial of this country's problems, as well as the one provoking the most intense emotional response and affecting the most lives, is the war in Vietnam. "The Ambush" by Captain James Morris is about the texture of the everyday lives of men fighting this war. Even though the essay is a straight personal narrative with almost no direct commentary from the author, the mundane terror of the events described suggests the extent of the dehumanizing savagery that is acceptable in war and how a man's psychology can be brutalized.

Another view of the war is provided in an editorial essay from Ramparts magazine, "The Redress of Their Grievances." But here the focus is on the effects of the war on those at home, specifically on the anti-war movement. This essay discusses the new definitions of "reasonableness" that this crisis has forced on Americans, and suggests how significant an historical occurrence the Vietnam conflict is, how its repercussions will be felt in the attitude of Americans toward their government for years to come. The issue of Vietnam also stands behind novelist Norman Mailer's essay on President Lyndon Johnson, although the President himself is the subject of the author's attack. This essay is a clever exercise in the rhetoric of damnation, one that sees the President as an expression of genuine Americana.

In an essay quite different from Mailer's, Paul Goodman attacks President Johnson's concept of a Great Society, suggesting that it is an impoverished notion, unworkable and hardly sufficient unto its need. "The Great Society" is complemented by an essay on real, not metaphorical, poverty by Peter Schrag. "Appalachia: Again the Forgotten Land" reports on a part of the United States that has been shut out of the middle-class paradise of creature comforts. Without being as theoretical as Goodman, Schrag too is attacking a society that calls itself great but leaves many of its people undernourished, poorly housed, and forgotten.

The last two essays illumine other aspects of the state of the nation. In "38 Who Saw Murder Didn't Call the Police," Martin Gansberg reports on the notorious murder of Catherine Genovese in a fine residential neighborhood in New York. The notoriety derives from the fact that 38 witnesses simply watched the murder or pretended not to hear the victim's screams as she was attacked three times within a 35-minute period.

The tableau soon became a popular image of the immorality of apathy. "In the Jungle" is novelist William Styron's first-hand account of the violence and chaos that engulfed the 1968 Democratic convention in Chicago. Writing "only a day or so after the event, [when] it is hard to be sure of anything," Styron uses vivid and violent images to convey the quality of the experience.

The short story for this section is "Survival," by M. F. Beal. It is about a lonely and frightened woman trying to retain her sanity in the midst of a society that seems to take away from her everything she feels is valuable.

CAPTAIN JAMES MORRIS

The Ambush

There were thirteen of us in the three-quarter-ton truck, myself included. I was the only American. We stopped for lunch at a big
Jarai montagnard village on Route 7.

Cowboy asked me to go with him to the house of a friend of his.
This longhouse, like all the others, was a split-bamboo and thatch
building set off the ground about five feet by large upright logs called
t'meh. The floor extended in front of the longhouse proper to make a
porch, against which a notched log leaned for stairs. Cowboy scooted

The Ambush. From *Esquire*, August 1965. Copyright © 1965 by Esquire Inc.
Reprinted by permission of Paul R. Reynolds Inc., 599 Fifth Avenue, New York,
New York 10017.

up it with ease. I lumbered after him in considerably less agile fashion. The lady of the house asked us inside and I ducked under the door. The effect inside was very pleasant. From the windows and through the bamboo walls the light filtered softly. The room was not cluttered. A few woven baskets and gourds hung on the walls. There was a square raised section in the middle of the floor that served as a fireplace, the smoke rising to the roof and slowly working its way out of the thatch.

The lady of the house gave us a friendly smile and offered us the floor to sit on. I leaned my AR-15 up in a corner and threw all my gear down beside it. Then I sat cross-legged on the floor. The split bamboo was resilient and pleasant to sit on.

Cowboy leaned his stuff up in the opposite corner and sat down too. He put his cowboy hat and wraparound shades on the floor beside him.

"Where's your friend?" I asked.

"He work in fields now, come back soon."

I started to ask if he was planting or what. Then I realized that Cowboy probably wouldn't know. He had been a soldier since he was twelve and probably hadn't worked a rice field in his life.

Perhaps warrior would be a better term than soldier for Cowboy. He had never been a member of a recognized army. His loyalties were to two things: money and personal friendship. I believed that personal friendship took precedence over money. I never had cause to change that belief.

He had commanded a Special Forces Strike Force Battalion for a year until he found out that being an interpreter paid roughly three times what a Battalion Commander got. He had been an interpreter for a year and a half. Cowboy was twenty-two years old.

He dived down into his pack and brought up a couple of cans of C's and pulled his canteen out of the carrier. "Let's eat," he said.

I got out two small C-ration cans, sliced ham and bread, and the little C-ration can opener. For reasons nobody now on active duty can remember it is called a P-38. The C rations and a couple of gulps of water made a pretty fair meal.

While we were eating, a little boy, about two, came in the door. He was wearing four bracelets on his left arm, and an anklet on each leg, an earring, and a Hopalong Cassidy T-shirt.

I said, "Hi, kid!"

He ran and grabbed his mother's skirts, looking back over his shoulder in apprehension. I guess he'd never seen anybody that big and blond before.

I rooted around in my pack and came up with a can of cookies and cocoa. I got up and opened the can and tried to give it to the kid. He grabbed his mother's skirts again and buried his head in her legs. I gave her two of the cookies and took one for myself. She smiled at me and gave one of the cookies to the kid. He took it and ran off, unsmiling.

I took the little envelope of cocoa and threw it back into my pack. Then I bent back the lid of the can and turned the edges under in a three-way fold, so it could be used as a cup without cutting your fingers on the edges. I gave it to the lady of the house and she smiled and nodded thanks. Later she would probably weave a wicker holder for it and throw away the lid altogether.

I always feel like some kind of condescending jackass giving my castoffs to the yards. But they take the gift as it is intended. They have marvelous dignity and never beg, but offer the hospitality of their homes, their food and their rice wine.

I went back over and sat down. "What time you think we ought to leave?" I asked Cowboy. I was beginning to think his friend wasn't going to show up.

"'Bout four," he replied.

It was one-thirty. "Okay, listen," I said, "I'm going to flake out for a while." I'd been up late the night before writing some kind of screwy report.

I awakened about three-thirty. Cowboy's friend had returned. He had changed into formal attire to meet the *Capitaine*. He was wearing a loincloth and an old U.S. Army olive-drab dress blouse. I suppose it had been lend-lease to the French and from there to one of the montagnard battalions.

"*Bonjour, Monsieur,*" I said, which almost exhausted my command of the language.

He cut loose a tremendous stream of guttural French, which Cowboy interpreted to mean that he wanted me to join him in some rice wine. My mind skittered desperately at the prospect, but I assented. It would have been uncourteous to do otherwise.

He brought the jug and sat it on the floor. Then he took out a long straw. We did not drink through the straw, but he siphoned off the *ou* into a couple of old Bière La Rue bottles.

The stuff tastes like a combination of sugar, water, and vomit. I tried to chug it down at a gulp, not breathing during the process. I couldn't kill it at once, but had to try again. Then I belched and smiled approval.

Naturally he offered more, but I informed him through Cowboy that I had a delicate stomach condition and could not continue.

Then rather more forcefully than was necessary I said, "Let's get started, Cowboy."

His grin was like a baby wolf's. He got up and put on his wrap-around shades and his cowboy hat sat down low on his nose. Then he took out that greatest of all South-east Asian status symbols, a Salem cigarette, and lit it. He held the filter in his teeth, James Dean fashion.

Once he got his image intact we walked out into the sunlight and went down the notched log.

The squad was good, handpicked without regard to rank or unit. Their faces were calm and their eyes were ready.

"Cowboy," I said, "how did you explain these soldiers to the village?"

"I tell them we go hunting."

I looked at Big Stoop with his front teeth out and his thirty-caliber machine gun in his arms. "With that?"

"Oh! They know that the soldier must take what gun he have."

It seemed a poor cover to me, but the montagnards are not used to questioning things. "Okay, let's go."

We went out the bamboo gate and past the long spiked fence, the defensive positions, punji stakes and watchtowers. We turned left to head back toward the rice fields.

Moving through the fields we automatically took up a kind of loose diamond formation, although we still carried our weapons slung. Once across the field we moved into the woods and waited. I unslung my rifle and leaned against a tree. Most of the others did likewise. We faced outward into the trees, weapons ready. I lit a cigarette. After we had waited about ten minutes I asked, "Any idea how soon he come?"

"Maybe ten more minute. He must wait so nobody know we go same."

"Uh huh."

Another cigarette later Cowboy's friend came across the fields carrying a Jarai ax for protective coloration. Once he was in the trees we grinned and shook hands all around again. Then the point man moved out, then Cowboy's friend, Cowboy, me and the rest of the squad.

The way was fairly rough and for the first kilometer I felt it: I had been in camp too long. After that it was fine.

The woods were open and green and the light was golden. We crossed a fair-sized stream, jumping from rock to rock, trying to keep our feet dry. I missed the last rock, slipped and my right leg went in the water up to the knee, making me feel like a graceless fool in front of the yards. That sort of thing never happened to John Wayne.

Once we showed *The Longest Day* at the camp. We didn't have a Cinemascope lens so everything was pretty narrow, but the yards didn't seem to mind. Cowboy drove out in his old three-quarter-ton truck with his wife and little girl and a few inlaws. About halfway through the picture he turned to me and said, "This John Wayne, he is paratrooper, he is cowboy, he is pilot. What he really do?"

I tried to explain what an actor was, but he didn't grasp the concept. I guess he thought all those flicks were documentaries.

Thinking about something else makes walking go easier. After we had gone about two kilometers Cowboy's friend, the agent, pointed at the ground. I went up to look. There was a small trail, a path really. It was covered with a fine grey gravel and wound along a slight rise through the luminous green wood. It looked like the path I had imagined Hansel and Gretel taking when I was a kid; pretty in the daytime, but dark and scary at night.

"He says every day, almost, one squad VC come by here."

"They come by day or by night?" I asked.

"Sometimes day, sometimes night."

"Does he see them?"

"Sometimes. Sometimes they make greeting."

I thought that was jolly.

"This is not a good place for ambush," Cowboy said.

"True. Let's get back away from the trail and walk along until we find a good place."

Cowboy nodded and gave instructions to the squad in Jarai. It sounded like a bad coughing fit.

Keeping the same order, we set off through the woods, moving parallel to the trail. The country was not good for ambushes. There was no commanding terrain. There was very little cover, but there was tall grass and some trees to hide behind. Finally we found a place that was less ridiculous than the rest, and set up.

Cowboy asked if I wanted to position the squad. "You are Captain. I must do as you order."

"You've set this thing up. As far as I'm concerned you're running the show. If I see something I don't like I'll let you know and we'll work it out."

Then I asked how he planned to set up.

"AR's on flanks. Machine gun in middle. All spread out with maybe five meter between each and get cover."

Aside from the automatic rifles and the machine gun, every man in the squad had either a Grease Gun or an M-2 carbine, all automatic weapons. Cowboy and I had AR-15's. An AR-15 looks like a cross between a Buck Rogers ray gun and a king cobra. It is six pounds plus of sudden death. It was a hell of a lot of firepower for thirteen men. We could take on anything up to a VC platoon with ease. Anything bigger than that was bad trouble.

I suggested to Cowboy that he put a one-man outpost out behind us so we wouldn't have any unexpected callers coming in from that way. He agreed.

Cowboy placed each man in position behind the best cover he could find. We were pretty well concealed by some tall grass. I chose a spot by a V-fork tree about fifteen feet from the trail and sat down cross-legged.

I took off my patrol harness and put it on the ground in front of me; then I opened the ammo pouches, took a magazine out of both of them and laid them where they could be reached easily. There were two magazines taped together in a U on the weapon itself, and eight more from the pouches, two hundred rounds in all. Then I unsnapped the snaps on the canteen carrier to avoid making the noise later in the night. The canteen itself was wrapped in a wool sock and would make no metallic noise against its cup when taken out.

Everything was ready. It was five-thirty. I opened a can of peaches with the P-38 and ate them with a dirty plastic spoon from my shirt pocket. By then it was getting dark. I rammed the can into the ground, olive drab side up, so the bright metal of its inside would not show; then turned the selector switch to full automatic and lay the weapon beside me.

You have to sit perfectly still and make no noise. None. So immediately you want a cigarette. You have to cough. Your throat starts to tickle and your nose itches. Your back aches, then your legs, then your shoulders, then your neck. When you do not react to this, but continue to sit still, the mind casts about for thoughts to amuse itself and pass the hours.

The moon rose to our front.

I started to shake uncontrollably. It was not cold and I was not afraid. It was a flat rush of adrenalin and the sudden knowledge that the ambush would go. I have had the same feeling since, and it has failed, and sometimes I have not had it and scored. But this was the first time and I was sure. Then the shaking passed and my mind was coldly detached.

My aching shoulders were hunkered for a long wait. I did not expect to see anything until three o'clock the next morning. The moon was high now and full and gold in the blue-black sky with the clouds turning to silver. The breeze rose and then died and the black silhouettes of armed men were passing quickly, quietly down the trail.

We were all firing. One faded from my sights. Tracers from the thirty-caliber weapons were ricocheting so high I thought the Cong were sending up flares. I fired up one magazine and then another. I kept firing. We all did. I wanted nothing to live out there. I felt nothing, neither elation nor horror, just the cold astringent calm.

I fired up five magazines before I stopped. Then everybody stopped and I called out, "Cowboy, let's check out the stiffs."

"Yes, sir."

We got up and moved onto the trail. The bodies were lying to the left, to the right, on the trail, cut down running. There were six bodies in all. Three had moved through and got away before we opened up. Later we learned that another died in a village the following morning.

I moved from one dark shape to the other, making sure they were dead. I fired a round into the ground by each man to see if he would move. None did. Cowboy moved beside a covering.

When I moved up on the last one, he raised up, his arms extended, eyes wide. He had no weapon. I said, "Good, we got a pris—"

Cowboy stitched him up the middle with his AR-15. He didn't even twitch.

"Goddamn it," I said, "we could have got some good information from that guy."

"Sorry," said Cowboy, "I get, you know, excited."

Nothing to do but shrug it off. I said, "Get their weapons and packs and we'll move out."

Cowboy was looking fearfully down the trail. "Maybe better we just get weapons. Must move fast now."

That sounded okay. When we got a report that the weapons had been picked up, I said, "We'll come back for the packs tomorrow." Cowboy didn't say anything, just moved. He really wanted to get out of there.

We cut straight cross-country through the brush and the creek, moving quietly and taking no known trail. We were back in the village by ten o'clock and the villagers loaned us a half-completed longhouse with a roof on it to sleep in.

I hadn't brought a poncho because I had expected to be all night in an ambush position and didn't want to be comfortable and go to sleep.

I flaked out on the bamboo floor with the yards, but it got cold pretty fast and I couldn't sleep. One of the yards had a spare poncho in the truck. He offered it to me. I declined. He insisted. I rolled up in it and wished for a pillow. Never satisfied.

The next morning we hired some villagers to go with us to carry back the Cong's packs and equipment.

The bodies still lay across the trail in their black shortie pajamas and their black sandals made from old truck-tire treads. Rigor mortis had set in and the ants were marching in straight lines across their bodies. They were so stiff we had to cut most of the equipment off.

I wanted to take the stiffs back with the rest of the gear. I figured it would make quite a stir when we kicked them out in front of the Ops Shack. Cowboy pointed out that there was hardly room for thirteen men, all those packs and six stiffs in the back of a three-quarter-ton truck. Besides, it might make some of the boys a little twitchy. I said okay and we left the stiffs on the trail.

Back at the village we gave each of the porters 20 piasters apiece, which is about twenty cents, and Cowboy slipped his buddy, the agent, one thousand in small, old bills when nobody was looking. Then we thanked everybody, shook hands, exchanged smiles, said *Bonjour*, and *Merci*, a few times, jumped in the truck and drove off.

There was no rush. We stopped for a beer in Cheo Reo and still made it to camp by noon.

THE EDITORS OF RAMPARTS

The Redress of
Their Grievances

In a deep-seated way, the dream of reasonableness has been the dream of America. Our laws speak of reasonable doubt, and our courts of what reasonable men might conclude. The Founding Fathers were steeped in theories of rational men, and Lyndon Johnson invokes the reasoned call of Isaiah. The men to whom the nation turns for guidance—Joseph Alsop, Eric Sevareid, Max Lerner —are listened to, when they are listened to at all, because they are, above all else, reasonable men.

Among them, certainly, is James Reston of the *New York Times.*

The Redress of Their Grievances. From *Ramparts*, December 1967. Reprinted by permission of the publisher.

Scottish by birth, patrician in manner, he has been by turns an excellent sports writer, a superb Washington reporter and a top bureau chief. No longer burdened with a bureau chief's duties, he functions today, from his seat near but not among the mighty, as the epitome of the reasonable man of America. He takes his responsibility seriously, normally employing a careful prose that avoids any suggestion of demagoguery or oversimplification, and when the subject is important—as were the anti-draft demonstrations at the Pentagon on October 21—the *Times* gives Reston the front page, as befits the most eminent staffer of the nation's most eminent publication.

The overwhelming majority of Washington demonstrators, Reston said, were decent, sincere and upstanding citizens—but they had allowed their protest to be tarnished by a tiny minority of left-wing extremists; the columnist saw two strains present: "one was native American; the other was alien."

Freedom of dissent, Reston argued, was of course vital—for despite the stresses of a little-understood war, the values of a democratic society are to be upheld; and most of the demonstrators understood that. "Moderate but concerned young university students," Reston wrote, came to Washington for what "was supposed to be a petition for the redress of their grievances." But Reston was openly shocked that the petition of the many should have been distorted in the public eye by the resistance of the few activists who violated the conduct agreement negotiated between the organizers of the march and the guardians of the Pentagon.

No one better embodies the tradition of reasonable dissent than another man very much like Reston: also at the top of his chosen profession, also patrician of manner and mild of speech, a man older than Reston and if anything more conservative in appearance and style.

Famed pediatrician Dr. Benjamin Spock is nothing if not native American: New England Presbyterian, descended from pre-revolutionary Dutch settlers in the Hudson Valley, son of the general counsel of the New York, New Haven and Hartford Railroad. He was on Yale's winning Olympic crew in 1924. He was an enthusiastic Navy lieutenant commander during World War II, and felt that America should have joined the war earlier.

Yet in Washington, it was Benjamin Spock who stood on the steps of the Lincoln Memorial and said that not communism but

Lyndon Johnson is the real enemy of America. It was Benjamin Spock who led the march to the Pentagon, and on the day about which Reston decried the "alien" strains of protest, native American Benjamin Spock was sitting on the ground in front of the Pentagon, surrounded by angry, shouting kids.

Surely this is a phenomenon to be pondered: these two men, the one defining alien ideas, the other clearly placing himself with a group of demonstrators whose threatened radicalism was enough to bring out thousands of armed soldiers.

Dr. Spock only recently rejected the dream of reasonableness; in 1964, he campaigned vigorously enough for Lyndon Johnson against Goldwater so that Johnson made a personal call from the White House, a few days after the election, to thank him. And for years, he has been one of the more distinguished leaders of the "responsible" American peace group, the National Committee for a Sane Nuclear Policy. Formed in the 1950's to fight the battle against nuclear testing, SANE did a patient and ultimately a magnificent job, making opposition on that one issue respectable and paving the public way for the test ban treaty ultimately negotiated under John Kennedy. Since then, it has edged its careful way into broader issues of peace and war, always careful of its associations—left-wingers have twice been purged—and maintaining strong ties to some Congressmen and other national leaders. One of its most moderate founders, Homer Jack, first scored the coup of recruiting the famous baby doctor Benjamin Spock; and if Jack may now look on himself as a latter-day Baron von Frankenstein, he had cause for pride at the time, for Dr. Spock's eminent respectability was a major factor in maintaining the reasonable image of SANE.

But the scene at the Pentagon does not mean that Spock has broken with SANE, nor SANE with Spock. For SANE itself is splitting, and while there are other factors (there are still red-baiters in SANE, and one of them has criticized Spock for the "ecumenical promiscuity" of the doctor's associations in the peace movement), the division is basically the same division that today separates Spock from Reston. It also separates other men of good will throughout the nation.

From college campuses to metropolitan downtown intersections, the nation was alight in mid-October with spiritual bonfires. It was reminiscent of the fiery single-issue morality of William Lloyd Garrison—an intensely clear understanding of a national evil coupled with an overpowering need to do something, anything, to give witness against it. Charging the Pentagon is not nice, and neither is burning draft cards; and voting with their feet is a posture with which most Americans are uncomfortable, let alone practiced. But to hundreds of thousands of citizens the war in Vietnam has become so incredibly monstrous, its goals so undefined, its methods so horrible, its escalation so relentless, that the moral imperative to oppose it has overbalanced the need for respectability; it demands a break in life style.

The men who maintain the American consensus are at a loss to explain the commotion in the streets. It becomes necessary for observers like Reston and television pundit Eric Sevareid to postulate the devil theory of "alien" forces at work which, if given their extremist way, would make a nightmare of their dream of reasonableness. But that dream is rapidly becoming its own nightmare, for Vietnam will no doubt be recorded in history as the reasonable man's war. Every decision, every intervention, every escalation was made reasonably and was justified with careful liberal rhetoric—until the slow and painful accretion of reasonableness built a bloody pyramid of madness, which the United States can now neither afford nor accommodate.

But obscene as it is, Vietnam is not the issue that has split SANE or made Mr. Reston wonder at Dr. Spock. The issue for Reston is how one operates within the system, and what manner of dissent is responsible. It is not good form to call the President a murderer for his saturation bombing policies; rather, one must discuss the fact that the bombing simply has no discernible political or military value.

Beneath this surface division on style, however, lies a most profound disagreement on the state of the nation at this point in late mid-century. Like most very serious issues, this division is reducible to rather elemental terms—elemental as a first year civics course. Those reasonable men who share Reston's vision of America are, if "the Establishment" is too redundant and simplistic a definition, the men who largely control our communications media, staff the legislative and executive branches of government, enjoy power in American business and financial communities. And once, though no longer, these men completely dominated academic and religious circles. These men believe that the democratic process is functioning adequately. Making sophisticated allowances for the complexities of society and the obvious problems in maintaining a democracy with so large a base, they believe that the constitutional fail-safe systems of checks and balances and separation of powers are working, that the press is fulfilling its function of providing responsible criticism, and that the orderly process of change essential to a democracy is available, at the polls, for all citizens. This is the full, perfect circle of the democratic system, and any attempt at effecting change which departs from the channels and assumptions of that system is not only disorderly but dangerous, since it tends to give a black eye to "responsible" dissent and creates an unhealthy polarization in society which feeds, in the popular phrase, the extremism of both left and right. It is all a little like the attitude of a teacher toward a student who talks during a fire drill; it does not matter what the student is saying—one simply does not talk during fire drill.

Ironically, the opposite view to Reston's articles of faith is held by large numbers of the young men and women who took Civics I relatively recently. They see that the democratic process is not functioning as promised in their textbooks—they see it malfunctioning, most agonizingly and inscrutably, as a result of Vietnam.

Macaulay might view Victnam as an intriguing, classic anomaly —a war remarkably unpopular with the citizens which is nonetheless prosecuted by a democracy, with the very segment of the population most violently opposed to the war's aims, the youth, being conscripted to do the fighting.

If this anomaly is difficult to grasp for some, it is a frightening and disillusioning reality to many, particularly to the young Americans who have the perspective to judge the system on its own terms —those who are still studying it instead of being caught up in it. They studied the separation of powers, but know what the Tonkin Gulf resolution meant to that principle. They believed in the theory of the general will, but cannot square it with the fact that there were at last Gallup Poll count 46 per cent of the American people formally opposed to the war—a condition which led the President, incredibly, to state that he worries at night over this dissent lest it divide the nation in its goals. They know the constitutional promises of freedom of individual choice and meaningful channels for dissent, but when the choice of dissenting from the draft is five years at hard labor, it is difficult to explain to a young man why the choices offered are meaningful or free. They know there is nowhere to go to petition for the redress of their grievances.

The catholic range of opposition to this particular war is both qualitatively and quantitatively unparalleled in American history— yet this remarkable public protest has in no way affected the conduct or the reckless extension of the war. If the administration had given even on a marginal issue—a permanent halt in bombing, for instance—the war's critics might have some feeling that the influence of their vast numbers had some effect on national policy. But for almost every escalation of dissent, there has been an escalation of the war. And, correspondingly, an escalation of political frustration.

As the mathematical percentage of the public opposed to the war passes the 50 per cent mark and the war grinds on, it may be difficult even for Reston to maintain that the democratic system is functioning at its best. The fact that there is frustration and anger and desperation in this country has nothing to do with the Gallup Poll; the democratic process, in whatever platonic spit and polish Reston envisions it, is not providing real political alternatives to the voters or allowing legitimate channels for the discussion of such alternatives. If you doubt that, ask somebody who voted for Johnson against Goldwater.

Richard Rovere, long before James Reston discovered the "alien" forces of protest, defined the function of the American Establishment as the setting of the limits within which debate can take place. Reading from left to right within those boundaries, you have the horizon of allowable views about the American system, dissent and the world. Underlying the current crisis of alternatives is the steady shrinkage of that consensus, with all the inevitability of an un-Sanforized shirt, during the long Cold War years. Today there is a great logjam in the liberal center, from the seniority system of Congress to the cautious criteria for the selection of platforms and candidates, in both parties, which has made it extraordinarily difficult (most people who have tried and failed would say impossible) for any anguished protest over contemporary inequities in the American system to find satisfaction through any available "normal" channel. The consensus by which this country operates is simply not programmed to deal with moral crises. And so new institutions of protest built outside the consensus have come into being—the Free Speech Movements, the Black Panthers, underground railways for boys attempting to stay out of the Vietnam war the hard way, by staying in the country.

This present consensus bears as much relation to a legitimate social contract for this society as does an atrophied limb to a whole man. However, it is this telescoped consensus that is the foundation, the divining rod, and the arbitrator of all things for those professional reasonable men who have assumed the burden of judging what is fit and proper for us all. This tends, unfortunately, towards a static, self-fulfilling circle of reasoning that has difficulty comprehending, let alone adjusting to, dynamic and unpredictable social situations at home and tumultuous forces abroad which may require the rethinking of American means and basic goals.

In a society which so values comfort and where conciliation (some would use the word co-option) is generally and usually successfully employed to smooth over any troublesome rifts in the consensus, there is little room for the indiscriminate exercise of moral indignation. In this sense, it is easy to understand how the uncompromising goals and populist tactics of the dissenters in the streets could be so repulsive to the comfortable, conciliatory and reasonable men whose material stake in life, along with their honest social and political beliefs, are all tied, in their entirety, to comfort, conciliation and reasonableness. But understanding is not excusing. It may not be a very genteel thing to say, but, dealing with even the morality America insisted upon at Nuremberg, there is a good case to be made for calling Lyndon Johnson a murderer. And if he is a murderer, he has many accomplices, all of them reasonable men.

Fortunately, there are also unreasonable men in America. The names read like an honor roll of conscience—Dr. Spock, religionists like Dr. Robert McAfee Brown, scholars like Noam Chomsky, pacifists like Daniel Berrigan. Together with over 100,000 others, they took part in the week of national activist protest in mid-October— convinced that as of now, the democratic process is incapable of responding to the intensity of today's moral crisis which has crystallized over Vietnam, and that the system must be confronted, changed, opened again before it is too late. Conscience, they insist —in a cry as American as the dream of reasonableness itself—is more human, more important, than can be any devotion to procedure.

This is why protest in America has gone into the streets. The disorderly process is the direct result of the failure of the orderly process. Thus to attempt to divide the protests into "good" or "bad" dis-

THE EDITORS OF RAMPARTS

sent, or to postulate "outside agitators," in the manner of a Southern sheriff placing the blame for "troubles" with his blacks, is to totally misinterpret the crisis.

During the hectic week of October, men and women of conscience, spurred by the maddening realization that they were leading normal lives while their government was performing monstrous acts in their name, went into the streets to wrestle with what Thoreau and Emerson came to recognize as the ultimate question of ethics —how to make moral energy effective on the earth. Whether they burned draft cards in Boston, or blocked an induction center in Oakland, or marched on the Pentagon itself, or simply picketed in sympathy with such acts, as was done in hundreds of other American cities that week, their actions drew a line between themselves and what they would let the government do in their name.

For the war represents the consummate contradiction of all American values. We stand for freedom, yet we support dictators. We believe in truth, yet Vietnam has been a living lie through each dishonorable, escalating step. We say we play fair, yet we are selectively exterminating a people incapable of matching our technology of death. We build a better world in Vietnam, yet we must make a wasteland to do it. It is a barren, bitter experience, one which shows at once the scope and the limit of American power, and when the President speaks of the agony and the loneliness of decision-making, one is immediately reminded of Captain Ahab.

Untenable in terms of the definition and traditions of American society, the war mocks our vision of ourselves. Increasingly, more Americans are coming to the realization that we cannot fight what amounts to, as distasteful as the word may be, a totalitarian war abroad and maintain democracy at home. Like a tumor on a small child, the Vietnam war has put all of American society in lopsided perspective. And it has raised other issues. The protest over the war is also a protest over the entire disproportionate nature of what has been happening in the United States: $30 billion dollars a year to feed a military tapeworm in Vietnam while Americans starve among affluence and riot in the shadow of skycrapers. If the system is working, the people who protest in the streets are saying, it is working for someone else.

The draft, more than any other single stimulant, has provoked the unparalleled rebellion now facing the administration. A war morally repellent to so many must now be fought by young men who oppose it—men who won't go, and don't know how to stay. When young people in America fear a knock on the door at night, this society is in deep trouble. It is in trouble because it is, in the final analysis, untenable in a democracy to use an amoral device like Selective Service to force men to fight an unpopular, unsanctioned war on which they have never even had the opportunity to vote.

The society at this juncture lacks a safety valve; the system seems to have lost the capacity to reassess its aims, provide fundamental alternatives, or even to consider them. It also lacks purpose and direction—unless it is in the chase of the great white, fading whale of the international communist conspiracy.

If reasonable men expect their system to work, time is running out for them. When society makes it clear that the traditional methods of dissent are ineffectual, people will turn to other, more disruptive, more desperate measures. It is the responsibility of men like Reston to show that the moderation they counsel has some effective connection with the urgent concerns being manifested. Failing that, their counsel is irresponsible. For they are then helping to maintain a politics of frustration which may turn into a politics of futility, and ultimately, tragically, a politics of violence.

It is the thesis of this essay that the reasonable man has become the enemy of this society at this time. His reason has been soured by compromise and his moral conscience traded for a conscience of conciliation. The capacity to ask fundamental questions appears to have been lost. The criticism of the war, in the mass media and in Congress, has been generally marginal and directed to practical, tactical critiques. The worst thing that reasonable men seem capable of saying about our attempt to control another people's destiny is that it is not working out very well; if we were winning, it would no doubt be considered a good war.

The frustrations from the government's posture in Vietnam feed the militancy of the right as well as the radicalism of the left. If Hubert Humphrey is correct, then so is Ronald Reagan; if we must send American boys to kill Humphrey's communists abroad, then why shouldn't we lock up the communists Reagan finds at home? Reston and Sevareid are correct in fearing that the very real dangers of polarization in society will feed the cause of the right. They argue that the polarization can be stopped by ending the militancy of the protests. But it is the reasonable men of the liberal center who have created the conditions that have brought this society to crisis, and it is dishonest of them to blame that crisis on those citizens protesting the immoral and irresponsible war which has become as destructive of American traditions as of Vietnamese lives. They cannot revitalize the system by simply wishing the left or the right away. If there is a danger of America becoming a garrison state, it is a real potential because the reasonable men in power for the last 20 years allowed what former President Eisenhower called the military-industrial complex to develop all out of proportion to our national needs. Since they had narrowed the channels of power and contained the efficacy of dissent by consensus, there were no unreasonable men in power to challenge their myopic assumptions. This lack of fundamental opposition to men—or ideas—in power has been the greatest danger stemming from the liberal consensus. Political decisions have been made without the benefit of strong and clashing political ideas —from the left, or from the right—and the inevitable result has been the stagnation and corruption of the center.

The war they perpetrated and escalated has now become intolerable, and it must end, or the result may be a form of permanent military chauvinism that even reasonable men will find themselves incapable of co-opting.

Back in 1949, when Arthur Schlesinger, Jr., published a call to American liberalism to enlist totally and uncritically in the Cold War, he used the phrase "the Vital Center" as a title, in reference to the pragmatic liberals (of whom Hubert Humphrey was the prototype) who would join the ideals of domestic social reform with uncritical support for the new, emerging military hard line. They supported Truman, who committed us in 1950 to underwriting the return of French colonialism to Vietnam—the first step towards our current involvement. The men of "the vital center" came to be the most enthusiastic of cold warriors, often rivaling those in the military.

This commitment to the communist devil theory seemed to harden in inverse proportion to the liberalizing trends within the communist world itself, and reflected a greater commitment to serving current power and private ambition than political principle. In the process, Cold War liberalism lost even the pretense of vitality in the pursuit of truth and change, and instead came to acquire the stench of decay. Hubert Humphrey represents the most perfect embodiment of this decay, and he is the symbol of perverse accommodation for that great number of grass roots liberals who make up a new class of the "reluctant revolutionaries." Their break was forced by a younger generation raised on the principles of liberal morality, but outraged by the crimes committed ostensibly in their name.

Of all the opponents of the war, the most desperate are the young men who oppose it, and who are being drafted to fight it. Even those who are not inducted are feeling the crunch of the system; they know that it is only their privileged deferment that allows them to avoid dying in Vietnam or going to jail with their contemporaries. They cannot glory in their good fortune. Moreover, they are conscious of being worked on by a Selective Service System that is designed to coerce them into a particular kind of life, just as it coerces others into a particular kind of death.

The Selective Service System no longer makes available to the public a document dated June 1965 entitled "Channeling." . . . It is a classic totalitarian document, its language cloaked in reasonableness, which makes it clear that the government has assumed the right to control and direct the life choices of young Americans by the manipulative use of the draft and its exemptions. When one subjects 30 million men to a totalitarian system, even if it is American and indirect, one must expect them to rebel. And that is precisely what has happened.

The young men who, in the face of the Selective Service System and the war in Vietnam, have moved to resistance are behaving responsibly. They are taking America's burden upon themselves, and they should be encouraged and supported in bearing it in every way possible. They are now the conscience of America, its new "vital center."

Every American must realize that resistance and militant protest is going to continue; it will grow as the war grows, and will not go away until the war ends. That is the nature of a moral imperative.

The increased militancy of the protesters does in fact represent a threat to the stability of society, but that is of small moment compared to the moral danger of the crime of silence which includes mumbling on the sidelines while the war machine moves inexorably on its way.

David Harris, former Stanford University student body president, summarized the inescapable tension brought about by the war: "If this country is going to police the world, it will have to imprison its youth."

NORMAN MAILER

Lyndon Johnson

In 20 years it may be taken for granted that 1964 was the year in which a major party nominated a major pretender to conservatism. It was a loss, and it was conceivably a horror, for 1964 was also a year in which a real conservative still had a great deal to say to the nation. He could have demonstrated with no vast difficulty that America was under the yoke of a monstrous building boom whose architecture

Lyndon Johnson. From *Cannibals and Christians* by Norman Mailer, published by Dial Press, 1966. Originally titled *"My Hope for America:* A Review of a Book by Lyndon B. Johnson." Copyright © 1966 by Norman Mailer. Reprinted by permission of the author and his agents, Scott Meredith Literary Agency, Inc., 580 Fifth Avenue, New York, New York 10036.

gave promise of being the ugliest in the history of man, that our labor unions had watered the value of labor until physical work had become as parasitical as white-collar work, and that our medicine had been overburdened beyond repair by a proliferation of wonder drugs whose side effects (with the notable exception of thalidomide) were still largely unknown—hence a delayed mass poisoning might yet be the fruit of this research. Our fruits, our vegetables, our cattle, had lost the opportunity to feed on native soil and organic food; the balance of nature, the fisheries, the economy of marine life, and the insect economies were being disrupted to the root by marinas and insecticides; our old neighborhoods and old homes were being—one could swear it—systematically demolished, and our educational system was glutted by a host of intellectual canapés: art appreciation, domestic economy, sexual efficiency, the modern novel, and so forth.

A real conservative could also have pointed out that the Civil Rights Act, no matter how imperfect and conceivably unconstitutional, was an act to be voted for, since finally there was a matter more important than the protection of property rights—it was spiritual rights: the Negro was entitled to his spiritual rights even if there were hard niggling costs to the rights of the Constitution. Finally, a great conservative could have noted that the health of Communism was its misery, that like all top-heavy structures its greatest danger was in its growth. Prosperity was Communism's poison, but attack from capitalism was its tranfusion of blood. So the time was open for a great debate. Should we go back to isolationism? Did we not already possess enough nuclear Doomsdays to protect ourselves, was it not perhaps time to recognize that the industrialization of the backward nations was a thankless venture which wise men would avoid? Might it not be best to let the Communists have Asia and Africa after all? Would they not strangle on the meal? Yes, America was perhaps ready to listen to the sophistications of a conservative, if such a man was there to appear in 1964.

But what a conservative came down the pike! Marooned in a hopeless traffic with hate groups and bigots, Southern bullies and oil pirates, offering a program of sinister hints that a Federal police force would protect the young ladies of our land on their walk through our streets at night; reasoning with all the homely assurance of a filthy sock that he would protect the past by destroying the present (as in those remarks about scorching the foliage in Vietnam in order to keep the guerrillas from concealing themselves); wasting the sub-

stance of his campaign in pointless technical arguments with the
Pentagon; and boring reconciliations and new feuds with the stricken
Moderates of his party—the alleged conservative candidate was
perhaps no more than a demagogue of the Right with a manly Christian air, a sweet voice, eyeglasses, and total innocence of a sense
of contradiction, a spirit so naturally conservative that on the grounds
of his home he raised the American flag with an electronic flag-
pole. Up at dawn, down at dusk, commanded the photoelectric cells
in the mast. Well, one couldn't vote for such a man. He pressed the
wrong buttons.

The mandate would go therefore to Lyndon Johnson. So most of
America had seemed to decide by the eve of election. But it was
nonetheless a vote heavy with gloom, and stricken with a sense of
possible bad consequence, for there was much about Johnson which
appealed not at all, and some of the evidence was intimate. He had
written a book. That is intimate evidence. *My Hope for America*,
he had called it. Now, of course, a book written by a high official must
not be judged by average standards, or one would be forced to say,
for example, that Jack Kennedy was not a very good writer and that
Bobby Kennedy, at last reading, wrote a dead stick's prose—his style
almost as bad as J. Edgar Hoover's. But even at its worst, the prose
style of Jack Kennedy (and his ghost writers) is to the prose style of
L.B.J. (and *his* ghost writers) as de Tocqueville is to Ayn Rand. It is
even not impossible that *My Hope for America* is the worst book
ever written by any political leader anywhere.

The private personality of L.B.J., as reported by the authority of
the best gossip, is different from his public presence. He is, one is
told, not too unlike Broderick Crawford in *All the King's Men*, roaring, smarting, bellowing, stabbing fingers on advisers' chests, hug-
ging his daughters, enjoying his food, mean and unforgiving, vindic-
tive, generous, ebullient, vain, suddenly depressed, then roguish,
then overbearing, suddenly modest again only to bellow once more.
It is somewhat like the description of an early Renaissance prince,
and if one looks hard at the photograph of the President on the cover
of *My Hope for America*, a leader of *condottieri* stands forth—hard,
greedy, exceptionally intelligent eyes whose cynicism is spiked by a
fierce pride, big fleshy inquisitive (and acquisitive) nose, thin curved
mouth (a boss mouth) and a slab of round hard jaw, deep dimple on
the upper lip, deep dimple on the chin. It is not a bad face altogether,
it is sufficiently worldly to inspire a kind of confidence that while no

age of high ideals is close at hand, yet no martyrs are to be tortured, for there is small profit in that.

It is a face and a concealed personality which could even, considering the Republican alternative, inspire a touch of happiness, if it were not for the public image—that boundless sea of overweening piety which collects here in this slim volume, this cove of Presidential prose whose waters are so brackish that a spoonful is enough to sicken the mind for hours. *My Hope for America* is an abominable, damnable book, and what makes it doubly awful is that nearly all of its ideas are blessed. It is in fact difficult to disagree with almost any one of them.

Who can argue on the side of poverty, or against justice, or against the idea of a Great Society? Let Barry Goldwater argue, not I. No, the ideals in this book are double-barreled, double-ringed, a double end of the cornucopia. More for the poor, more for the rich; more for peace, more for war; dedicatedly opposed to Communism, cautiously conciliatory; out to raise the income of poor nations, out to squash the economy of Cuba; all out for the Negro, all violence to be checked in city streets; all for the Democratic party, all for a party which includes Democrats *and* Republicans. There is even, and it is the achievement of this book, a curious sense of happiness running through its paragraphs. It is that happiness which is found at the end of the vision. It is as if the dream of Rousseau and Condorcet and Bakunin and Herzen and Marx and Lenin and Trotsky and John Dewey and the Webbs and Keynes and Roosevelt, Dreiser, and Darrow—name any of a hundred, any of that long stream of political engineers who dreamed of changing a material world by material means to make all men free and equal—had come down at the end to Little Ol' Lyndon, and hot damn, he had said, discovering Progressive religion in 1964, that's the ticket, that's the liver-eating ticket! And he was off to bring it off. And happy as a clam. That's the happiness which comes off this book. It is like a dream of heaven in a terminal ward.

For beneath this odd disembodied happiness is a prose more sinister than the most pious of Lyndon Johnson's misrepresentatations of his own personality; it is a prose which stirs half-heard cries of the death by suffocation of Western Civilization, it is a prose almost so bad and so deadening as the Georgian catechisms Josef Stalin used to hammer out: "Why is the Communist Party the party of the Soviet people? The Communist Party is the party of the Soviet people because . . ." It was enough at the time, reading Stalin, to keep from becoming a Communist. Now, reading Lyndon!—the horror is that one must still vote for him. But what a book is *My Hope for America.*

Examine it: 127 pages, a little more than 200 words to a page, most of the pages half pages or blank pages so that in bulk there are 17,000 words collected in 13 short chapters; they have titles like this —*President of All the People, A President's Faith and Vision, Building the Atlantic Partnership, This Developing World, Creative Federalism.* Each page of each chapter is divided into paragraphs. Page 8 has 12 paragraphs; the average page has four or five with a generous space between each paragraph. This is not because the remarks have the resonant echo of Pascal's *Pensées,* rather—one idea does not lead to another. So the space must be there. It is useful for burying whichever infinitesimal part of the brain died in the gas of the preceding phrase.

Yet every altruistic idea and every well-tuned moderation which Lyndon Johnson's political experience has put together over the years is somehow worked into the organum of his credo. It is impossible to disagree with a single one of its humanistic desires ("We know that we can learn from the culture, the arts, and the traditions of other countries"); it is equally impossible to feel the least pleasure at the thought these goods may yet come to be—just so bad and disheartening is the style of this book:

> Reality rarely matches dream. But only dreams give nobility to purpose. This is the star I hope to follow—which I know most of you have seen, and which I first glimpsed many years ago in the Texas night.

> When the helpless call for help—the hearing must hear, the seeing must see, and the able must act.

> It is an America where every man has an equal chance for the well-being that is essential to the enjoyment of the freedom that we brag about.

> The Gulf of Tonkin may be distant Asian waters, but none can be detached about what happened there.

High-school students will be writing essays on these paragraphs. One's stomach turns over. It is certain that if Barry Goldwater had written the same book, everyone would be agreed his style was a menace. Still, what is quoted up to here is still English, English more or less. It is in the depth of the real prose articulated by Johnson and his corps of ghost writers that the heart of the darkness resides. For Johnson is not a writer and has no wish to be. He is a communications engineer. He uses words in interlocking aggregates which fence in thoughts like cattle. At bottom, the style consists of nothing but connectives and aggregate words—that is, political phrases five words long which are one aggregate word and so should be hyphenated. Example:

> And it is one-of-the-great-tasks-of-Presidential-leadership to make our people aware that they share-a-fundamental-unity-of-interest-and-purpose-and-belief.

The essence of totalitarian prose is that it does not define, it does not deliver. It oppresses. It obstructs from above. It is profoundly contemptuous of the minds who will receive the message. So it does its best to dull this consciousness with sentences which are nothing but bricked-in power structures. Or alternately a totalitarian prose slobbers upon an audience a sentimentality so debauched that admiration for shamelessness is inspired. But then, sentimentality is the emotional promiscuity of those who have no sentiment:

> When I was a child, one of my first memories was hearing the powder go off on an anvil on Armistice Day. I remember the terror that flowed from the *Lusitania*. I remember seeing boys come marching home, and the welcome we gave them at our little schoolhouse. When Pearl Harbor was attacked . . .

There is one expanding horror in American life. It is that our long odyssey toward liberty, democracy and freedom-for- all may be achieved in such a way that utopia remains forever closed, and we live in freedom and hell, debased of style, not individual from one another, void of courage, our fear rationalized away. We will all have enough money and we will all have a vote. The money will buy appliances made of plastic, and the money will buy books just as bad as *My Hope for America* or *The Conscience of a Conservative*.

The dream of democracy—that the average man possesses riches within himself worthy of a lord—will evolve into some anomalous electronic shape of human, half genius, half lout, and the liberation of existence will not take place. Only the buildings will continue to be built—bigger housing for all, slum clearance, urban renewal, Edward Durrell Stone, until we will look as if indeed we lost a war, as if we had been bombed to the ground, and built ourselves up again just so quickly and cheaply as the barracks could be slapped together.

"In the next forty years," writes Johnson, "we must rebuild the entire urban United States." But who will do it? Whose vision will prevail? Which head of horror may condemn generations not yet born to look at faceless buildings and roofless roofs, the totalitarianism stealing in from without, from the formless forms and imprisoned air of a new society which had lost the clue that a democracy could become equable only if it became great, that finally the world would continue to exist only by an act of courage and a search for style. Democracy flowers with style; without it, there is a rot of wet weeds. Which is why we love the memory so of F.D.R. and J.F.K. For they offered high style to the poor. And that is worth more than a housing project. That is the war against poverty.

Still, Lyndon Johnson must be given a vote. Because *My Hope for America* contains one good sentence, one more than Barry Goldwater could claim. This sentence reads: ". . . the wall between rich and poor is a wall of glass through which all can see." It inspires a corollary which is almost as good—the space between hypocrisy and honest manner may not forever insulate the powerful from the poor.

PAUL GOODMAN

The Great Society

A reasonable function of government is to see to it that the conditions of life are tolerable. In modern societies this might involve
considerable government intervention, to prevent or remedy social
and physical evils, like urban poverty, exploitation of labor, traffic
congestion, air pollution. But such a safeguarding function is entirely
different from government trying to make life excellent, to make society moral, civilized, or magnificent. Intellectual or moral excellence
is not a likely province for rulers of any breed, and certainly not for
American politicians who have risen to power by speaking banalities,

The Great Society. From *The New York Review of Books,* October 14, 1965.
Reprinted by permission of the author.

making deals, and pandering, and who stay in power by avoiding the risks of sharp definition, imagination, scrupulous integrity, or even too much wit. Political arts have their use, but they are not the way to spiritual excellence.

Yet the last three administrations have kept dabbling in this direction. President Eisenhower, who was hardly literate, ordered a commission to map our National Goals, and under him government agencies began to improve the school curricula and speed up intervention in scientific research. John Kennedy, who was stylish and had academic connections, called us to service and he wanted us to be respected for our civilization as well as our military and economic power. He was a champion of art centers, neo-glassic architecture, and concerts at the White House; above all, he speeded up the harnessing of academic social sciences to government policy. And now Lyndon Johnson, who is culturally noted for monograms and driving fast, is going to inaugurate for us The Great Society.

I do not think this was only a campaign slogan. Even if it were, we must note the change in slogans. "Fair Deal" and "New Deal" used to refer to political economy and were a legitimate bid for votes; "New Frontier" and "Great Society" are more spiritual. (Barry Goldwater, correspondingly, threatened to restore us to Moral Order.) In any case, the President has carried his slogan over into 1965, and when his oblique eyes become dreamy and his voice avuncular on the theme of our future greatness, I am insulted by his pretension.

Do not misunderstand me. When the President speaks of trying to dissolve hard-core poverty, assuring equal rights, opening to every child the opportunity for an education, or coping with the blight of cities, I assent. (It is said that this populist strain in LBJ is authentic, and I hope so.) But that is not the program of a great society but of any decent society. It should be urged modestly and executed resolutely. There is no cause for fanfare in doing justice where we have been unjust, conserving where we have been vandals, and spending for neglected public goods what a small country like Denmark or Holland provides as a matter of course.

But the fact is that every element of The Great Society, including its war on poverty and its conservation, is contaminated by, compromised by, and finally determined by power lust, greed, and fear of change. No good thing is done for its own sake. Let me give half a dozen examples—I could give a hundred. The drive to schooling, even in its propaganda, is not to liberate the children and to insure that we will have independent and intelligent citizens (this was the educational aim of Jefferson); it is apprentice-training of the middle class for the corporations and military, and a desperate attempt to make slum children employable and ruly. Beautification and area development are treated as adjuncts of the automobile business. We will curb the billboards but multiply and landscape the highways that destroy country and city both. Eighty per cent of the billion for Appalachia is going for highways. Yet almost acute emergencies, like air and water pollution and the insecticides, are bogged in "research" because of hostile lobbies and because there is no money to be made of them. The cities are overcrowded, yet farm policy persistently favors food-chains and big plantations and drives small farmers out, so beautiful, vast areas are depopulating and returning to swamp. In the cities, housing, renewal, and community development are tied to real-estate bonanzas, the alliance of national and municipal political machines, and even the aggrandizement of the Welfare bureaucracy. In the crucial test case of Mobilization for Youth in New York, the move toward grassroots democracy was swiftly crushed and brought under professional control, staffed by City Hall, Washington consenting. (As Edgar and Jean Cahn have pointed out, in the War on Poverty, as in all wars, the invading army insures its own welfare before that of the occupied population.) In communications, there has ceased to be any attempt to decentralize television and get some variety, if not foliage, into the wasteland. Indeed, by temperament President Johnson hankers for consensus and managed news; he says he welcomes responsible criticism, but it's an angry welcome; and the projection of his personality and ikons is beginning to resemble the style of Russia or Cuba. In forwarding the fine arts, the government neglects the traditional, useful, and safe method of underwriting standard repertory and editions of the American classics, but it toys with the obnoxious official art of Arts Councils, glamorous culture centers, and suppers for the famous. Meantime, free lances are bulldozed from their lots and it is harder for creative people to be decently poor in their own way. The Department of Justice keeps whittling away at civil liberties, and the emasculation of Congress proceeds. The arms budget continues to increase. Now a space-ship will explicitly become a new grotesque weapon, and we explicitly use the adventure of exploration for propaganda. And it is hard to believe the President's moral commitment to civil rights at home when he dispatches marines and bombers to subjugate foreign peoples whose civil rights threaten what he sometimes calls the Free World and sometimes our National Interests.

Perhaps most alarming is the bland affirmation of clashing contradictories, as if people were already imbeciles. When we bomb hospitals and burn villages, the President is bound to make an unusually tender announcement about cerebral palsy (and the marines give out candy). When we allot 1.7 billions for a new space weapon, our astronauts are at once sent on a world tour for peace.

The theory of The Great Society is obvious enough. Lyndon Johnson came in during an unparalleled prosperity, with a consensus of businessmen and liberals and, seemingly, money for everything, including tax cuts to encourage investment. He made a fairly graceful capitulation for the Negro protest. Thus, The Great Society could re-invest unprecedented profits in new fields, including the public sector; could provide unskilled and semi-skilled jobs; and could consolidate the votes of the urban poor. But if we examine this happy formula, we find that money, power, and fear of change are the determinants. We do not find the magnanimity, disinterestedness, and imagination of a great society. Worse, it is less and less an American society. Instead of tackling the political puzzle of how to maintain democracy in a complex technology and among urban masses, it multiplies professional-client and patron-client relationships. Worst of all, if we watch, during ten minutes of television, the horrors of the world, the piggish commercials, and the nightly performance of the President, we do not see even a decent society. As the Connecticut Circuit Court recently put it succinctly, in clearing some tabloids of charges of obscenity: "Coarse and puerile these tabloids are, but so is much of our civilization. We doubt that they will pollute the social atmosphere."

Nevertheless, the concept of a national mission cooked up by the past three administrations is not merely a fraud. It is an ideology made necessary by contemporary history. In the first place, there has developed a dangerous vacuum of political-moral values, dangerous especially for the young. To give an important example: there must be *some* human use of our galloping high technology better than the infinite expansion of a hardware Gross National Product; affluence is no longer enough. One purpose of the big slogans has been to meet this moral demand and yet contain it, as we have seen, in the control of the same leaders and corporations. So far, the official moralists have not hit on anything believable, but that may come.

Secondly, however—and this, I think, is the essence—there must be some general ideology, whatever it is, to give a warrant to an amazing new grouping that has emerged in our society, the American Establishment. For this purpose, The Great Society might prove good enough, and it is virulent.

An Establishment is the clubbing together of the secular and moral leaders of society—in industry, the military, labor unions, the cities, sciences and arts, the universities, the church, and state—to determine not only the economy and policy but the standards and ideals of the nation. The role of an Establishment is to tell what is right, accredited, professional, British (German, Russian, etc.), and to rule out what is not (not *Kultur*, not Leninist, etc.). An important part of an Establishment is a large stable of mandarins to raise the tone, use correct scientific method, and invent rationalizations. Also, the literate mandarins write the speeches.

There is no doubt that such an interlocking accrediting club has attained enormous power in the United States. Its genius is to go round and round and be self-enclosed. The job in the want ads says "M.S. required," for industry respects the university; but meantime the university is getting contracted research from industry and the government. Cities or settlement-houses will get funds from Washington if they employ accredited staff. (I am laying stress on school credentials because education is probably the biggest business in the country; there has been no such class of monks since Henry the Eighth.) Retired generals become vice-presidents in charge of contracting; they know whom to talk to and how. A broadcaster seeks his license from the F.C.C., but the administration has a healthy respect for the power of the broadcaster—hardly one license has been rescinded. Meantime, by F.C.C. mandate, a commercial sponsor cannot censor the program he sponsors, but he does have the right to expect that it will not tarnish or jar the image of his firm. Tax-exempt foundations support what *is* art or research, as recommended by those who are accredited, and they will underwrite a pilot project if it is carried out by a proper institution. But woe to a project that has nothing to recommend it but that it is a good idea, and whose inventor carries his office under his hat. In principle such a project cannot exist, and soon it does not exist.

Now our country has had neither a traditional aristocracy nor a totalitarian dogma, so it is not easy for the American Establishment to find moral justification for so much omniscience and exclusive power. It has really thrived on quiet expansion and being taken for granted, like creeping socialism. It is not surprising that its ideology should be mere campaign slogans, future and hortatory, half public relations and half corny dreams.

But however hazy its justification, the personnel of the Establishment has specific properties: it must be rooted in the baronial institutions and it must be conspicuously idealistic. It was with uncanny precision—in fact, the candidates are pre-selected for him from 25,000 *vitae* by computer—that Johnson chose John Gardner as Secretary of Health, Education, and Welfare. Gardner was the head of the Carnegie Corporation, and he is the author of a book called *Excellence*.

Thus, the process of spelling out and implementing the vague national mission is as follows: From the Establishment, the President chooses task forces. The task forces think up programs and these are given for execution to those accredited by the Establishment. It is not astonishing, then, if a major function, if not purpose, of The Great Society is to aggrandize the Establishment, the education barons, the broadcasting barons, the automobile barons, the shopping center barons. In a youth employment project, more than three-quarters of the appropriation will go for (accredited) staff salaries and research; not much is left for wages for the kids. Of course, sometimes there is an hilarious exception, as when some SNCC youngsters I know got $90 a day as consultants at a conference on poverty in Washington.

So a practical definition of The Great Society is: to provide professional employment and other business for card-carrying members of the Establishment. *This* is not a fraud.

Of course, The Great Society is strictly for domestic consumption. Abroad, our friends are drifting away because we have lost our reputation; persuasion gives way to brute force. Thus, by a grim devolution, The Great Society turns out to be a liberal version of the old isolationism of Fortress America.

In conclusion, let me return to a thought mentioned above, the need to fill the moral vacuum. The technical, urban, and international premises of modern life have changed so rapidly and markedly that the old elites, who cling to their power, inevitably seem morally bankrupt, especially to the young. I have no doubt that this is the case everywhere—it has been persistently reported from the Soviet Union during the last ten years—but since ours is the most advanced country, we reveal the moral bankruptcy worst.

By the middle of the administration of Eisenhower, it was impossible for a public spokesman to say "the American Way of Life" with a straight face. And there occurred the flood of social criticism, often devastating, which left us morally dank indeed. It was in this context that the President's Commission on National Goals made its report. But it was a feeble effort that influenced nobody, certainly not the young. The beat generation withdrew. And there began the spiritual defection of college youth from the corporations that has increased steadily. (In 1956, according to a survey by David Riesman, the great majority of collegians wanted to work for a big organization. Just now, at Harvard, more students want to go into the tiny Peace Corps than into business!)

John Kennedy hit on the Posture of Sacrifice, which was what young people wanted to hear, something to give meaning to the affluent society. But apart from the token of the Peace Corps—filled largely, as it turned out, by youth of the upper middle class—he could not produce anything to sacrifice *for*, not with so many credit cards around. Indeed, when they asked what they could do for their country, many of the best youth found that they wanted to serve precisely against the government, sometimes illegally, in the Negro movement and protesting against fall-out. And the majority of the returning Peace Corps itself have proved to be critical of the society they have come back to.

The Great Society, as we have seen, started with more moral ammunition: an electoral campaign against Black Reaction, a bill for Civil Rights, a war against poverty. Yet once again many of the best youth have remained unconverted. During the nominating convention, the militants of the Freedom Democratic Party rejected the Humphrey compromise. Shortly after the electoral triumph of The Great Society, the students at Berkeley raged in their thousands. This year, there have been student troubles on a hundred campuses, East, Middle West, and even South. The Students for a Democratic Society have thrown themselves into undermining precisely the War on Poverty, which they consider undemocratic and insincere.

And both many students and many teachers seem to want to undermine even the war for the Free World in Vietnam. Some writers refused to go to the President's party.

In brief, as a moral incentive for youth, The Great Society, like its predecessors, is unpersuasive. It does not square with the obvious facts; it is too corrupt. Fatally, it avoids the deep problems that demand real changes. The political-moral problems that deeply interest youth are of the following kind: How to use high technology for human advantage? How to regain substantive democracy in modern cities and with mass-communications? How to get rid of the Bomb and the whole atmosphere of the Cold War? How to be educated without being processed? How to work at something worthwhile outside the rat-race of an infinitely expanding GNP? How to avoid 1984?

The Establishment in America and its President do not cope with these questions because they *are* morally bankrupt.

PETER SCHRAG

Appalachia: Again the Forgotten Land

Once again Appalachia is becoming America's forgotten land. Seven years and more than seven billion federal dollars after John F. Kennedy brought the region to national attention, grand solutions have soured into new problems, the exploitation of land and people continues, and even the best and most hopeful efforts are jeopardized by a war 10,000 miles away and by ugly political machines all too close to home.

Because of the work of a handful of dedicated people—VISTA workers, Appalachian volunteers, and local residents—some hope

Appalachia: Again the Forgotten Land. From *Saturday Review*, January 27, 1968. Reprinted by permission of the publisher and author.

has returned with the mounting welfare checks, and some sense of the possible is growing even in the most remote creeks and hollows. But now the programs that have been most effective—many of them aimed at giving the poor a measure of choice and control—are threatened by the politicians' response to local commercial pressures and by the rapacious demands of the strip-mine operators. Efforts at regional development are being directed by distant planners and small-town chambers of commerce, while individuals trying to organize the poor are called agitators and Communists, and are driven from the region under agreements between state politicians and national poverty officials who have become politically too weak to resist.

Appalachia, the original American frontier, extends from southern Pennsylvania to northern Alabama, covering 182,000 square miles of land rich in coal, timber, sandstone, natural gas, water, and some of the most magnificent scenery on the continent. In 1966, nearly 100 million tons of coal worth close to $400 million were mined in Kentucky alone. Where the strip mines have spared the hillsides, the folded mountains, covered by white oak, pine, walnut, beech, and other trees, extend in all directions to the blue-gray horizon. But in the half-abandoned coal camps that adjoin the sulphur-polluted creeks, on the streets of the little towns, and in the welfare offices, the poverty of the people stands in brutal contrast to the wealth of the land. Along the winding roads, the rotting carcases of abandoned automobiles lie alongside smoldering coal dumps and the decaying tipples of exhausted mines, and in the brown and yellow streams, once rich with fish, the sad trash of poverty accumulates in rusty piles.

Appalachia, now growing its third welfare generation, has counties where more than a third of the population is unemployed, where the government check—social security, welfare, aid to dependent children—is the prime source of income, and where some men are so far from their last job that it cannot properly be said that they have a trade at all. Here the average adult has a sixth-grade education, three-fourths of the children who start school drop out before they complete the twelfth grade, and the statistics of human pathology—tuberculosis, silicosis, infant mortality—are so high that they do not belong in the Western world at all.

Everything has eroded: The best of the resources flow forever downstream and toward the industrial cities of the North. Heavy rains wash the topsoil from the hills and turn the rivers into muddy torrents, the coal fires the mills of the North and the generators of the TVA (which is the prime buyer of Appalachian fuel), while the most skilled and ambitious of the young leave the hills and hollows to find work in Cleveland, Chicago, or Detroit. "We've been the great pool of manpower for the Northeast," said a poverty worker in eastern Tennessee. "And the pool has been turned on and off at will. The rest of the country gets automobiles and the gadgets of affluence. All this region gets is silicosis."

Appalachia's coal regions enjoyed a brief, uncertain moment of prosperity during and immediately after World War II, when the war economy and the pressure of John L. Lewis's United Mine Workers brought decent wages, hospitals, and pension plans. But when the war boom ended, many of the mines closed, leaving the survivors of a single-product economy without resources or useful skills. The coal industry ultimately returned to prosperity with a rising demand for fuel, but it did so as a highly efficient, mechanized enterprise. Using modern equipment, 140,000 men can now dig more coal than 700,000 did twenty years ago. And while many of the deep mines continue to operate, frequently under enlightened management, a substantial part of the industry is now stripping the mountains, cutting or blasting away the topsoil and vegetation—which spills down the slopes—to get at the coal beneath. Each year the strip mines of Kentucky scar some 12,000 acres of land, leaving the bare cliffs of the high wall above and the sliding soil banks on the hills below.

The legal basis for this damage rests in the so-called broad form deed: Before strip mining became prevalent, thousands of mountaineers sold their mineral rights to coal and land companies for a few cents an acre, entitling the companies to remove minerals and holding them harmless for any damage except that incurred through malice. The courts have held that this immunity extends even to the uprooting of graves and the destruction of the homes and gardens that are occasionally covered by slides. Under the broad form deed, said a mountaineer, "they've dug up the dead and buried the living." Although several states have enacted strip-mine laws requiring operators to restore the land, and although many companies are diligently trying to comply, enforcement is often difficult or ineffective.

In West Virginia, a new statute now entitles property owners to collect triple damages from the coal companies, but in the mountains of eastern Kentucky that state's law has had little effect. Kentucky's new governor, Louie B. Nunn, received support from the strip-mine interests in the 1967 election, and it is unlikely that he will be overzealous in enforcing or strengthening it. Under his predecessor, Edward T. Breathitt, state officials experimented with techniques of restoring the hillsides, but even they admitted privately that where the slopes are steep, there is no possible way of eliminating slides and reclaiming the land. In the mountains of eastern Kentucky, the only effective hope for conservation appears to be the elimination of the strip mine altogether. (Last month, the day Breathitt's term expired, he approved a set of tough regulations, limiting strip mines to slopes of less than 28 degrees; if those regulations stand, they will severely restrict strip mining and will represent a major victory for conservation in the region.)

In this sad economy of food stamps and subsistence, the coal company is no longer the great employer—and hence the paternalistic provider—it used to be. Gone are the days when the company owned the buildings, ran the store, and furnished the services, and even the most naïve have now abandoned the hope that some day "the mines will open up again." What remains is the condition of dependency: Through a half-century of rural industrialization, the once-independent mountaineer was reduced to reliance on a single enterprise, and, when it no longer required his labor, to nothing except the dole. The public payroll, and most notably the public schools, now furnish the prime source of employment. In Appalachia, schools mean jobs for bus drivers, clerks, lunchroom employees, coaches, and teachers, and hence they represent the most important source of political power at hand. In the isolated mountain counties where kinship and tribal loyalties overshadow the abstractions of political ethics, the school superintendent is often a political boss who controls contracts for insurance, construction, and fuel, appointment to other offices, and employment in the system.

In Breathitt County, Kentucky, for example, Marie Turner or her husband have held the school superintendency for more than forty years, and thus they also control most of the other offices the county has to offer. There are similar machines in other areas, and although many people feel that people like the Turners have been benevolent bosses—Breathitt County, someone said, would have fallen apart without the Turners—they have been bosses neverthe-

less. At a time when Appalachia was out of the national consciousness and the mountaineer was a figure for mythology and amuse-
ment, the Turners did what they could for their people. The *quid pro
quo* was patronage and power.

The American romance with the happy hillbilly came to an end
in the early Sixties. Prompted by Mr. Kennedy's concern with Appalachian poverty—which he saw first hand in the 1960 West Virginia primary—Americans began to discover the misery behind the
moonshine. Television crews and magazine writers swarmed to the
hills in such numbers that one Kentucky motel owner began to conduct photographic safaris to hollows that he promised "ain't been
worked yet." While bands of hungry, desperate miners roamed the
coal regions dynamiting trains and bridges, Congress passed the Manpower Development and Training Act, the Appalachia Redevelop-
ment Act, and a variety of other measures designed to bring the here-
tofore invisible poor some share of the affluence that most Americans took for granted.

Although the federal poverty program was aimed at all indigent
Americans, Appalachia came to symbolize, along with the urban
ghetto, the most pressing item on the nation's social agenda. As a
consequence, special funds have been appropriated for the construction of Appalachian highways, water facilities, and hospitals; the
distribution of surplus food has been augmented through a food
stamp program which enables the poor to purchase more groceries
than their welfare checks would otherwise permit; unemployed fathers have been given jobs, at $1.25 an hour, in a "work experience
and training" program (they are generally called "happy pappies");
young men and women have been enrolled in the Job Corps and the
Neighborhood Youth Corps; vocational education has received increased support, and large sums have been made available for the
education of the disadvantaged, which, in the mountain counties,
means almost everybody.

To anyone visiting Appalachia now, these programs have clearly
had an effect: new roads and vocational schools are under construction or already in use; the happy pappies have planted trees on hillsides that had been covered by strip-mine soil banks; medical facilities
are more accessible; the school dropout rate has been reduced (partly
because federal funds are keyed to enrollment); and there appear
to be fewer obvious signs of malnutrition than there were three years

ago. In some families, the money earned by adolescents in the Youth Corps has become the most important source of income. It has also become a source of pride and respect. "After those kids received their first pay check," said Don Roarke, the director of a four-county Youth Corps in eastern Kentucky, "they were dressed better, they held their heads higher. You could see the difference." At the same time, the graduates of many vocational programs are finding jobs as heavy-machine operators and mine technicians, a few of them in the mountains, others in Northern cities.

For many more, however, the existing programs serve only to hide the misery: The new highways are beginning to make it possible to cross large portions of Appalachia without seeing a tarpaper shack or a coal dump; the food stamps run out before the end of the month, and the schools, though far better than they used to be, still remain a blind alley, graduating children who are approximately two years behind the national average on standardized tests. "The bare gut essentials are now being met," said Tom Gish, the editor of the Whitesburg, Kentucky, *Mountain Eagle*, who is undoubtedly the most outspoken and dedicated journalist in the region. "By and large people are getting fed and getting coal for the winter. If you go back to the early Sixties when there was mass hunger and violence, then you can say there's been improvement. Peace has been restored."

But the peace is shaky, and the economy remains dependent on the federal government. President Johnson's recent declaration that "the dole is dead" was, to say it mildly, premature. Poverty remains endemic: Median family income in eastern Kentucky is $3,505, and Gish predicts that if poverty funds are reduced there will be more violence. In the county seats, the prosperous get roads and water lines and sewers, but only a few miles away the privies stand alongside the dirty creeks from which people draw their water, rain turns the unpaved roads into muddy ruts, and the youngsters can't go to school because they have no shoes.

The prime beneficiaries of government funds appear to be the swelling banks, which are afraid to invest their deposits in anything but government bonds; the small businesses; and the politicians. For all their ignorance and isolation, the economic and political interests of Appalachia have a highly developed knack for using outside help to perpetuate the existing structure and the conditions of dependency. In Perry County, Kentucky, a political enemy of a former county school superintendent used his influence as director of a poverty project to help elect a new school board and oust the superintendent; the new administration then rewarded him with the directorship of another federally financed program administered by the schools. In other areas, the directors of happy pappy programs discourage their charges from participating in community action groups that threaten local political machines, and in almost every community the traditions of nepotism are so powerful that many people still regard the poverty program as a source of employment rather than as a means of upgrading the skills of human beings and the social health of the community. "Jobs are coveted so much, and loyalties to kin are so strong," said a poverty worker in Kentucky, "that it's pretty hard to persuade anyone that you have to pick people on merit."

Although some training programs have brought new skills and confidence, and although many children who had once gone hungry through the school day are now receiving hot lunches (sometimes even in the most remote one-room schools), many school officials have refused to appoint outsiders, preferring to promote politically faithful employees to the uncertainties of new blood and new ideas. In one community, a group of men who were enrolled for training in construction and maintenance composed a letter to Washington:

> We were in the building and maintainence class under MDTA that took up on April 10 and ended September 29. They told us each day we would have 2 hours of electricity, pluming, carpentry and painting but for the most of it all we did was paint school buildings and repair and cover the roofs of the schools. When some of the men bucked on painting so much they was told if they didnt like it they could leave. To start we was told the government would buy around a thousand dollars of lumber a month for us to work with we unloaded plenty new lumber and racked it up on the racks. For awhile we used some then we was told we could buy it for 25 cents a foot and then they said it wasnt for sale but it still got missing. In electricity all we had were 9 days, on our certificate of training it says we got 320 hours. They just didn't care much if we learned a thing or not we was just putting in time. Now we are in worse shape than when we started and we got knocked off the food stamps for 30 days. We didnt get the training they said or the permanent jobs they promised at the start. The only jobs we have heard about are temporary and a long way off. A man with a family in school cant just leave out at the promise of a job.

Given these conditions, the most promising idea for Appalachia has been community action—training individuals to organize local groups for social improvement, community welfare, and self-help. As

originally conceived, the Community Action Program (CAP) of the
Office of Economic Opportunity was to include "maximum feasible
participation" of the poor: Community action agencies were, if possible, to be free from domination by local politicians. In some areas
of Appalachia, the program worked effectively, despite the suspicions
of county officials: Community centers have been built, small mar-
keting cooperatives (selling quilts and other local products) have
been organized, and new leadership has developed. In the eastern
Kentucky counties of Leslie, Knott, Letcher, and Perry, a four-county
Community Action Program (LKLP), which includes poor people
as well as sympathetic county judges, has established a network of
depots to inform people of their welfare rights, of new training programs, and of the availability of medical facilities. Among other
things, LKLP operated a transportation system to bring the sick
from the hollows to the area clinics, it is training local people in
welfare work and social service, and it has prompted a number of
projects to clear the region of decaying bridges and abandoned coal
tipples.

Despite such successes, however—and there are others—many
CAP agencies have been captured by established interests or abandoned after local battles destroyed embryonic organizations before
they had a chance to function. Many of those that survive must strad-
dle an uncertain line between ineffectiveness and the dangerous
course of challenging the established order. Recent Congressional
action, moreover, indicates that control for all local CAP agencies
will be given to local elected officials, thus making CAP—in Appalachia, at least—the biggest potential pork barrel since the invention of
rivers and harbors.

Because of the limitations of the Community Action Program,
some of the most effective community work has been done by VISTA
(Volunteers in Service to America—the domestic Peace Corps); by
the Appalachian Committee to Save the Land and People, which has
been fighting the strip mines; by the long-standing Council of the
Southern Mountains; and by the Appalachian Volunteers, a private
organization which originated among students at Berea College, but
which is now fully autonomous. Originally, the Appalachian Volunteers (AVs) concentrated on the repair of schoolhouses, the distribution of books—more than a million were collected and placed in
mountain schools—and on other community work. The AVs and
VISTAs, who often work together, have moved into isolated moun-

tain communities—places named Marrowbone and Cave Ridge, Clover Fork and Horse Creek—have come to know the inhabitants, and are helping to create new organizations and a new sense of confidence: adult education groups, nursery schools, community centers, craft shops, and, most significantly, a belief that choices are available and collective action possible. "These are the first people," said a woman in the mountains, "who promised to do something, and then did."

What they have done, among other things, is to arouse the suspicions and fears of the established interests. In the past year, the AVs have become increasingly involved in the strip-mine issue and in tax reform, helping to organize protests, transport people to meetings, and warn affected property owners when the strip-mine bulldozers were coming. In their zealousness, some have talked, none too privately, about overturning local political structures and establishing some vague new order; a few were poorly trained or offensive in dress or manners. As a consequence, they have been labeled Communists and agitators (though many are natives of the region), and they are now threatened with the suspension of all federal support.

The precipitating incident took place in the summer of 1967 when a small Pike County, Kentucky, farmer named Jink Ray, supported by his neighbors (and, later, by Appalachian Volunteers), stood in front of the bulldozers of the Puritan Coal Company, which had come to strip his land. Within a few days the matter had become a regional *cause célèbre* and threatened to develop into a mountain shoot-out. Under the new Kentucky strip-mine law, Governor Breathitt lifted the company's permit, ordering the state's Department of Natural Resources to determine whether the slopes to be mined exceed the statutory limits. Two weeks later, after several conferences among Pike County officials, the county sheriff, in a midnight raid, arrested an AV fieldworker named Joe Mulloy and two organizers for the Southern Conference Education Fund on charges of violating a Kentucky sedition law. (The man charged with the prosecution was a former president of the Independent Coal Operators Association who was then a candidate for state office.)

In indicting the three, the Pike County grand jury concluded that "a well organized and well financed effort is being made to promote and spread the communistic theory of the violent and forceful overthrow of the government of Pike County" and that "the employees of the Appalachian Volunteers and other federally financed antipoverty programs have collaborated and cooperated with known communist organizers to help them organize and promote the violent overthrow of the constitutional government of Pike County." The grand jury, said Harry M. Caudill, the Whitesburg attorney who is probably the most eloquent spokesman for the mountains, "was certain that the revolution was about to begin in Pike County, and that the neighboring counties, in domino fashion, would then fall to the enemy."

Although the sedition law was quickly declared unconstitutional by a federal court, the Pike County affair reinforced suspicions not only about the Appalachian Volunteers, but about everything that smacked of community action. In many eastern Kentucky counties VISTA workers are no longer welcome. In West Virginia, Governor Hulett Smith, while praising the VISTA program in mental health, charged the AVs with "misconduct" and demanded an OEO investigation. In Kentucky, Governor Breathitt (who could not succeed himself as governor but was nonetheless involved in the political campaign) demanded and received assurances from OEO Director Sargent Shriver that some current OEO grants to the Appalachian Volunteers would not be renewed, and that the cancellation of other federal support for AV activities would receive "most serious consideration." In Hazard, Kentucky, a few months later, an exasperated staff member of the Community Action agency declared that "we're still trying to beat this Red rap. People in the Work Experience and Training Program have been told that if they had anything to do with us they'd be off the rolls."

What is most in jeopardy now is not merely the budget of the Appalachian Volunteers (who are trying to find private funds to replace their uncertain federal support), but the principle of independent community action itself. The efforts of the past three years have (in some areas at least) generated a degree of independence that will be difficult to arrest: Even before the poverty program began, the Appalachian Group to Save the Land and People, composed entirely of mountaineers, had begun to campaign for stricter stripmine laws and for the imposition of a severance tax on the minerals that now flow untaxed from the region. In the creeks and hollows, residents have stopped bulldozers, sometimes with their bodies, sometimes with shotguns and dynamite. When Youth Corps funds ran out during the 1967 Congressional debate on the poverty program, the staff members in many Appalachian communities came to work anyway, and when Shriver announced the curtailment of AV support, the residents of a number of mountain communities signed letters and telegrams of protest. This fall, for the first time in history, teachers in an eastern Kentucky county went on strike for higher pay. Nevertheless, if prime responsibility for the Appalachian portion of the war on poverty is delegated to the established regimes, the basic political arrangements will remain unchanged: Every dollar in federal funds will make the politicians that much stronger.

And yet, even if Appalachia's poor achieve greater political power and independence, the problems will persist. "You can't have real community action," said a Kentucky CAP director, "until you have economic choice." To date, regional development has meant a few highways and hospitals, not jobs. The area's topography and its unskilled population make it unattractive to industry, leading to the desperate suggestion that the best program is training people so they can move away. "They want to regard these towns as breeding grounds," said Robert Cornett, who was Breathitt's director of area development. "I'm losing faith in the planners. They're always looking for big solutions. You have to do it slowly with roads and health and small businesses, woodworking industries, or maybe poultry."

People like Cornett hope to encourage the construction of new housing (which is desperately needed) through the pooling of public and private resources, and to foster greater local concern for development. "You have to use what's here, to improve the power structure, not tear it down." So far, the results have been meager. In some of the county seats, even the most proper people are still unpersuaded that poverty really exists, or that it would persist if the unemployed just had enough character to work. "I grew up here in Hazard," said a staff member of the local CAP, "but I never noticed the poverty until I went outside. I never saw it."

Perhaps the chief consequence of the recent programs in Appalachia is the realization that poverty and exploitation, isolation and ignorance, are not susceptible to left-handed solutions, that they are linked to the general affluence, and that they raise moral questions which strike at the very heart of America's willingness to bring a decent life to all its citizens. What do the Combs and Caudills, the Napiers and Brashears of eastern Kentucky think, after the food stamps run out in the third week of the month, when they hear the President declare that the "dole is dead"? What kind of judgment does one make about a nation that can spend close to $500,000 to kill a Vietcong but less than $150 a month to support the family of an unemployed miner who lives in a place called Stinking Creek? How great is a society that permits the systematic, mechanized defacing of its hillsides while it encourages the natives of these same hills to move into the slums of Detroit? "People expected this thing to be solved in six months," said Perley F. Ayer, the chairman of the Council of the Southern Mountains. "But in education alone we're 5,000,000 years behind."

It is difficult to cheer the results of Appalachian development or the war on poverty: The harmonious interplay of poverty, politics, and the welfare mind combine to frustrate even the most valiant effort. But it is even more difficult to criticize the intent of these programs or the officials who are charged with running them. They have been forced to live with a limited and reluctant mandate that prohibits them from anything more than making poverty bearable and, if possible, invisible. The vested Appalachian interests in the status quo—coal companies, railroads, banks, local bar associations, insurance agencies, politicians—are so vast that they represent a fair cross section of American society itself. Their stockholders and beneficiaries live all over the nation; they help sustain our affluence. If Appalachia hasn't changed, it may be in part because too many are dependent on it as it now is. "The reason little has happened," said Ayer, "is that America doesn't have its heart in it."

MARTIN GANSBERG

38 Who Saw Murder Didn't Call the Police

For more than half an hour 38 respectable, law-abiding citizens in Queens watched a killer stalk and stab a woman in three separate attacks in Kew Gardens.

Twice their chatter and the sudden glow of their bedroom lights interrupted him and frightened him off. Each time he returned, sought her out, and stabbed her again. Not one person telephoned the police during the assault; one witness called after the woman was dead.

That was two weeks ago today.

38 Who Saw Murder Didn't Call the Police. From *The New York Times*, March 27, 1964. © 1964 by The New York Times Company. Reprinted by permission.

Still shocked is Assistant Chief Inspector Frederick M. Lussen, in charge of the borough's detectives and a veteran of 25 years of homicide investigations. He can give a matter-of-fact recitation on many murders. But the Kew Gardens slaying baffles him—not because it is a murder, but because the "good people" failed to call the police.

"As we have reconstructed the crime," he said, "the assailant had three chances to kill this woman during a 35-minute period. He returned twice to complete the job. If we had been called when he first attacked, the woman might not be dead now."

This is what the police say happened beginning at 3:20 A.M. in the staid, middle-class, tree-lined Austin Street area:

Twenty-eight-year-old Catherine Genovese, who was called Kitty by almost everyone in the neighborhood, was returning home from her job as manager of a bar in Hollis. She parked her red Fiat in a lot adjacent to the Kew Gardens Long Island Rail Road Station, facing Mowbray Place. Like many residents of the neighborhood, she had parked there day after day since her arrival from Connecticut a year ago, although the railroad frowns on the practice.

She turned off the lights of her car, locked the door, and started to walk the 100 feet to the entrance of her apartment at 82-70 Austin Street, which is in a Tudor building, with stores on the first floor and apartments on the second.

The entrance to the apartment is in the rear of the building because the front is rented to retail stores. At night the quiet neighborhood is shrouded in the slumbering darkness that marks most residential areas.

Miss Genovese noticed a man at the far end of the lot, near a seven-story apartment house at 82-40 Austin Street. She halted. Then, nervously, she headed up Austin Street toward Lefferts Boulevard, where there is a call box to the 102nd Police Precinct in nearby Richmond Hill.

She got as far as a street light in front of a bookstore before the man grabbed her. She screamed. Lights went on in the 10-story apartment house at 82-67 Austin Street, which faces the bookstore. Windows slid open and voices punctuated the early-morning stillness.

Miss Genovese screamed: "Oh, my God, he stabbed me! Please help me! Please help me!"

From one of the upper windows in the apartment house, a man called down: "Let that girl alone!"

The assailant looked up at him, shrugged, and walked down Austin Street toward a white sedan parked a short distance away. Miss Genovese struggled to her feet.

Lights went out. The killer returned to Miss Genovese, now trying to make her way around the side of the building by the parking lot to get to her apartment. The assailant stabbed her again.

"I'm dying!" she shrieked. "I'm dying!"

Windows were opened again, and lights went on in many apartments. The assailant got into his car and drove away. Miss Genovese staggered to her feet. A city bus, O-10, the Lefferts Boulevard line to Kennedy International Airport, passed. It was 3:35 A.M.

The assailant returned. By then, Miss Genovese had crawled to the back of the building, where the freshly painted brown doors to the apartment house held out hope for safety. The killer tried the first door; she wasn't there. At the second door, 82-62 Austin Street, he saw her slumped on the floor at the foot of the stairs. He stabbed her a third time—fatally.

It was 3:50 by the time the police received their first call, from a man who was a neighbor of Miss Genovese. In two minutes they were at the scene. The neighbor, a 70-year-old woman, and another woman were the only persons on the street. Nobody else came forward.

The man explained that he had called the police after much deliberation. He had phoned a friend in Nassau County for advice and then he had crossed the roof of the building to the apartment of the elderly woman to get her to make the call.

"I didn't want to get involved," he sheepishly told the police.

Six days later, the police arrested Winston Moseley, a 29-year-old business-machine operator, and charged him with the homicide. Moseley had no previous record. He is married, has two children and owns a home at 133-19 Sutter Avenue, South Ozone Park, Queens. On Wednesday, a court committed him to Kings County Hospital for psychiatric observation.

When questioned by the police, Moseley also said that he had slain Mrs. Annie May Johnson, 24, of 146-12 133d Avenue, Jamaica, on Feb. 29 and Barbara Kralik, 15, of 174-17 140th Avenue, Springfield Gardens, last July. In the Kralik case, the police are holding Alvin L. Mitchell, who is said to have confessed that slaying.

The police stressed how simple it would have been to have gotten in touch with them. "A phone call," said one of the detectives, "would have done it." The police may be reached by dialing "O" for operator or SPring 7-3100.

Today witnesses from the neighborhood, which is made up of one-family homes in the $35,000 to $60,000 range with the exception of the two apartment houses near the railroad station, find it difficult to explain why they didn't call the police.

A housewife, knowingly if quite casual, said, "We thought it was a lover's quarrel." A husband and wife both said, "Frankly, we were afraid." They seemed aware of the fact that events might have been different. A distraught woman, wiping her hands in her apron, said, "I didn't want my husband to get involved."

One couple, now willing to talk about that night, said they heard the first screams. The husband looked thoughtfully at the bookstore where the killer first grabbed Miss Genovese.

"We went to the window to see what was happening," he said, "but the light from our bedroom made it difficult to see the street." The wife, still apprehensive, added: "I put out the light and we were able to see better."

Asked why they hadn't called the police, she shrugged and replied: "I don't know."

A man peeked out from a slight opening in the doorway to his apartment and rattled off an account of the killer's second attack. Why hadn't he called the police at the time? "I was tired," he said without emotion. "I went back to bed."

It was 4:25 A.M. when the ambulance arrived to take the body of Miss Genovese. It drove off. "Then," a solemn police detective said, "the people came out."

WILLIAM STYRON

In the Jungle

It was perhaps unfortunate that Daley, the hoodlum suzerain of the city, became emblematic of all that the young people in their anguish cried out against, even though he plainly deserved it. No one should ever have been surprised that he set loose his battalions against the kids; it was the triumphant end-product of his style, and what else might one expect from this squalid person whose spirit suffused the great city as oppressively as that of some Central American field marshal? And it was no doubt inevitable, moreover, a component of the North American oligarchic manner—one could not imag-

In the Jungle. Reprinted with permission from *The New York Review of Books*, September 26, 1968. © 1968 The New York Review.

ine a Trujillo so mismanaging his public relations—that after the catastrophe had taken place he should remain so obscenely lodged in the public eye, howling "kike!" at Abe Ribicoff, packing the galleries with his rabble, and muttering hoarse irrelevancies about conspiracy and assassination, about the *Republican* convention ("They had a fence in Miami, too, Walter, nobody ever talks about *that!*") to a discomfited Cronkite, who wobbled in that Oriental presence between deference and fainthearted suggestions that Miami and Chicago just might not be the same sort of thing.

That is what many of us did along about Thursday night in Chicago—retreat to the center, the blissful black interior of some hotel room and turn on the television set. For after four days and nights in the storm outside, after the sleepless, eventually hallucinated connection with so many of the appalling and implausible events of that week, it was a relief to get off the streets and away from the parks and the Amphitheater and the boorish, stinking hotel lobbies and to see it as most Americans had seen it—even if one's last sight was that of the unspeakable Daley, attempting to explain away a shame that most people who witnessed it will feel to their bones for a very long time.

Yet, again, maybe in the immediate aftermath of the convention it was too bad that Daley should have hogged a disproportionate share of the infamy which has fallen upon the Democratic party; for if it is getting him off the hook too easily to call him a scapegoat, nonetheless the execration he has received (even the New York *Daily News*, though partly of course out of civic rivalry, carried jeering stories about him) may obscure the fact that Daley is only the nastiest symbol of stupidity and desuetude in a political party that may die, or perhaps is already dead, because it harbors too many of his breed and mentality. Humphrey, the departed John Bailey, John Connally, Richard Hughes, Muskie—all are merely eminent examples of a rigidity and blindness, a feebleness of thought, that have possessed the party at every level, reaching down to those Grant Wood delegates from North Dakota who spilled out from the elevators into my hotel lobby every morning, looking bright-eyed and war-hungry, or like Republicans, whom they emulated through becoming one of the few delegations that voted against the pacific minority Vietnam plank *en bloc*. It has been said that if various burdensome and antiquated procedural matters—the unit rule, for instance—had been eliminated prior to this convention, the McCarthy forces might have gained a much larger and more significant strength, and this is at least an arguable point of view; for a long while I myself believed it and worked rather hard to see such changes come about (some did), but now in retrospect it seems that the disaster was meant to be.

Recalling those young citizens for Humphrey who camped out downstairs in my hotel, that multitude of square, seersuckered fraternity boys and country club jocks with butch haircuts, from the suburbs of Columbus and Atlanta, who passed out Hubert buttons and Humphrey mints, recalling them and their elders, mothers and fathers, some of them delegates and not all of them creeps or fanatics by any means but an amalgam of everything—simply well-heeled, most of them, entrenched, party hacks tied to the mob or with a pipeline to some state boss, a substantial number hating the war but hating it not enough to risk dumping Hubert in favor of a vague professorial freak who couldn't feel concern over Prague and hung out with Robert Lowell—I think now that the petrification of a party which allowed such apathy and lack of adventurousness and moral inanition to set in had long ago shaped its frozen logic, determined its fatal choice months before McCarthy or, for that matter, Bobby Kennedy had come along to rock, ever so slightly, the colossal dreamboat. And this can only reinforce what appears to me utterly plausible: that whatever the vigor and force of the dissent, whatever one might say about the surprising strength of support that the minority report received on the floor, a bare but crucial majority of Americans still is unwilling to repudiate the filthy war. This is really the worst thought of all.

Right now, only a day or so after the event, it is hard to be sure of anything. A residue of anguish mingles with an impulse toward cynicism, and it all seems more than ever a happening. One usually sympathetic journalist of my acquaintance has argued with some logic but a little too much levity that the violent confrontations, like the show of muscle among the black militants, were at least only a psychological necessity: after all, there were no killings, few serious injuries, had there been no violence the whole affair would have been tumescent, impossibly strained, like *coitus interruptus*, and who would have had a bruise or a laceration to wear home as a hero's badge? As for myself, the image of one young girl no older than sixteen, sobbing bitterly as she was being led away down Balbo Avenue after being brutally cracked by a policeman's club, is not so much a memory as a scene imprinted on the retina—a metaphor of the garish and incomprehensible week—and it cannot be turned off like the Mr. Clean commercial that kept popping up between the scenes of carnage. I prefer to think that the events in Chicago were as momentous and as fateful as they seemed at the time, even amid the phantasmagorical play of smoke and floodlights where they were enacted.

One factor has been generally overlooked: the weather. Chicago was at its bluest and balmiest, and that gorgeous sunshine—almost springlike—could not help but subtly buoy the nastiest spirit and moderate a few tempers. Had the heat been as intense and as suffocating as it was when I first arrived in the city the Tuesday before the convention began, I feel certain that the subsequent mayhem would have become slaughter. I came at that time to the Credentials Committee meeting in the Conrad Hilton as one of four "delegate challengers" from Connecticut, presenting the claim that the popular vote in the state primaries had indicated that 13 delegates out of 44 should be seated for McCarthy, rather than the 9 allowed the McCarthy forces by John Bailey. Although logic and an eloquent legal brief by Dean Louis Pollak of the Yale Law School were on our side, the megalithic party structure could not be budged and it was on that stifling day—when I scrutinized from the floor the faces of the hundred-odd cozy fat cats of the Committee, two from each state plus places like Guam, nearly all of whom were committed to the Politics of Joy and who indeed had so embraced the establishment mythopoeia that each countenance, male or female and including a Negro or two, seemed a burnished replica of Hubert Humphrey— that I became fully aware that McCarthy's cause was irrevocably lost. Nor was I encouraged to hedge on this conviction when, sweating like a pig, I made a brief *ad hominem* plea in summation of our case, finished, and sat down to the voice of the Committee chairman, Governor Hughes of New Jersey, who said: "Thank you, Mr. Michener." Later, the governor's young aide came up to apologize, saying that the governor knew full well who I was, that in the heat and his fatigue he must have been woolgathering and thinking of James Michener, who was a good friend of Mr. Hughes—a baffling explanation which left me with ominous feelings about life in general.

When I returned as an observer to Chicago the following Sunday, the lobby of the Conrad Hilton resembled a fantasy sequence in some Fellini movie, people in vertical ascent and horizontal drift, unimaginable shoals of walleyed human beings packed elbow to elbow, groin to rump, moving sluggishly as if in some paradigmatic tableau of the utter senselessness of existence. It took me fifteen minutes to cross from one side of the hotel to the other, and although I endured many low moments during the convention, I think it was at this early point, amid that indecent crush of ambitious flesh, that my detestation of politics attained an almost religious passion.

The Conrad Hilton is the archetypal convention hotel of the universe, crimson and gold, vast, nearly pure in its efficient service of the demands of power and pelf, hence somehow beyond vulgarity, certainly sexless, as if dollar hustling and politicking were the sole source of its dynamism; even the pseudo-Bunny waitresses in the Haymarket bar, dungeon-dark like most Chicago pubs, only peripherally distract from the atmosphere of computers and credit cards. Into the Hilton lobby later that week—as into the lobbies of several other hotels— the young insurgents threw stink bombs, which the management misguidedly attempted to neutralize with aerosol deodorants; the effect was calamitous—the fetor of methane mingled with hair spray, like a beauty parlor over an open sewer—and several of the adjoining restaurants seemed notably lacking in customers. Not that one needed any incentive to abandon the scene, one fled instinctively from such a maggot heap; besides there was much to study, especially in downtown Chicago on the streets and in the park, where the real action was, not at the convention itself (I only went to the Amphitheater once, for the vote on the minority report), whose incredible atmosphere of chicanery and disdain for justice could best be observed through television's ceaselessly attentive eye.

Since I somehow felt that sooner or later the cops would make their presence felt upon me more directly (a hunch that turned out to be correct) it appeared to me that they deserved closer scrutiny. They were of course everywhere, not only in the streets but in the hotel lobbies and in the dark bars and restaurants, in their baby-blue shirts, so ubiquitous that one would really not be surprised to find one in one's bed; yet it was not their sheer numbers that truly startled, as impressive as this was, but their peculiar personae, characterized by a beery obesity that made them look half again as big as New York policemen (I never thought I might feel what amounted to nostalgia for New York cops, who by comparison suddenly seemed as civilized as London constables) and by a slovenly, brutish, intimidating manner I had never seen outside the guard room of a Marine Corps brig. They obviously had ample reason for this uptight façade, yet it was instantly apparent that in their sight not only the yippies but all civilians were potential miscreants, and as they eyed passersby narrowly I noticed that Daley, or someone, had allowed them to smoke on duty. Constantly stamping out butts, their great beer guts drooping as they gunned their motorcycles, swatting their swollen thighs with their sticks, they gave me a chill, vulnerable feeling, and I winced at the way their necks went scarlet when the hippies yelled "Pigs!"

On Tuesday night I left a party on the Near North Side with a friend, whom I shall call Jason Epstein, in order to see what was going on in nearby Lincoln Park. There had been rumors of some sort of demonstration and when we arrived, at a little before midnight, we saw that in fact a group of young people had gathered there— I estimated 1,000 or so—most of them sitting peacefully on the grass in the dark, illuminated dimly by the light of a single portable floodlamp, and fanning out in a semicircle beneath a ten-foot-high wooden cross. The previous night, testing the 11 P.M. curfew, several thousands had assembled in the park and had been brutally routed by the police who bloodied dozens of demonstrators. Tonight the gathering was a sort of coalition between the yippies and the followers of a group of Near North Side clergymen, who had organized the sit-in in order to claim the right of the people of the neighborhood to use the park without police harassment. "This is our park!" one minister proclaimed over the loudspeaker. "We will not be moved!" Someone was playing a guitar and folk songs were sung; there was considerable restlessness and tension in the air, even though it was hard to believe that the police would actually attack this tranquil assembly which so resembled a Presbyterian prayer meeting rather than any group threatening public decorum and order. Yet in the black sky a helicopter wheeled over us in a watchful ellipse, and word got back to us that the police had indeed formed ranks several hundred yards down the slope to the east, beyond our sight. A few people began to leave and the chant went up: "Sit down! Sit down!" Most of us remained seated and part of the crowd began singing "The Battle Hymn of the Republic." Meanwhile, instructions were being given out by the old campaigners: don't panic, if forced to the street stay away from the walls and blind alleys, if knocked to the ground use your jacket as a cushion against clubs, above all walk, don't run. The time was now about twelve-thirty. Vaseline was offered as a protection against MACE, wet strips of cloth were handed out to muffle the tear gas. The tension was not very pleasant; while it is easy to over-dramatize such a moment, it does contain its element of raw threat, a queasy, visceral suspense that can only be compared to certain remembered episodes during combat training. "They'll be here in two minutes!" the minister announced.

And suddenly they were here, coming over the brow of the slope fifty yards away, a truly stupefying sight—one hundred or more of the police in a phalanx abreast, clubs at the ready, in helmets and gas masks, just behind them a huge perambulating machine with nozzles, like the type used for spraying insecticide, disgorging clouds of yellowish gas, the whole advancing panoply illuminated by batteries of mobile floodlights. Because of the smoke, and the great cross outlined against it, yet also because of the helmeted and masked figures—resembling nothing so much as those rubberized wind-up automata from a child's playbox of horrors—I had a quick sense of the medieval in juxtaposition with the twenty-first century or, more exactly, a kind of science fiction fantasy, as if a band of primitive Christians on another planet had suddenly found themselves set upon by mechanized legions from Jupiter.

Certainly, whatever the exact metaphor it summoned up, the sight seemed to presage the shape of the world to come, but by now we were up, all of us, off and away—not running, *walking*, fast— toward Clark Street, bleeding tears from the gas. The streets next to the park became a madhouse. The police had not been content to run us out of the park but, charging from the opposite direction, had flanked us, and were harrying people down the streets and up alleys. On a traffic island in the middle of Clark Street a young man was knocked to his knees and beaten senseless. Unsuspecting motorists, caught up in the pandemonium, began to collide with one another up and down the street. The crowd wailed with alarm and split into fragments. I heard the sound of splintering glass as a stone went through the windshield of a police car. Then somehow we disengaged ourselves from the center of the crowd and made our way down Wells Street, relatively deserted where in the dingy nightclubs Go-Go girls oblivious to the rout outside calmly wiggled their asses in silhouette against crimson windows.

It hardly needs mention that Daley might have dealt with these demonstrators without having to resort to such praetorian measures, but violence was the gut and sinew of Chicago during the week, and it was this sort of scene—not the antiseptic convention itself, with its tedium and tawdriness and its bought and paid-for delegates— that makes its claim on my memory. Amid the confusion, I recall certain serene little vignettes: in the lobby of the Pick-Congress Hotel, Senator Tom Dodd flushing beet-red, smiling a frozen smile while being pounded on the back by a burly delegate, steelworker type, with fists the size of cabbages, the man roaring: "I'm a Polack! We know how to ride that greased pig, too!" Or the visit I made—purportedly to win over delegates to McCarthy—to the Virginia delegation, where I was told by at least three members of the group that, while nominally for Humphrey, they would bolt for Teddy Kennedy in a shot (this helped to convince me that he could have won the nomination hands down had he come to Chicago).

But it is mainly that night-scene out of Armageddon that I recollect or, the next day, the tremendous confrontation in front of the Hilton, at the intersection of Michigan and Balbo (named for Italo Balbo, the Italian aviator who first dumped bombs on the Ethiopians) where, half-blinded from the gas I had just caught on the street, I watched the unbelievable melee not from the outside this time but in the surreal shelter of the Haymarket bar, an hermetically sealed igloo whose sound-resistant plate glass windows offered me the dumbshow of cops clubbing people to the concrete, swirling squadrons of police in Panavision blue and polystyrene visors hurling back the crowds, chopping skulls and noses while above me on the invincible TV screen a girl with a fantastic body enacted a comic commercial for BIC ballpoint pens, and the bartender impassively mooned over his Daiquiris (once pausing to inquire of a girl whether she was over 21), and the Muzak in the background whispered "Mood Indigo." Even the dénouement seemed unreal—played out not in the flesh but as part of some animated cartoon where one watches all hell break loose in tolerant boredom—when an explosion of glass at the rear of the bar announced the arrival of half a dozen bystanders who, hurled inward by the crush outside, had shattered the huge window and now sprawled cut and bleeding all over the floor of the place while others, chased by a wedge of cops, fled screaming into the adjacent lobby.

I left Chicago in a hurry—like many others—pursued by an unshakable gloom and by an even profounder sense of irrelevance. If all this anguish, all this naked protest, had yielded nothing but such a primitive impasse—perhaps in the end best symbolized not even by the strife itself but by a "victorious" Hubert Humphrey promising us still another commission to investigate the violence he might have helped circumvent—then the country truly seemed locked, crystallized in its own politics of immobility. There were to be sure some significant changes—removal of the unit rule for one—at least partially brought about by those who worked outside the establishment, including many amateurs in politics; had they been effected in less hysterical circumstances they might have been considered in themselves prodigious achievements.

And there were some bearable moments amid all the dreck: the kids going to bed unblanketed on the cold ground by the fires in Grant Park when I came back just before dawn after our encounter with the police in Lincoln Park, the crowds by the hundreds hemmed in by National Guard troops (themselves Illinois plow-boys or young miners from places like Carbondale, most of them abashed and ill-at-ease—quite a contrast to the brutal belly-swagger of the cops—but all of them just as ignorant about the clash of ideologies which had brought them up here from the prairies); or the next night when again there was a vigil in the park and over a thousand people, including protesting delegates from the convention, came bearing candles and sat until dawn beneath the stirring leaves, singing *Where Have All the Young Men Gone?* as they waved their candles, a forest of arms; or the moment in the daylight, totally unexpected, when a busload of children, no more than six or seven years old, rode up from somewhere on the South Side with a gift of sandwiches for the demonstrators and slowly passed by in front of the park, chanting from the windows in voices almost hurtfully young and sweet: "We want peace! We want peace!" But these moments were rare and intermittent and the emotional gloss they provided was unable to alleviate not just the sense of betrayal (which at least carries the idea of promise victimized) but the sorrow of a promise that never really existed.

M. F. BEAL

Survival

Lillian twitched the white nylon dress from the shower head and fluffed the skirt briskly. With small grunting explosions of breath and snatches of hummed sound she twined slip straps, tucked hems, waistlines even; tied, buttoned, and zipped herself into her day's routine, watching all the time the ragged crest of firs beyond the window and their illuming tips. Dawn, then suddenly day and sun and a stirring wind. She released one last satisfied throat-sound, then flicked off the light and strode from her room-and-a-half to her

Survival. First published in New American Review #3, 1968. Reprinted by permission of M. F. Beal, c/o Marvin Josephson Associates, Inc. Copyright © 1968 M. F. Beal.

Burger Hut. The slam of the birch door punctuated her engagement with the day.

"Whew!" she spat, pausing. It was still night in the Hut. The long counter was islanded by stale smoke, white enamel surfaces glaring stingingly; a stale patter of grease slicked from the grill. The floor, impenetrably scuffed and mounded at the door with red mud, had a look of failure. A lone customer stirred his coffee in grating circles.

So she shouted hello to Helen, somewhere behind frying bacon, hotcakes, and the lone coffee drinker, and began to clean for the day, or at least to tidy. She turned off lights, nodding as surfaces were again reduced to function. She swept with orderly strokes, humming on the downbeat, shoes squeaking. She watched the highway, went out with the wire broom and swept toward the road shoulder, inspected passing cars and glared as they passed, knowing their occupants needed a good hot breakfast as she began to sense her own emptiness. Finally, a small headache creeping up, she unreeled the hose, watered red and white petunias, flushed the walkway and went in for breakfast.

The customer looked from his plate and nodded as she planted elbows around her coffee cup and tried the first sips with a great taking-in of air. "Uhm." The radio played a war song, vaguely familiar. She thought for just an instant of Harry. There was kitchen clatter, then car sound. Pursing her lips, turning curiously, she saw the purple and cream Plymouth pull up to the house next door, this time with a U-Haul.

That guy, she thought, looking over the partition at Helen. Must be broke . . . Why doesn't he . . . "Say," she said aloud when Helen saw her staring, "fix me something, will you? Don't tell me what, just—something." She sipped the cooling coffee. Must be broke, moving in with her. He never will learn . . .

The customer rattled the morning paper and hunched back over the ruins of his breakfast.

"What's happening?" she asked. The radio buzzed with the DJ's insistent voice. She flicked it low. "What's happening?"

The customer looked up, back down. "Oh, more of the same."

"Yeah?" She slid down the counter toward him and he looked up, startled. Helen brought her breakfast as she stared at the newspaper around his arm. "Thanks, hon," she said, turning to the eggs and hashbrowns. With obvious hunger she began to fit them between her dark wet lips.

*

She drank her second cup of coffee and stared at the purple and
cream Plymouth parked in front of Helen's house. It belonged to
Helen's ex-husband. The day before as Helen worked her shift she
said he'd called again, wanting to come see her. Helen asked Lillian
what to do. Helen was a pushover; married twice to the guy and
twice divorced and still willing to listen when he called. Lillian
couldn't get across to her that she had to give up on a bad thing.
So this morning he came, bright and early, carrying something or
other under his arm. Well then, at least he wasn't broke. Thank God
for small favors.

As she watched the car, her own husband's hard-to-remember
face flitted through her mind and she tried to fix it for a moment;
hadn't seen or heard from him in nearly fifeen years, since two weeks
after he left her and Harry, so whenever she thought of him it was
of an aging boy with still-curly hair and a mad grin bursting to display
his strong, even white teeth. She sucked egg residue from her mo-
lars and sipped again, reflectively.

"That's disgusting," the customer was saying sharply, batting
the paper with a folded five-dollar bill. "How come they put stuff like
that right on the front page?" It was a picture of an oriental face
bundled about with print fabric and splayed, stick arms. A woman,
one guessed, because below the shut dead eyes a smaller child's face
watched with erupting tears.

"Yeah," she said, running her ragged red nail across it as if to
pin down or make contact with the message.

"And it says here it's just a setup, anyhow, propaganda," the
customer said, and paid.

She made change but failed quite to grasp how a picture of a
dead woman could be propaganda. "Izzen it awful," she mumbled,
flicking the radio dial loud and calling out: "Bye now," as the door
shut tinkling.

Harry was dead. It was months already since his coffin had been
returned.

The tiny transistor belched magically, a cornucopia of noise. The
DJ, a grown man's larynx surrounded by a teen-age mind, rambled
about "oar tewn" and "lewcal proide" and how it would be "gosh,
great" if we all got out to line the highway when the visitors from

Neuhoftal, "oar sister city from across the waves" arrived in their motorcade.

Motorcade brought a sudden tinselly feeling to Lillian, a recollection of colored floats and summer sun: "Let's see, where did I put those signs they gave me?" She dumped her empty cup into the tepid suds behind the counter where it drifted down clattering. "Uhm." Sifting through dusty inked cardboards, adding-machine tapes, and ball points, she finally found the C of C offerings:

WELCOME
SISTER CITY DELEGATION
FROM
NEUHOFTAL, GERMANY

When she had set them against the heating flyspecked glass, she ran outside to inspect; the motorcade would pass right by, see her place . . . behind her the DJ's voice mounted: "and I got to thinkeen, wouldn't it be noice if we could greet these visitors with just a word or two in their own language, just somethccn simple, hello in German . . . so you out there who know German, give us a call, will you? And here's the German National Anthem . . ."

To the opening strains, as if cued, the purple and cream car pulled away from the curb and she could see the face of Helen's ex-husband squinted in concentration as he crossed traffic. Her eyes traced his passage, her scalp heated, and she realized she was still mad from last night. Twice married, twice divorced, almost forty; the business with Helen and her husband had been going on for . . . eleven years, as long as Lillian had her Burger Hut. And last night suddenly she found herself unable to feel Helen was just a mixed-up kid. Her own involvement in the thing came to her too; she saw how she'd been used by them both. She felt the righteous fatigue of the victimized. The answer was clear: forget the bastard. Find someone who'll realize what he's got. She got nowhere pressing this solution; it was not the direction which interested Helen. Helen's passivity frustrated her, yet excited her protective instincts. Still when Helen finished cleaning the grill the night before, Lillian was tired to the bone. "I'm just a doormat," she said to herself.

The DJ was having a phone interview with a quavery-voiced old man: "*Willkommen*, that's what my dad used to say. He was from the old country, he was from . . ." he rummaged his memory for a moment, uselessly, then the DJ asked him to spell it, to pronounce it.

Lillian bagged the newspaper with one hand and lined it even at the end of the counter while with the other she ran the rag in damp circles. The photo of the dead woman and the crying baby held her eyes: how did she die? She bent closer to look for darker gray spotting which might be blood but it was unclear what was the print of the dress and what the wound. Harry, on furlough before being shipped overseas, told her about wounds, about how the wounded he'd talked with said they never felt the one that hit them. His sergeant, who had a bayonet scar running down and across his chest from shoulder to hip, said he'd felt a series of sharp blows, had run on past the Japanese who'd done it, then found himself on hands and knees . . .

Helen came from the kitchen, took off her apron, and sat at the counter with a cup of coffee. She had on a bright pink dress and looked very young; from the radio a woman's voice sharply countered the DJ's: "I don't know what the correct form of greeting in Germany is now, but it used to be 'Heil Hitler'!" the phone clicked firmly. A car pulled into the Burger Hut lot and disgorged a man, woman, and child. As she took their order for burgers, she sensed Helen behind her rising to return to the grill; on impulse she turned, smiled: "Why don't you stay put, dear, I'll run this order." She was rewarded by a blank look as Helen wandered, obedient, to a seat. She felt somehow that she had protected herself from further violation.

The frying of the order and setting of places, cutting of beefy tomato slices, spearing of pickles, took her time. She wiped the ketchup and offered it, poured coffee, and milk for the little girl. Then, almost an afterthought, took Helen a fresh cup. Behind the kitchen partition the patties sizzled, filling the room with their tentatively meaty odor; humming wafted like steam, as if in the act of cooking Lillian realized herself. She spread buns with soft butter, took them in and set them on warmed plates, removed the finished burgers swiftly and slid them in front of the waiting family. She watched eagerly as they bit in.

"Good burger," said the man, after a moment. The woman nodded.

Lillian licked her lips and smiled. "Oh, I love a good burger," she said, richly endowing the u of burger. "I'm real fussy about the burger I serve. People come all the way from Portland . . ." Satisfied, she drifted away, to Helen and the cooling coffee; Helen, perched sullenly over the cup, looked up and smiled unwillingly but Lillian dismissed her temper: "Well, hon, want to talk?"

And so Helen told her:

He had called last night after she got off about coming by. She didn't know what to think. She told him they were through, really through this time—just what she and Lillian had talked about. But he sounded miserable. She remembered they'd had more than one good time together and she hated, anyway, to hear anyone that miserable. Wasn't that right?

Lillian sucked her coffee without comment.

This morning he came by earlier than she thought he would and caught her in her housecoat—oh, everything had kind of been beyond her. He brought a red shorty gown. She hadn't liked that, it was compromising. But after all, he said, it wasn't as if . . . He had a new business deal with a fellow he'd met a few weeks before: his own car and fifteen hundred to cover operating expenses, twenty-five hours a week collecting from coin-ops. One-twenty-five a week right now, more as new users were added to the route. It sounded really good this time. There was, of course, the past . . .

But her eyes glowed. Lillian sipped coffee and saw Helen warm to the excitement of remarriage. He got to her, thought Lillian. That son of a bitch. But it was hopeless to remind her how it had been.

"It's your life," she said shortly, and not even that could put Helen off: "Oh wouldn't it be wonderful if this time we worked things out?"

"Hey, who are you trying to kid? It hasn't worked twice; you've got to forget it and go on."

She got up to refill coffees for the family and to talk about french fries, about how she made her own instead of just using frozens; and when the little girl had loiteringly finished her milk and the bill had been paid, Helen was back in the kitchen. She felt bad. The sun was climbing; on the radio the DJ talked in terms of a half hour and played the German National Anthem again: "Now wouldn't you be threlled if you were going into Neuhoftal and they were playeen the 'Star Spangled Banner'? So I think it's kinda noice if we . . ."

She gathered herself and moved briskly into the kitchen. "Helen?"

Helen looked up from dishes, focusing milkily.

"Helen? Let's make a nice plate of deviled eggs."

*

She hummed as she set things out, pleased with her briskness. She worked well, and working satisfied her; she forgot in it, passed over the bad and incomplete. Once it had bothered her to do filthy work: cleaning the Men's and Ladies' had been agony. Then gradually she had seen how it was all the same, a contribution. It had to be done. She would do it well, would incorporate it and make of it something explanatory. If anyone asked, she could say how clean toilets were part of the Good Burger.

The DJ reminded them of the passage of time; he had a reporter stationed down the line and by phone traced the visitors. Lillian began to hurry. She saw, beyond specked windows, early parade watchers: two boys and a small girl in a droopy pinafore. Coffee. Buns warming for burgers. Fresh cream in the pitchers; refills on ketchup, mustard. Sugar. Salt. Onions to chop. Moisture stood out on Lillian's lip; Helen abandoned her humming.

Then as she sliced down hard she felt the blade sever flesh; her stomach turned, blood spurted. Lillian stared unbelieving at her thumb even as her lip rode up over her teeth. "Uhm."

Helen came over, stared, fumbled at it with napkins. "God, so deep. Press it." The blood was very red, thick. It hurt. Lillian thought of how Harry had said wounds did not hurt. Well maybe big ones. They blotted and drew the napkins away, inspected, blotted. They ran cold water over the wound, then finally, when Helen located the aid kit, wrapped it well with gauze and adhesive. "It'll be wet in a minute," Lillian said, laughing shakily. "Oh I know," said Helen.

She went back to work, her thumb throbbing. Harry.

She had not seen him; the coffin was sealed. At one point she was desperate to know what, just what, had happened. He died of multiple fragmentation wounds. What were they? She ached steadily behind the eyes. You could not keep them out of it. A long time ago she had talked with an older woman whose two sons died in the Second World War. "You could not keep them out of it," the woman said, without much force. Later, when Harry left school to join, claiming it was only a matter of time before they got him anyway, she understood what the woman meant and adopted it for herself. "You can't keep them out of it."

Yet again the German National Anthem came on, and this time after the last strains the DJ announced triumphantly the visitors were entering town. "So get out there, welcome them folks. Show them you're glad to see them. *Willkommen*, that's the exprayssion. *Will-kommen*."

It was true; passersby had stopped, sensing a commotion down the long street. Without thought, Lillian and Helen took off their aprons and went out. People stood two deep at the curb, their excitement stirring the air; cars filled with cruising teen-agers pulled to the sides and halted, young faces gaped from the windows, as much at the footbound onlookers as at anyone who might suddenly arrive. They stared at each other in a confusion of transistor voices chiming the same message, wondering at a sense of history. Lillian longed for something to hold on to, perhaps a flag. Down the highway voices swelled; they strained to hear. Their eyes caught movement; the sun, glinting, hit them in its reboundings from glass and chrome. A Motorcade! Red firetrucks and grinning firemen; ambulances with frosted sides; the mayor's car; chief of police; motorcyclists, leather-clad; a float by the Elks: "*Willkommen!*" and pretty girls and a deeper, nearer voicing.

They strained at the sounding syllables as it all drew near, caught and held the sounds: Villl ko mmennnvil komm men villll kkoommm mmeeenn so their throats took it up: VILL KOO MMEN VILL KOO MMEN . . .

That lunchtime the Burger Hut took in one hundred fifty-four dollars, and Lillian, returning from the bank, realized with astonishment her accounts, savings and checking, held over nineteen thousand dollars. Nine of it was from Harry's insurance; there had been the eight hundred dollars used for his funeral, the rest she had. But ten thousand she had made on the Burger Hut. Suddenly she understood she would not have to worry about money. If she needed anything, she could go out and get it, and not think twice about expense. She fingered the hem of her sweater as she wondered what she might need or desire; oh, some stockings, of course; some underpanties, a new lipstick. But what else? She could not think of any other desire that had enough force to excite her imagination. Still she would have to do something with all that money.

With a dull feeling she remembered how, when Harry was small, she had wanted things: dresses, shoes, jewelry, a car . . . once she slid halfway into a nasty affair over a mouton lamb coat. Then that all seemed to pass and it had been instead a question of meeting bills and keeping ahead of creditors when she couldn't; teeth to be fixed, never-ending lunch money, money for movies, notebooks; then date money. Finally money for college. Now all that was permanently ended; she herself could not quite understand how so much money had come her way. They said the war had cut down unemployment. It was true she had more business lately.

She helped Helen set up for the evening and then let her take off a few hours before her evening's work; with a cup of coffee and the final edition she settled herself to wait for late-afternoon coffee-breakers.

The first thing she noticed when she opened the paper was the photo of the dead oriental woman with her crying child. She briefly thought she was seeing it for the first time; the hours collapsed as if it was still morning. Then she shook herself, realized it was simply a rerun, leaned closer to study it again.

It told her nothing new; it was imperfection: dull, hazy, confused. How did the woman die? The big wounds did not hurt, Harry said. Her finger throbbed under the damp gauze. The woman never felt a thing. The child's face was as if split in two, unhealable. *How did the woman die?* Stick arms utterly destroyed thrust from the rag bundle dress whose pattern was so obscure you could not make out the wound's sign.

In the last week before his senior year, on a cool evening as they drove home, a four-point buck ran in front of the car and Harry stopped dead, pulled out his Winchester levering the action, and fired in an instant, bringing the deer down in midleap. They walked together into the rhododendrons, she saying again and again over her heart's pounding: "You got him. I saw him go down."

The buck lay bedded and still breathing in thick bracken, red blood sprouting lazily, bright petals on dry ferns. *What will we do?* she asked herself as he bucked upward and fell back over and over, looking at them and dragging himself on windbroke legs. "What will we—?" Harry slit the brown throat. The hair parted white, then ran pink-red like the sprouting petals; a sheet spilled on Harry's wrist, a black clot of hemorrhage slid to the ferns. The buck kicked and was still. They stood back together, briefly appalled by death.

In his last letter Harry said: "I know it's not a nice thing to talk about but yesterday I killed a VC. He was six feet away and I figured I'd better cut him down before he got any closer."

When the buck's ribs were still, and quickly as the dusk fell, Harry cut the white belly and spilled the ropy guts onto the ground.

Bits of fir needles, bracken, dust clung as they rolled and oozed; the deer's dulling eye unblinkingly collected its own freight.

There was an odor. Lillian drew back, placed herself beyond the sense of it touching her, but still she saw her son's arm in the deer's gaping chest, prizing first the liver to steam in the cooling air, then the frothy lungs.

"Got him right here, see?" he asked with a craftsman's awe. "He went right down, wouldn't have gone more than ten feet before he bled to death. Probably never felt a thing."

She was amazed there could have been so much inside the body; the heap of viscera glinted in the last light as Harry's boot touched it. He kicked duff and it dulled, reduced to indistinguishable refuse.

"There," he said, shouldering the deer, grunting under it. "You'd never know anything had happened, would you?" He was grinning, blood was on him, dark streaks down his arms and in black moons around his nails. That was the next to last time she saw him.

"Hey, Lil, wake up." The lights snapped white.

"Oh," she said, coming alive, lips recurving over licked teeth. "Hi." It was Helen, returning. "Say," she said as Helen tied her apron, ". . . fix me something, will you?" She went on firmly, ". . . don't tell me what, just . . ."

"I know, a surprise."

She watched Helen's face as it bobbed above the grill and the sizzling of food brought an evening warmth to the Hut. Her face seemed bland, resolved; Lillian wondered briefly what Helen had been thinking. She poured herself another coffee, straightened salts and peppers, and sat before the cup. She felt strange yet. Maybe she needed a vacation. But she could not think of any place to go.

Suddenly she knew something bad was going to happen; it welled up like tears. I'd better get out, she thought, rising and walking swiftly to her room-and-a-half, shoes rapping the floor with a panic beat. *My God.* She felt faint. She found herself in her darkened bathroom, a ghostly face in the mirror. She snapped on the light.

Her face swam up like the face of a stranger and to still the pounding in her temples and throat she leaned on the sink, close, almost eye to eye. It was as if she asked *Who are you? What are you doing here?* She saw how terror had blurred all the planes of the face in the mirror—terror, advancing age, and ignorance; how it had all settled the fine wrinkles around the eyes into unbelieving blankness and set the fine recurving lips loosely in rouged laziness. *I have just been going on and on*, she realized with terror. *On and on. And all these things have been happening.*

Tears burst from her. Her mouth hung, a cry pushed up behind her teeth and she held it, watched the face in the mirror, closed her eyes and let it come, impersonal. At first it was thin, small, but it rose larger and came again. She cried and cried. Her whole face ran wet, jerking, slippery with tears and mucus, loud; she cried, tears burst again, her shoulders jerked, shook, twisted but without relief: *my God I will not feel better when I stop this time* she thought in panic. Her wet face chilled, split again with new grief.

So she stopped, exhausted.

It was deadly dark outside but she could hear fir limbs chafed by an awakening breeze. She hung to the lavatory rim as her clock beat out the time; she listened for what seemed hours. Something calm and cold was building itself in her and slowly she understood parts of it; as in a ceremony of puberty, she was passing from one world to another. All she had left behind: courtship, marriage, childbirth, abandonment, even the loss of her son, came swimming up again. These are all I have, she thought wonderingly. I've tried to do right and it's all been taken from me.

Then she knew how the woman had died, she had died in pain and final understanding of the violation of her body; she had died knowing her body was broken. Harry, too. He had in the last moments understood life was amnesiac, death real.

"Lillian?" The opened door slashed the strong life odor of food across the room. Oh yes, she thought. Helen. My surprise. "Right there."

She realized Helen was coming into the room. "Hey," Helen's voice asked, "what's up?" Helen stood behind her. "Oh, Lillian. It's Harry, isn't it."

Lillian patted at her hair and tried to move but an overwhelming weight held her to the lavatory basin; she felt she knew what she was going to hear:

"Oh, Lillian, I've thought it over and I realize you're so right about me and him. I've got to give it up, I've got to go on. You and I, we've both got to go on, we've got to live."

Lillian felt something deep in her throat respond even as her scalp crawled with a sense that things were slipping from her, that as fast as she learned she forgot. *No* she thought. *No.* But the incantation faded and instead came the image *surprise* and she thought *Friday; probably Helen's cooked fish and chips.*